AT THE BARRICADES

AT THE BARRICADES

FORTY YEARS ON
THE CUTTING EDGE OF HISTORY

WILFRED BURCHETT

WITH AN INTRODUCTION BY
HARRISON E. SALISBURY

Times
BOOKS

Published by TIMES BOOKS, a division of
Quadrangle/The New York Times Book Co., Inc.
Three Park Avenue, New York, N.Y. 10016

Library of Congress Cataloging in Publication Data

Burchett, Wilfred G   1911-
At the barricades.
Includes index.
1. Burchett, Wilfred G., 1911-
2. War correspondents—Australia—Biography.
I. Title.
PN5516.B87A33   1980   070'.92'4   [B]   80-5133
ISBN 0-8129-0925-9

Introduction

by Harrison E. Salisbury

WILFRED BURCHETT IS a man who defies classification. There is hardly a war or revolution in the past forty years at which he as a journalist has not been present. There is hardly a left-wing movement with which he as a radical (or "progressive," as he likes to call himself) has not sympathized. In his ceaseless travel he has met most of the diplomats and national leaders of his time and most of his fellow correspondents. There is probably no other man living who was on intimate terms with both Ho Chi Minh and Henry Kissinger.

Wilfred Burchett's life has been filled with conflict and controversy. He has launched libel suits against persons who have called him a subversive and a KGB agent wearing the masquerade of a foreign correspondent. He was given refuge by Prince Sihanouk in those halcyon Cambodian days before the fatal American "incursion" which started that lovely country down the slide into genocide. For years he was a man without a country, denied admission to his Australian birthplace.

Burchett has always possessed a gift for friendship. Few are the journalists who met and worked beside him in World War II in China and Burma or with the U.S. Fleet in the Pacific who did not become his enduring friends. The same was true in controversial postwar days in Germany, Eastern Europe, Korea, Southeast Asia, and, more recently, revolutionary Africa.

Burchett was born in Australia in 1911 of English emigrant stock. His boyhood was spent, for the most part, in rock-hard conditions, his family oscillating between economic disasters—sometimes working at the Burchetts' traditional building trades, sometimes scratching out a living on farms. Burchett was a child of the Depression much as his fellow generation in America. His early years radicalized him before he left Australia, but it was not until after World War II, when he was serving as correspondent of Beaver-brook's London *Daily Express* in Berlin, that politics began to bulk larger in his life than hard-nosed, action-filled reporting.

By this time Burchett was one of the best-known and ablest of English correspondents. He had done epochal reporting from China, had survived and written about an incredible "long march" with the British fleeing Burma into India ahead of the Japanese, and had scored a sensational scoop by being the first correspondent to enter Hiroshima and bring to the world the story of the A-bomb and the horrors it left in its wake—the first details of radiation illness (denied for a long time by official U.S. sources). It was the beat of a lifetime, and Burchett's almost laconic account of how he achieved it by boarding a train jam-packed with hysterical Japanese is a classic.

The cold war pushed Burchett across the line from objective reportage to partisan of radical causes, although it is notable that he never quite cut his connections with conventional newspapering even in the controversial days when he turned up on the North Korean-Chinese side at the Panmun-jon truce negotiations. Here Burchett quickly became a major news source. He had access to the North Korean-Chinese negotiators and often gave American correspondents inside information which they could not pry out of the U.S. negotiating team.

In many ways Burchett reminds one more of the old-fashioned pre-1917 radicals than those of today's highly ideological confrontations, a Lincoln Steffens or a John Reed with an Australian accent. Those who search this book for philosophical explanations of Burchett's positions will be disappointed. To one who has known him for many years this seems no accident. While there are few radical causes which Burchett has not espoused, his own beliefs are difficult to classify. Was or is Burchett a member of the Communist party? He has never said, but he did once declare that he would not sue for slander if he was called a Communist.

Burchett spent the late 1940s in Central Europe and the Balkans. There he reported on the purge trials imposed on Communist leaders in Bulgaria and Hungary by Stalin and his sinister police chief, Lavrenti P. Beria. It seems clear that at the time he accepted the basic postulates of the trials. Even today he does not seem entirely convinced that those exhibitions were mere extensions of the paranoiac terror which Stalin had long since imposed upon the Soviet Union.

Yet, a few years after Stalin's death (although he probably would not now so put it), he found himself at such odds with Soviet policy that he became more and more uncomfortable in Moscow. In part this grew from his sympathy for the Chinese Communists and in part from his interest in evolving revolutionary movements in Southeast Asia. Over a long period, beginning with the Korean war, he was supportive of the tough dictatorial regime of North Korean leader Kim Il Sung, hardly a person in whose breast much milk of human kindness had ever flowed. At the same time Burchett was on terms of intimacy with high Chinese party figures and an ardent admirer of the late Premier Chou En-lai and Ho Chi Minh of Vietnam. During the Vietnam War Burchett threw his energies into reportage and propaganda in aid of Hanoi and was close to the North Vietnamese leadership, Ho Chi Minh, Premier Pham Van Dong, and General Vo Nguyen Giap. He became a personal friend of Prince Sihanouk and strongly supported the Sihanouk regime. During this period Burchett often sharply criticized the Soviet Union and its policies, especially what he considered its tepid attitude toward national liberation struggles. A complex man, as this recital indicates.

Even before the war in Vietnam ended, Burchett had begun to turn against the policies of Peking, feeling that the Chinese in their quarrel with Moscow were siding against revolutionary forces in the former Portuguese African colonies and elsewhere.

After a long absence from Hanoi Burchett emerged once again as a supporter of the Vietnamese regime and its Cambodia policy. This put him sharply at odds with China and once more in line with Moscow's position.

This résumé supports the theory that Burchett is an individualist so far as radicalism is concerned. If his sympathies have a polarization, it is toward the cause of struggling, backward, emerging nationalist regimes, typified by Cambodia and Vietnam. His inclinations clearly derive from his own difficult Australian youth.

Burchett's autobiography is a cornucopia of adventure and politics. One need not share Burchett's often-shifting radical inclinations to be rewarded by the human details of his life's odyssey. He is a product of the passionate conflicts of the twentieth century. Born into backcountry poverty, he sallied forth almost accidentally to take a front seat on the stage of world history. He has written an engrossing account, regardless of whether we take his political professions at face value. One can only wish that occasionally in his swift movement from country to country and from war to war he had found a bit more time to pause and tell us about himself and how these events affected his own thinking. But he has always been a man on the run, tomorrow's headlines eternally on his mind.

Burchett's conventional journalistic companions have found him a well-informed, useful source and a warm and decent friend. They almost always could check out a report or a rumor with Burchett regardless of whether it fitted Communist ideology or party propaganda. On most occasions they got a straightforward answer, one which was trustworthy and which stood the test of time. In written reportage it might be a different story. Burchett was an advocate, and he wrote in support of the cause to which he adhered at a given moment.

It should not be assumed from the foregoing that Burchett was in any sense a flibbertigibbet. He was not. But changing situations constantly changed his appreciations. In a world in which Communist and revolutionary movements became increasingly fragmented, in which Stalin's once-monolithic Communist world split and split and split again, Burchett moved where his humanist sympathies led him. If his positions seem far from any Hegelian logic, this is because in the age in which we live simplistic dogmas have lost their *raison d'être*. Burchett, thus, can be seen as sui generis, a radical who moves through a changing milieu, lending his sympathy to one cause after another not because of some Marxist doctrine, but because he believes in the underdog whatever the continent, whatever the color, whatever the creed. He is, in short, the iconoclast of contemporary radicalism.

Contents

AT THE
BARRICADES

1

━━━◄●►━━━

Blasted Visions

A DISTANT BOOM and familiar whine ended in a sharp whack and pillar of black smoke a couple of hundred yards down the road. Another boom and whine. Some flames with the smoke this time as the bang went off closer to us but missed the road by about fifty yards. Peasants packed a few bags of rice and other belongings into an oxcart and rushed into shelters dug between the blackened ruins of a few huts—all that was left of Tan Bien hamlet, wiped out three nights previously by Khmer Rouge commandos. (The term "Khmer Rouge" [Cambodian Reds] was first used in 1967 by Prince Norodom Sihanouk to describe an ultraleftist faction of the Cambodian Communist party which had taken to arms against his neutralist regime. This faction rose to power during armed struggle, from 1970 to 1975, against the U.S.-backed regime of General Lon Nol, who had seized power by a coup d'état against Sihanouk on March 18, 1970. The Khmer Rouge was overthrown by a Vietnamese-backed insurrection in January 1979.)

"Better head back," said Huynh Van Luan, member of the People's Committee of Vietnam's Tay Ninh Province, who was accompanying me in December 1978 on Highway 22, which leads southeast from the frontier with Cambodia's Kompong Cham Province through Tay Ninh City to join up with Highway 1—and straight on to Saigon (now Ho Chi Minhville).

I had pedaled back and forth along Highway 22 many times, starting fifteen years earlier on the first of my four wartime visits to the Vietcong-controlled areas of South Vietnam. Then it was bordered by dense jungle. Branches meeting overhead for most of the way from the frontier toward Tay Ninh City provided near-perfect protection from the prowling spy planes. Gibbon apes, flocks of shrieking parrots, and myriads of other birds

3

used to cheer bicycle-borne and foot travelers on their way. Since then, tens of thousands of acres of virgin jungle had been defoliated, napalmed, or bulldozed out of existence. Gibbons and birds had been blasted or roasted as the B-52s passed over in their extermination bombings. Survivors among the furred and feathered community had long fled from whatever jungle remained in its original state.

Until we turned back, our target had been a triangle of still-existent jungle situated roughly between a line linking the villages of Lo Go and Xo Mat and the frontier where Tay Ninh Province makes a small bulge into Kampuchea. There I had visited various central organs of South Vietnam's National Liberation Front (Vietcong) in the early days of its armed struggle.

Before leaving Tay Ninh City, Huynh Van Luan had warned: "We might not make it. Pol Pot [leader of the Khmer Rouge until December 1979] has some Chinese one-hundred-thirty-millimeter cannon along the frontier where it runs parallel with Highway Twenty-two at less than ten miles' distance. His gunners can easily bracket us as we approach the Lo Go-Xa Mat area." He was right. Had we not stopped to check on what had happened to Tan Bien hamlet, Huynh Van Luan grudgingly admitted that "by a fluke" the first shot would have been "bang on target."*

We spoke to a peasant, Nguyen Van Mau, sitting dejectedly on a log, holding a rope at the other end of which was an ox guzzling at some recently beheaded rice stubble. "They came in yelling and firing their guns around three in the morning," said Nguyen Van Mau. "They were after our rice and cattle, grabbing what they could and setting fire to the houses. Our lads, who had been guarding the fields—half of which had not been harvested—counterattacked and drove them off. But by then everything was ablaze. Nobody was killed, but we had some wounded by bullets and burns." The hamlet had been evacuated; the villagers, relocated farther back from the frontier. Some had returned early that morning to collect what remained and could be carried away. Much ripened rice still stood in the fields.

Huynh Van Luan explained that Tan Bien was one of more than 100 hamlets and villages evacuated from the Tay Ninh frontier areas, involving more than 70,000 peasants and 35,000 acres of abandoned land. From September 1977, 1,181 civilians had been killed, about 800 of them women and

---

* The incident was given added significance seventeen months later after a Chevrolet minibus in which a three-member Australian film crew and I were traveling was ambushed on May 7, 1980, only forty miles from the Cambodian capital, on the Kompong Chnang-Phnom Penh road. Automatic rifles and Chinese-made B-40 bazookas were used at a range of about seventy yards. Our lives were saved by the Vietnamese driver who drove us out of the field of fire despite a bullet through his cheek and wounds to his neck and shoulder. The twenty-strong commando group was rounded up within a matter of hours, their leader conceding that I was the object of the attack. It was the first time any vehicle had been ambushed on that stretch of the road since the overthrow of the Pol Pot regime. With this in mind, the Vietnamese concluded that the unusual shelling in Tay Ninh, December 1978, was also intended for your author.

children. I mentioned that during four years of residence in Cambodia I had visited the frontier with Tay Ninh innumerable times and had always been struck by the friendly cross-border relations among the frontier people.

"It used to be like that," replied Luan. "For a very long time relations between the peasants on both sides were good. But in recent years the Pol Pot authorities pushed their people back, ten to twenty miles behind the frontier. They started building military posts along the hundred miles of frontier between Kampuchea and Tay Ninh Province. By the end of last year five of their divisions and three independent regiments had been stationed along the Tay Ninh section of the frontier alone. Instead of friendly peasants on the other side, we now have bands of commandos who kill our border villagers often in the most barbarous manner. Attacks at divisional strength have also been launched deep into our territory."

In addition to the problem of resettling 70,000 peasants—out of a total population of 800,00—Tay Ninh had to look after 30,000 refugees who continued to pour in from across the border in Kampuchea. From 1970 on, Cambodian nationalists have insisted on the use of the more phonetically accurate Kampuchea as the name for what the English-speaking world knew as Cambodia, and of Khmer for Cambodian.

Later in the day we headed for one of the province's four refugee centers. In the Tan Chau resettlement area were some 6,500 Khmer, 900 Hoa (ethnic Chinese), and 600 Cham (a Muslim minority people settled in Kampuchea from the ninth century on) refugees. Among the Khmer I found a former schoolteacher, Madame Nuth Thi, whom our family had known during our four years' residence in Phnom Penh. To my first standard question as to why she had fled, she gave what was an almost standard reply: "I couldn't stand the killings. Doctors, teachers, anyone with education, were being killed. Up to 1977 it was only those who had directly served the Lon Nol or Sihanouk regimes. From 1977 it was anyone with education."

"Did you actually see anyone killed?"

"Yes. Five schoolteachers were beaten to death with hoes before my eyes. At each blow they were cursed as reactionaries. To be educated and, later, even to be literate were considered 'reactionary.' There were no books left— they all were burned. I never read anything from the time I left Phnom Penh. All we knew was work: digging canals, irrigation ditches, fishponds; working twelve or thirteen hours a day every day of the week—no Saturdays or Sundays off. Anyone who complained was taken off at night and not seen again. We learned to be dumb, to suppress even our sobs at night. Weeping was considered criticism of the regime. Child spies crawled up into the roofs at night or listened under the floors to denounce anyone heard whispering or weeping. We got used to working in silence and suffering in silence.

"Family life was ended. We sometimes saw our children at mealtime, but they slept in special barracks at night. It was said that this was for 'education' —there was shouting of slogans, but no education. There was no way of learning the fate of friends and relatives. Travel was totally prohibited."

Nuth Thi rightly considered herself one of the most fortunate of the refugees. In the evacuation of Phnom Penh, ordered by the Khmer Rouge when they entered the city on April 17, 1975, she managed to keep her family intact during the seventeen-day trek from Phnom Penh to a village in Kampuchea's easternmost Svay Rieng Province. Later she shepherded them all, including a desperately ill husband and six children ranging up to fourteen years, in a perilous all-night flight across the frontier into neighboring Tay Ninh Province.

They had escaped early in 1978, and her husband was still in a Vietnamese hospital. As for what struck her most when she crossed the frontier, she replied: "I saw that people were happy. There were markets, and people went freely along the roads, talking and laughing. We were immediately treated with great kindness, given food, medicine, and clothing. My country has become a terrible place. By day I still hear the curses of our oppressors, and by night the muffled sobs of our people."

The Khmer at Tan Chau were growing rice and had just reaped their first harvest. The Cham had settled in as blacksmiths and other handcraftsmen; the Hoa had set up small market booths, having been given cash advances to buy stocks of cigarettes, matches, soap, and other items of daily life. It was in the market that I met Madame Yap Mor, a small bobbed-hair woman, crouched over an odd assortment of wares. She was from Mimot in Kompong Cham Province, a mile or so across the frontier from Tay Ninh. Why had she come? "In early 1978 they started killing more people than ever," she replied. "My husband was killed, and they threatened to kill me."

"Why?"

"My husband was accused of having contact with the Vietnamese."

"Did he?"

"Everyone in the Mimot area did. We have always had friendly relations. But they took him off and killed him. I was told I must say he died of illness or I would also be killed. I couldn't pretend I didn't know he was killed, and I couldn't hide my grief. One night I fled with my twelve-year-old son, leaving four other children behind. I've since heard they all were killed because I ran away."

At this point she started weeping, as did the girl interpreter, and the interview ended.

One of the most unbelievable stories from the Tan Chau center, which later turned out to be only too true, came from Sen Mat, a husky thirty-five-year-old Cham, exuding strength and vitality and—despite everything—cheerfulness. Why had he come?

"Because the Khmer Rouge started killing all the Cham," he replied.

"Why would they do that?"

"They objected to our women wearing their hair long like the Vietnamese and said we must be under Vietnamese influence." The *Angkar* ("Organization"), in the name of which everything was done in the Kampuchea of the Khmer Rouge, had decreed that women should wear their hair cropped at not more than one inch long and that clothing must be exclusively black! "They also tried to make us eat pork, although they know this is against our religion."

"Most of those to whom I have talked say they never got any meat—only rice gruel," I observed.

"Traditionally many Cham are blacksmiths," replied Sen Mat. "The Khmer Rouge worked us very hard but knew they had to give us extra food. They stood over us with guns while we swallowed some pork. But they knew we hated them for it.

"At the beginning of 1976 they asked all the Cham in my area of Kompong Cham Province to assemble at Coc Pho. They said they wanted to consult with us about various problems. Everyone had to pass by a table and give his name and hamlet. I was one of the last and saw that one thousand one hundred sixteen had been listed before me. Then the table was taken away, and troops hidden among the trees opened up with mortars and heavy machine guns. When the firing was over, there were just eight of us left. We pretended to be dead and escaped at night.

"We went to another place and started working as smiths again, but we were determined to escape. We left as a group in March [1978]. Right at the frontier, the Vietnamese gave us everything we needed, even money to buy a forge." He took me to the smithy where half a dozen of his comrades were hard at work. Stripped to the waist, some were smelting down bomb and shell casings in a forge powered by an ancient bellows, others belting the molten metal into axheads and sickles.

And so the atrocious tales continued, the horror magnified by the conversational tone in which they were related and the lack of emotion from those gathered around to listen. It was clearly a way of life—and death—to which they had become conditioned, as was also the lack of interest in the continuing thumps of exploding shells about fifteen miles distant. "So much regular shelling is most unusual," muttered Huynh Van Luan, as we headed back toward Tay Ninh City. "Pol Pot's obviously preparing for some more mischief."

Driving back to Ho Chi Minhville, I realized I was caught up in one of the most miserable months of reporting ever experienced till then. It had started off badly enough and was getting worse. How to explain to my left-wing readers and supporters all over the world that Asian socialist states were at each other's throats and that the foulest barbarities were being committed in the name of "socialism" and "revolution"? And this in gentle, peace-loving Kampuchea? How could the "oasis of peace," as it was known under the rule of Prince Sihanouk, a model of religious and racial harmony, as many of us thought and wrote, have been transformed into a slave-labor concentration camp and slaughterhouse?

Because of a missed plane connection to Hanoi, I had to stay overnight in Ho Chi Minhville on my arrival there from Paris on November 30, 1978. Local press officials wondered whether I might seize the occasion to pay my last respects to Thanh Nga, who was to be buried the following day. Thus, I learned, to my horror, that Vietnam's most talented and universally loved actress had been assassinated four nights earlier. A few hours later I joined a line of white-clad mourners, most of them weeping, to file past the coffin, place some incense sticks into a bronze urn, and bow before the portrait of the late actress.

The previous year Thanh Nga had ignored repeated telephoned warnings not to play the role of Trung Trac, the elder of the legendary Trung sisters who, in A.D. 43, headed an insurrection which briefly threw the Chinese Han dynasty out of Vietnam. She played the role but was temporarily incapacitated after a hand grenade was thrown onto the stage on March 13, 1977. She later continued to act despite grenade fragments in her right shoulder. The second warning was that she would be killed if she accepted the lead role in Huy Hanh's play about a tenth-century heroine, Queen Duong Van Nga, who inspired a young general to raise an army to expel the Chinese Sung dynasty invaders. After the performance on November 26, Thanh Nga was driven home by her husband, Dong Lan. Gunmen waiting outside their garage shot first Dong Lan, then Thanh Nga, killing both. A few months earlier a Peking *People's Daily* editorial (July 12, 1978) had accused Vietnam "of fanning national hatred by anti-Chinese propaganda in digging up the historical fact that some Chinese feudal rulers had committed aggression against Vietnam. . . ."

While I was flying to Hanoi the following day, more than half a million Vietnamese from all over South Vietnam, reinforced by several delegations from the North, attended Thanh Nga's funeral—one of the greatest in the history of Saigon. The assassins were not caught. When I asked the local press people who was responsible, there were tight smiles and the advice "Ask anyone in the market!" Typical replies were: "Better go to the Fifth District [formerly Cholon, twin city of Saigon with an overwhelmingly Chinese population]"; "Bad elements among the Hoa"; "Ask Peking." The huge funeral seems to have been a dignified and restrained affair. There were no reports of hostile acts against the more than half million Hoa residents of the city.

After the formalities of accreditation and program arranging in Hanoi, I returned to the South, visiting, among other places, the Mekong Delta province of Dong Thap, one of those hardest hit in that year's disastrous autumn floods. Eighty thousand Vietnamese refugees from Kampuchea had arrived there since the Pol Pot regime had taken over. Thousands of others had been killed trying to escape. Almost all who did arrive were in lamentable physical condition. (In Ho Chi Minhville, I had been informed that 80 percent of the 268,000 Vietnamese who managed to make it to Vietnam were in a condition of semistarvation.) Close to the frontier areas were the same familiar explosions from 130 mm artillery shells, coming in from the Kampuchean side of the frontier, as at Tay Ninh.

Toward the end of my trip I visited the Lang Son Pass area in the extreme north, the traditional route for China's land invasions of Vietnam for the past 2,000 years. Lang Son City is about 100 miles northeast of Hanoi. For the first 45 miles the road leads through lush rice fields of the northern sector of the Red River Delta; then gradually it climbs to reach towering mountains which signal the approach to the pass. The last 30 miles of narrow, winding road lead through gorges where rugged mountain slopes drop down to within a few hundred yards and less of the road. It is a wildly beautiful landscape, a country friendly to the defender but implacably hostile to the invader. In late December 1978 the road was dotted with family-sized groups—mainly Nung-Thai tribespeople—moving back from the frontier areas with their oxen and buffalo or squatting around roadside cooking fires. At the provincial headquarters in Lang Son there was news which sent me speeding nine miles farther north to Dong Dang, only two miles from the frontier and the first station inside Vietnam of the only railway line linking Vietnam with the outside world, through China.

There were two special reasons why I should remember Dong Dang. Almost twenty-four years earlier (on March 3, 1955, to be exact) I had traveled from Dong Dang to Hanoi on the first train to reopen the China–Vietnam railway since the Vietnamese section had been destroyed by Vietminh guerrillas eight years previously. It was a great triumphant occasion. The locomotive bore portraits of Chairman Mao and President Ho; carriages were decked out with red bunting and banners hailing the victories of the Chinese and Vietnamese revolutions and the eternal, indestructible unity between the two peoples. A great symbolic moment.

The other souvenir of Dong Dang was more personal and less pleasant. As I was returning to Hanoi in early May 1955, after a drama-packed journey to the Bandung Conference of Afro-Asian nations, my passport was duly stamped at Dong Dang station, as the first entry point into Vietnam by rail from Nanning. I put it in my pocket and never saw it again.

At the time of the conference I was based in Hanoi. I left for Bandung on a plane carrying North Vietnam's premier, Pham Van Dong. Because of bad weather, we had to make an unscheduled refueling stop at Singapore, where the plane was sent off to a special parking area for four hours while my passport was temporarily confiscated and the British-Singapore authorities decided what to do with me. On arrival at Djakarta I was greeted with the news that the UPI had reported that if Burchett tried to reach Bandung via Hong Kong or Singapore, he would be arrested. During the conference I was warned by colleagues not to return through Hong Kong or Singapore because although there were no grounds to arrest me, the local authorities would at least impound my passport.

In any event, I flew back over the top of Singapore with Chinese Premier Chou En-lai as far as Kunming in South China, took another flight across to Nanning, capital of China's Kwangsi Province bordering on Vietnam, and thence by train to Dong Dang. From there I drove by car to Hanoi, to discover on arrival that my passport was missing. Vietnamese authorities to whom I reported the loss later told me they suspected it was stolen by agents at the Dong Dang guesthouse, where foreign travelers into and out of Vietnam usually had a meal and rest (as I had done) while awaiting their car or train. Mine was the latest of a series of mysterious losses, but by the time the inquiry reached the guesthouse the "birds had flown." My request to the British consul for a new passport was referred to the Australian government, which refused to issue one and maintained that refusal for seventeen years.

My arrival at Dong Dang station on Christmas Eve 1978 was my first visit since that 1955 trip. Preceding me by half an hour was a group of Vietnamese railway liaison personnel from the international checkpoint of P'ing-hsiang, the last station on the Chinese side of the frontier. The Chinese authorities had severed the rail link the previous day, expelling the Vietnamese at twenty-four hours' notice.

Station master Nguyen Tien Tat read me the message he had received from his Chinese opposite number at P'ing-hsiang, the previous day:

> I would like to inform you that that part of the railway line lying in Chinese territory from the junction with the China–Vietnam line is gravely damaged. This will be detrimental to the passage of trains. For this reason, on December 22, the Chinese minister of railways has informed us that . . . until further notice all passengers, luggage, parcels, and cargo sent on this international railway from and to Vietnam are temporarily halted. Passenger and freight trains between P'ing-hsiang and Dong Dang will cease functioning as from this date. All personnel from the Vietnamese side working at the P'ing hsiang railway station are no longer required. . . ."

Than Van Tong, deputy chief of the Vietnamese liaison team, had been stationed at P'ing-hsiang for thirteen years—ever since the opening of the line. We recalled the great celebration that day at P'ing-hsiang. An enormous banquet had preceded the departure of the inaugural train. Six hundred Vietnamese railway workers were the guests of honor. They feasted and exchanged toasts in "seven different kinds of wine."

"It was very different this morning," said Than Van Tong. "We have always tried to maintain the old friendship. But when we went to say good-bye to the station master and thank him for past cooperation, all he could say was: 'Have you got everything ready to leave?' We waved to the personnel as we left, but they turned their heads, and there were no answering waves."

The next morning I visited Nam Quan and the famous Friendship Gate, which—although now a misnomer—marks the historic frontier between Vietnam and China. The Lang Son–Dong Dang road is relatively straight with plains on the western side and the mountain slopes to the east much farther from the road than those south of Lang Son. But between Dong Dang and the frontier, the mountains closed in on the road again, and their steep slopes were crisscrossed with freshly dug trenches and dotted with artillery replacements. To reach Nam Quan, where the Vietnamese had their forwardmost frontier post, our car had to negotiate tank traps, made of big chunks of rock cemented together, blocking the road, with just enough room for a jeep to squeeze past on one side. The real Friendship Gate, an ancient Chinese-built arched gateway under which I had passed a quarter of a century earlier on my first visit to Vietnam, was unattainable. The road leading to it was blocked by a barbed-wire barricade. On a mountain peak the Chinese had seized four months earlier, directly overlooking the Vietnamese forward post, a huge radar antenna had been set up to scan the Vietnamese rear, twenty-four hours a day.

Lieutenant Nguyen Tien Hoa, deputy commander of the Nam Quan border post, with a nut-brown skin and an impression of calm combined with acute alertness, spoke of the distressing scenes to which he had been witness during the previous months as Hoa refugees piled up in the area, awaiting their turn to cross into China. "There were tearful farewell scenes between family members leaving and those who had decided to stay, each trying to persuade the other to change their minds."

Regarding the current military situation, Hoa said, "It is tenser than ever since the closing of the railway. Road and rail links between our two countries no longer function. There is shooting all along the border, and the Chinese have occupied some of our peaks."

On another peak opposite to that on which the Chinese had set up their radar station, Vietnamese had established fortified positions in what was obviously an "eyeball-to-eyeball" confrontation. I asked Lieutenant Hoa what typical Chinese military activities were. "Building roads and hauling artillery into position along their side of the frontier," he replied, "seizing high ground on our side, and making raids to capture military or civilian personnel." When I had asked the railway personnel from P'ing-hsiang what sort of material had been arriving in the period immediately prior to their expulsion, they had told of heavy artillery, mountain guns complete with mule teams, and large numbers of the stocky Mongol types of ponies that the Chinese use for their cavalry units.

What struck me in driving back to Hanoi was the lack of any movement of Vietnamese troops toward a front which seemed to be approaching flash point. In Hanoi I found few responsible cadres who shared my pessimism as to an imminent explosion along the northern frontier. Hanoi seemed more concerned that Pol Pot forces had launched three divisions against Tay Ninh Province on December 23, driving close to the outskirts of Tay Ninh City— just 60 miles north of Ho Chi Minhville. Vietnamese forces had driven them out two days later and then launched a generalized offensive against the other sixteen Khmer Rouge divisions massed along the length of the Vietnamese frontier. The offensive was gathering strength as I flew back to my Paris base at the end of the year, deeply depressed.

Regardless of the rights or wrongs in the China-Vietnam-Kampuchea confrontation, the main part of "my" world, in terms of reporting and engagement, was falling about my ears. Writing from the scene over a period of nearly forty years, I had successively supported Kuomintang China's resistance to Japanese aggression; Mao Tse-tung's Communists against the Kuomintang in China's Civil War; People's China when it aided the North in the Korean War (although this brought me into conflict with the United States and Australia, which, under the UN flag, had earlier intervened on the side of South Korea in what was essentially a civil war); the states of Indochina in their national independence struggles against France and later the United States. The material and social sacrifices involved were an acceptable price, I felt, to pay for my own concepts of professional integrity. Together with other progressives, I had rejoiced when, within the space of three weeks in April–May 1975, the peoples of Cambodia, Vietnam, and Laos, backed by People's China, won their respective national liberation struggles. My activities were switched to Africa, especially the struggles in the former Portuguese colonies and their implications for the rest of southern Africa.

Now my Asian friends were at each other's throats—each waving the banner of socialism and revolution—and I was again in the thick of it. It was a shattering blow to a vision of things acquired during the previous four decades, including my certainty as to the superior wisdom and morality of Asian revolutionaries.

Back in Paris, despondency was compounded by frustration. The *Guardian* (formerly *National Guardian*) of New York, the newsweekly in which my reports had regularly appeared for many years, had not published my reports from Vietnam, nor was the editor interested in any material about the situation in Kampuchea. I was faced with the extraordinary situation in which I was deluged with letters and telephone calls from *Guardian* readers in the United States and elsewhere, asking why my voice and opinions were not heard about what was the most explosive situation in the world at that moment. Ironically, these were from readers who were not even informed that their correspondent had spent the whole of that fateful month of December 1978 along Vietnam's frontiers with Kampuchea and China—the only Western journalist in the world to have done so.

If any readers had a right to know what was going on in the Vietnam-Kampuchea-China triangle—and at least a partial explanation—it was those of the *Guardian*. Most of them, including thousands who contributed financially toward its survival, had "graduated" in the protest movement against U.S. involvement in the Vietnam War, of which movement the *Guardian* was the most articulate and effective voice. But the editors were now suppressing reports from their own correspondent—and widely acknowledged specialist on the area—and even the fact that he had been there.

On January 23, 1979, *The New York Times* published an op-ed page article in which I gave my impressions of the impending Vietnam-China crisis. It was one of the rare warnings of what was to happen twenty-five days later, when China invaded Vietnam along the land frontier between the two countries. In its January 31 issue the *Guardian* published, in garbled form, the only material from my Vietnam journey—an interview with Prime Minister Pham Van Dong.

I did what most journalists who value their integrity would do: reached for the telephone, asked for the editor—and resigned. After twenty-two years of regular cooperation as by far the longest-serving *Guardian* staff member, it was a wrench. But suppression of such information on such a subject was an abdication of editorial responsibility. It was also an unacceptable violation of my own perhaps unorthodox concepts of journalistic ethics. These were formed by my life and background, some details of which are set forth in the chapters which follow.

2

New Worlds for Old

MY ANCESTORS ON THE paternal side seem to have been moderately respectable and God-fearing people. Until they were bitten by the wander bug in the mid-nineteenth century, they divided their time as far back as there are any records between yeoman farming and building houses in the Surrey-Kent counties of Old England. One diligent delver into family affairs discovered that there had been a "biscuit-tin full of notes, letters, documents, including birth and marriage certificates, official copies of extracts from registers, etc., bundles of family letters . . . neatly docketed as to contents. Some of these letters were in Hebrew, others in Spanish, and a few in German Yiddish. . . ."

Although the mysterious biscuit tin was escorted to Australia in the early 1850s and apparently zealously protected at first, it was subsequently lost. Thus some family skeletons could rest in peace.

One who had a peep into the biscuit tin refers to Josiah, as one of the "earliest English Burchetts." The only one who fits more or less in time and place is a Josiah "of humble birth" who was "at the age of fourteen taken by [Samuel] Pepys, the then Secretary of the Admiralty, about 1680, into his service as body servant and clerk. After remaining with Pepys for more than seven years, he incurred his master's displeasure, apparently by insolence, and was discharged in 1687." *

Despite "three most abject letters" of apology, the insolent Josiah remained sacked. But somehow he had so ingratiated himself with the upper crust of the British Establishment that eleven years after having been sacked by the great Pepys, he had replaced him to become the first-ever permanent Secre-

---

* *Dictionary of National Biography* (London: 1882), p. 16.

tary of the Admiralty and remained in that post for an all-time record of forty-four years.

My great-grandfather James Burchett, who brought his family out to Australia, was mixed up in early trade union agitation in England and in Australia, and the records show that he was once court-martialed in England "for firing his rifle without due cause, thus calling out the whole regiment." *
Why did he bother to emigrate? There does not appear to have been any compelling reason, except for his having been caught up by the great wave of emigration to the New World which started in the 1850s. James had started life as a bricklayer but had worked his way up to master builder. He had three brothers: George, Edward, and Charles—all in the building trade, except George, who was a technical draftsman.

Edward and Charles had rushed off to California to fill their pockets with gold. They quickly made fortunes—by building homes for those who "struck it lucky" in the California gold fields. James was about to follow them when brother George returned on leave from Paris, even wealthier than the other two. George, it seems, was an outstanding draftsman-architect. James was about to return to Paris with George when news came of a fabulous gold strike in Australia. He fell for the glitter of gold and the lure of the New World, bitterly regretting it later. The family left London's East India Docks in September 1853 on the *Fairlie*, which sailed into Melbourne's Port Phillip Bay 147 days later. Among other things he accomplished by this hazardous and grueling voyage was to ensure that his great-grandson, the author of these lines, was born not an Englishman, a Frenchman, or an American— although such were distinct possibilities—but an Australian. For as the Bible records such matters, James begat Caleb, who begat George, who begat Wilfred—all begotten in Australia except Caleb, who, at the age of ten, had arrived with his parents.

Not finding any gold nuggets lying around in the streets—James followed one of the family's traditional pursuits of building houses. It was a bust-and-boom period with James usually losing more by the busts than gaining by the booms. By the time Caleb grew up he decided to try the other family pursuit of farming.

At this time—the early 1860s—battles raged between the "squattocracy" and the "selectors." In Victoria, 33 million acres of the best land had been grabbed by the squatters.

A struggle to "unlock the land" developed, as the would-be smallholder settlers challenged the squatters. It was waged most strongly in Victoria and eventually resulted in the passing of legislation which opened up some 1.3 million acres for selection.

---

* Sir Ronald East, *More Australian Pioneers, The Burchetts and Related Families* (Melbourne: privately published, 1976), p. 4.

By the time the type of land James considered suitable was available he was nearing sixty, and it was young Caleb—already married to Amy Stroud and with four children—who managed to get a "selection" of 320 acres at a place called Poowong, in South Gippsland, about 60 miles east of Melbourne. The third of Caleb's children (later increased to ten) was George Harold, who became my father.

The inaccessibility and ruggedness of the country and the prospect of dealing with a mass of almost impenetrable forest and undergrowth were the reasons for the South Gippsland area's being the last in Victoria to be opened up for selection. Not even aborigines dwelt in these steep, inhospitable, and forest-covered hills. The only way to clear the land was by ax and fire, controlled burns, as the latter were called. By the time Caleb had secured his land it was too late in the season to contemplate a burn, so he took on some building work, investing his earnings in forty young calves which he could collect at his convenience.

The hazards were many—even during the frequent trips that had to be made between Poowong and Melbourne to collect stores, grass seed, and other necessities. Caleb noted that to kill half a dozen poisonous snakes on a single trip was commonplace. He wrote of one trip with his cart and faithful mare, Polly:

> An item appeared in the press about the death of a settler attacked by dingoes [an Australian wild dog which hunts singly or in packs]. I noted that in my memory, but it did not trouble me until some months later. I was returning from Melbourne with a load of stores and, as night came on and the road was very bad, I camped on the top of "Tinpot Hill." I fed and secured my mare to a sapling and, propping up my cart, crawled into my bunk for the night. Sudden as a night attack came the unmistakable howl of the wild dogs. I listened fearfully for there was evidently a good pack of them, and they were advancing in my direction. I thought of the newspaper story, then of my poor tethered mare and then of myself. In another minute or two they would be upon us. The human voice, I had read, would frighten even a lion. I had no firearms. . . . Alighting from my cart I stood out in the darkness and yelled and shouted to the full extent of my vocal strength. I distinctly heard the patter of their feet as they turned and fled in the opposite direction and I followed them with volley after volley of sounds till their voices were lost in the night.*

The next morning he saw the "sprawling marks of the great feet of a pack of dingoes—perhaps a dozen in number," where they had skidded to a stop and headed in the opposite direction.

Caleb was a small man with a big heart, plenty of guts, and tough muscles.

---

* *More Australian Pioneers, The Burchetts and Related Families*, pp. 72–74.

Working on his own with ax and slasher pitted against primeval forest and impenetrable scrub, he carved out a promising farm in the first years. But later he had to admit defeat in that first long round, despite the efforts of his children, who, as muscles developed, worked at his side. Dingoes ate the livestock; rabbits ate the grass; prices were too low for the excellent cream and butter produced by as many survivors of the original forty calves which the dingoes had permitted to grow into milk-producing motherhood. Investments in wire-netting fences to keep out the rabbits, topped by rows of barbed wire high enough to deter the agile, leaping wallabies, meant high-interest loans, repayments of which were difficult to meet in lean seasons. When they were not met, the banks were liable to move in and seize the property.

About fifteen years after he started his assault on the forest, Caleb led his tribe back to Melbourne—the tenth and last child having been delivered and a revival of the building trade having started. The small dairy herd at what had been named Hazeldeane was sold, and the cleared land leased out for grazing. Caleb had worn himself out trying to cope with the ever-intensifying problems. One out of every three of his generation of settlers in the South Gippsland area abandoned their selections. Caleb at least held onto his land.

Half a century after Hazeldeane was abandoned for the first time, I found myself doing with my father, George, exactly what Caleb had been doing nearly sixty years earlier: hacking away with ax and scrub hook at thirty acres of the only uncleared patch of virgin forest and scrub left among what was by then hundreds of thousands of acres of valuable dairying, cattle, and sheep-grazing country around Poowong. Because it was steep, unkempt, and impossibly misshapen, nobody had given it a second look in all the decades which followed the opening up of South Gippsland. "It's worth nothing but the rabbits and trees for firewood," the owner warned when we inquired whether it might be for sale. This did not inhibit him from driving a hard bargain when he found we were in earnest. We had no money for even the most modest deposit, but it was agreed that if we could raise a stipulated sum within six months, the ugly duckling would be ours. "And be sure *you* keep the rabbits," said the owner!

Just when the option was agreed on, I was offered a job on the farm of a friend of some relatives, at one pound per week and keep. It was agreed I should take it, while my father—highly accomplished in all arts of the main family trade—should keep an eye open for building work. Earnings would be counted as the date for expiration of the option approached. "My" farm was at a place called Dollar about thirty miles east of Poowong. The owner was a newly married dairy farmer named Harrison, cross-eyed and tough. His opening remarks were: "There's plenty of hard work to be done here. You're on two weeks' trial, and if you don't suit, there's plenty of others around."

Why we should have been in such a predicament is a long story. Briefly,

Caleb's move back into the building business, which seemed to prosper at first, blew up in what was known as the land boom crash. The bottom dropped out of property values; banks and investment companies went bankrupt; thousands of families were ruined overnight. Building came to an abrupt halt. For the Burchetts, there was still land. The family accompanied Caleb back to Hazeldeane. This time Caleb's two brothers-in-law joined in. With many strong arms to help, grass and clover soon dominated the original clearing again, while axes and controlled burns tore into the remaining forest. After a few years, old and new pastures were flourishing, a pedigreed herd had been built up, and there was relative prosperity.

The dingoes had been driven back by organized hunts; the wallabies had retreated as forest and scrub gave way to axes and controlled burns; rabbits were kept down by massive trapping and confined by netted fences. Then, on February 1, 1898, came what is still referred to in the area as the Great Fire. After describing the devastating swiftness of the fire's advance from the time it started in midafternoon of a blazing summer day, an eyewitness noted:

> As it advanced, the heat engendered a strong wind which ripped off the sapwood from the old trees and hurled flaming pieces hundreds of yards away. The whole countryside in an incredibly short time was thus engulfed in fire and smoke. . . . People immersed themselves in dams or underground wells. Parents covered their children with wet bags, or perhaps sheltered them with the family in a hole. Young men fainted while carrying water in the terrible heat. Older folk collapsed under the strain while young children were terrified by the roar of the fire. The full blast of this terror encircled the Hazeldeane homestead. There was no chance of escape if the house caught fire. As burning sapwood showered down on the clearing the Burchett boys checked its advance by beating out the flames with their wet hessian bags.
>
> By nightfall the fury of the first onslaught had abated, but danger continued and a constant vigil was necessary. Great trees standing in their thousands on the hillside were still alight, burning brightly throughout their whole height. . . .
>
> Morning revealed an unbelievable state of devastation. Fallen trees littered the blocks with logs and black ashes from the fire. As far as the eye could see, not a blade of grass existed. There were no signs of cattle. . . . Fences were non-existent. . . .
>
> The pioneers in the past had suffered and overcome many setbacks, but never had they been so grievously afflicted. . . . The few cattle left could not be fed. . . .*

The pedigreed Jersey herd, built up so carefully over the years, was entirely destroyed; the costly investment in fencing, reduced to ashes. The backbreaking work of "picking up"—dealing with all the enormous grounded

---

* *Ibid.* The Hazeldene Selection, E. E. Straw, pp. 117–19.

tree trunks—had to be done all over again and on an unimaginable scale!

With characteristic optimism and energy, the seven Burchett brothers threw themselves into a full year's work of restoration, not overlooking the fact that the fire had made a clear sweep of one flat bit of ground which could easily be converted into a full-sized cricket field. This they proceeded to do on Saturday afternoons with the help of some of their younger neighbors, later constituting seven-elevenths of the redoubtable Poowong cricket team.

Three years after the Great Fire there was another tragic blow with the death of Clement, then twenty-one, the eighth child of Caleb and Amy. Smitten with a sudden attack of pneumonia, he died before adequate medical help was available. (The other six brothers went on to live well into their eighties and nineties.) Another blow, which started the breakup of the family, came a few months later. The revenue from a reconstituted dairy herd, plus homegrown vegetables and abundant rabbits, was just sufficient for a modest existence, but there was no margin to put aside for such a large family. The soil proved exceptionally favorable for potatoes, and in the early nineties potatoes were fetching a high price in Melbourne. The boys cleared the stumps from a large field, plowed it, and sowed potatoes. The first season in virgin soil, they had a bumper crop. They dug and bagged them, then purchased a special wagon to take them to the railway station and on to Melbourne. Ten days later the eagerly awaited letter came from the selling agent. Instead of a fat check, there was a letter explaining that since potato prices had slumped, the amount received was not sufficient to cover the agent's expenses. A bill was enclosed for two shillings and sixpence!

This was too much for my future father, George, and his inseparable younger brother Franklin. They returned to Melbourne, and with a few sovereigns donated from the family's reserve fund, they took off as steerage passengers for Western Australia, where gold had just been discovered. Digging for gold, they hoped, would be more remunerative than digging "spuds," and in any case it would be more fun. And if there was no gold, they could emulate Great-uncles Edward and Charles in California by building homes for the lucky ones. (George and Franklin, having learned to make bricks—and to lay them—had also served their apprenticeship as carpenters in Melbourne before the land boom broke, and George had even taken a night school course in architecture.) They ended up digging for gold, but it was always at a more elusive depth than their meager finances permitted them to follow. The results of their first strike were invested in a winch to haul out the dirt, then in dynamite to break up the rock and a pump as they struck water. But the "rich seam" was always a few feet lower. In the end they gave up and returned, Franklin to prospect new ways of making a living in Melbourne, George to escort his bride, Mary-Jane Evelyn Davy—the sole positive result of the Western Australian venture—to Poowong.

Apart from elder brother James, who had settled on part of the original Hazeldeane homestead, the other brothers had gone. George took up 120 acres of Caleb's original selection, starting by building a house. It was there that I spent my life from September 16, 1911, when I was born. I was proficient at milking cows, trapping rabbits, and riding bareback, but notorious also for riding a cow to school while most other children rode ponies. I was the youngest of four, the others in order of ascending age, being Winston, Amy, and Clive.

The year 1919 was memorable for two things: Uncle Edwin and some cousins returned safely from the war, and we had a record crop of potatoes, which I helped gather and bag. Fifty tons were sent off in the first shipment. I remember my father's startled face when the agent's letter arrived and the payment was in postage stamps. The end of the war had caused a glut in the potato market. My father gulped and said, "If that is the price of peace, we can't complain." After setting aside a good stock for family consumption and the next season's seed, the rest was fed to the pigs. The next year I had the mournful task of tramping around the farm with my father, straining at the heads of yearling calves stretched out on the ground, holding their throats taut while my father drew a knife across them, ending their lives in a gush of dark blood. It was a vain attempt to stop a mysterious disease known as swamp fever from spreading. Of a thriving herd of pedigreed Jerseys, we saved only the skins.

For a long time my parents had considered giving up the farm, not only because of the recurrent setbacks but because they wanted at least some of the children to have secondary education. The loss of the dairy herd, which had taken twenty years to build up, was decisive. The farm was sold, and we went to Ballarat. I was the only one who resented leaving the open spaces to be crammed in between brick walls—as I imagined a city at that time. I was bribed into acquiescence by the promise that there would always be a cow to milk and ride—even in Ballarat—as there was for the first few years. With the money from the farm, my father bought a block of land and building materials. With the aid of Clive—a quick learner with so many generations of builders' blood in his veins—a five-room cottage was soon taking shape. Originally intended for us, it was sold before completion at an attractive price.

The purchaser was entranced by the wealth of built-in cupboards, virtually unheard of in those days; the placing of windows to exploit the view most effectively; and all the little artistic touches to please my mother. The agent who handled the sale was delighted. He had made a good commission and knew there was a big market for original houses of that type. More houses were built for sale while we lived in a modest rented cottage. As funds accumulated, we started to build our own home—an ambitious project. It was one of the first houses, if not *the* first one, built in Australia of reinforced concrete. Once the foundations were laid, it grew in spasms—according to the rhythm of other work and the availability of ready cash. When a house was sold, we poured a lot of concrete.

My parents, heartily seconded by Clive, decided that because he was nearing seventeen, he had passed the age to enter secondary school. Only very advanced people in the 1920s thought that girls merited more than primary education, so hopes were centered on brother Winston and me as far as secondary education was concerned.

Three years after arriving in Ballarat, we moved into our handsome two-story house. Shortly afterward, Amy—by then eighteen—complained of a pain in the upper part of her arm. She had fallen from a horse before leaving Poowong and had occasional twinges of pain. Now it was constant. After consultation it was recommended that an eminent—and very expensive—specialist in Melbourne be consulted. The trouble was diagnosed as sarcoma, a rare type of bone disease. Only very expensive radium treatment could help. My father rushed back to Ballarat to raise every penny possible, including what the bank would advance with the new house as security.

After some months a pale ghost of my sister was brought back. She had heard an imprudent surgeon whisper, "Amputation is the only chance." She pleaded to return home, where she died after a few days. My mother, exhausted from weeks of day-and-night bedside vigil, fell seriously ill and lay at death's door for months. My father was ruined financially. Winston left school to work in an iron foundry.

The day came when the bank manager and his agent came to seize the house. After a few polite words to my father they began looking over the furnishings. After an hour or so the manager totted up his evaluation of the furnishings, argued with my father about the value of the house, subtracted all this from the debts—property values having dropped by 30 percent in the meantime—and proved there was still a substantial amount owing.

"You'll be hearing from us again," said the manager as he left. "I don't want to be too hard. You can stay on for a few days until you find another place. Of course, none of the things marked down may be removed or harmed. Inform me of your new address and when you are leaving." My father's face was ashen as he stumbled inside after seeing him to the gate.

"We still have ourselves and the children," murmured my mother.

Some days later, with the few belongings the law allowed us—beds and a minimum of crockery and kitchen utensils—we moved to a tumbledown three-room cottage on the shores of Ballarat's Lake Wendouree. It belonged to someone who sympathized with our plight and offered it rent-free if we would totally renovate it with materials that she would supply.

It was a bitter period. Fortunately, after we had repaired the lakeside cottage, there was an upsurge in building activities. We earned modestly and were able to pay back the worst of the debts.

For a few years, life went fairly smoothly. Clive got married, and we all helped build him a house. Then the real Depression hit. The sudden drop in property values a few years earlier had been but a herald of disaster to come. As a primary producer Australia was among the first countries to suffer from what turned out to be the World Economic Depression, and although the building trade was the first and hardest hit, virtually all branches of economic activity soon began to suffer. Like tens of thousands of other young Australians, I took to the road, a swag (pack) on my back, looking for seasonal work. I quickly picked up the knack of jumping the rattler (leaping into moving railway freight cars and avoiding the police) for a free ride for 100 or so miles. My first aim was the rich fruit-growing areas of Mildura, more than 300 miles northwest of Ballarat on the Murray River. Rumor had it that there was a great dearth of labor for the fruit-picking season. But it was only a rumor. My home for the next six months was under an outsize gum tree at Bruce's Bend, a big curve in the Murray River, where the borders of Victoria, New South Wales, and South Australia come together.

I lived by catching fish, exchanging the surplus from my own consumer needs for flour and salt from a nearby shop, eating grilled Murray cod and catfish and damper (swagmen's unleavened bread of flour, salt, and water, cooked on any bit of flat tin on an open fire). After confirming the impossibility of any seasonal work in the Mildura area for the foreseeable future, I decided to return home.

The railway police, tolerant toward the unemployed leaving the big urban centers, were very vigilant in preventing them from returning. Hitchhiking was the next best thing. Having covered the last fifty-three miles over hilly country in twenty hours—with a heavy pack—I turned up in the small hours one morning at our Wendouree house, scaring the living daylights out of the only occupant: brother Winston. My parents had returned to Poowong, my mother to look after Grandfather Caleb, then entering his nineties, my father on the lookout for whatever meager farming or building work was available.

After some months' tramping around, doing a few odd carpentering jobs and some agricultural work, I got a letter from my father suggesting I come to Poowong, where "there was plenty of potato digging to be had." Another 140-mile hike with an emotional family reunion at the end of it. After the backbreaking work of digging an uncle's big potato crop there was nothing more to do but trap rabbits for food and pelts.

It was then that we started prying into the bit of virgin forest and scrub which lay between the property of my uncle and a neighbor—and it was the prospect of having our own little farm that led me to earn a few pounds as a farmhand for the Dollar Harrisons.

The day started at 5:00 A.M., initiating me into early-morning working habits that the passage of almost half a century has not changed. First job was to get the thirty cows into the sheds for milking an hour later. After that and breakfast came a good eight hours in the field before the evening milking. The main field work was to clear up the back hill. This meant grubbing out stumps from the original forest and clearing up the secondary growth which had sprung up after its destruction. At first muscles ached and hands got badly blistered from mattock and ax handles. But muscles soon toughened; blisters turned into calluses.

Harrison, a surly man of few words, said nothing at the end of my trial period, so the weekly pounds piled up. On one unforgettable morning, Harrison turned up to mutter that a number of parcels had arrived for me and I must sign some papers. There were half a dozen large volumes of *The New Popular Educator*, edited by Sir J. A. Hammerton, sent as a gift by brother Winston. (He had opened a lending library, based on the family stock of books, plus what he could persuade friends to contribute.) These splendidly bound books opened a new world to me. They dealt factually, if in capsule form, with an enormous number of subjects in the form of "outlines" of history, philosophy, science, political systems, courses in foreign languages, and a dozen other subjects—including journalism. This was a subject which quickly caught my interest, especially the role of the foreign correspondent "with the world as his beat."

As the months went by, I started to swallow those volumes, including the language courses, French, Italian, Spanish, and German. Morning and evening milking sessions were excellent for reflecting on what I had read the previous night on philosophical and kindred subjects. If I swung my fern hook or wielded the ax with extra vigor, it was because I was muttering the declensions of a German verb. The Harrisons never overcame their suspicions that my improved humor was somehow obtained at their expense.

After nearly six months, by which time I had the back hill ready for plowing, the long-awaited letter from my father arrived. Through a succession of building jobs he had earned enough for the precious deposit. What I had saved could go toward buying a horse. "Come quickly" was the message, so we could cut as much scrub as possible during what was left of the summer.

The morning after my arrival money was counted out, papers were signed, and we became the legal owners of thirty acres of virgin bush. The days and months that followed were among the happiest in my life till then. With ax and scrub hook we attacked the wall of undergrowth and the smaller trees. Although there were almost forty years between us, my father and I worked in a similar rhythm, both of us physically and muscularly stronger than our ages.

This part of the family saga at least had a happy ending. We had a "good burn," and from the grass and clover sown in the ashes moistened by timely autumn rains we had a "good strike."

Within six months of launching the assault on the wilderness, we had something starting to look like a farm, a very beautiful little farm, what with a generous fringe of bush we had left along the first creek, framed by the tall blue gums and blackwoods left for shade. All the bigger trees had survived the flames, and within a few weeks their leaves were growing again. Beneath them was the brilliant green of the fast-growing grasses.

We decided to name our property Greenhaven, the fittest expression of what it meant to us at that time. Grandfather Caleb had died by that time— at ninety-two—and his little cottage, by unanimous consent of the family "council," was dismantled and rebuilt, with some additions, on Greenhaven. So we had a home again and an assured means of existence. It had all been done with our bare hands—plus some honorable help from Jimmy, the chestnut gelding bought with my Dollar pounds.

3

Distant Pastures

A S THE GRASS continued to grow at Greenhaven, there was time
for books again, especially during the long winter nights. I renewed
my study of languages and exercise books became fat with multilingual
vocabulary. During rest periods, while we cleared the back hill for the plow,
swigging cold tea with backs against a blue gum, disscussions with my father on political affairs took up more and more of our time. Until the shock
of our crash he had been a liberal-conservative and had even stood as the
endorsed Nationalist (conservative) party candidate for Ballarat in 1925.
But the continuous family misfortunes had shaken his earlier beliefs and
caused him to ponder the ills and injustices of the day. He was indignant
that Clive—an excellent carpenter—had to cycle fifteen miles, twice daily, to
break stones for railway ballast for a pittance insufficient to feed his wife
and baby, and that tens of thousands of other skilled tradesmen were forced
to do the same thing.

Our tea-break exchanges were enlivened by the formation of the Poowong
Discussion Club at the initiative of our local Irish blacksmith, a newly arrived butter factory manager, the local schoolmaster, and a few other kindred
spirits. Speakers were invited from Melbourne once a fortnight to speak on
topical and controversial subjects. At the in-between weekly meeting we discussed the previous lecture. As the elected secretary I had to keep the minutes of each meeting. It was my first "intellectual" task and one which made
me punctiliously respect facts.

Our club was popular with the poorer farmers and a handful of the well-
to-do ones. They contributed to pay the hire of the hall and the transport
expenses of the speakers. Gradually the club became known to progressive

intellectuals in Melbourne, and our lecturers included some well-known and much-traveled university professors. Years later, when I went to live in Melbourne, I learned that it had been considered something of a distinction to be invited to speak, although none of them ever received a fee. The lecturers appreciated the fact that the members of our audience, rarely more than fifty, were in deadly earnest. Questions, often framed in awkward, stammering language, came straight from the hearts and minds and revealed the problems bothering people everywhere in those days. Fascism was in power in Italy; Nazism was on the rise in Germany. Because we once invited a known Communist and on another occasion a university professor lately returned from the Soviet Union, the club was branded "subversive" by some extreme rightists. Superpatriots of the Returned Soldiers League took up the matter; an officer from the nearest police station came to investigate and found there was nothing to discover. Thus, although like cabbages, we had sunk our roots into the soil, we did not entirely live the life of cabbages. As a by-product to enlightenment we were also introduced to the world of heresies and witch-hunters.

After a few years of routine and successful farming at Greenhaven, I developed a yearning for wider experiences. The way was eased for me to resume travels when Clive, by then with a wife and two children to support—and still unemployed—moved to Poowong, where Greenhaven was at least a sure source of food supply. My aim was 1,000 or so miles north of Melbourne—the sugarcane fields along the New South Wales-Queensland border. Cane cutting, I knew, was very hard, but highly paid, seasonal work. It was a long and adventurous trek north, and my experience at jumping the rattler stood me in good stead, as did the ease with which my legs could take me thirty to forty miles a day when there were no rattlers to be jumped.

At the end of one particularly weary day, when my swag weighed heavy but my tucker-bag (food bag) was empty, I crossed a branch of the Clarence River, about ninety miles south of the Queensland border, onto Harwood Island. Sugar plantations stretched as far as the eye could see. A mile downstream from the river crossing was a factory which, by the treacly odor of the smoke puffed out from its chimney, could only be a sugar mill. Bundles of cane were being loaded onto a barge from horse-drawn carts. Watching the work and making entries in a notebook was a burly middle-aged man with a bushy mustache. As I stood looking, he turned to me and said gruffly, "What do you want?"

When I explained that I was looking for work in the cane fields, if possible cutting cane, he asked if I'd come to join a gang. When I replied that it was my first time in cane country, he said, "You haven't got a chance. It's a job you've got to learn. You can't just walk into it, coming off the road like that." I explained I was used to timber cutting, and wielding a cane knife should not be all that different from using an ax. "You'll never get a start," he said, and asked what else I could do. When I said I was a good milker, he replied, "I'll give you a try . . . fifteen shillings a week and keep with a week's trial. You can learn all there is to learn on the cane fields—on my time," and he gave a short laugh.

I sank onto my swag, appalled at the thought of working for even less than Harrison had paid at Dollar. "Make it twenty-five and I'll take it," I replied. "I'm a good general farmhand."

He roared with laughter. "Easy to see you're a newcomer. Nobody's ever paid twenty-five bob for a milker around here. I can get all the help I need off the road for ten bob; I don't know why I even offered you fifteen." Tired and hungry, with the soles practically worn off my shoes, I was in no position to bargain. So I hired myself out to the meanest man I've ever known.

Robber Ryan, as I later learned he was called, beckoned to a surly young man whose cart had just been unloaded. Nodding toward me, he said, "Drop him off at the shed on the way back. I'm trying him out as a milker." The driver turned out to be one of Ryan's three sons.

My quarters were a tiny space, separated from the rest of a big barn by a partition of split bran bags, roughly stitched together. There were two beds in it, one for a teenaged lad I was soon to meet. Beds consisted of more split bran bags, strung together on wattle poles like stretchers. More sewn bags made a blanket for each bed. There were no sheets. I was shown a tap in the yard where I could wash and the cow sheds, where I would be expected in an hour's time.

The only good impression in the first couple of hours were the cows. They were high-quality Illawarra Shorthorns, a crossbreed developed in Australia between Shorthorns, famous for their excellent beef, and Jerseys, no less famous for their high-quality milk. I was not surprised to learn that this was one of the best dairy herds in New South Wales and that Robber Ryan was one of the wealthiest farmers in the rich coastal area.

My roommate, Harry, was a slim, cheerful lad who had been getting the cows in when I arrived. Between us we had more than half the herd of thirty milked before two of Ryan's sons turned up. They stood over me as I milked, then tried each cow to make sure I had stripped the last drop of milk from their udders. When the boss arrived as the last cows were leaving the bails, the sons reported that I was "okay" as a milker.

After dinner Harry told me something of the Robber and our work routine. We would be up around 4:00 A.M. to get the cows in and fed so that milking, separating, and breakfast would be over in time for work in the fields at 8:00 A.M. "No one stays long at this joint," Harry assured me. "You won't either." At seventeen, he worked between sixteen and eighteen hours a day, six days a week (eight hours on Sundays) for five shillings a week and keep. As to why he stood it, he explained that he was an orphan, brought up by an uncle who was only too glad to be rid of him and had sent him to Ryan. Harry had twice run away back to his uncle, only to be soundly thrashed each time, then sent back to Ryan for a second beating!

Breakfast was a surprise. The milk served with the tea and porridge, from one of Australia's finest dairy herds, was thin and bluish. I could hardly believe my eyes and taste buds. It was the skim milk left after the separation of the cream—the stuff you serve to pigs, but never to human beings. It was something I have never been served at a farmer's table before or since. The Robber drank his tea black and ate only meat for breakfast, but the rest of the family also used the separated milk. That should have been enough for me to pack my swag there and then, but I wanted to stay at least long enough to make contact with the cane cutters.

The cutters had been at work for an hour or two before Harry and I arrived on the scene that first morning. What an impressive sight! Long, parallel lines of blue-black cane lay among the golden thresh. At the head of each line was a man hacking into what looked like a solid green-topped dark wall. Ten of them were in a row, backs bending rhythmically, the sun catching the flash of their heavy knives, now at ground level as the cane was severed from the stumps, now high up as the tops were decapitated with a backhand slash. Harry and I had to gather the cut cane and pile it onto the carts for hauling to the barges. It was awkward work. Every six to eight inches is a sharp little bud, and since the only way of carrying half a dozen ten-foot sticks is to hug them against your body, undershirts would be reduced to tatters in no time. Better to strip to the skin like the cutters, but there were more scratches and blood than skin after the first few hours. Harry assured me I would soon toughen up.

In midmorning the cutters knocked off for a "smoke-oh," and their cook came out with a harvester can full of tea and a platter piled high with buttered scones and cakes. Harry and I were invited to join in. They were fine-looking men with golden-bronzed bodies and rippling arm and shoulder muscles. They seemed a kindly lot who got on well together. They worked as an autonomous team with no boss or foreman standing over them. They were paid according to weight of cane cut, the weekly paycheck divided equally among the ten cutters and the cook. Each morning a different cutter would act as the pacemaker, the others honor-bound to keep up. Since the cane lay in rows behind each cutter, it was easy to see who was lagging behind. But no accounting was made of this when the check was divided up. "We're mates, not bloodhounds," one of them expressed it when I asked what happened to those who could not make the pace on any particular day. The cane cutters, together with the sheep shearers, were the "big men" of agricultural work, by far the highest paid—earning what then seemed to me the fabulous sum of fifteen to twenty pounds a week while the season lasted.

After several months, during which the cutters occasionally let me try my hand at cutting, one of the most physically exacting jobs I have ever tried, my work with Robber Ryan came to an abrupt and glorious end. The cutters had left, to return only when more fields were ready for cutting. Months later Harry and I had to strip the thresh from the last field to be cut. Stripping is one of the worst jobs in cane growing. As the cane ripens, the leaves within which it is swathed shrink ever closer to the stalk. This has to be torn off by human hands—or had to be in those days. The leaves have serrated edges, and those dropping down from the green crowns lacerate the stripper's neck and arms, while the dry thresh tears at the hands. Deep inside a stand of cane not a breath of air can penetrate, and the sweat dripping into the myriad tiny cuts and scratches is a minor form of torture. On that last field our task was complicated by the fact that the bottoms of the cane stumps had been eaten away by rats, leaving a fine powder which drifted up into our noses with an unpleasant irritant effect. When I mentioned this to Ryan, he flew into one of his furious rages.

"Rats be danged," he roared, glaring at Harry and me. "There's no rats in my fields, and don't go spreading stories that there are."

I was unaware of the implications, and Harry did nothing to enlighten me. But when I casually mentioned it to the cook a few evenings later, he exploded. "What? Rats!" He called the others together. "Hey, there's rats up at the Robber's number three field, according to our mate here."

"We'll look at that field in the morning," one of the cutters said, "but why the devil didn't you tell us before?"

The next morning, after milking and breakfast were over and Ryan was roaring out his orders as usual in the backyard, along came ten grim-looking cutters, with the cook trailing behind. "There's rats in that number three field of yours," one of them said.

"Who's been telling you that rubbish?" yelled Ryan, giving Harry and me a murderous look.

"We've just been to give it a routine check," replied another cutter. "It's riddled with rats and will have to be burned."

"Burned," shouted Ryan. "I'll see you off my property first. That's my cane, and if you don't cut it, there's plenty of others that will."

"If you don't burn, we'll report to the union, and the field will be declared black. Not a gang in Australia will touch it, and you know it. . . . And there's another thing," he said, turning to Harry and me. "You boys better not touch that stuff again. That rat dust is really poisonous, and you can land up in the hospital, if not the morgue."

Around the campfire that night, the cutters turned on Harry, asking why he had continued stripping—and let me do it—when he knew the field was rat-ridden. "Because he threatened to beat me half to death if I let on about it," he said.

The cook swore softly and said, "The old bastard knew about them all the time then."

I had assumed that Ryan had reacted because he would lose his crop by burning. But no. "The fire destroys only the thresh and all sources of the dust. Then we'll cut it, but Ryan will get about ten percent less than the prime rate because it's been burned."

The climax came next day. Using the pretext that Harry had used a kerosene lantern to light his way home after taking the horses to the back paddock, Ryan rushed at him, shaking the nearly empty lamp.

"You little bugger, you thief you," he shouted, aiming a blow at Harry's head with the lantern. "I filled it only two days ago, and now it's bone dry, you blasted cur, you." He threw the lantern to the ground and picked up a pair of steel hames, to aim a murderous blow at the boy's head. Harry managed to dodge, but the blow caught him squarely on the shoulders, and he almost fell. Ryan, mad with rage, prepared for another blow—but was pushed aside by one of the brawniest of the cutters, who had just come into the yard. He gave the bully a push—not a punch—on the chest that sent Ryan sprawling to the ground.

"None of that here, you bastard! If you want to hit someone, hit me." And the cutter rolled up his sleeves to reveal muscles like footballs. Robber Ryan picked himself up, grabbed his hat from where it had fallen on a pile of fresh horse dung, and headed back for the house without a word. "You're not a man, you're a dingo," the cutter shouted after him. "And if there's any more of this stuff, we'll have your farm declared black now and forever more."

When we told the cutter what the row was about, he swore softly and said, "I'd never have believed it if I hadn't seen it with my own eyes and worked on this hell farm myself. You chaps ought to get out of here as soon as possible."

The cane cutters were the first organized workers I had met, and I admired their independence and, above all, their comradeship and the way they stood together and supported the weak against the strong. The incident over the rat-ridden field made a deep impression.

The cutters promised to find Harry a decent job under union protection, and I was to work for a while for a neighboring cane farmer, where I at least had my own room, with a proper bed, sheets, and blankets, not to mention whole milk with my tea and porridge.

It was a pleasure to be in a totally different atmosphere with a decent couple who made me feel like a member of the family. World War I injuries prevented the husband from doing heavy work. So I did the plowing, with a single-furrow plow and a pair of flighty horses which actually insisted on trotting, taxing my stamina to keep up with them and manipulate the reins. The first furrows were very crooked, but gradually we got the job done and the cane planted. By then I had completed the whole cycle of cane production—even if I had done it backward.

The next cutting season was still some months distant, and I decided to try city life for a change, hitchhiking my way down to Sydney. To look at the space devoted in the newspapers to those offering work and those seeking it was very demoralizing. For carpenters, or anyone else in the building trade, there was absolutely nothing. Eventually, like so many of the unemployed in those days, I tried to sell vacuum cleaners, payment by commission on sales only. Even for the privilege of plodding around the streets with a heavy demonstration model in my hand, I had to invest an alarming proportion of my savings in clothes and shoes. Trying by a crash course in sales technique to sell goods to unwary housewives that they cannot afford must be one of the lowest forms of existence.

But during this period—the end of 1934—of tramping the streets of Sydney something happened which affected my future career. I used to spend my Sundays in the Sydney Domain, a big park one section of which was a Sydney equivalent of London's Hyde Park Corner, upholding the tradition of free speech for anyone who could attract an audience and even those who could not.

One Sunday, November 18, 1934, an enormous crowd had gathered around one meeting which dwarfed all others. I wormed my way as close as possible to a lorry that served as a platform where an old man, with a short white beard and parson's collar, was speaking with surprising strength and passion for his age. It was all about a man whose name I had vaguely seen referred to in the press and about the injustice of the government's trying to prevent him from entering Australia:

> The people believed that the World War was to save democracy, but the harvest they have reaped is fascism, or the menace of fascism. . . . Fighters for peace are banned in our country, and the shame is made even greater by attempting to justify that ban by a test in a foreign language. If Jesus Christ were to come here to preach peace on earth and goodwill to all men, our police chiefs and politicians would try to stop Him, because He was an alien and did not know every European language, at least not Gaelic.

Pointing to a taxi that was slowly making its way through the crowd toward the lorry, he said, "Here comes our guest, whose entry they tried to prohibit. Let us rejoice that our struggle has not been in vain. Let us carry on the fight. . . . My time is up. I have finished. Thank you." *

With these words the old orator collapsed. A doctor appeared and pronounced him dead. A cloth was spread over the body, but not before a man with a ragged mustache and his leg in a plaster cast was lifted out of the taxi and hoisted high enough to gaze on the face of the Reverend Albert

---

* Egon Irwin Kisch, *Australian Landfall* (Australia: Macmillan Press, Limited, 1969), p. 86.

Rivett for the first and last time. After two short speeches paying tribute to his lifelong activities for good causes, the man with the ragged mustache and leg in plaster was lifted onto the seat on the lorry and introduced as the Czech writer and antifascist journalist Egon Irwin Kisch. His first words were:

> My English is broken, my leg is broken, but my heart is not broken, for the task which I was given to do by the anti-fascists of Europe is fulfilled when I speak to you, the anti-fascist people of Australia. Albert Rivett died in the execution of his self-imposed duty. His name, so far honored only by Australians, will now be honored among European anti-fascists also, and if I write a book on Australia, then a cross of remembrance will be erected therein to the brave man of God—this I promise.*

Every sentence of this rather comical-looking man was punctuated with applause and cheers from the crowd of 20,000 who had gathered in the Domain on that memorable day.

The Kisch affair left an indelible impression. Because it was crucial in shaping my life and attitude toward my subsequent profession (although I could have no inkling of that at the time), it demands more than a passing reference. Since an account of the affair was rated among the 152 most significant reporting events in the history of Australian journalism from 1771 to 1975, it is worth a mention on its own merits.† Of course, I was among the crowd escorting Kisch away from the Domain, thus taking part in my first political demonstration. The next day I went to the public library to read about him and the reason for the excitement created by his arrival in Australia. Egon Irwin Kisch was a journalist and author, born in Czechoslovakia but living in Germany at the time of Hitler's takeover. He had been jailed by the Nazis for his antifascist writings but was later released and expelled. So much for the man, but why the passions aroused by his visit?

November 1934 marked the centenary of the founding of the city of Melbourne. The conservative Australian government of the day decided to mark the occasion with what the left considered a jingoistic display of the military might of the British Empire. The year 1934 was a somber one on the international front. Fascism was on the march: Italy was poised to attack Abyssinia (Ethiopia); Hitler was on the rampage, persecuting progressives and Jews at home and preparing for war abroad. The militarists were in control in Japan; Manchuria (now Northeast China) had been invaded in 1931, and Japan had walked out of the League of Nations the following year. Although the British policy of appeasement was still four years away, the

---

* *Ibid.*, pp. 87–88.
† See Harry Gordon, *An Eyewitness History of Australia* (Adelaide, Sydney, Melbourne, Perth Brisbane: Rigby Limited, 1976).

Australian government was already firmly headed on that course, in both Europe and in Asia. The government considered Japan the most stable force in Asia and was committed to supplying the raw materials for Japan's fast-expanding arms industry. The Soviet Union, not the fascist powers, was seen as the main enemy.

Thus, the fact that the star visitor to the Melbourne centenary celebrations, the Duke of Gloucester, was bringing with him the top brass of the British Military Establishment was construed by the left as banging the drums of war threats against the Soviet Union, rather than an attempt to defuse the increasingly tense international situation or to warn the nascent Rome-Berlin-Tokyo axis against military adventures. The Australian section of an international Movement Against War and Fascism decided to organize a counterrally in the form of an antiwar congress to be held in Melbourne, November 10–12, 1934. The keynote speaker was Egon Irwin Kisch. Since the climax to the centenary celebrations was to be on Armistice Day, November 11, with the duke unveiling a Shrine of Remembrance to Australia's World War I dead, the government understandably regarded the counter-attraction as a highly undesirable provocation. Leading antiwar activists, ranging from nonviolent pacifists to militant Communists, on the other hand, regarded the centenary celebrations as a cover to whip up militarist sentiments and the shrine to honor the dead of one war as a hidden recruiting device for renewed slaughter.

Constitutionally the antiwar rally could not be banned, but the attorney general, Robert (later Prime Minister Sir Robert) Menzies, was instructed to ensure that neither Kisch nor the second most important guest speaker, George Griffin, an Irishman who lived in New Zealand, should be permitted to land in Australia. What followed led to some of the most exciting events in Kisch's stormy career. From beginning to end the Australian saga was high drama as his description of the departure from Europe makes clear:

> A king has been murdered. Alexander II of Serbia, who came as the guest of France but yesterday, was shot on arrival at Marseilles. Not only he: Foreign Minister Barthou was sitting on the car beside the King, and also met his death.
>
> The assassin was sabred down. In his pocket was a Czechoslovakian passport. Accomplices, who had been with him in the same hotel, had shown Czech passports too.
>
> Raids on Czechoslovaks and Yugoslavs: 418 brought before the Prefecture in Marseilles alone, in Paris more than 300. . . .
>
> Posters of the "Action Française" and other fascist leagues shriek: "The Aliens are Guilty. . . . Down with the Red traitors, the agents of Moscow! Out with the Aliens! . . ."
>
> A man walks through this unleashed, suspicious Marseilles, and he does not feel at all comfortable. He is going from the station to the wharf of the

P & O Company. He wants to leave France today. He has a Czechoslovakian passport. He is neither a monarchist nor a fascist! Quite the contrary.
Will the liner take him? Will it? *

The P & O liner *Strathaird* did take him. His Czech passport was in order,
stamped with a valid Australian entry visa. In the meantime, Attorney General Menzies had issued his "ban Kisch" orders. The star delegate was not
permitted to land at Fremantle, where he was to take the train to Melbourne,
and thus missed the antiwar congress. By the time the *Strathaird* dropped
anchor in Melbourne a Kisch Defense Committee had been formed. For the
second time Menzies stated, "Kisch will definitely not set foot on the soil
of the Australian Commonwealth. . . ." On arrival the *Strathaird* was surrounded by a flotilla of small boats displaying banners demanding that Kisch
be allowed to land. A delegation of lawyers, parliamentarians, writers—
accompanied by journalists—boarded the ship, where the banned Czech held
a lively press conference. This prompted another declaration by Menzies:
"Any actions on behalf of the excluded person will be senseless and futile.
. . . I declare for the third and last time that he shall not set foot on the
soil of the Australian Commonwealth." Menzies was wrong, as so often in
his long political career.

As the *Strathaird* started to pull away from its berth, Kisch jumped overboard, injuring his leg. Police rushed to seize him, the liner put its engines
into reverse, and despite protests from Kisch and his supporters, he was
hustled back aboard. The *Strathaird* headed for Sydney, with placards on its
hull: "Kisch, deported by Hitler 1933—by Lyons, 1934." (J. A. Lyons was
Australian prime minister at the time.) The liner was stopped before berth-
ing at Sydney to allow a doctor aboard. She diagnosed two fractured bones
and protested that the patient had not been hospitalized in Melbourne.

An application for habeas corpus was lodged with the Supreme Court of
New South Wales. The presiding judge, Justice Herbert Evatt (later a very
distinguished secretary for external affairs and chairman of the Australian
Labour party), found that the detention aboard ship was illegal, ordered the
release of Kisch and the *Strathaird* captain to pay the costs. But from the
stretcher on which he was being carried ashore, Kisch was transferred to a
police car and whisked off to Sydney's Liverpool Street police station. Here
was played out the most ridiculous part of the whole farce. Kisch was informed that he was to be submitted to a Dictation Test. Menzies had dug
this up as his last trump card.

Under the Immigration Restriction Act of 1901, the government had the
right to exclude "undesirables" if they failed to write fifty words of a European language "as dictated by a designated official." Since it was known that

---

* Egon Irwin Kisch, op. cit., pp. 7–8.

Kisch was proficient in an unknown number of European languages, official-dom was in a dilemma as to which one to choose.

At the Liverpool Street police station Kisch was confronted by an Inspector Wilson, who handed him a fountain pen and said, "Write down what Constable McKay will read to you in the Gaelic language."

"In Gaelic," shouted Kisch for the benefit of his supporters massed outside. "But you will make the whole of Australia a laughingstock. . . ." He was handed a piece of paper, and as Constable McKay started to dictate what was purported to be some Scottish Gaelic prose, Kisch started to write a letter of protest. The fountain pen was without ink! Another was produced, and the farce continued, Kisch refusing to write. A form was made out to the effect that he had failed the test, Inspector Wilson proclaimed that he was under arrest, and he was led off to a stinking cell.

Another appeal was launched, and pending the hearing, a Sydney magistrate, rejecting the contention that Kisch was such a dangerous person that he might escape surveillance if released from jail, set him free. He went almost directly from his police cell to the Sydney Domain.

How could I fail to be influenced by what I had seen with my own eyes, heard with my own ears, and learned by my detailed perusal of the press? Kisch measured up to the best of my idealized concepts of what I had read in *The New Popular Educator* about the work of a foreign correspondent "with the world as his beat"—plus! Here was a man who stood up for the underdog, with the ability and courage to get the true facts on vital issues back to the public. I went to celebration meetings at which he spoke and described in masterly fashion the situation in Nazi Germany, the persecution of the Jews, and the danger that Hitler would lead us into a new world war. The man himself, modest, cheerful, and a splendid sense of humor, with the physical and moral courage he had so graphically displayed, became my "instant hero."

Also impressive were the instinctive Australian sympathy for the underdog and suspicion of authority which came to the fore and the quality of the organization which channeled such sentiments into effective action. It was the working people, through their trade unions, and progressive intellectuals, writers, journalists, lawyers, university professors who were the vanguard of the "Defend Kisch" movement.

The first appeal was rejected, but subsequent actions went up and down the various courts until five judges of the Sydney High Court, after a week's deliberations, decided by four to one that an immigrant could not legally be tested in Scottish Gaelic. Another action was started by the government. While it was being heard, a couple of sailors from the German ship *Mosel* dropped into a Sydney pub and leaked the fact that their ship was leaving that evening and the brig had been prepared for a "very special prisoner." Later a friendly constable urged a taxi driver to rush the news to Kisch's lawyer, A. B. Piddington, K.C., that Kisch was to be put aboard the *Mosel* that evening. He was to be shanghaied, in other words, and handed over to his mortal enemies.

Announcing the fact that he had received news of a fact "so incredible, so . . . so . . . ," Piddington collapsed in court. Press rumors had been that Kisch was to be sentenced that day—and deported. With Piddington's collapse, the magistrate adjourned the hearing until the following day, by which time the *Mosel* had sailed with its brig empty. Kisch was sentenced to six months' "hard labor" as a prohibited immigrant but was freed on bail pending still another appeal.

By this time, whatever went on in the courts, the government had totally lost its case as far as public opinion was concerned. As Kisch had predicted, it had become the "laughingstock of the world." Eventually Menzies was glad to drop the case. By trying to ban him, the Australian government had given Kisch and the cause for which he struggled a thousand times more publicity than could ever have been expected from the antiwar congress. And hundreds of thousands of Australians, including me, received a lesson in politics—enlivened by the spectacle of the long arm of Nazism into Australia —that they would never otherwise have dreamed of.

At about the time the excitement over the Kisch case was beginning to wane, word came from Poowong that my uncle's house, adjoining Greenhaven, had burned down and that Burchett and Sons were to rebuild it. Our farm was just holding its own. The building job would give us work at our own trade for a good three months. Thus, I packed my swag again and headed south into the salt breezes from the Pacific and the clean pungent smell of the gum tree forests.

4

---◄◆►---

Away From It All

THANKS TO CAR LIFTS and a couple of train jumps, I covered the 500 miles home in four days. With a violet haze over the giant blue gums topping the back hill, a dozen sleek cows and some young stock browsing on the front slope, and, as I got closer, the house surrounded with roses, geraniums, hydrangeas, and other flowers, the little farm looked very beautiful.

My parents looked better and younger than for years. My father immediately rushed out to kill a duck for supper. We strolled over the farm while I had to repeat everything I had written in my letters and fill in the omissions. Everything had to be gone over again when Clive dropped in a couple of hours later. (During my absence he had built his own home in the center of Poowong township.)

After a day's rest we started clearing away the debris from my uncle's burned-out home. There was not much left. A timber house built by my father thirty years before, it had caught fire when a gasoline-fed pressure lamp exploded. The furniture had been saved, but there was one terrible loss—the trunk in which old Caleb's diaries had been stored. Within a few days we were laying the foundations of a spacious new house.

What happened over the next eighteen months or so was a rare joke on the capitalist system and an odd turn of fortune's wheel for us. My uncle, like most of the farmers in our district, had insured his house against fire in the years of prosperity. In those days insurance agents were anxious to boost house values and urged owners to insure to the maximum so as to earn the fattest commissions for themselves. Moreover, although as a result of the slump, property values went down drastically, the insured value remained the same. Building costs had also gone down in sympathy with the drop in property values. When my father worked out the estimates for the new house, my uncle discovered that the cost would be appreciably less than the check he had received from the insurance company. Houses, in fact, "were worth more dead than alive," a matter that was slowly digested by the local farmers as they chewed over matters on market days.

Every few months after that, there were mysterious fires. Not even the most diligent insurance inspector could find an iota of incriminating evidence, but at the cattle pens on market day the question "Have a good burn?" or "Expecting a good burn?" provoked roars of laughter. An astute inspector would have noted that the spacing between fires coincided precisely with the speed with which the Burchett family could replace those burned, the rhythm speeding up when another family of builders moved into the area. The farmers were getting their own back on the banks that had plagued them for so long. For the inconvenience of camping out in the barn for a couple of months, they were getting new houses with a bit of extra money thrown in. The sudden drop in real estate values which had caused my father's downfall more than eight years earlier now restored the family fortunes.

To build five or six houses a year meant full employment. Winston sold his lending library in Ballarat and came to join us. A cousin who had learned the building trade from my father twenty-five years before temporarily turned his farm over to a brother and got out his carpentering kit again. Splitting into two teams, we built two or more houses simultaneously so that delays in deliveries of bricks or timber did not hold up the overall work. A proportion of our previous earnings which the Ballarat bank had confiscated was now coming back to us through the insurance companies, most of them owned by the banks. We were able to pay off our debts on Greenhaven.

The miniboom in building was not at the expense of our interest in international affairs. Throughout 1935 and 1936 the Poowong Discussion Club had been the center of passionate debates about the Italian invasion of Abyssinia, the victories of the Popular Front in Spain and France, the start of the Spanish Civil War, the rising arrogance of the militarists in Nazi Germany and Japan—all those things which Egon Irwin Kisch had been warning about.

We had acquired a small delivery van, which I drove to Melbourne every week, taking produce to the central market, returning with urgently needed building materials. Visits were timed to coincide with weekly meetings of the Australian Writers' League, set up by progressive intellectuals opposed to war and fascism. Famous writers, like Nettie and Vance Palmer, and others to become famous, such as novelist Robert Close and short story writer Alan Marshall, and top journalists Gavin Greenlees and Kim Keene came to read extracts from their new works or discuss writing and journalistic problems. There was also time to have weekly lessons in Italian from the wife of the owner of an international bookshop where one could buy left-wing newspapers and magazines from European countries. My thoughts turned more and more to seeing what was going on in the Old World for myself.

By the end of 1936 the building jobs started tapering off. My fortunes had improved to the point that I could contemplate further travels—overseas. Winston, whose receipts from the sale of his library were intact, decided to join me. He was then twenty-eight, I was twenty-five—both unmarried and unattached. We found the cheapest and most interesting route was that taken by the French Messageries Maritime line, via the Pacific, Panama Canal, and West Indies to Marseilles.

With little money and lots of good advice we boarded the *Pierre Loti* on the last day of 1936, bound for Nouméa in New Caledonia, where we would change ships. There were two rapid disillusionments. Instead of a healthy smell of tar and salt, as described by Jack London, Joseph Conrad, and other sea lovers, there was a stuffy, rubbery smell mixed with a public-lavatory type of deodorant. The second more serious shock was that I understood not a word from the French stewards, nor did they understand me except for a few monosyllables of the *oui*, *non*, and *bon* category.

The third, most shattering disillusion was not long postponed. As we bounded, in a jaunty, rollicking sort of movement toward the Sydney Heads, the rubbery, deodorant smell grew unbearably strong. After we passed through the heads and the wretched craft started to plunge and roll in the open ocean, things got worse. I made for the lavatory, but the ship always moved in the opposite direction from that which my sense of balance dictated. Winston, who had been drinking in the sea air, found me on my knees in the sickly-smelling lavatory, retching my heart out. He helped me to our cabin.

Wiseacres have told me, "It's all psychological. If you think you're going to be seasick, you'll be sick. It's all in the mind." They could not have been more wrong in my case. Toughened as I was by my travels and good physical condition, my only worry had been about Winston, who was considered the least hardy of the family. The final whispered words of advice from my parents were to be sure to look after him, take cups of tea to his cabin, as he was almost certain to be poorly at first. That I, the hardened traveler and train jumper, could ever be seasick never entered my head. But I was terribly, terribly seasick, and I have never entirely overcome this humiliating malady.

After a few days ashore at Nouméa, eating ravenously, I recovered my confidence. The *Pierre Loti* had been built for the Black Sea (a glorified lake as I then imagined), whereas the *Ville d'Amiens*, on which we were to continue the voyage, was six times as big and built for transoceanic travel. But there was the same sickly, rubbery smell, and I neither ate nor left my bunk during the two days between New Caledonia and the New Hebrides.

From the New Hebrides on, my internal affairs deteriorated. A cargo of copra had been loaded, and the rancid smell, as it rotted in the hold, added to my miseries. Tiny, black, sharp-nippered copra bugs, which came aboard with the cargo, immediately abandoned it for human flesh. I can't say they singled me out, but I was more available than anyone else. For eight days I ate nothing at all.

In the early-morning hours of the ninth day a tantalizing fragrance wafted in through the porthole. Imperceptibly it gradually imposed itself on the foul odors that had plagued me. Good was triumphing over evil. The rolling and pitching had ceased. After I dragged myself with difficulty up the iron ladder to deck level, there was a vision of peaceful sea. But even the sight of the long, rolling swells made my entrails writhe in agony as though there were nothing but razor blades inside. The ship's engines had been slowed down, and globes of phosphorus, like large, translucent oranges, floated lazily past the bow. By the time a horizon was discernible Winston had arrived, astonished to see me at the ship's rail. A faint smudge appeared in the clear sky; then a rosy cloud detached itself from the horizon to reveal a purple peak, almost completely swathed in mist: Orohena, Tahiti's highest mountain, seemingly rising straight up out of the sea.

As the sun rose higher and the ship headed toward a gap in a coral reef, against which the rollers were dissolving into cream, another smaller peak appeared through gossamer veils of cloud. Gradually an island took shape. An invisible hand suddenly whipped away the clouds in a dramatic unveiling ceremony—and there was Tahiti, in all its emerald and purple majesty. A mirror-smooth lagoon, as we passed through the gap in the reef, was dotted with outrigger canoes. My internal convulsions ceased when we entered the lagoon.

The fragrance borne to us by the offshore breezes was now enough to make the senses reel—a blend of tropical perfumes of which the main ingredient was from frangipani blossoms. The port-capital of Papeete began to take shape, and we floated directly toward it. It was there that I was to be abandoned, put ashore as scurvy-ridden sailors from the whaling fleets were half a century earlier. We went to make one final appeal to the captain, but he was adamant.

"*Non, messieurs. Non!*" he said. "Two days from Nouméa to the New Hebrides you didn't eat. Eight days to Tahiti you didn't eat. After Tahiti we have eighteen—maybe twenty—days to Panama. *Non!* No doctor and no captain would take the responsibility of carrying you farther. I have radioed our company's agent to make arrangements with the authorities for you to stay ashore. But at your own expense." Turning to Winston, he said, "You may continue or stay as you wish. But your brother must stay ashore. Your tickets will be good for the next boat or the one after that . . . whenever your brother is well enough to travel. *Au revoir! Bon séjour à Tahiti!*"

And that was that. An hour later we went down the gangway with our baggage, through a gauntlet of Tahitian beauties, glistening jet black hair flowing to their waists. They competed to place garlands of frangipani and hibiscus blossoms around our necks. Humiliated at being the cause of such a disastrous upset to our plans, I was in no mood to appreciate the welcome or the smooth beauty and inviting smiles of the Tahitian girls. The great adventure on which we had invested such hopes—not to mention money— had foundered badly. The next boat would be in six weeks, and even the most modest hotel expenses would eat up all our slender finances—and more. The terrible thought that we might have to turn back weighed on both of us. It was still early morning, and we went to a Chinese restaurant, where I ate two enormous steaks.

Strolling through the streets, we came across an agency which advertised little huts along the coast for very reasonable prices. Why not rent one and fend for ourselves? The agent was very sympathetic—after one glance at me —when we explained our plight. "I think I have just the thing," he said, and invited us to jump into his car and have a look.

It was a dream. On the shore of the lagoon, about six miles from Papeete, was a large symmetrical hut with a roof of thatched coconut fronds and walls of pleated bamboo. One large central room opened into two smaller ones at each end. Beds and furniture were covered with dust, but everything needed for housekeeping was there. In a lean-to outside was an outrigger canoe, with a long bamboo fishing rod and line lying in the bottom. Along the beach and in the garden behind the hut were coconut and banana palms and paw-paws.

Beyond the lagoon lay the surf-lined reef, and beyond that was the serrated profile of Moorea Island. We could hardly believe our ears when the rent was quoted at the equivalent of about ten Australian shillings per week. Canoe, garden, and all the fruits therein, as they ripened, were included. The agent explained that the hut had been built a couple of years earlier as a "chief's residence" for the filming of Nordhoff and Hall's epic *Mutiny on the Bounty*. He had never rented it before, but "in view of your unfortunate situation. . . ." We hastened to move our baggage in before he changed his mind.

By late afternoon, having cleaned up, dusted the furniture, and inspected the cooking arrangements, we could relax on a coconut log and admire the spectacle of the sun disappearing behind the magic isle of Moorea. The polished waters of the lagoon were painted with swiftly changing colors for half an hour after the red disk of the sun completely disappeared. Suddenly it was all over. The colors faded into the jet black of tropical night while the lagoon water lapped gently at our feet.

Over a supper of fish and salad bought in the Papeete market we discussed our rapidly changing fortunes. Our lodging for the six weeks until the next boat came would cost us only three pounds. Food in the market, we had already discovered, was incredibly cheap, and I was sure we would soon be eating our own fish. Things were not so desperate after all.

Just before dawn the next morning, while Winston was still asleep and I was struggling to launch the canoe, Natua appeared, as unexpected and unannounced as she appears in these pages. Pronged fishing spear in hand and the frankest of smiles, she offered her free hand in greeting. Around the lower part of her slender body was wrapped a blue and white pareu; higher up was a tiny bra of the same cloth. In between was a generous band of honey-colored skin. Her waist-long hair glistened with coconut oil, perfumed with frangipani. She was the daughter of a fisherman neighbor and had seen me gathering hermit crabs for bait and struggling with the canoe. After expertly helping me with that, Natua threw in her spear and, having clambered in after it, started to initiate me into the art of handling a Polynesian canoe. It was easy to handle once you got the knack of countering each thrust of the paddle by leaning toward the stabilizer. This was explained in rudimentary French well suited to the state of my own.

By the time the sun started to warm our shoulders we were halfway to the reef, skimming over sparkling green water so clear that every detail of the delicate coral formations twenty or thirty feet below was clearly visible. After an hour's brisk paddling we reached the reef, against which Pacific rollers were crashing, sending flurries of tamed water across the coral outcrops into the lagoon. An anchor was thrown overboard and trailed until it hooked into the coral. Natua unhitched her skirt and slid into the water with her spear, while I manipulated the long bamboo rod to flick the line back and forth into the surf as the other fishermen were doing.

Lithe as a fish, her hair streaming behind, Natua moved in effortless grace in the deep pools between the coral clusters, jabbing her spear into a fish as it flashed past, pinning it to a coral cluster, and, with a kick of her legs, curving up to the surface to brush her prey off the barbed prongs into the canoe. A pause to catch her breath and flash me a smile, and down she went again. By the time the sun had chased the clouds from the peaks of Orohena the bottom of the canoe was covered with flapping fish. Natua clambered aboard, wiped her body with the pareu, fastening it into place again with a deft twist of the fingers. She had difficulty in believing me later when I revealed that hers was the first nude female body I had seen.

Winston was more than a little surprised at the contents of the canoe. With a wave of her hand Natua left as soon as the canoe was beached to her satisfaction, refusing to take any of the fish and, to my considerable disappointment, without any arrangements for a further meeting.

Suspended over the back entrance to our palace was an enormous bunch of bananas that Winston had removed from one of the palms during his inspection of the garden. Together with copious servings of fried fish, some of them contributed to our first cost-free meal. My thoughts went back to my gum-tree home at Bruce's Bend on the Murray, but the image was soon replaced by that of naked Natua among the coral clusters.

By chance, on our first morning walk, we found that a neighbor was a French art historian, Professor Paul Nordman, and his ravishingly beautiful Tahitian wife, Marguerite. From him we learned that our little village of Faaa had been the home of Gauguin. His house had been burned down, together with its priceless murals and other paintings, for fear of contagion from leprosy of which he died. Nordman's most prized possession was a lewd wooden carving of a lecherous-looking Polynesian male with an out-size detachable penis, which he said was a typical, but rare, example of Gauguin's wood sculpture. The professor was to escort it to Paris on the *Commissaire Ramel*, the same Messageries Maritime liner on which we were to continue our travels.

Taking a path which led from the coastal road toward the mountains, we were astonished at the profusion of oranges, plantains (cooking bananas), mangoes, paw-paws, breadfruit, guavas, and other fruit which grew on common land, where everyone could help himself. On every side were the violent splashes of color which held Gauguin captive and which he so masterfully transferred to his canvases. Lunching under a mango tree, our feet cooling in a brook and eating the fruit as they fell into our laps, we decided that Tahiti had the good fortune not to possess important minerals or other raw materials to incite the despoilers of man and nature. Unlike New Caledonia, with its fabulous riches of nickel and chrome, mined by local and indentured labor under conditions bordering on slavery, or Fiji, where the discovery of gold had brought similar exploitation by British and Australian mining companies, Tahiti seemed relatively untouched and unspoiled.

Nearing our palace in the late afternoon, we were astonished to hear music and the sound of women's laughter. Inside there was great activity as Natua and two other young women swept floors and dusted furniture to the music of an old gramophone which we had not even noticed. After giggling introductions, we understood that the other two were Natua's sisters, who spoke no word of French. A few minutes later, chairs and beds having been returned to what was now an impeccably clean hut, they all took off with peals of laughter at our attempted thanks.

Later that evening Natua returned with a few toilet articles wrapped in a reserve pareu. She became my first love, and the Tahitian idyll was complete. For me at least. (Winston, whose departure from Australia was partly the result of a broken love affair in Ballarat, heroically resisted the classic antidote, devoting himself to the practical exercise of journalism, the rudiments of which he had studied by correspondence. Discovering that Charles Nordhoff and James Norman Hall, authors of the trilogy *Mutiny on the*

Bounty, Pitcairn Island, and *Men Against the Sea,* were in Tahiti, he spent some time interviewing them and, with Professor Nordman's expert advice, collected other materials for use in his first foray into that precarious profession.)

In those days there were virtually no tourists. Those who did come stayed in Papeete. What we experienced was life as lived by the Tahitians, with not a shadow of commercial exploitation of their talents and customs. Our immediate neighbors were happy people, as people can be happy when nature is generous and economic and social stresses are virtually nonexistent. Nature was superabundant. Not only were fish, fruit, wild pigs, and jungle fowl to be had for the taking, but much of the food fell into one's hands. Coconuts fell when the milk was still good to drink and the flesh ready to be grated and squeezed into delicious cream for salads and coffee. Mangoes plopped to the ground at the optimum moment of ripeness. Even fish, at times, actually jumped into the canoes! On certain nights which Natua and other fisherfolk could predict, fish for which light exercised a fatal attraction surfaced. On such occasions the lagoon was transformed into festoons of glittering diamonds as groups of canoes wove back and forth, lights from coconut fronds flaring up and dying away, new flares immediately replacing those that died. The fish popped up, like corks from champagne bottles, toward the light. Many jumped clear over the canoe into the water on the other side, but a proportion landed in the bottom or were knocked out by paddles in midflight.

Those were gala nights. Shouts of triumph echoed from group to group and back to shore until the stock of frond torches was exhausted or the fish had plunged to the nether depths again.

Gala nights were followed by gala days, as the villagers left for the Papeete market with their harvest. It was one of our great events to ride on the gaily painted charabancs bringing the villagers to and from the Papeete market. These were always jam-packed, trussed-up pigs and poultry squealing and screeching on the roof, and a cross-section of everything Tahiti produced crushed in between the passengers inside. There were sure to be a few musicians, with their instruments, among the passengers. After the first mile or two the musicians would strike up, and a few people would shyly give voice. Someone would invariably produce a wicker-enclosed gallon bottle of red wine, which, passed from seat to seat to seat, quickly loosened inhibitions and voices.

So the golden days and velvety nights passed, and departure time loomed nearer. In the first week I had recovered my weight and was perfectly fit. No doctor or sea captain could refuse me. There was an unexpected reprieve when New Caledonian dockers went on strike and the *Commissaire Ramel* was held up for two weeks. Natua proposed a walk around the island. We started off at dawn one morning while the cool night breeze was still blowing seaward with the magic fragrance which the name Tahiti still evokes. We rested at midday under the shade of breadfruit trees and continued in the cool of the evening till we came to an acceptable inn. It took us a week of easy walking, with plenty of time for swimming, to circle the island.

By the time we returned the *Commissaire Ramel* was on its way to put an end to our Tahitian idyll. The community decided to prepare a feast, partly in belated celebration of the marriage of a village couple, partly in honor of our departure. We provided the wine and rum; they provided whole pigs and chickens and mountains of fish, all cooked together over hot stones in a deep trench, the various meats and fish arranged in layers, separated by wads of green banana leaves and with upper layers of breadfruit, plantains, taro roots, and sweet potatoes.

There were no speeches, only a gargantuan orgy of eating and drinking, punctuated by shouted anecdotes—which Natua could not, or would not, translate, but which always produced roars of laughter. By filling themselves to capacity, the villagers were bestowing their blessings on the not-so-newly-weds and saying good-bye to adopted friends, who for some absurd and incomprehensible reason, were leaving their incomparably happy and hospitable community.

To leave the next morning was not easy. But it had to be. If there were other things in life besides the cows and potatoes of Poowong, there were also other things besides beachcombing and lotus-eating in Tahiti. When the moment of farewell came, there were tears and flowers cast into the water as the gap between the *Commissaire Ramel* and the Papeete wharf widened.

Gradually the curve of the ocean blotted out Natua, the beaches, and plantations, and finally the still-cloud-swathed peak of Orohena. It was one thing to have Natua and Tahiti disappear from my line of vision, quite another to dismiss them from my thoughts and emotions. Natua's name—like many in Tahiti—was almost certainly an approximation of a French term that had caught her parents' fancy. In her case "nature." If so, it could not have been more perfectly chosen. As distinct from her sisters, who could have been Gauguin models, she was slender and fine-featured, a European-Polynesian blend of rare beauty. Her joys came from the simple things —the vivid colors of a fish, a particularly symmetrical clump of coral, the lapping of the lagoon waters, the discovery of a new melody brought back from voyagers to the myriad islands of Polynesia. She was as much a part of the sensuous Tahitian setting as the perfumed frangipani and multi-colored hibiscus. The weeks spent with Natua in such a setting were the happiest in my life till then. Personal tensions and world problems shrank to a very tiny spot on the horizon.

For the youth of my generation, the future in Australia seemed bleak in the extreme, and any meaningful future was nonexistent. During the first months of the Depression we thought the situation would soon improve. But the months grew into years, and the years piled up until many accepted Depression as a chronic, normal state of affairs.

There was no discussion as to what sort of job or profession a lad would like to follow on leaving school. The question was whether there would be a job, any job. Our fate, many of us felt, was doomed to be a hand-to-mouth existence at best. I was convinced that I would never be able to marry and have my own family. With my strict Wesleyan-Methodist upbringing this barred any approach to a girl, as without marriage in view an approach was immoral! Winston's love affair ended when, despite betrothal sealed by a cheap engagement ring, the years went by without his gaining any prospects of supporting a wife and family. Honor required that he release his girl while she was still of marriageable age. Methodist morals precluded pre-marital sex. Clive had married when the future seemer relatively normal but had ended up breaking stones, as in the convict days, to earn less than the minimum needed to feed his wife and kids. There was no starvation in Australia, as I later came to know it in Asia, but there was the deadly, humiliating hopelessness of the breadwinner who could no longer provide for his own.

Suddenly, for me in Tahiti, all this faded away into a distant background. Everything was at my hand for the reaching: love, beauty, abundance, and warm human relations. Natua's almost innocent frankness in bed made short shrift of my Methodist inhibitions, as her generous nature made light of my inexpertise. For months later, in the fog and smog and hard pavements of London, I was obsessed with the idea that there were two worlds—Tahiti and the rest. What a fool to have abandoned that of Natua for the other!

5

Back to Reality

THE HARSH REALITIES of life soon reasserted themselves. Aboard the *Commissaire Ramel* were not only Professor Nordman and his lovely wife, Marguerite, but a young Australian couple, Sam Aarons and his friend Esme Odgers, bound—as was discreetly revealed after they learned we had mutual friends—for Spain to join the International Brigade and fight against the Franco fascists. During the two months in Tahiti we had been completely cut off from news. Sam and Esme brought us up-to-date on the worsening international situation, also that there were more unemployed than ever at home. Egon Irwin Kisch was already in Spain as a correspondent with the anti-Franco Republican forces. This news touched a sensitive nerve. My most closely guarded secret, kept from my family, including Winston, was that I intended also to try to get to Spain. I could not visualize myself squeezing the trigger with a human being in the sights, but I thought of doing a stretcher-bearer job or making some other nonviolent contribution to the antifascist struggle. The only person to whom I confided this deeply secret resolve was a schoolmate from my Ballarat days, Ken Miller, who, to my great astonishment, I rediscovered during my Melbourne forays, was the editor of the *Guardian*, the weekly organ of the Victoria branch of the Australian Communist party. He encouraged the idea but said, "You'll probably be more useful with a rifle. In any case, before you set out, you'd better join the party." He produced an application form for membership and said, "I'll sponsor you."

I mentally noted that being a Communist had imposed great strains on my old schoolmate. At twenty-four, his face was lined, his hair streaked with gray. I said I would think it over, realizing that joining such a party was an act not to be taken lightly. In the end I filled in and mailed the

47

form. In return I received a free copy of the *Communist Manifesto* and a copy of *Anti-Dühring*, by Friedrich Engels, with a request to return the latter with my comments. In the meantime, my application for CP membership was being considered. At my stage of mental, moral, and ideological development, I was repelled by the violent language of the *Manifesto* and could not make head or tail of *Anti-Dühring*. I returned it after futile struggles with the first chapter, explaining as best I could in a brief note my incompetence to comment. There was no follow-up to my application! But this did not affect my resolve to go to Spain.

We parted company with the Australian couple in Marseilles, Sam Aarons to survive his service in the International Brigade and later to become head of the Communist party of Western Australia; Esme Odgers to win praise for her running of a camp for Basque refugee children near the French-Spanish frontier.

England was in the throes of "coronation fever." George VI was to be crowned because of elder brother Edward's determination to marry the American divorcée Mrs. Wallis Warfield Simpson. Loyal Commonwealth subjects who could afford it were converging on London for the attendant pomp and ceremony.

In the "Situations Vacant" columns of the London newspapers I discovered that carpenters were not in demand but that the travel agents Thomas Cook and Sons were in need of temporary staff, preferably with knowledge of foreign languages. My family background, level of education, lack of personal recommendations produced nothing but frowns from Thomas Cook's staff recruiter. He brightened up when he learned that I knew French—at least functional, thanks to Natua and practice on the *Commissaire Ramel* —and that my Australian accent could even be an advantage. Of all Commonwealth citizens, Australians were the most fervent when it came to the pageantry of Empire. They would be flocking to England in the tens of thousands. What was needed was an ability to understand French railway timetables and hotel guides and to talk back to the Australians in an accent they understood. So I had a job.

It was a strange feeling, turning up on a gray Monday morning at Cook's main office, then in Berkeley Square, for my first white-collar job. Officially I was a tourist clerk at the princely sum of three pounds a week, from which I paid ten shillings for a tiny room in Soho's Charlotte Street. Winston left on a roundabout return route shortly after the coronation. In the meantime, I had enrolled at the Polytechnic School of Languages, attending classes five nights a week in French, Spanish, Italian, and German; later I added Russian. My weekends were mainly spent at the Linguists' Club in Kingsway, which ran foreign-language conversation courses.

My attempt to get to Spain fared no better than that to join the Australian Communist party. A few weeks after arriving in London, by an incredible coincidence—in an underground lavatory—I encountered one of the only two Australians I knew were in England. It was Bob Burns, a Sydney lawyer, whom I had met on the *Ville d'Amiens* with his friend, a trained nurse Honey McRae, both on their way to Spain. "Did you go to the party?" he asked after our first exclamations of pleased astonishment.

"What party?" I asked, thinking I had missed some convivial get-together of homesick compatriots.

"The British party, of course, King Street," he replied, assuming, as many did, because of my undisguised sympathies, that I was a party member. "What an experience!" he continued. "We went in and knocked at the reception window. It slid open about two inches, and a horse-faced girl asked who we were. When we said, 'Australian comrades,' she snapped, 'Colonial Department,' and slid the window shut. At the 'Colonial Department' they treated us like creatures from outer space. A fat chance we have of getting to Spain."

My own effort was made in a note wrapped around a few shillings handed in at a big rally for the Spanish Republicans at London's Trafalgar Square. The note explained that I did not have money to contribute, but I was a candidate for the International Brigade. (By then Hitler and Mussolini had sent in troops, and I had no qualms about using a rifle.) When the note arrived in the hands of the woman appealing for funds, she consulted for a moment with her comrades at the base of the Nelson column and then said, "Here is a donation of very precious value. Will the comrade who sent it in please come to the tribune at the end of the meeting?" At that I felt I was already on my way to Spain. My name and address were taken, and I was assured some "comrades" would visit me. They did—very solemn-faced and justifiably suspicious, as I recognized later. I had neither letters of recommendation nor support from any organization. There was no one in London—or anywhere—to vouch for me. At best, from their viewpoint, I could be a freebooting adventurer, at worst a spy trying to penetrate their ranks. There was no follow-up. But since I had offered my life, rejection rankled.

When the coronation season was over, I was transferred to another department of Thomas Cook's. Later, because of my rudimentary knowledge of Russian—rare in an Anglo-Saxon in those days—and because the assistant manager was an Australian, I got a job with the London office of Intourist, the Soviet travel agency. This lasted only a few months because of a diplomatic quarrel between England and the Soviet Union which resulted in virtually all travel—tourist and otherwise—drying up. By chance, I was carrying with me a letter from the head of the travel agency in Melbourne which had arranged the Melbourne–Marseilles–London tickets. (He was a remarkable Russian émigré, named Patkin, who had been a prominent Menshevik and had given me a letter to his counterpart in the travel business in Paris, a Russian émigré friend of his, presumably with the same political convictions.)

My meager savings permitted a trip to Paris, where I intended to pursue the possibility of going to Spain and, if that failed, to get a job in Paris with Patkin's friend on the basis of my travel agency experience and languages. I failed on both counts. The tenuous French contacts I had been able to establish were adamant that as an Australian I must be sponsored by the British Communist party. With the clouds of war already gathering, the tourist trade was in the doldrums, but Patkin's friend, impressed by my fluency in French and German, gave me a letter to his opposite number in London who ran the Palestine-Orient Lloyd travel agency. It specialized in handling emigrant traffic out of Germany to Palestine and the United States and was obviously linked with one of the Jewish émigré relief agencies. My knowledge of German and natural sympathy with the plight of the Jews, backed by the "secondhand" letter of introduction, clinched the job.

At the Linguists' Club, in the meantime, I had met a Jewish refugee from Hitler Germany. Intelligent and cultured, she confirmed everything that Kisch had said about the persecution of Jews, communists, socialists, trade union leaders, and any who opposed Hitler's racist, reactionary policies. We soon discovered lots of similar interests, and the result was that I married Erna Hammer at the Hampstead Heath registry office in September 1938 and for good measure adopted her two daughters of a previous marriage, thus ensuring them a secure haven in England.

Less than two months after our marriage a seventeen-year-old Polish lad named Hershl Grynszpan shot Ernst vom Rath, third secretary to the German Embassy in Paris, who died two days later. Grynszpan said he acted to avenge the fate of tens of thousands of Polish Jews, deported from Germany under the most inhuman conditions. On November 10, 1938, wholesale pogroms were launched against Jews throughout Germany. Within a few days it was estimated that at least 35,000 Jews had been arrested, including 8,000 in Berlin alone. Among them were Adolf Hammer, my brother-in-law of a few weeks, and many clients of Palestine-Orient Lloyd. Communications with the Berlin office were cut, so I offered to go find out what had happened to the firm's Berlin office and clients and what I could do for my brother-in-law.

Several factors made it easier for me to go than others. By then I spoke German fluently, I was not Jewish, and as an Australian I needed no visa. Within a few days I was on my way, with lots of names and addresses either memorized or written in a coded form. My wife warned me of the need for extreme vigilance in avoiding the attentions of the Gestapo. (Its activities were not much publicized in England in those days.) Of course, it was dangerous, but I was relieved to be doing *something*. The war in Spain was going badly. Like all other progressives, I had been sickened by Munich and Chamberlain's betrayal of the people in that "faraway country" Czechoslovakia.

A room had been booked for me in Hotel am Zoo, in the very center of Berlin's West End. Two shops opposite were boarded up with rough planks, their windows having been shattered a few days earlier in the "spontaneous" anti-Jewish outbursts. In fact, as I soon learned, Hitler's Brownshirts, with motorcycle sidecars filled with brickbats, roared up and down the Kurfürstendamm and other main streets, hurling their missiles through Jewish shopwindows, urging the crowds to loot and spill a little blood. The entrance to the hotel bore the inscription *Eintritt der Juden Verboton* ("Entrance of Jews Forbidden").

Around the corner from the hotel was Joachimstalerstrasse, where my wife's parents lived. My first call was to present myself there and ask about Adi. They believed he had been taken to the Sachsenhausen concentration camp. Another ten-minute stroll, and it was clear why there had been no contact with the Berlin office of Palestine-Orient Lloyd. Shattered plate glass lay mixed with tourist literature on the floor; planks were nailed crisscross where the office front had been. Scrawled on them in white paint were the words *Schmutzige Juden* ("dirty Jews").

The next visit was by taxi to a street corner near one of my coded addresses, a solid stone villa set in a lovely garden near the Tiergarten. After I had rung a couple of times, the door opened a few inches. A beautiful, but ashen-faced, young woman with blond hair coiled high on her head opened the door farther after I insisted I had just come from London to see Herr Grünstein. I was ushered into a library. After a few minutes a distraught man came in and introduced himself as Herr Grünstein and the beautiful woman as his wife. The atmosphere was abnormal, to say the least. Herr Grünstein kept passing his hands through his hair, muttering to himself, and paying no heed to what I was saying. As his wife tried to calm him, I repeated that visas had been obtained and travel arrangements made for him and his brother and their families to proceed to London and wait there until their American immigration visas came through. He stared at me with bulging eyes, continuing to mutter to himself. There was nothing to do but leave my hotel address and room number with his wife and advise her not to call from their home telephone.

Hardly had I returned to the hotel, dog-tired from travel and the shock of Berlin, than the phone rang. It was Frau Grünstein, begging me to return immediately. The urgency of her voice and the uncanny scene I had just left wiped away my tiredness. Mingling with the Kurfürstendamm prostitutes and late-night strollers and making sure I was not followed, I took a taxi to another corner near my destination. This time the door was quickly opened. Coffee, sandwiches, and a bottle of cognac had been set out on a table in the library. Herr Grünstein came in, more composed and a shade less ashen. He grasped my hand, begging forgiveness for his impoliteness. "Two minutes before you rang at the door the first time, my brother shot himself. His wife was just telephoning the news when you rang. . . ." In the pause, broken by his wife's muffled sobs, he poured three large cognacs. Still unaccustomed to anything stronger than beer, I gulped some down. "This evening he got an order to report to Alexstrasse, the main Berlin police station at Alexanderplatz. You understand what this means? The concentration camp! He always swore he would kill himself first—and he has. He today—why not us tomorrow? I was too shocked to listen or talk when you came. Please tell us again." As I repeated the message, he paced up and down, glancing at the window every few moments, clenching and unclenching his fists.

"Ten days ago your news would have saved us all. Now I fear it is too late. Ernst is dead. His wife will certainly be arrested the moment the police arrive. It's the property they want, and now it all goes to her. We also may be arrested at any moment."

"But you can leave at any time," I pointed out. "Your visas are waiting in the British Embassy."

"It's not that easy now," he said wearily. "We can't leave without an Unbedenklichkeitsbescheinigung, and who can tell how long that will take after what's happened in the past few days?"

It was the first time I had heard this monstrous word, but it became only too familiar in the months that followed. It referred to a certificate testifying that all obligations toward the Reich had been fulfilled. Only with this document could other steps be taken to leave the country. In effect it meant that Hitler's agents were satisfied they had got their hands on every mark's worth of their victim's assets at home and abroad.

All I could advise the Grünsteins was to try to get a letter from the British Embassy that their visas were awaiting them and to start working on that unmentionable document. They thanked me for the ray of hope brought at their darkest moment, and I left.

What I did not then know was that while I was traveling to Berlin, Hermann Göring, economic dictator of Nazi Germany, had promulgated a decree ordering German Jews to pay a collective fine of the equivalent of 83 million pounds sterling, ostensibly as "collective punishment" for the assassination of Vom Rath. Anyone leaving the country had to produce the certificate with the monstrous name as proof that all "debts" to Hitler had been settled.

After a few days and a couple of dozen interviews, plus others with lawyers, the picture became clearer. A very high proportion of Berlin's Jews had been carted off to concentration camps in the two or three days following Vom Rath's death. Most of them were just served with notices to present themselves to "Alexstrasse" or some other designated police station.

With typical German reverence for the law they did this—including my brother-in-law. They could be released—in those days it was still possible—only by proving that they had another country to go to and that they had paid their "debts."

If they had not left Germany within a stipulated time after release from the camps, they could be locked up again, and chances for a second release were zero. The *Unbedenklichkeitsbescheinigung* could be applied for only after release from the camp, and only with that in their possession could they apply for a passport. The key document to start the process of getting someone out of a camp was a consular letter, pledging to give a visa if a valid passport was presented. With any visa at all in a valid passport, the holder could get out of Germany and also obtain a French or Dutch transit visa.

Tracking down the lost threads of the agency's clients took me to distant corners of Germany, to places as far apart as Hamburg, Breslau, Frankfurt am Main, Königsberg in what was then East Prussia, and to *gleichgestaltet* ("integrated") Austria. I was always the diligent tourist, never neglecting the chief cultural attractions in any place I visited, gathering copious tourist literature from the Hotel am Zoo for wherever I was going and requesting the staff to make the hotel reservations.

In many of the old tourist guides, together with museums, art galleries, and cathedrals, synagogues were listed among the attractions. Most had been burned or blasted into ruins. Nine of the twelve Berlin synagogues had been destroyed between November 10 and 12, 1938, and it was proportionately the same wherever I visited.

As far as the civilian population was concerned, the dominant impression was of grayness, gray-clad, gray-faced people, many with pinched cheeks and sores on their lips from Göring's "guns before butter" policy. A huge sign at Vienna Airport exhorted the Austrian people to cast aside their laziness and work hard for *Reich und Führer*. The streets of Berlin and Vienna were full of strutting, arrogant gray-uniformed Wehrmacht officers or those in the elegant black uniforms of the SS, saluting each other like automatons with outflung arms and a shouted *"Heil Hitler."*

On one memorable occasion, as I lunched in Berlin's Haus der Vaterlands restaurant, a few bars of martial music crackled over the loudspeaker, and then the high-pitched, ranting voice of Hitler took over. It was one of his ferocious tirades against "Herr" (President Eduard) Beneš of Czechoslovakia. Diners laid down their knives and forks and listened in glum silence. I kept eating, the noise of my cutlery alarmingly loud when the Führer stopped for breath. Two black-clad SS men, regulation six-footers, came in and strode over to my table, thumbs in belts, glowering at me. I tried to look unconcerned. Hitler started again, spitting out the words "Herr Beneš" every few seconds. I continued munching and picked up the menu.

The table jumped with the crash and rattle of plates as the fist of one of the thugs landed near the remains of my sausage and mashed potatoes. *"Der Führer spricht,"* he shouted while the other gave me a murderous stare. Pretending ignorance, I reached for some more sausage. Their hands shifted to their pistol butts. Diners started to look the other way. *"Ausweis,"* roared the table thumper. I shook my head, and he roared again, *"Ausweis! Dokumente!"* It had gone far enough. Even the most ignorant foreigner could understand *Dokumente.* I laid my Australian passport on the table. The one who had shouted picked it up and looked inside. *"Verfluchte Auslander* [a bloody foreigner]," he shouted to the diners as if to explain why they had not struck me dead on the spot. They examined the registration stamp, swayed forward slightly from their belted waists in an ironic bow, shot their arms out like robots, and, with a *Heil Hitler,* spun around on their heels and marched out. There were smirks of satisfaction all around the restaurant. It was a tiny victory—not to be repeated too often. (Had the waiter testified that I had ordered my meal in fairly good German, it could have turned out differently.)

Shortly after that incident, I landed late at night in a blinding snowstorm at Frankfurt am Main Airport. There was difficulty in getting through by telephone to the person who was supposed to meet me. A young airport official suddenly appeared and offered his help. I gave him another number for precaution's sake, and by the time he had discovered that no such number existed the passenger bus had gone. Could he ring for a taxi to take me to my hotel? He would not hear of it. His *Kameraden* were just finishing up, and he would ask them to take me into town. First we all would take a little drink together. The fact that I was an Australian had made a very favorable impression.

It was difficult to refuse. We went to the barracks type of living quarters of one of his friends, and soon Ernst, Kurt, Rudi, Pauli, and Wilfried—as they insisted on calling me—were gathered around a bottle of schnapps and many bottles of beer. They could have been blood brothers: blond, stocky, tanned, and blue, blue eyes. I was introduced as a *wunderbarer Kerl,* a wonderful chap—Australian. The first toast was to "my" prime minister, Oswald Pirow, who had left Germany that very day (end of November 1938) after numerous speeches of admiration for Hitler and his policies. I was able to fumble that one by pointing out that Pirow was South African. But they remembered similar speeches by Robert Menzies, premier of my own Australian state of Victoria during a visit some months earlier, so I swallowed a glass for Mr. Menzies, for the first and only time in my life.

There was worse to come. The previous night Ernst and Pauli had *fertig gemacht* ("bumped off") a Jewish tailor who lived on the road into Frankfurt by hauling him onto the road, beating him up, and then running their car over him as he tried to get to his feet. If I wanted to see some real fun, they knew where there was another we could "get" on the way into town. By this time I was thoroughly alarmed. Pleading great fatigue (it was already 2:00 A.M.) and an early-morning engagement, I threw myself on their generosity and hospitality to get me to my hotel as soon as possible. With shouted expressions of eternal friendship, Rudi, who had been in the Condor Legion in Spain, took down a huge photograph of one of the legion's Junker bombers. Each of them autographed it as a souvenir of my historic meeting with German *Kameraden!*

In front of the airport two cars were parked. To mark the end of this notable international encounter, they kicked the headlights out of one, and we clambered into the other. After a long and scary drive on the snow-covered road, they delivered me to my hotel, where they frightened a sleepy night clerk into giving a "friend of the Führer" the best available room. They escorted me upstairs and arranged the autographed photo on the dressing table.

My work in Frankfurt was soon over. At the home I had tried to telephone from the airport, both husband and wife had been arrested. I had wanted to inform them that entry permits for Australia had been arranged for the whole family. In three other cases, the husbands had been taken off. There was nothing to do but note the facts, visit a museum, and return to Berlin. The Condor picture was left embedded in a pad of dust on top of a very high wardrobe. No such souvenir was needed to remind me of one of the most disagreeable evenings I have ever spent.

After two weeks I flew back to London to report on the fate of Palestine-Orient Lloyd's clients, but also with the glimmerings of a plan. Starting with tourist and travel problems, we had been plunged into a man-made tragedy of enormous proportions from which we might salvage the handful of victims that fate had made our clients. (There were about half a million Jews in Germany at that time, and apart from a few specialized Jewish agencies, not a finger was being lifted to save them.) It would need some unorthodox arrangements, paying out more money than could be recovered from many of the clients, but it was certain that the travel agency could call upon international Jewish aid committees for financial help. That aspect was outside my operational orbit.

(After a long report on my experiences the Poowong Discussion Club swung into action. Archie Buchanan, the butter-factory manager, guaranteed jobs for my brother-in-law and his wife, a chemist specializing in the transformation of casein—a by-product of skim milk—into adhesives and synthetics. Because of this sponsorship, Adolf and Gerda Hammer were snatched from the gas ovens and eventually founded a flourishing company of manufacturing chemists in Melbourne. In a special variant of poetic justice they succeeded in converting the decreamed milk of Poowong cows into a glue highly prized by Australia's wartime aircraft industry and thus scored a minor personal revenge against their Nazi persecutors. The club also supported other humanitarian organizations in urging the government to be more lenient in granting visas to refugees from Hitler Germany. They, and those they were trying to help, represented a fair cross-section of their respective communities—except the political left. To get "politicals" out of Hitler's Reich by that time was an impossibility, nor were there any organizations, to my knowledge, even trying.)

My chiefs in Palestine-Orient Lloyd, one of whom was a naturalized German Jew, approved my plan, and for the next couple of weeks I made the rounds of some Central and South American consulates in London before flying back to Berlin. As a result, the relatives of arrested clients began to receive letters from any one of half a dozen Latin American countries informing them that in "accordance with their request," they could now receive a visa on presentation of their passports at the Berlin consulate of the country concerned.

In most cases the letters were invalid. They had been paid for at prices varying according to the scruples of the consular official, usually on the understanding that the visas would never be claimed. For a substantially higher fee, a visa could be stamped in, but on the understanding that it would never be used to enter the country concerned. The Nazi authorities could not care less whether the visas promised in the letters were ever delivered. With a valid passport, transit visas were easy to obtain for countries like France, Holland, and sometimes England, where local committees would find temporary solutions for them. A proportion of them already had visas awaiting them for the United States. At the worst, there were a few places like Shanghai and South West Africa (now Namibia) where they could go without visas. (Whatever the future promised there it was better than the gas ovens.)

The system started working, and I had the satisfaction of seeing some of the clients on their way out of the country, others like my brother-in-law out of the concentration camp and completing formalities to leave.

One cold and gray day in early March 1939, I was on my way to an appointment when I suspected a "shadow"—something I had long been expecting. Avoiding what had become known as the Deutsche blick ("German glance")—a quick look over one's shoulder from time to time—I noticed that someone stopped a few shops behind me every time I stopped to gaze in Kurfürstendamm shopfronts. I strolled across to Kantstrasse and caught a bus to Unter den Linden. The last passenger to get in was my shadow.

For an hour or so I wandered around the Deutsche Museum at Kaiser-Wilhelmsplatz, cogitating over the situation. My usefulness in Germany was obviously coming to an end. London had left it to me when to quit. The shadow was sitting in the museum entrance inspecting his shoes as I bought some postcards and shook hands with the curator, thanking him heartily for his help in the past and explaining that I would soon be returning to my own country, where I hoped to write about the magnificent German cultural heritage so well preserved and presented in the many museums and art galleries I had visited.

Back at the hotel—still followed—I found my baggage had been searched. There was nothing to find but art books, museum guides, and other evidence of my interest in German art and culture—not forgetting a fine collection of German toys acquired in Nuremberg. My suitcase was always ready for instant departure because of my constant travels, so the reports of my searchers and shadow would agree that I was on the point of leaving, as I did that same evening. I had done nothing illegal, but my dogged interest in potential Jewish émigrés, coupled with leaks from some Latin American consulates, were sufficient to arouse Gestapo suspicions.

During the long wait at the frontier I pretended a nonchalance that I was far from feeling as security officers worked their way down the passenger car. Had the Gestapo contacted the frontier police? A grim-looking pair entered the compartment with a *Heil Hitler* and the frigid politeness that Nazi officials wore like a mask. Two guards with pistols stood outside. A glance at the passport photo, a long icy stare, and the couple stalked out with my passport to enter the next compartment. After some minutes I heard a muffled sob, and almost immediately, a young couple, deathly pale, stepped out onto the platform. Behind them, pistol at the ready, was one of the two guards. It was more than two hours before the security officers returned with my passport. The young couple did not come back. After another half hour the train wheels began to turn. The slow sighs of the locomotive echoed my own deep sighs of relief as we glided out of that vast concentration camp to which Hitler had reduced Germany.

What to do next? By the very nature of my work, contacts, and travels during four months in Germany, I had an insight into what was going on that few other foreigners had. Little that I had seen made headlines in Fleet Street, but I was certain that Hitler was bent on war. To base my career on trying to sell European tours as the war clouds gathered was absurd. The Palestine-Orient Lloyd emigration business had dwindled to a trickle, although this was partly compensated for by a big departure from England for the United States of young men of military age—many of them Jewish, including some directly connected with the travel agency—who had no faith in the "peace in our time" rubbish. The official complacency, and pretended unawareness of what was going on a few hundred miles away, were unbearable. My wife was pregnant, and I wanted our child to be born in Australia, so we set off for Sydney—again on a Messageries Maritime liner—across the Atlantic and Pacific oceans, to arrive in early July 1939. My two adopted daughters, Renate and Ruth, were in a boarding school in Abergavenny, Wales.

Three months prior to our arrival Robert Menzies had become prime minister, and he gave the lead, based on his own visit to Germany, in presenting Hitler and the Nazis in the most favorable light. The gist of his message was that Germany was the one truly civilized country in Europe—you only had to cross the frontier into decadent France to realize it! Trains ran on time; everything was clinically clean; order reigned; stories of persecution of Jews and concentration camps were vastly exaggerated. That was the official line from Prime Minister Menzies, repeated at all official levels and in the press. It was more than I could stand. From a small country school where I had taken a job as carpentry instructor, I wrote letters to various Melbourne newspapers depicting Nazi Germany as I had seen it from a unique vantage point and stating my conviction that Hitler, far from being a "man of peace," was preparing to unleash war at any moment. The letters were not published.

Shortly after Hitler attacked Poland and Chamberlain got around to declaring war, some editors remembered the fellow who had been bombarding them with letters and who could be by-lined as "one of the last Australians in Germany before the war." I was called in by Neville Smith, features editor of the since-defunct Melbourne *Argus*. "We have inside information of a split in the Nazi leadership," he said. "What we need is an article about Göring. Can you write it?" I replied that I had enough anecdotes about Göring plus factual material for several articles.

"Great," he said. "We need to show Göring the family man, the popular figure. Quite different from Hitler. The country gentleman, English squire type, loves hunting and all that. Not one of the Hitler-type fanatics." I pointed out that Göring was perhaps more dangerous than Hitler because he was cleverer. He was hated as much as Hitler by ordinary people partly because of the huge personal fortune he had amassed by robbing the Jews and the assets of Austria.

"We've heard confidentially," said Neville (with whom I later had excellent professional relations), "that Hitler's to be replaced by Göring and the war will be called off. Maybe not right now, but we have to start preparing public opinion." This was the lunacy being peddled at the time by Chamberlain diehards at the British Foreign Office and passed on to Commonwealth newsmen in London. Of course, I refused, but in the next Saturday magazine section there was a portrait of a jovial, smiling Göring with a staff journalist's account of what a decent, human, un-Nazi chap the German really was!

At that time I had not much idea how newspapers were run, but I was horrified at the thought that had I been on the staff, I might have had to write that sort of article or be in trouble with the editor. But the experience did launch me ino journalism. The first major article published under my name was called "Roads of Conquest." Published in the second number of a brand-new journal, the Sydney *Sunday Telegraph*, on November 26, 1939, it showed that the *Autobahnen* which Menzies praised so highly were strategic military highways, specially built to carry heavy tank traffic and move masses of motorized troops at high speed to jumping-off points not only for the invasion of Poland, as already proved, but also for the invasion of France and especially the Low Countries six months after the article was published. I argued that the development of the *Autobahn* was an integral part of Hitler's *Blitzkrieg* tactics. There were immediate requests for MORE.

To my great astonishment and unintentionally I became a journalist, starting off retroactively as a foreign correspondent since everything I wrote at first was based on my experiences abroad. The manner of my entry into journalism and my early experiences have given me food for thought ever since and, to a certain extent, have remained guidelines for my activities.

It is not a bad thing to become a journalist because you have something to say and are burning to say it.

There is no substitute for looking into things on the spot, especially if you are going to write on burning international issues of the day.

Make every possible effort to get the facts across to at least some section of the public.

Do not be tied to a news organization in which you would be required to write against your own conscience and knowledge.

6

Foreign Correspondent

To RELATE my German experiences of the previous few months to anything within the ken of easygoing, tolerant Australians was very difficult. To talk of the Gestapo, concentration camps, and the lower depths of human beastliness while the blue smoke curled up and lamb chops sizzled in a pan on a weekend picnic—it all seemed too fantastic, too remote and unreal. The cultured Germans could simply not behave like that. But once we were at war, the pendulum swung to the other extreme. Superpatriots were calling for the annihilation of the German race. Two wars in less than twenty-five years—it was too much. There were no Nazis, only Germans, or inversely, there were no Germans, only Nazis.

However, having *been there*, I found plenty of outlets for what I had to say not only for articles about Germany, but for features on Tahiti and New Caledonia, where my wife and I had been stranded for two weeks by a dockers' strike. Within six months I had a regular place in the Literary Supplement of the Melbourne *Age*, one of the best of its kind in Australia. I was invited to contribute to periodicals dealing with Asian-Pacific affairs and to take part in discussions with specialists in these fields.

Japan was on the rampage in China as a prelude to carving out by force of arms a "Co-Prosperity Sphere" in Southeast Asia. Among the intended victims, as most of my Asian-Pacific specialists agreed, was underpopulated, mineral-rich Australia. But 1940–41 in Australia was like a replay of 1938–39 in England, with Menzies playing Chamberlain's role. By shipping minerals and scrap iron to Japan, the Menzies government was helping forge weapons for further Japanese expansion which would be directed against Australia, among other victims. During my enforced stay in New Caledonia I had found plenty of Japanese activity, assessing not only the importance of the island's nickel and chrome deposits but also the capacity of its deep water harbors. New Caledonia was no mean prize in itself, but as a base for the invasion of Australia—only 800 miles distant—it was of great significance. I managed to interest a few Australian newspapers—and Australian Associated Press, the leading news agency—sufficiently for them to finance a reporting trip there. So on New Year's Eve 1940 I was again aboard a French vessel bound for New Caledonia—but no longer the wide-eyed "boy from the bush." I had been as deeply shocked by the Nazi-Soviet Pact as by the West's Munich. It did not require Hitler's invasion of the Soviet Union to swing me wholeheartedly behind the Allied war effort. In taking my first step abroad as a foreign correspondent, it was as a militant against the Berlin-Rome-Tokyo axis.

It was not difficult to find evidence of Japan's interest in New Caledonia. This, as well as the revolt of the free French there against the pro-Nazi Vichy administration, was described in detail in some articles and my first book, *Pacific Treasure Island.* While in New Caledonia, I received a cabled reply to a request made on the day after Britain declared war on Germany—to contribute my experiences and qualifications to the war effort. I was invited to join the foreign-language monitoring service of Australia's newly formed Department of Information, aimed at countering the propaganda of Hitler and his allies. I cabled immediate acceptance on condition that this would not interfere with my freewheeling journalistic activities.

My job was to monitor Axis broadcasts in German, French, and Spanish, reporting on anything new or significant. It was interesting at first to put to practical use the time I had invested in language studies. But being slouched over a desk at night, listening to what Berlin, Rome, Vichy France, and Tokyo were saying about the war, was a poor substitute for being on the spot. I decided to get into more active journalism and to confirm, by on-the-spot observation, my conviction that Japan was on the verge of entering World War II.

By the time Hitler invaded Poland, Japan had occupied all the ports of China. Within just one year, in one of the greatest road-building feats of history, the Chinese had hacked out 600 miles of road over the wild mountain ranges of the southernmost mainland province of Yunnan to link Lashio, the northernmost railhead from the port-capital of Rangoon in Burma, with the southernmost terminus of China's road communication system at Kunming, capital of Yunnan. At the same time another 600 miles of road, linking Kunming with the Kuomintang wartime capital of Chungking, had been widened and surfaced. In late 1939 the Roosevelt administration decided to push military supplies along what became known as the Burma Road. No sooner did they start moving than Japan protested to Britain that the passage of military supplies through a British colony (Burma) was an unfriendly act which must be halted. Menzies, for Australia, was later to boast that through the Councils of the Empire he had put pressure on Britain to give in to the Japanese demands. The Burma Road was an "offense" that could "anger" Japan into striking retaliatory blows—even at Australia. If the price to be paid was sacrificing China to Japan, so what? So the road was closed politically as soon as it was opened functionally.

By mid-1941 Britain, dependent on war supplies from the United States, had to cede to Roosevelt's pressures and reopen the Burma Road. My ambition was to be among the first to travel over the reopened road and to be in China when the Japanese—as I was convinced they would—entered the war. With advances from the New Caledonia book and some contracts for feature articles, I left Australia in mid-August 1941, with typewriter and camera, for Rangoon.

There a cheerful Chinese consul exchanged a letter covered with red seals, given me by his counterpart in Melbourne, for another with still bigger red seals to be presented to the Chinese representative of the Burma Road Authority at Lashio, less than 100 miles south of the Chinese frontier. The Lashio railhead was the real starting point of the Burma Road. The boom-town atmosphere was not reassuring. One could only marvel at the wealth being dissipated by the Chinese drivers of the road convoys. They filled the restaurants and shops, gorging themselves with the best food and liquor, buying luxury goods in unlimited quantities.

After I waited around for a few days in an improvised hotel, a Captain Wang of the Chinese Air Force presented himself and said he was driving through to Kunming and would be glad to take me with him. Early the next morning we were on our way, not on the back of a truck as I had envisaged, but in the staff car of Captain Wang, a slim, responsible person. He was a patriot who wanted to push on with the war against the Japanese. As a liaison officer with General Claire Chennault's "Flying Tigers" (mercenary American fighter pilots hired by Chiang Kai-shek initially to protect supply convoys on the Burma Road from Japanese air attacks) he had been sent to Lashio to investigate the interminable delays in getting badly needed equipment up to Chennault's main base at Kunming. Wang had been allotted one of those swaggering drivers I had seen around Lashio, but after the first few miles, he took over at the wheel, and to my relief he turned out to be a first-rate driver.

At the top of the first 5,000-foot ridge after we crossed the border, Wang stopped the car so we could look back over the pass we had climbed from the beautiful valley below. The slope which we had negotiated looked like a statistician's chart with sharp brown zigzags laid against the mountainside from the velvety-shadowed valley to sunlit summit. A few paces from where the car halted a group of people, apparently from one family, was working. A venerable old chap in a thin blue shirt and trousers, with a goiter as big as a football extended halfway down his chest, wielded a hammer which looked as heavy as his emaciated body. His wife—or daughter—a teenage boy, two younger girls, and a toddler with padded pants, each armed with a hammer according to his or her size, pounded away at clusters of stone that the old man broke off from a granite outcrop just back of the road. Even the toddler, a hammer clasped in tiny fists, banged away at the chunks of stone and helped pile the small ones in neat piles by the roadside.

That group symbolized much of what I later learned to respect in the Chinese people: a discipline and intensity of labor combined with pride in a job well done and a natural dignity which shone through in the most undignified circumstances, as well as the feeling of generations of continuity, as exemplified by the old man and the toddler, working at the same task with equal intensity. How different from the image in Lashio of the racketeering drivers, flashing wads of money from hauling contraband goods for themselves and their Kuomintang bosses. The Burma Road had been built—and was then being kept in repair—by hundreds of thousands of pinched-faced peasants with their bare hands, carving this lifeline out of rock and mountains with hoes, hammers, and homemade blasting powder, carrying every pound of rock and dirt for the road and its facing in little bamboo baskets. They chiseled perfect roadrollers out of solid rock, hauling them up and down until earth and rock were padded down hard so that truck convoys could pass with guns and bullets to kill the Japanese invaders.

As we started off again, there seemed nothing but serried dark green mountain ridges, rising one above the other until lost in the clouds. As Wang headed directly for the first massive mountain wall, I wondered where we would find the pass. There were no passes—and obviously no tunnels. We zigzagged up to the top of a ridge and zigzagged down again, running along valleys for short stretches before heading for another somber wall blocking the sky. The human effort and sacrifice that had gone into all this were mind-boggling.

It was not the munitions that I had seen piling up on the Rangoon wharves that were in the convoys we passed. Priority was reserved for goods that yielded the highest returns on the black market. Captain Wang started a private war against the racketeers. He would race his Chrysler staff car dangerously close to the cabin of a truck, yelling to the driver to pull over to the side, if necessary waving his pistol until the truck stopped. Then he would clamber over the cargo, pulling out cases and bales of everything from whiskey and cigars to quinine and condoms, usually hidden under boxes of munitions and airplane parts. The drivers were always wide-eyed with astonishment, but Wang berated them and covered reams of paper with names of drivers, truck numbers, and types of contraband, then set out to overtake the next convoy.

It took four days to reach Kunming. The Japanese had heavily bombed the city two days earlier. At the city outskirts, survivors in one hamlet were softening up the rubble to which their homes had been reduced to make sun-dried bricks for rebuilding. Captain Wang did not leave me until he had arranged for me to continue on to Chungking in a postal truck. Reclining among mailbags in an open truck with nothing between me and the blue sky was the sort of journey I had dreamed of. It was strange after the official disbelief encountered in Singapore and Rangoon as to the possibility of Japan's striking into Burma, Malaya, or anywhere else in Southeast Asia to find Chinese troops moving down the Burma Road toward the border. At some villages little bands turned out to cheer them on their way with fiddle, fife, and trumpet. When they passed a halted convoy, some of the slender troops in tattered uniforms and worn shoes peered wonderingly and enviously at the shiny crated artillery pieces in some of the trucks. The heaviest weapons they carried for a whole battalion were three-inch mortars and Bren-type light machine guns.

Late on the evening of the fifth day out of Kunming the truck trundled down a bomb-pitted, dusty road to the edge of the swirling brown waters of the Yangtze. Across the river, through shimmering mist, Chungking looked like a dream city. Tier after tier of white buildings rose above each other from the steep bank, the topmost disappearing into the mist.

Mailbags and I were transferred to a crowded ferryboat, well upstream from the city. As it entered the swirling current, the overcrowded ferry seemed as helpless as a bottle in a whirlpool. With the bow headed upstream and the engines chugging at full force, we were carried downstream at a furious rate and were soon well below the city, hurtling—or so it seemed to a novice—with alarming swiftness toward the infamous Yangtze Gorges. After anxious moments, the laboring old boat freed itself from the worst vortex of the current and began imperceptibly to inch its way upstream and enter the calmer waters of the northern bank.

Long before the stout tethering ropes were flung ashore, it was clear that Chungking was indeed a "dream city." It was my first taste of the reality of war, and it was shattering. Laconic Japanese communiqués monitored back in Melbourne, reporting attacks against "military targets" in Chungking, were no preparation for this. The white buildings were only façades. From the water's edge, the windowless, roofless, backless shells, propped up—as could be seen later—by stout bamboo poles, looked like a screen set for some "end-of-the-world" fantasia.

At the water's edge pairs of husky porters awaited the ferry, competing to shout out bargain rates for the privilege of carrying passengers and their baggage in sedan chairs up the hundred or so steep steps to street level. Further progress was by man-pulled ricksha, the exclusive means of transport in those days through Chungking's narrow, winding streets. The consul in Rangoon had written down the address of the press hostel. A ricksha puller plucked it from my hand and bounded from shop to shop until he found someone who could decipher the characters and give the directions. With a whoop of triumph he started trotting toward our destination.

A wave of bombers had laid strings of bombs along the length of the street overlooking the river. On the one side were the façades, and on the other hillòcks of rubble. But even this ragged street testified to the vitality of China. It was crowded with bustling people, everyone doing something—clearing rubble, carrying, buying, selling, women sitting on blocks of rubble, breast-feeding babies. Only the children looked different from those in other towns and villages I had passed along the Burma Road. The faces of even the very young were old and grave, as if they had shouldered responsibilities beyond their age before they had learned to laugh and play. Things were upside down. The older folks had preserved their cheerfulness and sense of humor, but days and nights of Japanese bombings for months on end had wiped the smiles from the faces of the children.

The press hostel was a line of single-room dormitories in front of some still-intact substantial buildings which housed the Ministry of Information. Chungking was completely isolated in those days, and I was welcomed as a fresh breeze from outside by officialdom and the dozen other journalists there. The latter—in mid-September 1941—included those who had already made—or soon would make—their names as journalists and writers: Leland Stowe, Theodore "Teddy" White, Harrison Forman, Jack Belden, Betty Graham, and others. They were astonished that I had traveled over the legendary Burma Road and were especially interested that I had seen Kuomintang troops moving toward the Burma frontier. In exchange for my impressions, they were generous with their assessments of the situation in China. They were not very complimentary toward either Chiang Kai-shek or the regime he headed.

One of my first calls was on Sir Frederick Eggleston, one of the small group of Asian-Pacific specialists I had known from Melbourne, now Australia's ambassador to China. His first secretary was Keith Waller, also well known from the Melbourne days. Eggleston and Waller gave me their views on the internal situation, which coincided with those of the press corps. Conservative Sir Frederick warned me against taking at its face value anything coming from Hollington K. Tong, deputy minister for information in charge of the press and intimate friend of Generalissimo Chiang Kai-shek.

"If you really want to know what's going on," he said to my great astonishment, "go see Chou En-lai. He's the only man around here who will give you a straight answer to a straight question." Chou En-lai, then considered third in the Communist party hierarchy after Mao Tse-tung and Chu Teh, was in Chungking as head of the Communist party's liaison office with the Kuomintang. The united front between the two was more "fiction than fact," the journalists had told me, and the fault lay with Chiang Kai-shek, not Mao Tse-tung. Sir Frederick, in more diplomatic terms, confirmed this.

I asked for—and got—an interview with Foreign Minister Quo Tai-chi as to what would be China's reaction to a Japanese invasion of Southeast Asia. His reply was a miniscoop and propelled me into Fleet Street. China would become an ally of the anti-Axis powers and be prepared to send troops beyond its frontiers to aid its new allies.

Australian editors had been so skeptical of any important news breaking in that area—or perhaps of my ability to handle it—that I was limited to air-mailing features. But this information was of such major political importance that I cabled it at my own expense to the London *Daily Express*. Within a few hours came a cable from the foreign editor asking me to become its Chungking correspondent. Apart from *The Times*—whose correspondent, Colin MacDonald, was away in Hong Kong—no other British newspapers were then represented in China. Reuters relied on the services of a local journalist whose close ties with the Kuomintang were well known. Accreditation, together with press collect cable facilities, was quickly arranged, and I became a full-fledged foreign correspondent. (Note for would-be foreign correspondents: There is no shortcut as effective as being on the right spot at the right time and, if possible, without competitors.)

A few months later came the stunning news of Pearl Harbor, which, because of the time difference, reached Chungking in the small hours of the morning of Sunday, December 7, 1941. Owing to the habits acquired from my early appointments with cows in Australia, I was the only journalist awake when the service messages started pouring in. Within hours China declared war on Japan (amazingly, until then there had been no state of war between the two countries in what Japan referred to as the "China incident"). For good measure, a few days later China also declared war on Germany and Italy and became part of the grand antifascist alliance.

The attack on Pearl Harbor and the United States' entry into the war were received with euphoria at Kuomintang headquarters. The relief that China was no longer alone in its war against Japan was natural. The Western powers, especially the United States, would be forced at last to halt their shipments of arms, oil, and other raw materials to Japan and step up supplies to China. It later became clear that the dominant group around Chiang Kai-shek believed that the Western allies would now deal with Japan, while the Kuomintang, with greatly stepped-up military supplies, could concentrate on wiping out the Communists.

On the morning following Pearl Harbor I had my first meeting with Chou En-lai. It had been arranged by his extremely intelligent and beautiful secretary, Kung P'eng. As she escorted me to the interview, Kung P'eng explained that we were being followed and that the compound where Chou En-lai had his headquarters also housed Tai Li, the dreaded chief of the Kuomintang Gestapo, who had an apartment overlooking part of Chou En-lai's office. She was warning me that from the moment I entered the compound I would be a marked man, and if that worried me, I could just keep on walking as if I were taking a morning stroll and she would go into the compound alone. Knowing that most of my colleagues maintained contact with Chou En-lai, I was not too worried.

We entered a three-story house and went straight into Chou En-lai's office, a spartan room with a few bamboo chairs and three-shelf bamboo bookcases. Suddenly Chou En-lai was there, gravely shaking hands as Kung P'eng made the introductions. First impressions were of dignity, wisdom, and calm. These were quickly reinforced by his simplicity of style and clarity of expression. Obviously my first question was how he foresaw the new development of the war and the Communist party's role in the overall Chinese commitment. The main part of his reply was to the effect that Japan would try to offset its drastic shortage of strategic materials—now that U.S. sources would be cut off—by seizing the countries of Southeast Asia. It was already entrenched in Indochina, exploiting that area's rice and rubber production. It would try to get its hands on Indonesian oil, Malayan rubber and tin, Burma's rice and oil. All these countries were colonies of France, Holland, and Britain. Only if they were granted independence now, or at least solemn pledges of independence once Japan was defeated, would the peoples of these countries have a stake in victory over Japan. If no such steps were taken, or pledges given, many might even yield to the argument that if there has to be colonial domination, better that it be Asian. The key to rapid defeat of Japan was to mobilize the people of the area against the invaders. This could be done only if they were convinced that by helping defeat Japan, they were winning their own independence.

As for the Communist party, it would use its influence for stepping up China's resistance to Japan on all fronts. Where Communist forces confronted the Japanese this would be done immediately. There were large Chinese communities in Southeast Asia, and if pledges of independence were given, the Communist party was ready to send instructors to help those communities wage guerrilla warfare.

Because the Sydney *Daily Telegraph* had asked me to cable Chinese reactions to Japan's entry into the war, I included substantial quotes from Chou En-lai's analysis and was crestfallen to receive a reply: UNINTERESTED CHINESE COMMUNIST PRONOUNCEMENTS. This was in sharp contrast with the interest in the United States and Britain in anything that the Chinese Communists had to say.

Another phase had started. My cabled dispatches appeared regularly in the *Daily Express* and in the Sydney *Daily Telegraph* and Melbourne *Age*, which published them by arrangement with the *Express*. After the Japanese attacked Hong Kong, the *Express* asked if I would join its team of war correspondents in the Asian area.

7

❧◆❧

Into Battle

ABOUT ONE WEEK after Pearl Harbor, the Japanese launched a major drive to split China south of the Yangtze River into two. In one of their rare actions at that period, the Kuomintang troops were putting up a stubborn fight. The *Daily Express* agreed that I should go down and cover the Battle of Changsha, the focal point of the whole action. By the time our small group of journalists and military attachés arrived the shooting was over.

It was clear the Kuomintang troops had fought well, and the Japanese were in full retreat, abandoning many of their dead. The residents of Changsha had been evacuated; buildings in strategic spots converted into fortresses.

At every street corner were machine-gun nests and small concrete pillboxes; houses and shops in some areas had been torn down to provide clear lines of fire; rubble from Japanese bombs had been cemented together for tank obstacles, and street barricades erected from paving blocks, iron bedsteads, and stout wooden doors. The Changsha victory was an example of the best that the Kuomintang troops could do by supplementing their meager arms with traditional ingenuity.

The decisive battle had taken place in a cemetery just north of the city where the Chinese had dug in with the same thoroughness displayed in the city fortifications. A fierce battle had obviously been fought around a little knoll, in front of which many Japanese bodies still lay in the grotesque postures in which they had fallen. There I received my first lesson in military affairs from the U.S. military attaché, Colonel David D. Barrett. Pointing at the bodies at the knoll and the hundreds of cartridge cases lying around the defenders' positions, he said solemnly, "That's how famous battles are

68

won. A few guys hanging on in a hole in the ground and just staying there. You can have planes and big guns, but in the end it just comes to that, a few brave men clinging to a bit of earth, firing their guns and prepared to die rather than give it up. The Japanese attack obviously foundered at this one spot."

Any doubts about the dimensions of the defeat were dispelled the next day, when we left on horseback to follow the line of the Japanese retreat to the Liuyang River crossing, twelve miles north of Changsha. It was terribly cold; the countryside was blanketed in frost, and the road slippery with ice. We were mounted on rawboned Australian nags, captured from the Japanese. The path of any retreating army is a mournful-enough spectacle, but that leading back from Changsha was particularly gruesome. Many of the corpses had a limb, usually an arm, hacked off. It was explained that it was important for Japanese soldiers to know that if they died a hero's death, their ashes would be sent back to the family in a little white casket. In the haste of retreat, since it was not possible to cremate whole bodies, at least a limb could be reduced to ashes if time permitted or be carried along to be dealt with as opportunity offered.

After examining another battlefield nearer the Liuyang River, where sanitation squads with masks strapped across their mouths and noses were busily dragging corpses together and burying them in mass graves, we were more than ever convinced that the Chinese had scored a first-rate victory. One body caught my attention; the escorting officer said he was a Japanese major. As he lay face upward, his jaws were not quite closed, and peeping out behind his teeth were five revolver bullets. Apparently he had been leading a charge, revolver in hand with extra bullets in his mouth when he was struck down.

On the white sandbanks of the Hsiang River, which we had to cross early the following morning to resume the homeward journey, there was an amazing spectacle. Word that the Japanese had been definitely driven back had spread like wildfire. Thousands of people were streaming back into the city. They had been piling up at the river's edge all night, awaiting daylight to be ferried across. Old ladies, in trim black toques and with bound feet in tiny slippers, were being carried down to the ferry in sedan chairs, their belongings piled up on the shafts. Family men trotted along, with their household goods packed in baskets, suspended at each end of a carrying pole, often a child in one basket and an equivalent weight of goods in the other. Wheelbarrows, piled with baggage, were being urged through the sand, one man yoked in front pulling, another between the handles pushing. Children hardly out of the toddler stage staggered along with loads appropriate to their precocious strength slung across their shoulders.

Soon after I returned to Chungking, the *Express* asked me to proceed to Burma and cover the Japanese invasion there. It had just started, the

Japanese having crossed the Isthmus of Kra, the slender waist of land which separates Burma from Malaya and Thailand. Singapore and Malaya had rapidly fallen to the invaders. The great guns of the "impregnable fortress" of Singapore were installed to fire at invaders from the sea and could not swivel around to fire at the unmannerly invaders who came from the rear by land. Britain's "Pearl Harbor" had come when the pride of the British Navy, the battleship *Prince of Wales*, was sunk together with the battleship *Repulse* by Japanese bombers off the coast of Malaya. After that the Japanese were free to invade that corner of Empire wherever they wanted.

Chiang Kai-shek knew the importance of helping the British to hold onto Rangoon and keep the Rangoon–Lashio railway line open. It was for this that he had sent his Fifth and Sixth armies—elements of which I had seen moving down months earlier—to help the British. As a major concession to the United States, Generalissimo Chiang had agreed that U.S. General Joseph "Vinegar Joe" Stilwell would be in overall command. My assignment was to cover the Chinese operations; Jack Belden had been assigned to do the same thing for the London *Daily Mail*, the *Express*'s greatest rival.

Imagine our surprise—in mid-January 1942—to find the Chinese troops still camped on their own side of the frontier. This was due not to any hold-down orders from Chungking, but to British reluctance to let them into Burma. The argument was that while the Japanese would inevitably be driven out, there was no certainty that the Chinese, once in, would ever withdraw.

Arriving at a desperately overcrowded Lashio, I was able to share a room with an American, Captain Wilson, whom I had met during my first stopover there. He was thinner and grayer than three months earlier. His job was to cut through graft, gangsterism, and squeeze to keep supplies moving up the Burma Road. He gave horrifying examples of corruption in T. V. Soong's Southwest Transportation Company, which, by then, had the virtual monopoly of hauling U.S. lend-lease supplies up the road.

The next morning I set out by road to Mandalay and thence by train to Rangoon to get myself accredited and obtain authorization to contact the Chinese. At Pegu, the last halt before Rangoon, a weary young British lieutenant of the Burma Rifles (British-officered local defense force) came aboard. The company he commanded had just been routed in the Mergui-Tavoy area, well to the south of Rangoon on the Isthmus of Kra. He was returning to headquarters for replacement of supplies. His was the first account I heard on the situation at the front, but it was typical of what I was to hear and see later. Everything had been lost when the Japanese launched a surprise night attack. His company had been assigned to protect an airfield. A demolition squad had laid explosives to blow up gasoline and other supplies in case it could not be defended. But no orders came from battalion headquarters when the Japanese were reported advancing, so thousands of gallons of gasoline and hundreds of tons of supplies fell into Japanese hands—together with the airfield—without anyone's having actually seen an enemy soldier. It was ascertained later that the detonations which had convinced the company that it was surrounded were caused by firecrackers which the Japanese had hung in trees and which were extensively used in their "psychological night attacks."

At British Army (Burma Command) Headquarters, a public relations officer, Flight Lieutenant Wallace Crabbe—late of the Melbourne *Herald*—handed me a sheaf of papers to fill out, and within ten minutes I was an accredited war correspondent with His Majesty's Forces in Burma. I left his office with instructions to get into uniform complete with war correspondent's badges and with a rail warrant and "movement order" entitling me to proceed to Lashio and present myself to a Colonel Hobson, who would put me in contact with the Chinese forces.

There were two air raids on each of the two days I spent in Rangoon getting myself fitted out. From a small hill near the famous gold-topped Shwe Dagon Pagoda, I watched nine bombers pass overhead, their silvery wings flashing in the sunlight. Almost immediately there was the sound of machine guns as three fighters pounced on them, and three bombers went into steep dives, trailing smoke. Everything seemed leisurely and unreal. The six remaining bombers glided on at the same altitude, and at two more intervals there was the rattle of machine guns, and the drone of the bombers ceased. Without any fighter escorts they were "sitting ducks" for the P-40 Tomahawks flown by Chennault's Flying Tigers (by then they were officially known as the American Volunteer Group, or AVG; later they were integrated into the U.S. Fourteenth Air Force, commanded by Chennault).

The next day two faster reconnaissance-type planes came over, perhaps looking for the AVG base. They both were shot down, the pilots crashing onto Rangoon's Mingaladoon airfield when their parachutes failed to open. The Japanese Air Force was obviously not doing as well as the ground troops, which were steadily pushing up the narrow waist of Burma southeast of Rangoon.

At Lashio, in my war correspondent's uniform, I presented my credentials to a captain who was Colonel Hobson's deputy. After perusing my accreditation card and other documents, including my cables from the *Express*, asking why I was not reporting on the activities of the Chinese troops reportedly in Burma, he explained that all talk of Chinese troops in Burma was "bullshit." Except for a small body which had come in by a caravan trail in the far northwest, the Chinese armies were still in China, spread out in camps stretching from Wanting, on the Yunnan-Burma border, all the way back to Kunming. He made it clear that as far as he was concerned, that was where they could stay. While the Japanese were pushing forward from Tavoy, meeting only token resistance from the demoralized units of the Burma Rifles,

four divisions of the Chinese Fifth and three divisions of the Sixth armies
were uselessly spread along hundreds of miles of the Burma-Chinese frontier.
They represented at least 70,000 battle-hardened troops, whereas the British
had altogther 12,000 troops, most of whom had never heard a shot fired in
anger.

Since there were no Chinese Army operations to report and censorship for-
bade explaining why, I returned to Rangoon (1,400 miles from Lashio) and
asked to see Governor Sir Reginald Dorman-Smith. When he heard that I
had just come from the border area, he decided to see me immediately. After
all, my boss, Lord Beaverbrook, was a key member of the British Cabinet
and Churchill's right-hand man. Tall and handsome, clad in cream flannel
trousers and a blue double-breasted coat with brass buttons, Sir Reginald
looked more like a cricket hero than the governor of an embattled colony.

Speaking of the military situation, he explained in confidence that if his
recommendations—to occupy a small strip of Thai territory in the Isthmus of
Kra—had been adopted, the Japanese would not have been able to invade
Burma from the rear. But permission came through far too late as the result
of bureaucratic bungling. By the time the go-ahead was given the Japanese
had already occupied the area, and the few companies of Burma Rifles sent
in were cut to pieces. I related in great .detail what I had seen of British obstruction and discourtesies to the Chinese in the frontier area. These were not
things I could report to my paper because of censorship, but at least he should
know about them. He took it seriously and had me escorted to a brigadier at
army headquarters, where everything had to be repeated. That brigadier sent
for another who was the chief liaison officer with the Chinese forces, who
cursed the incompetencies of his junior officers and said he would leave immediately to "straighten things out." When the two brigadiers questioned the
value of Chinese troops, I related what I had seen at Changsha.

The visit shook things up on the British side at least, and the first
Chinese troops soon started moving down to the front. Once the Japanese
had occupied the Isthmus of Kra and Moulmein, only 100 miles east of
Rangoon across the Gulf of Martaban, they could afford to leave Burma
alone for a while and concentrate on consolidating their position in Malaya.

On the night of my conversation with the governor, I stayed with some
friends in the Burmese quarter of Rangoon. It was near full moon, and
Japanese bombers started night bombing. They came over quite low that
night. The first sticks of bombs whooshed down to explode a few hundred
yards away in the city's main market. It was by then early February 1942,
and about half the population had left Rangoon. British activities (mainly
the Burma Rifles and the Royal Air Force) were being covered by O'Dowd
Gallagher, veteran *Daily Express* correspondent, whose eyewitness account
of the sinking of the *Prince of Wales* (he was on board) made newspaper
history. Since he was temporarily absent and there was still no Chinese action

to report, it was logical to have a look at that part of the war. It was chaotic. Bridges that should have been blown to halt the Japanese advance on Moulmein were abandoned intact, and others that should not have been destroyed were blown up, leaving British troops stranded on the wrong side. After token resistance at Moulmein the demoralized defense forces started pulling back again, and there was nothing to prevent the Japanese from moving against Rangoon at their leisure. I returned to Lashio.

On Februray 19 the Chinese divisions started crossing the frontier in strength, and on the following day civilians remaining in Rangoon were ordered to evacuate the city by noon of the twenty-first. (There was no relation between the two events.) Fighting my way down from Lashio against an impossible current to get into Rangoon for the final agony, I felt a whack on my back at Mandalay railway station. It was an old Australian friend, David Maurice, who worked for Imperial Chemical Industries in Rangoon. Useless trying to get to Rangoon, he said; the Japanese would be there within hours. He drew a graphic picture of the panic after the evacuation order, which had followed one issued twenty-four hours earlier, asking everyone to stay because the city would be "defended to the last." One of his colleagues had taken everything—including his billiard table—with him. Others buried their valuables, hoping to return soon and dig them up. Through lying, but comforting, communiqués and a preposterous censorship, the public had been kept in almost complete ignorance of the real situation until they were suddenly ordered to get out. Maurice happened to be passing the lunatic asylum when the inmates were being set free, warders beating them with sticks to hurry them along.

"I can still the faces of those poor bastards," he said. "Vacant, crazed faces. Terror imprinted on idiocy, cowering under the blows from warders chasing them out into a world they'd been cut off from for years. . . . Then the lepers and beggars were chased out. Looters were shot where they were caught. Apparently it's better to let the Japs have the stocks than to let people help themselves for once. Fires were burning everywhere, some started by fifth columnists to guide bombers to their targets, others by lunatics. Fielding-Hall, in charge of the city Welfare Department, took the blame for prematurely releasing the lunatics and convicts and shot himself."

With the fall of Rangoon the fight for the rest of Burma was largely meaningless. The Burma Road as China's supply link with the outside world was finished. The Chinese had no great incentive to fight once the main reason for their presence was lost within forty-eight hours of their being allowed into the country. Nevertheless, their Fifth Army and one division of the Sixth Army fought courageously, mainly in holding actions to enable the British to withdraw whatever forces had survived back to India. The *Express* had no interest in my covering Chinese military activities in what had become a "lost cause" as far as Britain was concerned.

With the British photographer George Rodger of *Life* magazine, I left Burma by jeep along the Hukawng Valley, thence by foot 130 miles over the steep, jungle-covered Naga Hills into India, following animal tracks and those used by Naga headhunters. The notes we made were later used to enable 40,000 refugees fleeing the Japanese to take the same route, sustained by air-dropped supplies. Still later, that previously uncharted route served as the basis for what became known as the Ledo Road, linking Assam with the Burma Road via the Hukawng Valley. Our considerable adventures with the jungle, leeches, and Naga headhunters were chronicled by George Rodger in *Red Moon over Burma* and in my own book *Bombs over Burma*. Some episodes from our trek, recorded when the events were still fresh in my mind, may be of interest. Before setting out, we had been warned by Clive North, the British political officer at Shinbwiyang, the last British-administered village on the Burmese side of the frontier with India, that we were setting out on a dangerous, uncharted course and the only people we were likely to encounter would be Naga, known for their habit of snatching non-Naga heads. But he was helpful in recruiting ten of them to carry our baggage (mainly food for an estimated ten-day trek) and guide us to India from a point where North correctly foresaw we would have to abandon our jeeps:

> We reached a sharp incline leading to a stream filled with huge sandstone boulders. We knew we were beaten this time. Nothing less than dynamite and rock-drills could have bust those boulders. Regretfully, we parked our Jeeps side by side, wrote a note to North as agreed, and sent it back together with the keys of the Jeeps by a Kachin policeman who had accompanied us. . . .
>
> With our haversacks, containing camera equipment and revolvers over our shoulders, we started off on foot. . . .
>
> We were hungry, having breakfasted only on coffee. We had had five hours' strenuous physical exercise, axe, pick and shovel work and we realized we had packed all our foodstuffs on the backs of our Naga bearers. Neither of us had done much walking for a long while. When I asked George what sort of walker he was, he replied mournfully: "I don't know. I always take taxis." *

With hindsight it was a foolhardy venture. No white men, to North's knowledge, had ever crossed from Burma to India by the route we were taking. It was little better than an animal track, tunneled through the undergrowth for miles on end. But the Naga and opium-growing Kachin who inhabited the Hukawng Valley—the full length of which we had traversed by then—had assured Clive North that the main track led straight

---

* Wilfred Burchett, *Bombs over Burma* (Melbourne: F. W. Cheshere, 1944), p. 203.

into India's tea-growing province of Assam. It was on the basis of this flimsy information that we had set out. We had also been crazy to send our porters ahead, certain at first that we would overtake them with our jeeps long before the vague evening rendezvous at a stream indicated on a crude map, agreed to by North and a Naga headman.

> We knew we couldn't catch our Nagas till evening—and we both had fears, unvoiced at first, but discussed as the day wore on. The Nagas had everything we possessed, including 200 rupees—nice silver coins which would string together beautifully around a Mrs. Naga's neck. They knew all the paths and were nearing their own country and villages. What if they chose to clear out and leave us? We didn't have a scrap of food and we knew there was no chance of picking anything up along the track. . . . North warned us that since 1939, the Government had been unable to send out its usual annual expeditions, and he had had reports that headhunting had started again.*

Our immediate problems came not from headhunters but other bloodthirsty creatures: leeches! They dropped onto our limbs from leaves and twigs and squeezed into our boots through the lace holes, dropping off only when they were fat and bloated with our blood.

> We were fearsome sights with blood streaming down our arms and legs. . . . It was getting dusk and we seemed to have gone down further than we'd climbed—which was disheartening for the morrow . . . when we thought we heard voices. Sure enough, we dropped down from one especially steep section, and there was a rushing torrent hundreds of feet below and blue smoke hanging low in the valley. We groaned with relief. Water to drink, water to bathe our feet; the Nagas were still with us; food, sleep.
>
> The Nagas . . . had exceeded their duties as porters. They'd built a rough shelter for us, and had packed all our belongings under cover. They had a good fire going and rice cooking. We had a wash in the river and sat around on the rocks with our feet and legs in the icy cold water. Leech bites, which were still bleeding, stopped when we washed in the cold water. . . .†

To avoid the worries of the first day, we established a routine by which I went on ahead with an extra "eleventh man" who had attached himself to the main group somewhere along the trail and carried the coffee-making equipment and a few cans of food. By the time George and the rest arrived we had a fire alight, coffee brewing, and construction of the night's shelter well advanced. My leg muscles, toughened by my wanderings during the Australian Depression years, quickly reasserted their form. On one

---

* *Ibid.,* pp. 203–04.
† *Ibid.,* pp. 205–06.

memorable occasion, I outstripped my eleventh man and ran into a band of really wild-looking Naga. I could hear them crashing through a shortcut and stopped short, thinking it was a leopard or tiger, tracks of which we had spotted around the previous night's encampment.

They stopped dead in their tracks on seeing me. There were three men and one oldish woman, with drooping, bared, shrivelled breasts. One old man had a steel-shafted spear, the rest had *dahs* (large, heavy jungle knives). We stared at each other and I managed a weak smile. The old man with the spear tensened as I put my hand in my pocket and they all looked at me with alarmed suspicion. I tried to muster a laugh and pulled out a handful of silver rupees. I handed them one each. They took them, but continued looking at me rather than at the rupees. The youngest one . . . to my amazement then produced a packet of cigarettes and stiffly handed them to me. I took one and—breaking my non-smoking habit for the moment—lit it. Tension immediately slackened. Mama decorously flung a one-piece garment over her body, covering up her breasts. The youth opened up a bundle of cigarettes— five in a packet—and offered me half a dozen packets. He seemed hurt when I refused, so I took them. We all laughed then, and it struck me for the first time that laughter is the only true international language. I gave them some more rupees, and pointed my camera at my own head and clicked the shutter. I handed the camera to the old man to look at, while I examined his spear, and after that we were on the best of terms. . . . We shook hands all round and they padded away, chattering in great excitement. George, who'd been out of cigarettes from Myitkyina (the last big town before entering the Hukawng Valley) onwards, was a bit staggered when I produced the cigarettes later that evening.*

On the sixth day out from Shinbwiyang, we met some British teaplanters in charge of a big gang of Indian workers clearing the jungle for campsites for a further contingent of workers destined to build a road roughly following the track which we had followed. They were amazed to see us. They wanted a full report on the condition of the track and primitive bridges across the numerous streams, the height of the water in those we had forded, the attitude of the "natives," and other details. Because we had been conscious of our trail-blazing role, we had noted such matters. The planter in charge impressed upon us that the well-being of tens of thousands of refugees might well depend on the accuracy of our report. It was hard for us to visualize women and children and the aged following in our footsteps.

As the Naga ate their way through their rice—which constituted 90 percent of the weight that each carried at the start and the weight of our tinned food diminished, we made better time, and on the seventh day we covered twenty-two miles to reach Tipang, connected with Ledo—our principal ob-

---

* *Ibid.,* pp. 206–07.

jective—by a light railway from a coal mine. The colliery manager miraculously produced some cold beer, and a second miracle occurred when an unscheduled supply train arrived to return to Ledo an hour later.

> The Nagas—at first terrified at the noise of the puffing, grunting engine— approached it with eyes nearly bursting from their heads. . . . We had a chain of interpreters who gradually broke Naga down through Assam dialects and Hindi to English. We asked the bearers if they'd like to jump in the train and ride with us to Ledo. They were very fearful until we got in, but then they followed. . . . We left them at Ledo station, from where they wandered off, hand-in-hand, looking at the modest wonders displayed in the shop windows.*

After arranging double pay for the porters and rice for their return trek, we were taken to the local British military commander, who had received a signal from General Headquarters, Burma Command—evacuated to Calcutta —to extract from us a detailed report on the state of the route, including walking time between stages, the type of soil, where stones suitable for road surfacing were available, and other specialized questions. By then it was a question not only of getting refugees out but of building what became known as the Ledo Road, to mount an Allied counterattack into Burma.

Upon arrival in Calcutta, I promptly went down with my first onslaught of malaria. A degree or two was added to my fever when I discovered that (a) because of garbled cables at the time of my accreditation to the British War Office, I had become *Peter* Burchett in the *Express* and that (b) many of my dispatches had never left the censor's office in Rangoon or in Maymyo, after it was moved there.

My career as a war correspondent had got off to a bad start. I realized— fortunately the foreign editor also—that this was inevitable where only nonaction, bungling, and defeats were the raw material for reports and zealous censors were at work to transform them all into victories.

---

* *Ibid.,* p. 211.

8

Frontline China

CALCUTTA WAS IMPOSSIBLE, except as a study of British colonialism in its decadence. As Rangoon had been a replica of Singapore, so Calcutta was a replica of Rangoon. "Dress for dinner, business as usual, stiff upper lip" was the order of the day. Dinner jackets—or officer's uniform—were obligatory for males, long evening gowns for the *memsahibs* in the restaurants of any hotels where officers, gentlemen, and war correspondents were likely to be accommodated. It was "bad form" and "defeatist" even to mention the disasters in Hong Kong, Malaya, or Burma.

The *Express* agreed to my returning to China, where fighting had broken out in the eastern provinces of Kiangsi and Chekiang. Early in June 1942 I flew over what was known as the hump, the 16,000-foot-high Himalayan "foothills," to Kunming, then on to Chungking. A fortnight later I left by plane and train to Hunan Province and from there started a three-month trip by bus, horseback, sedan chair, and foot through China's frontline provinces, covering the Kiangsi-Chekiang campaign. Together with Yang Kang, a noted Chinese woman journalist and poetess as interpreter, these travels extended from Chungking right across southern China to Foochow on the Pacific coast.

The Japanese forays into the Kiangsi-Chekiang area were typical "kill all, burn all, destroy all" operations, intended partly to terrorize people to stop supporting local guerrillas, partly to prevent them from reaping the summer-autumn harvest. We rode, marched, or were carried through areas where village after village had been burned to the ground; rice grinders, threshers, plows, and waterwheels smashed and the remnants thrown into cesspools. Paddy in the fields was prematurely yellow and drying at the roots because the irrigation terraces had been breached. In other places it was headless—the

Japanese had turned their horses loose to feed to their bellies' content on the ripening grain. We avoided staying overnight in towns because cholera was rapidly spreading.

There were only old people, women, and children to be seen in the countryside, able-bodied males having fled either the Japanese or the Kuomintang press gangs. We arrived in the heart of old guerrilla country where Mao Tse-tung had set up the Kiangsi Soviet and where the Long March had begun. One day, after an attack of bacillary dysentery had eased sufficiently to permit my mounting a horse again—I had traveled for several days in a wheelbarrow—our ponies slipped and slithered over a path cut out of a steep mountainside to squeeze through a narrow pass at the top—and there was the city of Nanchang spread out at our feet. The romantic walled city, even from that distance, could be seen as a blackened, flattened waste of rubble. It looked as if it had been beaten into the ground by giant bulldozers. As we got closer, it was clear that the city's 50,000 population had almost all fled.

Such were the scenes in endless variations that met our eyes as we made our way across the mountains toward the coast. There were no signs of the Kuomintang troops' having offered more than token resistance anywhere. As we approached the Kiangsi-Fukien border, in very wild, mountainous country, a local Kuomintang commander insisted on giving us an escort, including a Bren-gun team. The area was reputed to be infested with bandits, he said, but Yang Kang thought they were probably guerrillas harassing the Japanese rear. In any case, it was ideal terrain for bandits or guerrillas, and the Japanese operation had clearly petered out there. Mountain trails were littered with Japanese dead, putrefying bodies blackened with heat. Some had been hacked and mauled as if local peasants with primitive weapons had ambushed stragglers. Red-eyed women in one village told of how the people had hidden in the mountains as the Japanese approached, returning after they had withdrawn. But they came back too soon. The Japanese reappeared the same night, murdered the menfolk, raped the young women, and carried off all boys between ten and sixteen years.

During the campaign which we were following, but never quite catching up with, because there were no set battles, Japanese forces had captured a trio of newly built Chinese airfields in northern Chekiang and were then pushing toward the border of Fukien—the only coastal province they had not penetrated at the time. The roads leading to the airfields were jammed with trucks—not carrying reinforcements and supplies to the north or evacuating equipment from the airfields, but piled high with officers' personal belongings, with family members perched on top. Gasoline, which had traveled halfway around the world and across China to reach Fukien, was being wasted on trucks, loaded to capacity with suitcases, furniture, sewing machines, and, in some cases, officers' wives and concubines.

At Kienyang we waited nine days to see General Ku Chu-tung, area commander in charge of Chekiang-Fukien provinces. We had many questions to ask, but appointments were always fixed for "tomorrows" which never came. Refugees, students and missionaries among them, were pouring into the city every day. They all told the same tale: The Kuomintang troops had not fought.

On the long route back, fighting our way aboard overcrowded buses and bug-ridden riverboats, we stopped for a rest at Shao-kuan, the beautiful temporary capital of Kwantung Province, 120 miles north of Japanese-occupied Canton. To my surprise, Yang Kang arranged a dinner there with a colonel in the Kuomintang army. Unusually tall for a Chinese and very slender, he was obviously a "personality." After a few minutes of earnest conversation with Yang Kang, he took off his colonel's jacket and threw it onto a chair with a derisory gesture. Speaking in excellent English, he then started to brief me about the activities of the Pao-An guerrillas. Public mention of this extraordinary organization was taboo in Chungking. At a later stage in the dinner—by far the best we had enjoyed in our travels—two of the main Pao-An guerrillas joined us. Wang Tso-yao, a seemingly gentle, scholarly person, who headed the 5th Battalion, and the rugged, knobbly Chin Sheng, commander of the 3rd Battalion. Both had graduated in the Canton revolutionary students' movement of the 1930s. Their two battalions between them had already rescued, or helped to safety, thousands of Chinese and more than thirty British and Americans. They were constantly engaged in widespread harassment of Japanese garrisons. Among the three of them they explained how it was done—in one of the most memorable dinners of my life till that time.

The full richness of the evening could be savored only later, when I learned that the "colonel" was a certain Chiao Kuan-hua, a prominent left-wing journalist in Hong Kong until the Japanese invasion, who had himself been rescued by the legendary Pao-An guerrillas. He had immediately thrown in his lot with them, managing to use his infiltration into the Kuomintang army as his cover. Sometime after our meeting he was transferred from the guerrillas to Chungking, where he became one of Chou En-lai's most devoted and appreciated aides and married Yang Kang's sister—the beautiful and prestigious Kung P'eng. (The friendship started at that memorable dinner in Shao-kuan ripened throughout the years. After the People's Republic was founded, Chiao Kuan-hua became an assistant foreign minister [foreign minister in 1974], and Kung P'eng headed the Information Department of the Chinese Foreign Ministry. Yang Kang, in the years immediately following the setting up of the republic, continued her journalistic career, writing as "Observer" in the *Ren-min Jih-pao [People's Daily]*, organ of the Chinese Communist party.)

The remainder of the return journey to Chungking was uneventful. I arrived there in the first days of October 1942 in time for a breakfast meeting with Wendell Willkie, the Republican candidate in the 1940 presidential elections. He was accompanied by two very able officials from the U.S. Office of War Information, Gardner Cowles, publisher of the Des Moines *Register and Tribune* and *Look* magazine, and Joe Barnes, who later became foreign editor of the New York *Herald Tribune*. These two persuaded Willkie that I was worth talking to. It was due to them—the "homework" they had done before leaving the United States and the diligent digging from the moment they arrived in Chungking—that Western diplomats were amazed at Willkie's grasp of the situation almost immediately after his arrival. I found him a warm, unprejudiced person—very different from my preconceived image of a Republican presidential candidate. A crowd of half a million had turned out to greet him on arrival at Chungking, and my appraisal—written not too long after the event and thirty-five years before the dramatic turn in Chinese-American relations—was not too far off the mark:

> The scenes at Mr. Willkie's arrival in Chungking were mainly staged by the efficient Information Ministry, but no-one could have staged his subsequent receptions. He radiated goodwill towards China and the people felt that, and reciprocated. Wherever he went and spoke he was wildly acclaimed. After all, he was a symbol of the genuine friendship and sympathy American people had for China and the determination of his government to stand by China through this war against Japan. His visit was a cleansing wind that swept away many fears and suspicions that the Allies were to leave China, high, dry and defenceless. There was already plenty of goodwill towards America at that time. Best of all, for the first time since the Chinese capital had been established in Chungking, the bombing season had come—and almost gone—and there were no signs of Jap bombers. The only planes seen over the city were American. . . .
>
> Despite the loss of the Burma Road, supplies were still coming in, flown over the [Himalayan] "hump" by American transport planes. More and more U.S. military personnel were seen around Chungking. . . .*

Willkie was well advised enough to have a meeting with Chou En-lai in Chungking—as a substitute for a visit he had hoped to make to Yenan and a meeting with Mao Tse-tung. The nearest he got to Yenan was about 200 miles to the north, at Sian, the capital of neighboring Shansi Province. With other correspondents, I accompanied him to that ancient walled city which had been China's capital for almost 1,000 years. From there we went to the Yellow River Bend at Tungkwan, where the "River of Sorrows"—a

---

* Wilfred Burchett, *Democracy with a Tommygun* (Bombay: Thacker & Co. Ltd., 1946), p. 98.

good half mile wide at that point—abruptly changes its north-south direction and heads directly east to the sea. Tungkwan was a stage set for visiting foreigners, and Willkie was given the full treatment.

It bore little resemblance to the real war: a labyrinth of underground defense works, complete with medical stations; aboveground a few batteries of big guns overlooking Japanese positions on the opposite bank. From an observation post, Japanese soldiers could be seen nonchalantly strolling about on the far bank. Someone asked if the big guns ever fired. "No," replied the commanding officer. "If we fired, the Japanese would only fire back. That would do neither of us any good."

In the afternoon we were treated to a first-class military exercise, with a couple of battalions of Chinese troops, protected by a creeping artillery barrage, advancing up a valley to take an "enemy position." Military attachés found the artillery fire accurate, that from the heavy machine guns well directed, and troop movements well coordinated with the support fire. Then there was a march-past of a division of the elite First Army, commanded by General Hu Tsung-nan, considered one of those most likely to succeed Chiang Kai-shek in case of the latter's untimely death. It was hard to believe that the division could be part of the military organization that I had seen on the fighting fronts of Southeast Asia or in Burma. Company after company of big, well-fed troops in splendid uniforms, steel helmets, and gas masks goose-stepped past the reviewing stand. There were Italian, German, and Soviet tanks, Krupp heavy artillery, American howitzers, abundant troop carriers and jeeps. This one division had more firepower than all the rest of the units I had seen in China, taken together.

One of our guides at Tungkwan was Captain Chiang Wei-kuo, the generalissimo's youngest son. Trained in Nazi Germany, he must have felt at home with Hu Tsung-nan's First Army, which had been built up by Nazi military advisers. He chatted away with me in fluent English and German about his "exciting" experiences with the German Wehrmacht at the time of the takeover in Austria. During my trip into the southeast, I had spent a day with his elder brother, Chiang Ching-kuo, at Kanchow, capital of South Kiangsi. Ching-kuo had been Soviet-trained and once declared in Moscow that he would never return to China as long as his father remained in power. (But he did return and later succeeded him on Taiwan as president of the Republic of China.) Physically and temperamentally, the brothers seemed totally dissimilar, reflecting partly the difference of the societies in which they had lived part of their formative years. Ching-kuo was a burly fellow, whose measured style, slow reactions, and lack of social graces could class him as a bureaucrat of peasant origin (which he was obviously not), but he radiated some human warmth. Wei-kuo, slim and dapper like his father, was sophisticated, had fast responses and slick repartee, but one felt that behind his ready smile were ice and steel.

Early on the morning after our Tungkwan visit, Willkie, having completed that part of his 30,000-mile "one world" journey, left Sian for Washington, by way of Siberia. The rest of us returned to Chungking, where I found a telegram from the *Daily Express* strongly hinting at renewed military action in Burma. The Tungkwan charade proved to be my last image of wartime China. Hu Tsung-nan's splendid divisions were later used against Mao's Communists—never against the Japanese.

Of Blimps and Heretics

I T WAS A CLOUDY MORNING on October 25, 1942, when I took off in a DC-3 transport plane from Kunming, over the hump to New Delhi to obtain a new accreditation to India Command. Pilot Lieutenant Benjamin warned that as we would have to go up to 17,000 feet, I might have respiratory difficulties. In that case I should come up front and he would give me a few whiffs of oxygen. Only he and the copilot had masks connected to the lone oxygen cylinder—no masks for the radio operator or me. I should keep my eyes open for fighter planes—they could be only Japs. After the first hour I happened to glance at the radio operator—slumped across his desk. Shaking did no good. My feet heavy as bags of tungsten, I alerted Benjamin, who said, "We're pretty high up. I'll chance it and go down a couple of thousand feet." The radio operator came to sufficiently to stagger to the pilot's cabin for a few whiffs of oxygen.

We had started to make height again when the copilot grabbed Benjamin's arm and pointed south. Three fighter planes were heading our way. The DC-3 responded to Benjamin's urgent action at the controls, and we were soon lost to vision in friendly cotton-wool clouds. After that we landed at Dum Dum Airfield in the Ledo area of Assam, just in time to be hit by the first Japanese air raid on the Assam fields. The results were disastrous, and early the next morning all surviving planes—which included ours—were ordered to get off the ground and head anywhere south or east. It resulted in my eventually being disembarked in Karachi, where red tape prevented me from getting on a Delhi-bound train for another five days.

What with the effects of dysentery and a couple of more bouts of malaria during the Southeast China trip, the doctors found I was suffering from debility, undernourishment, fatigue, vitamin deficiency, and precursor signs of liver trouble. With vitamin injections, normal foods, and Delhi's invigorating winter sunshine, I was soon in form again, fit enough to proceed to Bombay and greet my wife and three-year-old son, Rainer, who were stopping off for a few weeks on their way to England, my wife having despaired of my ever returning to Australia. By the time censorship permitted disclosure of the arrival of their ship they were already installed in a Bombay hotel. There were scandalized looks and mutterings among some *memsahibs* in the hotel restaurant when the three-year-old, guided to me by his mother, pointed a finger and shouted, "Is *that* my father?"

I was rash enough to suggest that we all go to Calcutta for a couple of pre-Christmas days of jollification before I left to report on the first British counterattack into Burma. On the evening of the day before my departure my wife and I went to the cinema to see Charlie Chaplin in *The Gold Rush*, leaving the little lad asleep in our hotel room. Just as Charlie was wolfing his boot, twirling the laces like spaghetti around his fork, the screen went black and the sirens sounded. Because there had been no air raids on Calcutta, it had to be a practice alert, or so I thought. But we hastened back to the hotel. There was a tremendous rumpus there, the hotel staff banging brass gongs, people yelling and rushing about. From the terrace came the unmistakable deep rhythmic drone of Japanese bombers. We had to wake the boy and all go down to the basement. The bombs started to explode, and there was pandemonium—the main object of the raid and others that followed. Having arranged for my wife and child to proceed to New Delhi, I left the following evening to cover what was to be the start of the British counteroffensive into Arakan, the southwestern province of Burma which adjoined Bengal.

Christmas Day found Gordon Waterfield of Reuters and me at an advanced British headquarters on the Burma side of the frontier, being briefed about a "victorious" counterattack into Burma. The Japanese had been taken by surprise and were retreating. As evidence of their hasty flight we were shown an abandoned brothel in the village of Buthidaung. Thirty miles down the Mayu River from there was Rathedaung, the last important post before the strategic port of Akyab. A patrol had been into Rathedaung the previous night and found no Japanese. The brigadier who briefed us said that advance troops would occupy Rathedaung that night and then push straight on to Akyab. A big sampan was placed at our disposal, together with two Arakan oarsmen, a British intelligence officer—straight out from England—and a public relations major, our escort. Waiting for the tide to change, we heard numerous explosions, which Waterfield and I interpreted as a battle going on at Rathedaung. The intelligence officer thought otherwise and sent a dispatch back to the brigadier to the effect that the Japanese were evacuating Akyab and blowing up supplies. The following afternoon, while we were in midstream of the wide Mayu, we saw six fighter planes, flying very high but heading in our direction. My opinion was that they were Japanese Zeros and we should pull into the bank, thickly lined with bamboo at that point.

"No, no," said the intelligence officer. "They're our new Mohawks. They've got radial engines just like Zeros." Even when they circled above as a preliminary to going into their dives, he was still going on about Mohawks and a trick of the sun that made us see only the red of the British ·red, white, and blue disks.

I continued to argue with the intelligence officer. "I'll swear they're Zeros. They've got their wings well forward and have a squarish look. . . . I've seen plenty of them. . . ."

"It reminds me of a story my father tells," interrupted the major. "He was having an argument with the postmaster at Bedford, about some planes flying overhead. He said: 'They're Jerries, I tell you.' The postmaster got angry and said, 'Don't be foolish, man. Think I don't know our own boys when I see them.' "

We did not hear the end of the story because Waterfield interjected, "I'm sorry boys, they're Japs all right. There's the red disk."

"By God, they're coming at us," said the major, turning over on his stomach. Indeed, they were. After two passes by each of the six planes we all had been hit, except the major. Miraculously there was only one fatality, one of the unfortunate oarsmen, who were the most exposed. Both kept rowing as the planes roared down and cut loose with their machine guns and cannon. My own wounds were in the back, right arm, and right leg. The solid craft, with water oozing in from below-waterline bullet holes, was maneuvered into the bank, and we clambered up a steep, muddy bank to lie in some tall grass, while the PR officer set off for medical help. Days later, after an emergency operation to remove some of the fragments from back and arm and sew up a big gash in my leg, I was gradually moved back to the dressing station on the Ganges. After some good sleuthing by journalist chums my wife broke through military secrecy to learn the date and place of one of my transit stops. (The exigencies of security were such that the names of the intelligence and public relations officers were deleted from the manuscript of *Bombs over Burma* by the censors, and writing thirty-eight years after the event, I am unable to recall them.) Alas! Just in time to verify that I was alive and to see me borne away in a hospital train to another undisclosable destination. My leg wound was long in healing, as a result of the long hours I lay untended on the bank of the Mayu River.

The Arakan campaign was a fiasco. The Japanese had only withdrawn from Rathedaung to lure the British into a trap; the explosions we had heard at Rathedaung were part of a fierce battle from which the British had to retreat. Waterfield, I, and escorts had the "honor" of being among the first wounded in the abortive Arakan campaign. There was much criticism later of the British commander of the action. Among other things he had put his troops on half rations because of supply difficulties but took a large retinue with him for his own comforts, including a private kitchen and folding bath.

Eventually I was hospitalized in Bareilly, a pleasant enough place about 150 miles east of Delhi, on the southern approaches to the Himalayan foot-hills, where my wife and son, still awaiting news of the ship which was to take them on to England, came to comfort me with daily visits. One day as I lay, almost immobile with my plastered leg and bandaged back, mentally cursing—as had become my habit—the asinine incompetency of the British Colonial Establishment as I had seen it in action in Burma and India, a *Daily Express* colleague arrived. He thrust into my hand a dispatch which said I could read at my leisure and relay to the paper only when the subject matter could be released.

Thus, I learned that a Major Orde Charles Wingate had set out on a highly unorthodox operation into Burma. By chance contacts in the various hospitals through which I had transited and in Bareilly itself, I knew that the (British) Indian Army "Blimps" hated the guts of a certain Major Wingate. This led me to think there must be something good in him. By the time I was deplastered and unbandaged and recovered strength and mobility during some convalescent leave at beautiful Srinagar in Kashmir, I had learned the date on which a plane would be leaving for a secret air-strip behind Japanese lines in Burma to pick up the first of Wingate's re-turnees. The few days spent in Sumprabum, in a remote corner of Burma where the frontier nears that of China and of India, did not yield much that would clear censorship, but the fact that of all the correspondents in India, I had made the effort endeared me to Wingate, and this was made clear as soon as we met. My colleague's dispatch made a lead story in the *Daily Express*, and my own more modest follow-ups were well displayed.

In the eyes of the "old India hands," Wingate was a "crackpot" out to destroy the Empire. And it was not the first time. He had organized a guer-rilla army which had played a decisive role in defeating the Italians in Abyssinia in 1941, at a time when things were going very badly for the British in the Middle East. The secret of his success was that he had wrested a pledge from Prime Minister Churchill that Abyssinia would regain full independence once the Italians were defeated. Only in that way could he win over the support of the local population, essential to win the type of guerrilla war he proposed waging.

Churchill agreed because he was bent on the supreme task of winning the total war against the Axis powers. Field Marshal Archibald P. Wavell, in overall command in the Middle East, supported Wingate for the same reason. But the Colonial Office did not. It supported a plan to carve up Abyssinia between the then two British colonies of the Sudan and Kenya

once the Italians were defeated. Some historians give General Alan Cunning-
ham credit for defeating the Italians in Abyssinia because he mounted a
lightning offensive and entered the capital, Addis Ababa, on April 6, 1941.
But so did Wingate, together with Emperor Haile Selassie. Wingate had defeated 36,000 Italian troops, taking half of them prisoner, with a force of
3,000 Ethiopian guerrillas, led by 50 British officers and 40 ordinary troops.
Ethiopia, as Churchill authorized Wingate to pledge, remained independent.

In the meantime, Wavell had been replaced as head of the Middle East
campaign by the Empire-saving enthusiast General Claude Auchinleck, who,
so Wingate assured me, regarded him as a dangerous radical and Empire
wrecker.

While the German and Italian armies were chasing those of Auchinleck
back across the desert, Wingate was punished by being given the "silent
treatment" in Cairo. Of passionate temperament, he was plunged into a deep
depression and cut his throat. Saved by a miracle, he spent two months in
a Cairo hospital and then was shipped back to England and "put on ice."
When things started to go wrong in Southeast Asia, Churchill dispatched
the two men he believed most capable of handling desperate situations,
General Harold Alexander and Major Orde Charles Wingate, both under
the overall command of Wavell in New Delhi. Their general instructions
were to save what could be saved in Burma but at all costs to hold India.
Alexander took over command in Burma, and although it was too late to
beat off the Japanese, he did manage to extricate more British troops than at
first seemed possible. Wingate produced a plan for guerrilla activity which
had the immediate support of Alexander.

Over the heads of the incredible collection of "Colonel Blimps" who infested the (British) India Army Command, Wavell endorsed the Wingate
plan, and Churchill again authorized Wingate to pledge to the Burmese that
they would have total independence once the Japanese were beaten.

Wingate's plan was to carry out a supercommando operation by a number
of self-supporting columns striking deep into Japanese-occupied territory in
such a way that the Japanese troops in Burma would be fully occupied in
chasing them around during the vital campaigning season of 1942–43. If
they could be held off until the monsoon rains, vital time would be won to
overhaul the inept India Command.

Wingate was grudgingly given the most unpromising material—a battalion
each of British, Gurkha, and Burmese troops, the British being overage for
guerrilla warfare. They were put through rigorous training in jungle country
similar to that in which they would be fighting. At first, officers and men alike
regarded Wingate as a fanatical slave driver. Later, when they recognized
that he shared their hardships and worked twice as hard as anyone else, they
came to respect and then to worship him. What finally won them over was

the occasion when after a freak storm the camp was flooded and Wingate, clad only in his topee (sun helmet), spent most of the night swimming among the trees to make sure all his men were safe.

The Delhi Brigade continued to gripe about his unorthodoxy. Splitting men into columns, instead of keeping them in battalion and company formations for frontal assaults; depending on air-dropped supplies of food and ammunition, instead of securing a safe overland supply route—sheer madness! Twice during the training period Wingate was ordered to abandon the scheme, but by forceful argument he kept it going.

On February 6, 1943, after final rehearsal of airdrops, quick dispersal, and fade-outs, long night marches, and pinpoint accuracy at assembly points, Wingate's men were assembled at Imphal, ready to cross into Burma. General Wavell flew up with the news that the project would have to be called off. Because of the fiasco of the Arakan campaign, the objections to "wasting" more men and material had mounted.

"Just because the Japanese have chased us out of Arakan," argued Wingate, "is all the more reason why we should go in. If we do nothing else, I can guarantee to keep the Japanese tied up for a few months. My men will never again be as fit for action as they are at this moment. They are trained to the highest point of efficiency, and morale will never be higher. If we don't get into action now, efficiency and morale will decline." *

Wavell, by then a tired old soldier, but a man of vision and imagination—a long supporter of Wingate against the views of his staff—decided to back his own judgment. At the end of a fifty-minute debate he told Wingate to go ahead. In homage to the nature of the mission, Wavell reviewed and saluted the troops, and that afternoon the first columns started to cross the frontier.

Wingate and his men marched and fought their way for 1,000 and more miles with never more than a few days' rations in their knapsacks. Because of excellent cooperation with the head of the American air supply services, Lieutenant General Brehon Somervell, food, ammunition, extra weapons, rubber boats—called for by radio—were dropped with meticulous timing and accuracy, as required. Wingate accompanied his men through the worst of their adventures from their first swimming of the Chindwin into Burma proper until the day, nearly three months later, when, bearded, tattered, and emaciated, he volunteered to lead a small party in swimming back across the Chindwin in the face of expected Japanese fire, to rescue and escort to safety the remainder of his dispersed troops.

Of the 3,200 men and 1,000 mules he led into Burma on February 6, 1943, he brought out 2,400 men and 1 mule in early May. As promised, he

---

* Wilfred Burchett, *Democracy With a Tommygun* (Bombay: Thacker & Company Limited, 1946), p. 134.

had kept the entire Japanese Army in Burma chasing around, trying to locate and wipe out his columns, which the Japanese Command was convinced were elements of a major invasion.

When the force was ordered by Delhi headquarters to return and Wingate announced that the only way of recrossing the two great rivers, the Irrawaddy and Chindwin, would be to abandon all heavy equipment and eat the remaining mules, even some of his own officers were aghast. Wingate's logic prevailed over the objections of his field officers:

"The total weight of supplies I propose abandoning is about six tons. We must keep things in their proper perspectives. On the high seas in a single month we have often lost a million tons of equipment before any of it could be put to good service. Every pound of ours has performed good and valuable service, but to keep it longer is to jeopardise the safety of our men. Their lives and experiences are now of far greater value. Sufficient mules will be taken across the Irrawaddy to carry the radio charging sets. As long as the radio functions we can have fresh mortars, machine guns and demolition equipment dropped when we have crossed the river." *

Although the historic feat of Wingate and his men made headlines in the British press—as the only victory scored by Britain in the war in Asia—he was an outcast at the Delhi headquarters. Wavell had again been replaced by Auchinleck, and the silent treatment was repeated. No one at headquarters was even interested in reading Wingate's report. Day after day he waited in his sweltering Delhi hotel room, awaiting a summons from Commander in Chief Auchinleck. It never came.

For weeks I spent each morning with him, cheering him up and listening to his fantastic accounts of the obstacles his columns had encountered and how they had been overcome. We immediately became close friends, Having studied everything he could lay his hands on about the Chinese concepts of guerrilla warfare, he was keenly interested in everything I could tell him about China, especially my various meetings with Chou En-lai. Obviously he agreed entirely with Chou En-lai's concept as to what the colonial powers had to do to give the Asian people a stake in victory over the Japanese. It was what he had done in Burma and earlier in Abyssinia.

At our morning sessions I gathered material for a book, *Wingate's Phantom Army*, in the afternoon he was generally alone in his hotel room. Wingate was exhausted by his ordeal, depressed by being totally ignored when he wanted to get things moving for a more ambitious expedition to kick the Japanese clear out of Burma. It was midsummer, and the blazing heat of Delhi was enough to knock out men physically stronger than Wingate—even without the terrible strain to which he had been subjected. Later he assured me I had helped preserve his sanity by my daily visits.

---

* *Ibid.*, p. 136.

When he could stand the silent treatment no longer, he wrote a polite note to Auchinleck stating his need for a brief rest in the hills, asking if his commander in chief wanted to see him before he left. He showed me the secretary's reply to the effect that the great man was "frightfully busy" with staff conferences. "If and when" he returned, Auchinleck would try to see him.

Wingate left forthwith for the little hill station of Naini Tal, where he had been born just forty years earlier. No sooner had he left than headquarters was in a furor trying to find him. It happened that shortly after he left, I took the first part of my book on Wingate to the censor. Brigadier Ivor Jehu, the pompous and incompetent head of Public Relations (where censorship took place), already furious with me for the book outline which had obligatorily passed through his reluctant hands and aroused some interest at the War Office, shouted, "Where is that fellow? The beggar just dashes off without a word to anyone, leaving no address. He's wanted back here immediately." Explaining that I knew that Wingate had Auchinleck's permission to leave, but that no one had bothered to ask where, I gave Jehu the Naini Tal address. A few days later Wingate phoned me from his New Delhi hotel. When we met, he grinned and pointed to a new star to his DSO. "They'll be giving me an OBE next, and then I'll know I'm finished," he said jokingly. "GHQ is suddenly being nice to me. I just saw Auchinleck. He pinned on the star and said that Churchill wants to see me in London immediately. They've fixed a special plane; I'm off in the morning."

He was flown to London, dined with Churchill on the evening of his arrival, was promoted to Major General on the spot, and asked if he could leave immediately for Quebec as Churchill's adviser on jungle warfare. He was astounded to find that the press rated him after Churchill and Montgomery as number three on the list of England's current war heroes. The Quebec Conference was to decide, among other things, the strategy to be pursued in fighting the Asian-Pacific war and the roles to be assured respectively by the United States and Great Britain. At all costs, Churchill wanted Britain to be in overall command of the ground forces in the Southeast Asia area. Wingate was his trump card. When the new major general pointed out that his wife was in Scotland and he had not seen her for two years, prime ministerial machinery was set in motion. A startled Mrs. Wingate was almost snatched from her bed, express trains were halted and diverted, and she was rushed to a port to join her husband and Prime Minister Churchill. A waiting ship cast off, and they were on their way to Canada almost before she was able to draw breath.

By the time Wingate arrived back in Delhi, his topee discarded for the red-banded cap of a two-star general, great changes had taken place. A Southeast Asia Command had been set up under Admiral Lord Louis Mountbatten. Auchinleck's command was reduced to looking after supply and training. Wingate's plans, which Auchinleck never did look at, for an offensive to be coordinated with American and Chinese operations, were endorsed by Mountbatten and his U.S. counterparts. Everything needed in the way of men, planes, weapons, radio, and other equipment was at Wingate's disposal. He plunged into the work of planning a far more ambitious operation to drive the Japanese out of Burma as part of an Allied general offensive to clear them out of the Southeast Asian mainland. Wingate planned to combine everything that had been learned from the previous expedition with many innovations, such as the use of glider-borne troops.

Tragically he was killed on the opening day of this campaign, March 24, 1944, when a small RAF plane in which he was flying crashed into a mountain along the Assam-Burma border. He died because he always ran the same risks he asked his men to take—in this case supervising the operation in which glider-borne troops landed astride the Mandalay–Myitkinya railway on the first phase of the operation he had so brilliantly planned and prepared. Churchill equated his death with the loss of a battleship. For me it was the end of a precious friendship which we both were convinced would grow closer as the years went by.

By the time of his death I had been transferred to the U.S. Navy and its Marine Corps for the island-hopping operations in the Pacific.

10

Island Hopping

THE TERMS OF MY reassignment had been spelled out in a cryptic, but very typical, cable from *Express* foreign editor Charles Foley: PRO-CEED AUSTRALIA CONTACT EXPRESSER HENRY KEYS AND UPSPLIT PACIFIC CUM-HIM STOP BESTEST HUNTING. In practical terms this meant that a fellow Australian, Henry Keys, would continue to be accredited to General Douglas MacArthur's headquarters at Melbourne to cover U.S. Army operations. I would get myself accredited to Admiral Chester Nimitz at his Honolulu, Pacific Fleet Headquarters and cover the island-hopping operations, just getting under way by the U.S. Navy and its marine combat troops. Aboard a former Italian luxury liner, transformed into a troop transport, but then carrying Italian POWs to Australia, I traveled from Bombay to Melbourne. There was ample time to get my sea legs and reflect on my experiences, especially since the zigzag route taken to avoid submarines doubled the normal time of the journey.

If I had been mildly anticolonialist before, I was violently so after wit-nessing at first hand the grotesque inefficiency and rabid racism of the guardians of Empire in Burma and India. Human and intellectual contact was much easier with a Chou En-lai than the "Blimps" at Indian Army Headquarters in Delhi. Despite my conviction that a healthy new breeze was sweeping away some of the cobwebs in Delhi, helped along by "crack-pots" like Wingate and—to give him due credit—Lord Mountbatten, I was glad to be leaving. It seemed to me that I was going to an area where gen-erals and admirals could concentrate on fighting the enemy rather than each other, where military affairs had priority over the politics and diplo-macy of Empire saving.

The "grand strategy" was that under General MacArthur, U.S. and

93

Australian forces would advance from the south, pushing the Japanese back from the landmasses of New Guinea and the Philippines. Admiral Nimitz's forces would advance from the east by island-hopping operations. The two forces would converge somewhere to deal the final blow to Japan itself. By the time my accreditation facilities had been completed Nimitz had already taken his first two objectives in the Gilbert and the Marshall islands. Advance U.S. air and naval bases were set up on these islands as plans were made for the next moves. I found the atmosphere at Admiral Nimitz's Pearl Harbor headquarters one of quiet efficiency. The only "politics" seemed to be conjecture as to whether his forces or those of General Mac-Arthur would first get to Japan.

The first operation in which I could take part was the invasion of the Marianas Islands, where I landed with the 1st Provisional Brigade of the U.S. Marines. From then on there was no reason to complain of difficulties in getting close to action. I alternated between island landings or forays with the aircraft carriers of either the Third Fleet, under Admiral William "Bull" Halsey, or the Fifth, under Admiral Richard Spruance. These all were brilliantly planned and executed operations, and I formed a very high opinion of the qualities of the U.S. Marines and the carrier pilots and crewmen. They were briefed not to defend an empire, but to defend their own way of life, and they accepted the sacrifices involved.

After covering defeats and retreats, I found it exhilarating to be in a theater of victories and advances. I tried to do justice to this in my dispatches and in a special background report, which Lord Beaverbrook requested, as to the realistic perspectives of the war against Japan. The most impressive thing was the way in which the use of "floating air power" was mastered and handled with a sure touch and coordination of action among the task force units, supply units, and the fighting men at the fronts. The development of the aircraft carriers totally changed the concept of naval warfare, something which the British, despite their proud tradition of "ruling the waves," were slow to understand. I set down my feelings about this in a book mainly written while the great battles were still going on:

The most decisive defensive battles of the Pacific were won by aircraft carriers, without the supporting warships on either side coming to grips. The Battle of the Coral Sea, which blocked the Jap drive south to Australia and Port Moresby (New Guinea), and the Battle of Midway, a month later, which stopped the Jap thrust east to the Hawaiian islands were won by the US aircraft carriers, Yorktown, Lexington, Enterprise and Hornet. The few US carriers that the Japs had overlooked when they destroyed the backbone of the US Pacific Fleet at Pearl Harbor, backed up by some land-based planes, were sufficient to halt the second expansive phase of the Jap war program and, together with their work during the invasion of the Solomons, completely turned the tide of the Pacific war. After Coral Sea, Midway and Guadalcanal, the Japs never regained the strategic initiative in the Pacific.*

I had asked to accompany the 1st Provisional Marine Brigade in the Guam operation because it had been built around a former famous raider battalion commanded by Lieutenant Colonel Evans Carlson. He had served several years in China as a military attaché and had formed the nucleus battalion on his conception of how the Chinese Communist guerrillas operated. Once aboard the troop transport I found that Saipan would be attacked first and Guam a few days later. The resistance on Saipan was tougher than expected, so the marines were kept on board in case they had to be thrown into the battle. Days were spent in sunbathing and endless study of relief maps and a large Plasticine model of Guam, until the troops felt they knew not only every hill but every rock and tree in the sectors assigned to them. Nights were passed in uneasy sweating in the poorly ventilated troop compartments, and morale dropped as days and weeks went by—the necessity for radio silence denying us any source of news. Two colleagues, John Beaufort of the *Christian Science Monitor* and Bill McGaffin of the Chicago *Daily News*, and I cursed our fate that we had chosen the Guam, not the Saipan, operation. What would our editors think after five weeks' silence and no possibility of explanations?

Finally, word came that the invasion of Guam was to take place on July 21, that against Saipan having started on June 17. On July 20 we had the "condemned man's" banquet, steaks, hoarded for an eve-of-battle dinner. Last church services were held, letters written, card debts paid, and those who felt they could sleep turned in early. Beaufort, McGaffin, and I slept on deck.

We woke early with the fresh, sweet smell of land in our nostrils. Tiny red pinpoints of light drifted in lazy parabolas through the blackness ahead, disappearing momentarily as a white flash fanned out to monopolize the vision. Drifting lights and white flashes seemed unrelated to the swish-swash of the ocean as the ship glided through the dead-calm sea to an inevitable assignment with death for some aboard. As we advanced, the red pinpoints expanded and picked up speed until they looked like Ping-Pong balls bouncing back and forth in a tournament of Titans.

Soon the tossing red balls were associated with the booming of battleship guns and the return fire of shore batteries; the fan-shaped flashes were linked with hits on gasoline stores and ammunition dumps. Booms developed into deafening cracks as we glided closer to the scene of action, faint glows into scarlet fires, low-hanging clouds into smoke palls by the time anchor was dropped in the invasion assembly area, five miles offshore. Battleships, cruisers, and destroyers were leisurely steaming up and down,

---

* *Democracy With a Tommygun, op. cit.,* p. 214.

firing single salvos, which burst among drooping palms on the shore. Return fire seemed to have been silenced.

The transports dropped anchor in a cove, sheltered on the left by the high plateau of the Orote Peninsula, site of Guam's main airfield and the first target to be secured. Between the ship we were on and the peninsula, a battleship was firing across at the airfield from one side, and on the other, heavy warships were spouting tawny flames and mustard-colored smoke, while one by one the transports and supply ships edged into position for landing troops and material on the southern beachhead.

No sooner had the ship's screws stopped turning than a boat was lowered, and McGaffin, Beaufort, and I, together with the landing control officer for the southern beachhead, scrambled down a net of thick rope and sped away to the destroyer *Ringgold*, which was to act as the parent control ship, directing the assault waves and movement of supplies to the beachhead. The first waves were due to land at 8:30 A.M.; we were aboard the *Ringgold* at 6:30 as it moved in to within 2,000 yards of the beach.

By the time we had clambered up to the bridge another awesome phase of the softening up had started. Wave after wave of Helldiver dive bombers arrived, circling high above the targets, then winging over one by one, plummeting down in vertical dives to release their bombs, and continuing straight on down to zoom into strafing runs at palm-top level, before curving up to rejoin their formation. Blossoming pillars of dark smoke and earth rippled along the beaches before the thunderous succession of explosions caught up with them, as each wave of Helldivers delivered their quotas. Then came the Hellcat fighters in murderous strafing runs, the guttural coughing bursts of their machine guns adding a new note to this mortal cacophony.

It looked and sounded like an overkill of absurd dimensions. No enemy positions or living beings could possibly have survived. But it continued. When the dive bombers and strafers had completed their work with stopwatch precision, the warships opened up again, this time firing broadsides instead of salvos. The entire coastline disappeared as hundreds, thousands of tons of white-hot steel poured into that narrow strip of palms that fringed the beach. Not even the hermit crabs could still be alive.

But over Orote Peninsula black puffs of smoke showed that the enemy was still reacting, and one of the puffs glowed crimson as a Helldiver was hit and dropped like a fireball. Behind the flaming guns of the warships, landing craft and amphibian tanks (alligators) were buzzing around, forming into lines of departure, crammed with somber-faced troops in jungle greens with life belts around the waists.

The barrage from the warships increased in intensity as the first waves formed up behind the rocket-firing LCIs' (landing craft, infantry) gunboats. *Ringgold* ran up the flags for EXECUTE ONE—and the first waves moved off behind their LCI escorts. Lessons of the Gilbert Islands calamity, where the marines had taken very heavy casualties because the state of the tide had been misjudged, had been well studied, and the first assault waves were carried clear across the reef in amphibious tanks and weapon carriers, equally at home on land or water—as long as there was sufficient clearance over the treacherous coral. The LCIs could not continue past the reef line, but from there they smothered cliff faces and remnants of water's edge fortifications with withering rocket barrages that continued until the alligators were across the reef and well on their way to the shore, heading for passes blasted through Japanese underwater obstacles by heroic Seabee (CB, construction battalion) engineering units.

Spouts lifting up from the water when the landing craft were a few hundred yards from the shore proved that some defenders, at least, were incredibly alive and active. Two craft were soon dead in the water, three more were burning, but at exactly 8:30 on the control officer's stopwatch, the first line of alligators trundled out of the water and lurched across the sand strip to disappear into the line of shattered, decapitated palms.

The barrage from battleships and cruisers had eased off, and their big guns were firing at individual targets signaled by Kingfisher spotter planes, whose pilots, hovering over what was left of enemy strongpoints—including antiaircraft batteries—won the admiration of all of us in our "grandstand" seats aboard the *Ringgold*. Larger supply craft arrived at the reef to unload supplies from the first alligators to have returned from the beach to start a reef-beach shuttle service, hauling light artillery, ammunition, and other supplies.

By 11:00 A.M. Howard Norton of the Baltimore *Sun*, Beaufort, McGaffin, and I were ashore, inspecting the remains of Japanese frontline trenches and foxholes. By midday marines were feeling their way up woody gullies, trying to secure the high ground overlooking the landing beaches before nightfall, when the Japanese could be expected to launch a counterattack. Demolition squads were already blasting passages through the reef so that supplies, including heavy artillery and tanks, could be delivered directly to the beaches. The latter were littered with Mae West life belts, the first discards on any amphibian invasion, and a few torn and huddled clumps— all that was left of the last-ditch defenders who had covered the withdrawal of the main Japanese forces.

We found the brigade commander, Lieutenant Colonel Alan Shapley, headquartered in a palm-surrounded hilly bit of ground about 100 yards inland from the beach. He told us the going was "not too bad," casualties so far had been light. After a couple of hours ashore we returned to the *Ringgold*, which was also the press transmission ship, to get our reports written and dispatched. We returned to spend the night with a Seabee unit and observe the expected counterattack.

My main impression was of the tremendous scale and efficiency with which everything was being done. More munitions were used in the soften-ing-up process than would be flown over the hump into China in a year. Then there was the split-second precision of the successive phases of the operation. Anything I had seen of war until then paled into insignificance. It was impossible not to reflect on the enormous vitality and economic power of a country which could have recovered so quickly from the crippling blow struck by the Japanese at Pearl Harbor only two and a half years earlier. Virtually all the warships, transports, landing craft, tanks, and artillery had been built since then. No less was the military power which enabled the Americans to stage such operations every few months.

I was lucky to have companions of the quality of Johnny Beaufort and Bill McGaffin, experienced journalists with strong nerves, with whom I was later to share numerous carrier and landing operations. We dug a communal foxhole by enlarging a drain, stretching our waterproof tent halves over a couple of fallen breadfruit trees that lay across the top. After a long and exhausting day, sleep came quickly. At 10:00 P.M. we were awakened by a muffled put-puttering sound. Peeping out, we could see showers of golden rain cascading toward us from the hills, and immediately the explosions of what turned out to be 40 mm shells with which the Japanese were spraying the beaches.

Star shells from the destroyers lit up the hills, and naval guns started up again. Within seconds there was a frenzied medley of sound and flashes. It was like being in the middle of an exploding ammunition dump. First to the east, then to the west of our foxhole there was heavy firing, showers of tracers, and flashes of bursting hand grenades, their explosions drowned by those of artillery and mortar shells. Hugging the bottom of the foxhole when the sounds of battle came directly our way, we peered out through the bread-fruit branches when it receded.

By dawn everything had quieted down, and we went to find Alan Shapley, sitting as he had been throughout the night, a poncho wrapped around his shoulders, receiving field telephone reports from his forward companies. We asked how the brigade had fared. He mustered a weary grin and said, "I'm not certain yet. That's the worst deal I've ever had. They broke through to within twenty yards of here. I don't know yet how our boys managed to hold them. They knocked out four Jap tanks less than two hundred yards away." Later it became clear that there had been four separate attacks, the last a *banzai* type of suicide foray which carried the attackers right onto the beach and into the complex of foxholes. The only way to avoid confusion as to friend or foe was for every marine to fight back from inside his foxhole. A body count later in the day showed that 950 Japanese troops died that night, 600 of them in the *banzai* charge during which they had attached bayonets to long bamboo poles to jab into the foxholes. About 60 marines also died in that nocturnal action.

For the first five nights we did not sleep, having changed our foxhole, on Colonel Shapley's advice, to one alongside some 105 mm and 155 mm artillery pieces. We were kept awake by either their firing or Japanese counterfire with mortars and heavy machine guns. There were never any safe places on Guam or any other targets of the island-hopping operations. At the start of the battle for the Orote Peninsula the three of us were moving up a road leading to the airfield with Major Messer, one of Shapley's battalion commanders, and a headquarters platoon. Reaching the top of a quarry, half a mile from where the front was supposed to be, the communications squad started to link up its field telephone when there was a fusillade of machine gun and small-arms fire—at us. Three men fell; the rest of us leaped for cover. Beaufort jumped so far back that he fell into the quarry. Messer, McGaffin, a few headquarters men, and I dropped behind a small clump of breadfruit trees; several more took cover behind some crated Japanese aircraft engines alongside. Medical Corps men appeared from nowhere, carrying wounded behind the crates and giving them plasma, while we groveled in the dirt and bullets smacked into the front of the breadfruit trees. By the scope and direction of the firing, it was clear that a substantial wedge of Japanese had been overlooked by the advancing troops. Mortars joined in, the screaming shells lobbing just behind us in the quarry where Beaufort had fortunately found a hole to shelter in—alongside a small gasoline dump!

Crawling forward during a lull in the firing, I peered over a coconut log and saw a Japanese sniper firing from a platform near the top of a coconut palm. After grabbing a carbine dropped by one of the wounded, I took careful aim and squeezed the trigger. The whole top of the palm was blown off. My first awesome thought was that I must have touched off a hand grenade, until I saw the smoke trailing out of the barrel of a tank-mounted artillery piece pointing in the same direction. That was the only shot I fired in World War II or any other war. Except for a few unusual cases I respected the convention that correspondents do not bear arms.

The fight for Orote was the fiercest of the Guam campaign and as bitter as any in the Pacific until that time. The Japanese were entrenched in what, at first sight, seemed to be innocent grassy mounds. Underneath were shelters, reinforced by stout coconut logs, with ample space for thirty men, machine guns, and big reserves of ammunition. The firing slits were too small to throw in grenades or demolition charges. After heavy casualties in trying to deal with them, bulldozer blades were fitted to Sherman tanks, and the tops of the mounds were scooped off, the inmates mopped up with grenades and flamethrowers. It took ten days of grueling day-and-night combat without letup before the Orote Peninsula was considered relatively secure, and the men of the 1st Provisional Marine Brigade were pulled back for a few days' rest. They came back like sleepwalkers: eyes glazed and red from lack of sleep; jungle greens stained from the soil into which they had burrowed and the blood of many killed and wounded comrades. Their young-old faces covered with fluff and stubble, they stumbled back on the first quiet day since the landing to a rest area almost free of enemy activity. They looked as if they had fought to the limits of human endurance.

After the Orote action was over, we three newsmen transferred to the 3rd Marine Division to take part in what was expected to be a tough fight for Agana, the island's capital. In fact, it was an anticlimax. The only shot fired was to kill an enemy soldier hiding in a culvert. With the capture of Agana, organized resistance on Guam ended.

The next target was the Caroline Islands, a group which included what were considered the two most formidable Japanese island bases in the Pacific—Yap and Truk. Even pronouncing those short, squat names of what were believed to be unsinkable aircraft carriers produced awe among military men. To assault them was bound to be a costly operation. As a precaution against Japanese interference from the Philippines, the first island to be seized was Peleliu, the southernmost of the Palau subgroup, about 300 miles east of Mindanao, the southernmost island of the Philippines. I was to cover the Carolines operation from the aircraft carrier *Hancock*. Its commander, Captain Taylor, was a fine man, and we quickly became firm friends.

As a further precaution against Japanese interference, air strikes were planned against their air bases on Leyte, the next main island north of Mindanao in the Philippines, and against the fearsome bases of Yap and Truk. First great surprise when the pilots returned—there were no military targets on the bogeyman islands. Second great surprise—airmen picked up by the navy's very efficient air-rescue service from the beaches of Leyte a few days later reported that apart from guards around some airfields, no Japanese forces were there. The two pilots had been taken in charge by the Hukbalahap guerrillas, who were in effective control of the island. Before being picked up the pilots had inspected beaches for seaborne landing possibilities and found they were excellent. Captain Taylor had the two pilots rushed over to relate their experience to Admiral Spruance, in overall charge.

Spruance communicated these astonishing facts to Admiral Nimitz with the recommendation that the troops earmarked for Yap and Truk be diverted to occupying Leyte, thus marking a tremendous shortcut in the strategy of pushing on to Japan. Nimitz agreed and recommended the immediate invasion of Leyte to the amazed U.S. Joint Chiefs of Staff. There was a snag. General Douglas MacArthur, the former U.S. commander in the Philippines, had been promised the glory of liberating the islands. He had personalized this promised assignment by showering the islands with everything from leaflets to matchboxes bearing his handsome profile and "I will return" pledge. (What would have happened propaganda-wise had he crashed in a plane or been knocked over by a car in Melbourne seemed not to have bothered him.) But it was mid-September 1944, and MacArthur proposed to invade the southern tip of Mindanao at the end of the year in what would have been a slow, slogging march northward through heavily defended positions. Nimitz proposed hitting at undefended positions 400 miles to the north three months earlier.

At that moment the JCS were meeting with their British opposite numbers in what was called the Octagon Conference in Quebec. Everyone favored speeding up the war, but the JCS knew that to rob MacArthur of his supreme triumph would bring the smoldering Army-Navy rivalry to new heights just when interservice unity was never more essential. While the Fifth Fleet steamed back and forth in the vicinity of the Palau Islands, awaiting a decision, a compromise offer was made to MacArthur. If he could speed up his invasion plans and make Leyte by October 20, the job was his. Of course, he accepted, but this ultimatum-imposed decision did not inhibit him later from accepting accolades of praise for his "genius" in choosing Leyte to fulfill his "I will return" pledge. The gist of the dramatic exchange of signals among the Fifth Fleet, Pearl Harbor, Washington, and Quebec was available on board the *Hancock,* and those officers "in the know" were furious at the decision.

So the 1st Marine Division finally invaded Peleliu on September 15, and I covered the first phase from the back seat of a Helldiver. The idea of being with the carriers was that it was expected that the Japanese Navy would come out in force, as it had done during the Marianas battle, and the main story would be that of a major air-naval battle. But this did not happen, so the invasion itself was the main story. In those days there were three types of carrier planes: single-seat fighters and double-seat—in tandem—torpedo carriers and dive bombers. The back-seat man acted as machine gunner-observer, so pilots were naturally reluctant to take nonprofessionals. But one—on Captain Tyler's recommendation—agreed to take me and was given permission to leave his three-plane formation on the return journey to "dive-bomb" my dispatch onto the task force's transmission ship.

The first part was interesting enough. We roared off from the carrier deck, gliding smoothly upward till we came over the Palau group—odd-looking islands like clumps of dung dropped by some prehistoric monster. Below us battleships and cruisers were spouting flame, and ahead of them, clustered like bacilli on a medical slide, were the landing craft, trailing white tails as they headed for the beach. Low over the island, scores of planes were circling, diving, and strafing targets as ordered by the air coordinator. Jet black puffs of smoke were expanding into the air below and around us. My earphones buzzed:

"Safety belt strapped tight?"

"Roger."

"Parachute attached?"

"Roger."

"Hatch open?" I wound it open.

"Roger."

"Here we go!"

Then we tipped over at an unearthly angle and I thought: I can never stand it. Suddenly the bottom dropped away and I was hanging in the safety belt, the plane's nose turned down in a totally vertical dive. I was conscious of the altitude meter whizzing madly backward, black smoke puffs with scarlet centers blossoming all around, a plane plunging in flames on to an airfield beneath and a square patch of slightly rocking earth rushing to us at devastating speed as we hurtled from 12,000 to 2,000 feet in a few seconds. The plane started to buck and I was sure we were hit. Although I vaguely heard "Bombs away" and the nose was pointed upward again, we were still plummeting toward the ground in what I later understood was "mushing" as the power of the engine fought it out with the force of gravity and inertia of impetus. We pulled out over the tops of palm trees, causing a sickening rush of blood to my head that made me vomit. After two weaving, strafing runs at something or other, the sudden change in temperature from ice-cold with an open hatch before going into the dive, to sickly tropical heat as we skimmed over the coconut palms added to my discomfort. We gathered height again, while I finished off a handwritten dispatch, sealed it in a tube with a smoke signal attached, and we came down more gently this time to drop it, smoking satisfactorily, alongside the transmission ship.

It was a great homecoming to bump gently back onto the deck of the *Franklin*, where an enthusiastic servicing sergeant helped me out of the rear gunner's compartment with a welcoming smile. "Isn't she a sweet plane? Rides like a feather." He frowned when he peered inside and explained that according to established practice, I must clean it up myself.

My next assignment was aboard the *Lexington*, flagship of Admiral Marc Mitscher, a kindly gnome of a man, with eyes as blue as the sea and sky, his twin elements. His face, crisscrossed with tiny furrows from a life exposed to sea and wind, was dominated by shaggy fair eyebrows. Terse, but soft-spoken, a man easy to be silent with, he sat all day hunched in a swivel chair on the bridge, directing operations with a minimum of fuss and bother, his greatest concession to excitement in the heat of battle being to remove his peaked baseball cap and rub his balding pate. As distinct from the British, who had naval men in charge of their aircraft carriers, the Americans had airmen, of whom Mitscher was an outstanding example. His assignment this time included carrying out the first air strike of the war against Japanese-occupied Taiwan. Stiff opposition was expected because the Japanese had scores of airfields there. The predictions were correct.

The first day brought hundreds of air duels, with planes whirling and diving in a seemingly mad medley of combat in which the Japanese displayed their greatest combativeness since the Marianas battle. Apart from those destroyed over Taiwan, fifteen were shot down trying to attack Mitscher's task force, plus nine more by ship's gunfire at night. Pilots reported paddy fields and hillsides dotted with smoking funeral pyres of Japanese planes.

Early on the following morning (October 15, 1944) Japanese reconnaissance planes starting trailing the task force. Late in the afternoon came the warning that several hundred bomber and torpedo planes were heading in our direction. Flight after flight of Hellcats took off to intercept them, shooting down scores before they were visible from the flagship. But the evening meal was interrupted by the boom of the five-inch heavy antiaircraft guns. Enemy planes were diving down through heavy clouds to launch their bombs or skimming across the gray waters to fire their torpedoes. Many were shot to bits as they ran into the steel mesh which, like chain armor of old, encircled the ships in a close-woven pattern of exploding shells. Bombs threw up great spouts of water; torpedoes snaked their way through the fast-moving task force. The sun went down abruptly, but the spectacle only increased in intensity.

Red and white tracers streamed upward like colored snowflakes defying the laws of gravity. Crimson balls of fire burst in their midst as antiaircraft shells struck home. In what was probably the first kamikaze suicide attack, one Japanese tried to crash his plane on a cruiser alongside the *Lexington*, probably his real target. He blew himself up by diving onto the stern of the cruiser, starting a small fire. The debris was shoved overboard, and the fire quickly extinguished. Admiral Mitscher announced that 259 Japanese planes had been destroyed in the strikes and battles over the task force. Kamikaze attacks from that time on were commonplace.

Within a couple of days the softening-up process had started in the Leyte Gulf. Some small islands were seized on October 17 and 18, and four of MacArthur's divisions had carried out the main invasion of October 20, as planned at the Quebec Conference. Then came the electrifying news that the "Japanese fleet is out."

By dawn of October 24 the carriers of Mitscher's First Task Force were racing full speed toward where a Japanese battleship force was reported passing through the Strait of Luzon—between the northernmost main island of the Philippines and Taiwan. At about 200 miles' distance from the enemy battleships, word came that MacArthur was in trouble because rainstorms had caused his steel-mesh landing strips to sink into the mud and that the smaller escort carriers had come under attack from another Japanese naval force, which had unexpectedly negotiated its way through the maze of islands in the San Bernardino Strait between Luzon and Saniar. During a refueling slowdown I had transferred back to the *Hancock*. It, two other carriers, and their escort vessels were ordered to turn about and rush to the rescue, while the rest of Mitscher's force continued to engage the northern enemy force. A third Japanese battleship force had sailed through the Surigao Strait separating southern Leyte from Mindanao and was being engaged by the U.S. Seventh Fleet, under the command of Rear Admiral Jesse B. Oldendorf. Thus, the stage was set for the greatest air-naval battle of the war—the Second Battle of the Philippine Sea.

The carriers sped south, flying fish scudding from the racing bow of the *Hancock*, pilots munching toast and swilling coffee as they were briefed for targets. They would have to take off at maximum range with only an even chance of being able to make it back to the mother ship. Planes were prepared with greatest speed; there was not even time to attach extra wing tanks. The escort carriers to the south were under fierce attack. Thirty-three planes were launched within fourteen minutes, one plunging straight into the water. The pilot was saved, but the rear gunner went down with it. Other carriers were launching their planes, the long lines spread out like wild geese in flight. Precious gasoline would have been wasted had there been the normal circling to get into formation. Two hours later, by which time it was calculated the first wave would be over the target, the second wave was launched. Then came news that Halsey, having seen a good start made by Mitscher's task force in the north, had ordered a battleship squadron detached from it to race south and try to block the San Bernardino Strait and prevent the second Japanese force from returning the way it had come.

The *Hancock* group now had two tasks: rescue the escort carriers, and cripple sufficient enemy warships to slow them up and give the friendly battleship squadron time to block the San Bernardino Strait. With Oldendorf in position in the Surigao Strait, the Japanese fleet would be in a hopeless situation. Just under five hours after the first wave of *Hancock* pilots had taken off, the task force swung around into the wind to receive them back.

What tales the pilots had to tell! They had caught up with the battleship force off the east coast of Samar Island, north of Leyte and just south of the San Bernardino Strait.

Three battleships and a number of cruisers were hit in the first strike. But only three of the twelve Helldivers returned. Several landed in the water on the way back, and the crewmen were rescued. Others landed on the decks of the baby escort carriers.

The return of the second wave was another story. There was heavy rain and fog, and it was dark by the time the task force had maneuvered into the wind. Red and green wing-tip lights could be seen circling the carriers, but pilots had great difficulty distinguishing one ship from another and the exact distance from flight decks even when a carrier was identified. Planes ran out of fuel and plunged into the sea; others crashed into battleships and cruisers, discovering the mistaken identities too late. Many planes were lost, and although a number of pilots and gunners were rescued the next morning, losses were heavy. The name of General MacArthur was not popular for a few days—to say the least. Had it not been for the airy assurances that his land-based planes could deal with any enemy threats, the carriers would have stayed in the area, and the Japanese fleet would have been crippled with minimum losses. At least that was the view expressed with much energy by many officers and men on the *Hancock*.

The Japanese ships that had survived the two attacks headed full speed for the San Bernardino Strait. Mitscher's battleship squadron had to be content with picking off crippled survivors, including one heavy cruiser and some smaller fry. Pilots from the *Hancock* sank one battleship or heavy cruiser with two torpedo hits and a seaplane tender, which blew up and sank immediately after direct hits with 1,000-pound bombs. The pilots also claimed two torpedo hits on a Fuso-class battleship and bomb hits on a light cruiser. Another battleship or heavy cruiser was reported belching black smoke and settling at the bow after two torpedo hits.

From the rest of Admiral Mitscher's task force came news that four enemy aircraft carriers and three cruisers had been sunk. Shortly after we headed south for refueling, there was a radio intercept of a laconic remark from an *Enterprise* pilot: "Scratch one flattop"—he had just sunk a carrier.

The Second Battle of the Philippines was the last great air-naval battle of the war. According to the score totted up from reports coming through to the *Hancock*, fifty-eight Japanese warships were sunk or damaged. It was an awesome demonstration of the superiority of air power over the guns of the mightiest of battleships and their protective auxiliary vessels.

While MacArthur got bogged down in consolidating his Leyte beachhead, having failed to exploit the initial absence of the Japanese or the activities of the well-organized guerrillas, the Navy pushed on to the very gateway of Japan.

On August 6, 1945, I was shuffling along in the chow line for lunch with fifty or so weary U.S. marines at a company cookhouse on Okinawa. The radio was crackling away with no one paying much attention to it—as usual. A note of excitement in the announcer's voice as the cook's aide dumped a hamburger and mash on my tray prompted me to ask what was new.

"He's going on about some big new bomb we just dropped on the Japs. A lotta good that'll do us here!" (It was taken for granted that after Okinawa was "secured," the next job for those same units, and many more, would be the unimaginably costly invasion of the Japanese home islands.) Only by straining my ears was it possible to pick up a few snatches from the radio and learn that the world's first A-bomb had been dropped on a place called Hiroshima. I made a mental note that Hiroshima would be my priority objective should I ever get to Japan.

11

On to Hiroshima

A S DETAILS OF THE destructive power of the new bomb were released, I thought of conversations a few months earlier with the American playwright Robert Sherwood. During the invasion of Iwo Jima, Bill McGaffin and I had shared the (absent) admiral's suite on the *Bennington* with Sherwood, then a member of President Roosevelt's brain trust. A companionable and witty man, Sherwood managed to turn every conversation to the question of the reaction if some terribly lethal new weapon was used to shorten the war against Japan.

This was not just with McGaffin and me, but with senior and junior officers, carrier pilots, and ordinary seamen. The consensus was certainly "Anything to wind it up," accompanied by very uncomplimentary references to the enemy as the justification for using any weapon at all. It was generally felt that Sherwood must be referring to poison gas.

Opinion in naval circles at that time as to how the war would ever be ended was very gloomy. The admirals thought in terms of their own very considerable expertise: sea power, air power, marines admirably trained for swift, bitter assaults to secure beachheads or overrun islands. But even if Japan was occupied—and this was considered feasible if the Allies, principally the United States, were willing to pay the cost—how were the Japanese ever to be dislodged from their well-entrenched positions in China? By developing the raw materials and heavy industry in Manchuria (Northeast China) and exploiting the inexhaustible Chinese manpower, they could hang on forever. Thus, the idea of using some new, war-winning weapon was as welcome as the flowers of spring.

Stalin had promised his wartime allies at the Yalta Conference in February 1945 that Soviet forces would attack the Japanese in mainland China "within two or three months of the German surrender." Three months would expire on August 8, 1945, and on that date the Soviet Far Eastern Army attacked Japan's formidable Kwantung Army in Manchuria, forty-eight hours after the A-bomb was dropped on Hiroshima. Before both events the Soviet Union had relayed to Washington information that Japan was ready to quit the war. Revelation of this later raised questions as to the motive in dropping the A-bombs when the war was practically won.

In any case, Japan announced on August 14 its decision to quit, and a few days later I was aboard the troop transport the USS *Millett*, with part of the vanguard marine unit which was to be the first to land at the Yokosuka naval base. My objective was Hiroshima. One of my most precious possessions was a little Japanese phrase book which I hoped would help me find my way about by putting questions that would require simple yes and no answers. Having landed with the first wave of marines, McGaffin and I made straight for the Yokosuka railway station, where we jumped aboard the first Tokyo-bound train. We created something of a sensation. The surrender had not been signed. Although the train was packed, passengers cleared a space around us, gazing at us with a mixture of fear and curiosity, but not, we felt, with hostility. One who spoke English asked where we were going, and as the only place we could think of in Tokyo was the Imperial Hotel, he counted off the number of stops before we should get off. From the time the train passed through Yokohama, we traveled three or four miles through devastation which we thought must be without parallel in modern times. It was mainly the result of General Curtis Le May's B-29 fire raids. Mile after mile the train rattled through districts which had been among the world's most densely populated, mainly houses of wood and paper. There was nothing left but flat acres with some green poking through the ashes. Factories were reduced to pulverized concrete, twisted girders, and rusty, shattered machinery. We began to feel nervous, surrounded by people who were still technically our enemies, with the evidence of what our air power had done wherever we looked. But passengers stared stolidly at the ruins, showing no resentment at our presence.

We discovered that some colleagues, who had landed with MacArthur's airborne troops a few hours ahead of the marines, were installed at the Imperial, so we went to the Dai Ichi, the only other nearby hotel still standing. The manager, gazing at us as if we had dropped from the moon, explained that the hotel was full and "uncomfortable." When we insisted, he pointed out that we would be the only foreigners in a hotel full of Japanese, many of them "hotheads." Later he produced forms for us to fill in as if we had just arrived on a Cook's tour. He was nonplussed when he found we had neither passports nor visas.

Tokyo, in those first couple of days, was an example of how the people accepted anything—even surrender—from the emperor. A few days earlier every able-bodied male was armed—even with bamboo spears and old swords—to deal with invaders. But the emperor had told the people to behave and not "cause incidents" when the foreigners arrived. Now a handful of enemy journalists, without any occupation troops to protect them, could wander around and register at hotels without molestation.

McGaffin's and my interests now diverged. He had flown out specially from Chicago for the surrender-signing ceremony aboard the battleship *Missouri* on September 2. I was still bent on getting to Hiroshima. With the aid of my phrase book I was able to get to the Japanese official news agency (Domei in those days) and found that a train still went to where Hiroshima used to be. This was a great surprise because journalists had been briefed for months that the Japanese railway system had been brought to a halt by Le May's efforts. The journey would be long, difficult to say how long. Nobody, I was warned, went to Hiroshima. Domei received messages from its correspondent there by Morse code, but the correspondent had no way of receiving messages from Tokyo.

If I insisted on going, my English-speaking Domei man said, he would give me a letter to the local correspondent, asking him to show me around and to transmit my messages to the Tokyo office. All this could be arranged if I would take some food to the Domei man in Hiroshima. Back at Yokosuka a U.S. Navy public relations officer cheerfully dispensed a week's rations for me and a fortnight's for the Domei man, delighted at the prospect that one of its correspondents might get to Hiroshima ahead of one accredited to the Army. From there I went to Yokohama, where Henry Keys had arrived with a cable from the *Express* urging one of us to get to Hiroshima. Henry agreed to maintain contact with Domei's Tokyo office in case my madcap plan came off. The night before I left he gave me his .45 pistol and wished me luck. In the small hours of September 2, while some 600-odd newsmen were on their way to the *Missouri* for the surrender ceremony, I was on my way to Tokyo to board at 6:00 A.M. a train which would theoretically land me in Hiroshima within some fifteen to thirty hours.

The train was carrying elements of the Japanese Imperial Army away from their Tokyo barracks. Officers, big swords dangling between their legs, occupied the seating accommodation. I squeezed in among some ordinary soldiers on a platform—standing room only—at the end of a compartment. Having stuffed my military cap, pistol, and belt among my rations and purchased an umbrella to give an impression of civilian status, I was still clad in jungle greens. The soldiers were very sullen at first, chattering—obviously about me—in a hostile way. They brightened up when I handed around a pack of cigarettes. Several then offered me bits of dried fish or hard-boiled eggs in exchange. A major breakthrough came when I showed them the impressive scar on my leg, managing to get the idea across that it came from a Japanese plane in Burma, and that I was a journalist—my battered Hermès portable was evidence.

From then on it was smiles and friendship, more cigarettes against bits of fish—and even a drop of sake. They all had enormous bundles, and I understood later that they had just been demobilized, allowed to take from their barracks as much food and drink as they could carry, as well as their weapons, wrapped in blankets.

My fellow travelers, after the first few hours, started dropping off at various stops. After six hours I managed to get into the compartment and find a seat among the officers. Here the hostility was total. Among the passengers was an American priest, accompanied by armed guards. He had been brought to Tokyo from internment to broadcast to American troops on how they should behave in Japan to avoid friction with the local population, he explained, warning me in veiled tones that the situation in our compartment was very tense and that a false move might cost our lives. The officers were furious and humiliated at their defeat. Above all, I must not smile as this would be taken as gloating over what was happening aboard the *Missouri*. Watching those glowering officers toying with the hilts of their swords and the long samurai daggers that many of them wore, I felt no inclination to smile, especially since the train was in complete darkness when we passed through what seemed like endless tunnels.

At Kyoto, which the priest explained, as he was escorted off the train, was roughly halfway to Hiroshima in terms of time, the situation seemed bleaker than ever. After many more hours had passed and the interior of the train was pitch-black, I poked my head out of the window each time the train stopped and said, *"Kono eki-wa nanti i meska?"* According to my phrase book, this meant: "What is the name of this station?" I thus avoided my pronouncing the name of Hiroshima for fear of the effect it might have on my sword-toting fellow passengers. Dozing off between stations, I managed to awaken at each stop to repeat the question. In the meantime, a few civilians came aboard; one of them accepted a cigarette from me and offered me a welcome swig of sake. He must have guessed my destination. As the train started slowing down for another stop, he said, *"Kono eki-wa Hiroshima eki desu."* Since the compartment platform was crammed again, I climbed out the window, and he threw my knapsack after me.

The station, on the extreme outskirts of the city, was an empty shell, with an exit of improvised wooden gates. There two black-uniformed guards—with swords—grabbed me, probably assuming that I was a runaway POW. Trying to explain that I was a *shimbun kisha* ("journalist"), I opened my typewriter as proof, but they took me to a flimsy shelter and gave me to understand that I was "locked up." Because it was two in the morning, I had been twenty hours on the train, and it was just twenty-four hours since

I had left Yokohama, I was in no mood to argue. A woman heated some water to drink and gave me some peanutlike small beans, so I felt things were not going too badly. After sunup the guards read the letter addressed to the Domei correspondent, Mr. Nakamura, and my status obviously improved. No attempt was made to detain me as I stepped outside and returned to the railway station to get my bearings. It was on the fringe of the belt of heavy destruction. The central hall was intact but with roof and windows badly damaged. The rest—offices, waiting rooms, and ticket barriers—had been swept away. By then Mr. Nakamura had turned up, together with a Canadian-born Japanese girl who spoke excellent English. We followed a tramline toward buildings a mile or two distant.

There was devastation and desolation and nothing else. Lead gray clouds hung low over the city, vapors drifted up from fissures in the ground, and there was an acrid sulfurous smell. The few people to be seen in this former city of half a million hurried past each other without speaking or pausing, white masks covering mouths and nostrils. Buildings had dissolved into gray and reddish dust, solidified into ridges and banks by the frequent rains and heavy winds, as I learned later.

It was just less than a month since the bomb had exploded, and there had been no time for greenery to cover the wounds. Trees lay on their sides, roots sticking up into the air like legs of dead cows, yawning pits where roots had once been. Some younger trees were still standing, but leaves and smaller branches had been stripped off. Mr. Nakamura related what had happened:

"We had an alarm early in the morning, but only two aircraft appeared. We thought they were reconnaissance planes, and no one took much notice. The 'all clear' sounded, and most people set off for work. Then, at eight-twenty, one plane came back. It was taken for another photo plane, and the alarm was not even sounded. I was just wheeling out my bicycle to ride to the office when there was a blinding flash—like lightning. At the same time I felt scorching heat on my face, and in a tornadolike blast of wind I was knocked to the ground and the house collapsed around me. As I hit the ground, there was a booming explosion as if a powerful bomb had exploded alongside. When I peered out, there was a tremendous pillar of black smoke, shaped like a parachute but drifting upward, with a scarlet thread in the middle. As I watched, the scarlet thread expanded, diffusing through the billowing cloud of smoke until the whole thing was glowing red. Hiroshima had disappeared, and I realized that something new to our experience had occurred. I tried to phone the police and fire brigade to find out what had happened, but it was impossible even to raise the exchange."

In the center of the city I found that the buildings seen from the distance were only skeletons, having been gutted by the fire which swept through after most of the city had disappeared in a great swirling pillar of dust and flame. In the burned out Fukuoka department store (now rebuilt on the same spot) a temporary police headquarters had been installed. It was there that we went to explain who I was and what I wanted. The atmosphere was very tense and the police looked at me with cold hostility. (Visiting Tokyo-Hiroshima 35 years later, I met Mr. Nakamura who had miraculously survived the consequences of atomic radiation. He recalled that some of the policemen wanted us both summarily shot. In the end it was the head of the Thought Control police, Kuniharo Dazai—who outranked the others —who accepted my explanation, as had Nakamura immediately, that I wanted to report to the world what had happened in Hiroshima. It was he who arranged a police car to drive through the debris and to the only hospital which was still functioning. (Until he retired in 1974, Kuniharo Dazai was subsequently deputy minister at Japan's Ministry of Welfare and Public Health.)

From the third floor of the Fukuoka department store, as I looked in every direction, there was nothing to be seen but flat acres of ground, a few young trees, and some factory chimneys. Among the few gutted buildings still standing near the former department store was a church which, closer inspection revealed, had jumped into the air to return, practically intact, but crazily athwart its foundations. Low-level concrete bridges had also jumped off their piles, some spans landing back again, others dropping into the river. All balustrades and stone facings had disappeared from the bridges. There were no remnants of broken walls, no large chunks of rubble or blocks of stone and concrete, no craters, as one usually finds in a bombed city. It was destruction by pulverization followed by fire. The reason that some buildings were still standing in the center, according to the police, was that they were in the epicenter of the explosion, directly under the bomb as it parachuted down and thus in a relative safety zone as the explosive force expanded outward from the epicenter.

Our small group in an ancient car, piloted by one of the police officers, drove slowly across the city to the Communications Hospital in the outskirts. It was the only hospital to survive. If the evidence of the material destruction of the city was horrifying, the effects on humans I saw inside the hospital wards were a thousand times more so.

Stretched out on filthy mats on the floor of the first ward I entered were a dozen or so people in various stages of physical disintegration, from what I later knew to be atomic radiation. The head of the hospital, Dr. Gen Katsube (whom I was also able to meet during my visit thirty-five years later), assured me they all would die unless American scientists sent them some antidote for the terrible wasting disease that had stricken thousands of people since the bomb was dropped. In ward after ward it was the same. Patients were terribly emaciated and gave off a nauseating odor which almost halted me at the first door. Some had purplish burns on the face and body; others had bunched, blue-black, blistery marks on the neck. Dr. Katsube said he was completely at a loss how to treat them.

"At first we treated burns as we would any others, but patients just wasted away and died. Then people without a mark on them, including some not even here when the bomb exploded, fell sick and died. For no apparent reason their health began to fail. They lost their appetite, head hair began to fall out, bluish spots appeared on their bodies, and bleeding started from the nose, mouth, and eyes.

"The symptoms were of severe general debility and vitamin deficiency. We started giving vitamin injections, but the flesh rotted away from the puncture caused by the needle. And in every case the patient dies. We now know that something is killing off the white corpuscles, and there is nothing we can do about it. There is no known way of replacing white corpuscles. Every person carried in here as a patient is carried out as a corpse."

I asked about the masks people were wearing, and the doctor explained that at first, because of the vapors issuing from the ground and the vile sulfurous odor, plus the fact that people who had not been in the city when the bomb was dropped were stricken, it was thought that some type of poisonous gas had been used and still clung to the ground. So people were advised to wear primitive gauze masks. "Now we know it is not gas, but people are probably comforted psychologically by wearing them, so we have not discouraged this."

Around each patient squatted a few women, some with children, following my movements with hate-filled eyes. The patients were also mainly women and children, some bleeding from the nose, mouth, and eyes, others with halos of black hair, lying where it had fallen on their rough pillows. Others had large suppurating third-degree burns. I asked if anything could be done to improve hospital conditions. "We have no nurses," replied Dr. Katsube. "Most of them were killed immediately; others died through handling the patients; still others just left—went back to their villages. Now we can't admit patients unless relatives stay to look after them. We can only keep the wounds clean and try to provide vitamin-rich food."

The assistant city health officer, on a visit to the hospital, explained that those who sickened after the raid were, in most cases, those who had been digging in the ruins for bodies of relatives or household belongings. It was thought that some sort of rays had been released into the soil, so it was now prohibited to dig among the ruins. "We estimate there are still thirty thousand bodies under the rubble and dirt," he said. "They must remain unburied until we know how to deal with the main disease. This may result in other epidemics, but at least they will be of a kind we know how to deal with."

At one point Dr. Katsube, who was under great strain, asked me to leave. In good English, he said, "I can no longer guarantee your safety.

These people are all doomed to die. I also. I can't understand it. I was trained in the United States; I believed in Western civilization. I'm a Christian. But how can Christians do what you have done here? Send, at least, some of your scientists who know what it is so that we can stop this terrible sickness."

I could only explain that as a journalist I would faithfully report what I had seen, and that although not American, but attached to the Allied forces, I would do my best to get scientists who "knew" to be sent to Hiroshima as soon as possible. Japanese scientists, dissecting corpses in the hospital basement, confirmed that nothing they had discovered so far gave any clue to the origin of the disease or how to treat it.

Back in the center of the city I sat on a rare block of concrete that had escaped pulverization and typed my story. Some of the more blood-chilling details were deleted from my original text, but it appeared in the September 6, 1945, edition of the *Daily Express*, substantially as written, with the following headlines and introduction:

THE ATOMIC PLAGUE
"I Write This as a Warning to the World"
DOCTORS FALL AS THEY WORK
Poison gas fear: All wear masks
Express Staff Reporter, Peter Burchett
was the first Allied staff reporter to enter the atom-bomb city. He travelled 400 miles from Tokyo alone and unarmed [incorrect but the *Daily Express* could not know that], *carrying rations for seven meals—food is almost unobtainable in Japan—a black umbrella, and a typewriter. Here is his story from—*

HIROSHIMA, *Tuesday.*

In Hiroshima, 30 days after the first atomic bomb destroyed the city and shook the world, people are still dying, mysteriously and horribly—people who were uninjured by the cataclysm—from an unknown something which I can only describe as atomic plague.

Hiroshima does not look like a bombed city. It looks as if a monster steamroller had passed over it and squashed it out of existence. I write these facts as dispassionately as I can, in the hope that they will act as a warning to the world. In this first testing ground of the atomic bomb, I have seen the most terrible and frightening desolation in four years of war. It makes a blitzed Pacific island seem like an Eden. The damage is far greater than photographs can show.

I picked my way to a shack [sic!] used as a temporary police headquarters in the middle of the vanished city. Looking south from there I could see about three miles of reddish rubble. That is all the atomic bomb left of dozens of blocks of city streets of buildings, homes, factories and human beings.

STILL THEY FALL

> There is just nothing standing except about 20 factory chimneys—chimneys with no factories. I looked west. A group of half a dozen gutted buildings. And then again nothing. . . .

The dispatch then went on to describe the scenes in the hospital wards and what Dr. Katsube had said. I must have expressed myself even more strongly because Arthur Christiansen, the prestigious editor of the *Daily Express* in those days, wrote in his memoirs, *Serving My Time*, that "poor Peter" had been so overcome by the horror of it all that he (Christiansen) had personally taken a hand in editing the story. To his credit, despite some inserted errors, he used my "warning to the world" phrase in the headline. It was the main message I wanted to get across, but given the euphoria in the West about the monopoly possession of such a war-winning weapon, plus the justifiably strong feelings against the Japanese for their methods of conducting the war and treating Allied prisoners, it was not certain that I would succeed.

It was miraculous that the story got through as quickly and completely as it did. After my departure for Hiroshima, Tokyo had been placed out of bounds by General MacArthur. Allied personnel were forbidden to go beyond the Yokohama defense perimeter. Henry Keys was twice pulled off the Tokyo-bound train on his way to the Domei office. He then hired a Japanese courier to sit in the Domei office and rush any message from me to him at Yokohama. The greatest miracle of all was that Nakamura in Hiroshima so faithfully and accurately tapped out that long dispatch on his hand-operated Morse set to his Tokyo office.

My return trip was interrupted by finding at Kyoto station some pale ghosts of Australian POWs, who insisted that I should visit their camps in the Kyoto-Tsuruga area to persuade the inmates that the war was really over. "You must come and tell the others," one of them said. "Our mates are dying every hour. If you just show yourself and tell them what you've told us, you'll save lives. You'll give them that extra bit of strength to hold on." Their expressions, even more than their words, were very eloquent. I decided in their favor.

My belongings were collected, and I set out with them—first to the Domei office, easily located because one of the POWs had picked up a knowledge of Japanese. There I was able to confirm that my story from Hiroshima had indeed been received in Tokyo and handed over to the *Express*. The next few days were spent in a morale-boosting tour of the POW camps, where I was able—by freely using the name of General MacArthur—to persuade the Japanese authorities to improve food and other conditions. (I wore my correspondent's cap and strapped on Henry Keys's pistol for the occasion.)

By the time I arrived back Tokyo was in bounds, General MacArthur having received sufficient reinforcements to include Tokyo in his defense perimeter—but not enough to liberate the POW camps! From the station I had set out for the Dai Ichi hotel when I ran into a colleague who urged me to come with him to a press conference at the Imperial Hotel being given by some high-ranking American officers on the bombings of Hiroshima and Nagasaki, also A-bombed on August 9. Grimy, unshaved, and disheveled as I was, I accompanied him. The conference was nearing its end, but it was clear that the main purpose was to deny my dispatch from Hiroshima, which the *Daily Express* had made available to the world press, that people were dying from aftereffects of the bomb. A scientist in brigadier general's uniform explained that there could be no question of atomic radiation—which could cause the symptoms I had described—because the bombs had been exploded at such a height as to obviate any risk of "residual radiation."

There was a dramatic moment as I got to my feet, feeling that my scruffiness put me at a disadvantage with the elegantly uniformed and bemedaled officers. My first question was whether the briefing officer had been to Hiroshima. He had not, so I was off to a good start. I described what I had seen—and asked for explanations. It was very gentlemanly at first, a scientist explaining things to a layman. Those I had seen in the hospitals were victims of blast and burn, normal after any big explosions. Apparently the Japanese doctors were incompetent to handle them or lacked the right medications. He discounted the allegation that any who had not been in the city at the time of the blast were later affected. Eventually the exchanges narrowed down to my asking how he explained the fish still dying when they entered a stream running through the center of the city.

"Obviously they were killed by the blast or by the overheated water."

"Still there a month later?"

"It's a tidal river, so they would be washed back and forth."

"But I was taken to a spot in the city outskirts and watched live fish turning their white stomachs upwards as they entered a certain stretch of the river. After that they were dead within seconds."

The spokesman looked pained. "I'm afraid you've fallen victim to Japanese propaganda," he said, and sat down. The customary "Thank you" was pronounced, and the conference ended. Although my radiation story was denied, Hiroshima was immediately put out of bounds, and I was whisked off to a U.S. Army hospital for tests, following which I was informed that my white corpuscle count was down. I was also informed that General MacArthur was expelling me for having "gone beyond the bounds of 'his' military occupation." The diminution of my white corpuscles, which could have been a symptom of radiation, was finally put down to antibiotics given earlier for a knee infection. The expulsion order was rescinded because I was able to prove—with hilarious support by the Navy—that I had landed as an accredited correspondent to the U.S. Pacific Fleet, and it had set no restrictions on correspondents' movements.

By one of those extraordinary coincidences which diligent journalists have the right to expect from time to time, I learned, while revising this chapter, how lucky I was to have got my Hiroshima story through to London. George Weller, noted war correspondent of the Chicago *Daily News*, passing through Paris after his paper ceased publication in mid-1978, telephoned me. Our trails had crossed many times, but we had never met. To my surprise—after all, it was thirty-three years after the event—he congratulated me on my Hiroshima story. Why? Because he had done a far more thorough job on Nagasaki at the same time, but his series of articles never saw the light of day. When I told him what I was working on at that very moment, he dictated over the telephone from his Paris hotel what had happened. The gist was that he managed to get into Nagasaki alone and stayed there for three days, "looking at everything, interviewing eyewitnesses including doctors and other medical people. I wrote twenty-five thousand words, and as a good, loyal correspondent I sent it back to MacArthur's headquarters for forwarding—and the censors killed the lot."

After the Nagasaki episode George had not gone back to headquarters, but went off on a ship somewhere and was immobilized with a leg injury. After some time, astonished at not getting any acknowledgment of what had been a most commendable bit of journalistic enterprise, he queried his paper and discovered the articles had never arrived. They had remained at MacArthur's headquarters. (I did not know until a Washington reunion with Henry Keys in December 1979 that the censors also tried to kill my story. Henry, who is as tough as any in the profession, insisted that as the war was over, so was censorship. He refused a plea of "special case" and actually stood over the telex operator while it was transmitted.)

There was no real confirmation of deaths from atomic radiation for many months after my report was published in the *Daily Express*. General MacArthur's capacity for suppressing inconvenient truth was very great. (According to the Japanese Council Against A and H bombs, the Hiroshima bomb had accounted for 130,000 to 140,000 deaths by the end of 1945, that at Nagasaki 60,000 to 70,000. By 1950 the figure had risen to 300,000 for the two cities. During my visit to Hiroshima in June 1980, Dr. Kiyoshi Kuramoto, vice director of the Hiroshima Atomic Bomb hospital, informed me that there were still 370,000 A-bomb victims officially recognized as such by the Japanese Government. "This is far short of the real number," he explained, "because the Government requires that two persons, not related to the victims, must testify that the affected person was in one of the two A-bombed cities at the time of the explosions, or were there within the two weeks that followed. For many of those affected, it is impossible to provide witnesses."

"Recognition" carries with it free medical care and in extreme cases a disability pension. As for the genetic effects, Dr. Kuramoto said the full consequences could only be known after fifty to one hundred years.)

Once MacArthur had been forced to withdraw my expulsion order, I left for London for a family reunion and to meet the *Daily Express* bigwigs for the first time to seek the possibilities of a peacetime reassignment. The two girls had spent a relatively peaceful war in Abergavenny, but Erna and Rainer had a miraculous escape shortly before the victory over Hitler when a V-2 hit a school opposite their house near Hampstead Heath, causing heavy casualties. There were no great rejoicings when I explained that I would soon be getting out of my war correspondent's uniform—but to continue as a foreign correspondent.

12

That Old World Again

MY FIRST MEETING with *Daily Express* editor Arthur Christiansen was almost a disaster. He started by thanking me for my services—especially for ending up my war corresponding by a scoop like Hiroshima—and launched the idea that I work in the editorial department for a time, "getting to know us and how the paper works." A large, plumpish man, with a surprisingly benign expression, considering his reputation as Fleet Street's toughest editor, he continued: "We are thinking of a page that would handle foreign news in a tight, capsulized form—similar to *Time* magazine treatment. I thought of putting you in charge of that. . . ."

My body started trembling, my jaw shaking with such violence that I could not pronounce a word. Mumbling something, I stumbled out of the office, leaving Christiansen on his feet with bulging eyes. A few hours later I telephoned him from a tropical diseases hospital to explain that I had been seized with the first paroxysms of a bad attack of malaria. It was the only time I ever felt grateful for a bout of malaria, for if there was one thing I did *not* want to do, it was to be bogged down in the editorial offices of the *Daily Express* or any other paper. (After forty years of journalism I have still avoided this.)

By the time the specialists had pronounced my body exorcised of the sporozoa demons I assumed that Christiansen had been shocked into dropping the capsuled news page idea because I was offered a neat assignment from the *Sunday Express* to travel where I liked in Europe (my languages had served again) and write a weekly feature on how postwar Europe was being put together. (In my innocence I had assumed that the Beaverbrook empire worked as a monolithic and harmonious entity.) No sooner had my first feature appeared than there was a wrathful call from Christiansen. The upshot was that the *Sunday Express* "released" me back to Christiansen, who offered me an assignment in Berlin, which I accepted.

In fact, once the war had ended, I had speculated whether there would be any further basis for working with the *Express*. It was a right-wing paper with belligerently pro-Empire tendencies, whereas I had strongly anti-Empire, anticolonialist feelings which had grown only stronger because of my wartime experiences. I was also a committed antifascist as a result of my prewar experiences in Nazi Germany, very much a partisan of peaceful coexistence—having seen the alternative at Hiroshima.

There had been no problem in reporting for the *Express* during the war against the Axis powers. But what was going to be the line now the war was over? I had been amused, astounded, to see behind Christiansen's desk an almost life-size photo of Lord Beaverbrook—my boss for more than four years —hugging Joseph Stalin, of all people. I was assured by Christiansen that Beaverbrook—unlike some of his press lord colleagues—thoroughly disliked and mistrusted the Nazis, postwar or any other kind, and I would have to be very vigilant in reporting any signs of a Nazi resurgence. That would present no problem. The lord was also for maintaining and developing the friendly Anglo-Soviet wartime relations. No problems between us about that either. I was convinced that if the peace were to be kept during my lifetime and that of my children, extraordinary efforts should be made to foster normal, if possible, friendly East-West relations. On the issues which I would be covering it seemed there should be fairly smooth sailing.

Friends on the staff also said that as long as I avoided some of his lordship's pet phobias—such as any favorable mention of the British Council or India's Nehru—and in general kept as far away from Beaverbrook as possible, I would have no great difficulties. (I managed the latter part so well that in my eight years' service with the paper we never set eyes on each other.)

Thus, late at night on a freezing New Year's Eve 1945, I drove through the snow-covered ruins of Berlin's Kurfürstendamm to the Hotel am Zoo, now the British press headquarters. Champagne and schnapps were flowing as the journalists warmed up to celebrate the birth of 1946.

The spectacle on that first gray morning of 1946 was a reminder of what even conventional bombs can do to a city. All the way down the Kurfürstendamm, starting with the truncated steeples of the Kaiser Wilhelm Gedächtniskirche, were nothing but ruins. The cross streets were choked with rubble from gutted shops and apartment buildings. This was nothing compared to the area surrounding the Tiergarten, where for scores of acres there was not a single habitable dwelling. Twisted, crumpled, roofless, wall-less house after house, street after street—all the way from Budapesterstrasse to the treeless Tiergarten itself, a flourishing park when last I had seen it. It would remain for years to come an awesome monument to the horrors of war and the terrible retributions the Nazis had brought upon the German people.

It was soon clear that the ruins symbolized a general breakdown of society in Berlin—at least—and of corruption among the Allied occupation forces. Smuggling of art and other treasures out of the country by British and American officers, black-marketeering by the Germans were part of routine life. To the normal demoralization of a defeated people were added criminality and corruption as almost the sole means of survival. Contributing to the complexities was the fact that many officers—especially the British—had a notable class sympathy for their German counterparts, preferring them to their erstwhile "gallant Allies." In applying for my press card, I was subject to a long harangue by a colonel in British Public Relations about how awful it was that "good soldiers" like Colonel General Alfred Jodl (Hitler's former chief of operations) were being tried at Nuremberg when they could be "on our side." It was a common expression of opinion among staff officers of the British Control Commission.

A major reason for my having accepted the Berlin assignment was that this was the key point of East-West contact. It was where the senior officers and officials of the United States, Britain, France, and the Soviet Union discussed together, almost daily at some level or other, problems which could hold the key to war or peace in Europe—and the world at large.

During the first few months of the activities of the Allied Control Council —the supreme body of the wartime allies—it seemed that the unity which was the key to their victory could be maintained. The personalities of the Western commanders—General Dwight D. Eisenhower, Field Marshal Bernard L. Montgomery, and General Jean J. M. G. de Lattre de Tassigny— posed no problems for good contacts with the Soviet Marshal Georgi Zhukov. The agreed aims were explicit: Purge and punish the Nazis; emasculate Germany's future war potential; exact repayment in kind for partial reparation of the war damage. Such were the tasks as defined in the Potsdam Agreement.

By the time of my arrival the commanders had been changed, and the choice of the U.S. and British replacements hinted at policy priorities which might be at variance with the Potsdam decisions. For the United States, it was General Lucius Clay, whose reputed links with big business seem to have been confirmed later when he gave up his post and became director of half a dozen leading U.S. corporations. For the British, Field Marshal Montgomery was replaced by General Sir Brian Robertson, former director of the Dunlop Rubber Corporation of South Africa. Changes by the French and Russians seemed purely military: De Lattre de Tassigny by General Pierre Koenig; Marshal Zhukov by his former chief of staff, General Vasili Sokolovsky. Sir Brian had as chief political advisers two Foreign Office diplomats closely associated with Neville Chamberlain's lamentable appeasement policy, Sir William Strong and Christian (later Sir Christian) Steel. As chief economic adviser, Sir Brian had Sir Cecil Weir, former president of the Glasgow

Chamber of Commerce and director of the Schroeder, Weir and Company shipbuilding yards. His liaison officers were mainly naturalized Russians and British officers who had fought with the White Russian and British Army of Intervention in trying to put down the Bolshevik Revolution. They wore their czarist decorations to Control Council and other meetings. This was hardly conducive to good relations with their Soviet counterparts.

The main point of contention at the thrice-monthly meetings at the Allied Control Council was whether Germany was to remain a united entity or not. It was the central issue also at the regular meetings of the four foreign ministers in the first few postwar years. From skillfully evasive briefings the impression was given that it was a Soviet *nyet* that was blocking the united Germany concept which the Western powers were thought to be championing. In fact, it was the opposite. From the moment the question was raised, the Russians fought for a united Germany, and the West opposed it. Those of us who carefully watched the activities of the Allied Control Council and its related bodies and the manipulation of information on those activities knew that the public was being misinformed, but there was little to be done about it. Loyalty was in question with a "whose side are you on?" type of sneer if one queried the veracity of a press handout or the version of a Lucius Clay or Brian Robertson at the carefully stage-managed press conferences.

One can have honest differences of view whether a united or divided Germany was good or not. At the Teheran Conference in 1943 the United States proposed that a postwar Germany be split into five independent states. The Russians opposed the proposal. A year later Churchill and Anthony Eden went to Moscow and presented an all-British plan to divide Germany into three parts. Stalin and Molotov opposed this also. On May 9, 1945, immediately after the victory over the Germans, Stalin recalled that Hitler had boasted three years previously that among his war aims were the dismemberment of the Soviet Union. "But Hitler's insane ideas were fated to remain unrealized," said Stalin. "The course of the war scattered them to the winds like dust. Actually the very opposite of what the Hitlerites dreamed of in their delirium occurred. Germany is utterly defeated. The German troops are surrendering. The Soviet Union is triumphant, *but it has no intention of dismembering or destroying Germany.*" (Emphasis added.)

The initial U.S. intention was not only the dismemberment of Germany but its pauperization or "pastoralization," as it was spelled out in the plan drafted by Secretary of the Treasury Henry Morgenthau in the summer of 1944 and approved by President Roosevelt. An entry—on August 25, 1944—in the diary of James Forrestal, then secretary of the navy, makes this clear:

> The President said he had been talking with the Secretary of the Treasury on the general question of the control of Germany after the end of the war. He said that he had just heard about a paper prepared by the Army and that

he was not at all satisfied with the severity of the measures proposed. He said that the Germans should have simply a subsistence level of food—as he put it, soup kitchens would be ample to sustain life—that otherwise they should be stripped clean and should not have a level of subsistence above the lowest level of the people they had conquered. The Secretary of War [then Henry L. Stimson] demurred from this view but the President . . . finally said he would name a committee comprising State, War and Treasury which would consider the problem of how to handle Germany along the lines that he had outlined. . . . This was the beginning of the so-called Morgenthau Plan of pastoralizing Germany.*

The Russians showed no signs of going along with such Draconian measures. They were interested primarily in their own security interests and getting a generous share of German industrial equipment and other material in reparations to help compensate for staggering damages inflicted on their economy by the Nazis.

By the time Truman, Attlee, and Stalin met in Potsdam in August 1945 Morgenthau had resigned after eleven years as treasury secretary, and no more was heard of his plan. The nearest practical move toward unity at Potsdam was acceptance of the principle of the desirability of a centralized government of a united Germany and the setting up of five central administrations to run the economic affairs of the whole country. The Russians pushed hard to have these set up and working under four-power control.

France, which had not taken part in the Potsdam Conference, was even more adamant than the British in opposing anything which hinted at central administrations in any form. General Koenig refused even to stay in Berlin, flying back and forth to Control Council meetings from his headquarters in Baden-Baden. He ordered the term "Reich" ("state") to be abolished from all signs in the French Occupation Zone. *Reichsbahn* and *Reichpost* became *Deutschebahn* and *Deutschepost*. Since the contribution of General de Gaulle's Free French to the overall defeat of the Nazis was minimal—this is implicit in France's exclusion from important Allied wartime policy conferences, including Potsdam—its membership in the Allied Control Council was more by courtesy than performance. The Russians could be excused for their suspicions that France—not bound by the Potsdam decisions, as its delegates never tired of repeating—was brought in to veto policies to which the United States and Britain were committed but did not want implemented. It is inconceivable that the United States and Britain would have accorded such prerogatives to France unless they were used to advance Anglo-American policies.

The East-West wrangles within the Control Council and subsidiary bodies,

---

* *The Forrestal Diaries*, Walter Millis, ed., with collaboration of E. S. Duffield (New York: Viking Press), 1951, p. 10.

which took up most of the time of my first year's reporting from Berlin, were well publicized in the Western-controlled German press and delighted the hearts of all former Nazis and their sympathizers. The attitude of important elements among the Western occupation authorities from almost the first days was to bolster, praise, and even curry favor with this most reactionary section of German society. They were made to feel that they were the real heroes, the pioneers of the fight against communism. The West had made a mistake from the start by not fighting together with the Germans to bring the Soviet Union to its knees. In Berlin it was taken for granted that if you spoke English, you would immediately sympathize with German "sufferings" at the hands of the Russians. Even at Allied clubs it was considered "bad form" to mention the record of German troops in occupied countries or concentration camps and the gas ovens.

As I saw it, the West was playing a dangerous game. Despite official disclaimers, Washington and London were working for an East-West split by the formation of a separate West German state. This would lead to an eventual attempt by one side or the other, with its respective backers, to bring about reunification by force. This would inevitably lead to either outright war or the enormously costly arming of rival blocs and a permanent center of tension in the most explosive part of Europe. Influential Germans, by then being groomed for key posts in a West Germany which was already on the drawing board, were being briefed to the effect that the country would be temporarily divided but would be reunited through the "liberation," by one means or another, of Soviet-occupied eastern Germany by the Western powers.

As the time approached for what was expected to be a crucial Moscow foreign ministers' conference in March 1947, the *Daily Express* published my dispatch (February 6, 1947) that U.S. and British plans for setting up a separate West German state were far advanced. I gave substantial details on the type of state which eventually emerged (except that I had Frankfurt instead of Bonn as the capital). The story caused a sensation, was immediately denied by the British, but only half denied by the Americans. An extremely wrathful Christian Steel sent for me, exclaiming that my story was "outrageous," that I was "playing into the hands of the Russians" and there was not "a vestige of truth in it." Since I had received the "leak" from a member of Steel's own Political Department, I felt I could remind him—with details—that it was not the first time I had found him uninformed about matters within his province.

One of the difficulties for journalists was that the Western powers in Berlin, especially the U.S. and British, had one policy which had to look good for public opinion—implementing the Potsdam Agreement and maintaining correct relations with the Soviet Union—and another real policy of nonimplementation of the Potsdam Agreement and pushing relations with the Soviet Union to a point of rupture.

On grounds of "not helping the enemy," journalists were supposed not only not to challenge official versions of what went on at four-power meetings but also to turn a blind eye on all sorts of rackets going on among Allied officers at all levels. So many high British officials were involved that the chief of the Civil Affairs Division of the British Military Government, Julian Simpson, sent for a special team of detectives from Scotland Yard to investigate and help prosecute high-level racketeers within the British Control Commission. Within a few weeks Tom Hayward, who headed the team, had a casebook involving heads and deputy heads of the Civil Affairs Division and high-ranking officers—including one of the highest. In one instance, crateloads of valuable German furniture and carpets had been flown back to England; more crates for the same destination were awaiting plane space at Gatow Airport in the British sector of Berlin. Simpson and Hayward demanded prosecutions, and the files were sent to London. For reasons of prestige—"What would the Soviet-licensed press in Berlin say?"—it was decided to hush up the whole thing. Simpson resigned and returned to his native Australia. Hayward was transferred away from Berlin to where he could busy himself with less important personalities. As a result of the Simpson-Hayward investigations, however, some checks were made in homes in England, and a few crates of carpets, oil paintings, and other valuables were flown back to Germany.

One British public safety official in what was then known as the British Occupation Zone, who objected to prosecuting the small fry while the big ones went unscathed, told me, "Every time I'm asked by a superior to investigate some soldier for 'flogging' a few cigarettes, I open up my files and say, 'Let me go after these fellows, and I'll take on the little ones later.' And in that file I have some of the biggest names in the British Zone."

13

***

Carving Up Germany

UTTING GERMANY IN TWO was a long and painful operation. The Western corporation lawyers who drafted procedural documents were such masters of their craft that it was difficult to arouse an
editor's interest in any particular phase of the surgery. But there were some
agreed guidelines—considered indecent to mention in the presence of American or British policy practitioners—which, if violated, could not but have
grave consequences. One such was Article 14 of the Potsdam Agreement,
fathered by a document known as JCS (Joint Chiefs of Staff) Directive
1067, agreed to by Roosevelt, Churchill, and Stalin at Yalta.

Article 14 stated that Germany was to be treated as a single economic
unit and spelled out seven specific fields in which common policies should
be applied, the first of them "in mining and industrial production and allocation. . . ." The Russians proposed setting up a joint board to supervise
overall coal mining production and allocation, pooling the important brown
coal deposits of Saxony in the Soviet Zone with the hard coal deposits in
the Ruhr. The British objected that the Ruhr would be "subsidizing" the
Soviet Zone because of greater efficiency. Teams of experts sent to the main
coal-mining zones to check up on mining methods found in the Soviet Zone
that production was running at about 75 percent of peacetime partly because it was opencut mining and less damaged by bombings, while the
Ruhr was only up to 30 percent. Installations of the deep underground
coal mines had been badly damaged.

The British claimed the Russians were driving both machines and miners
too hard but were otherwise impressed with the progress. The Russians
claimed the British were only playing at mining in the Ruhr. They recommended that miners be given increased rations, Nazis be removed from

key positions, an immediate effort be made to improve miners' housing, and the trade unions be given more say in settling production and other problems. The British were shocked at what their officials privately said was "an inkling of what to expect if the Russkies get into the Ruhr." At that stage neither the Americans nor the French were too much worried about that.

Official British policy up to the end of 1946, at least, was for the "socialization" of the Ruhr. But under pressure from General Clay, the British started to backtrack. The trump American argument at social functions was: "We're here to teach the Germans democracy, aren't we? How can the British be allowed to impose socialist doctrines on their part of Germany?"

A few Labour party appointees to the British Control Commission put up a mild rearguard fight. But Clay produced Konrad Adenauer, then in a minority in the Christian Democrat leadership, to launch a violent and well-publicized attack against any socialist measures and a plea for private enterprise so that Germany "can play her rightful role in the European economic recovery."

Although by mid-1947 it was obvious that socialization of the Ruhr was already a dead letter, this was strenuously denied in London and by the British Control Commission in Berlin. In issuing one of the many denials, a commission spokesman conceded that "there is a difference of opinion between the Americans and ourselves on this question. . . . The American view is that . . . the Germans must be given a chance to express themselves on the subject." In fact, General Clay had no such intention of letting the Germans decide for themselves. This was made clear by what happened on the question of socialization in Greater Hesse—which, together with Bavaria and Württemberg-Baden, made up the U.S. Occupation Zone. At the constituent elections on June 30, 1946, Social Democrats and Communists won fifty out of the ninety seats. A Constitution was drawn up which included an Article 41, providing for the socialization of heavy industries and public utilities. The local U.S. military government protested at this article, but the Greater Hesse government stood firm. The matter went up to General Clay, who ruled that the Constitution must not be voted on as a whole, that Article 41 must be the subject of a separate plebiscite.

The Greater Hesse voters were thus asked whether or not they wanted their *Land* ("state") to expropriate and manage the iron ore and potash mines, the iron and steel industries, electric power plants, and railways, even when the headquarters of some of these companies were outside their own *Land*. General Clay was confident that when spelled out in such stark and uncompromising clarity, Article 41 would be rejected by an overwhelming majority. But as in so many other matters where the real wishes of the German people were concerned, Clay was wrong. The plebiscite was held on December 1, 1946, and approved by more than 70 percent of the voters, a greater majority than for the rest of the Constitution. Clay then vetoed the offensive Article 41. "The people of Germany as a whole must decide such major issues," he said, reversing his earlier opposition to anything that smacked of centralism or infringing on the sovereign rights of the *Länder*.

Clay's first argument against British plans for the Ruhr was only that it would be "undemocratic" for the British military government to impose socialization measures. When the electors of North Rhine-Westphalia— where the Ruhr is situated—did vote solidly for socialization and a law to implement this was passed by the Landtag on August 6, 1948, Clay again insisted that Germany must be considered as a whole. By that time Britain was so deeply involved in the Marshall Plan that Foreign Secretary Ernest Bevin meekly gave way and British Military Government vetoed the Ruhr socialization bill.

For journalists and other on-the-spot spectators, there was a drama being staged simultaneously at two levels. On the upper stage the East-West split was being enacted; on the lower stage was the process by which the United States was gradually swallowing and digesting the British and French zones to create the single West German state after its own image. (The process— by such devices as creating an artificial food crisis in the British Zone, for instance—was described in detail in my book *Cold War in Germany*.)

The final carving up of Germany was a major act of surgery which brought the former Allies to the brink of war and implanted a permanent state of crisis in the heart of Europe. The instrument chosen was currency reform, the sixth of the seven points of Article 14. It was *the* issue on which at least a thread of unity could be maintained.

Everybody agreed that there must be a new currency. The old marks had been run off the Nazi printing presses by the billions and were added to by Allied occupation marks. They both were worthless. Farmers were reluctant to exchange their produce for notes with which they could buy nothing to keep their fields cultivated or their livestock fed. Manufacturers had no incentives to rebuild, obtain raw materials, plan, and produce goods. The conscientious worker who put in his eight hours a day at a factory or an office found the money he earned would buy fewer goods than he could obtain by a few minutes' activity on the black market—which was what a sizable proportion of his fellow workers were doing.

From the beginning of 1948, stories began to appear in the British- and American-licensed press in Berlin that the Russians were printing their own notes and were about to introduce new currency in their zone. I was informed by the deputy chief of a department of the British Control Commission that he had "indisputable proof" that the Russians had already distributed new notes to banks in the Soviet Zone. But he had not seen them, nor could he give any information about quantities, date of issue, or distribution. His Soviet opposite number was equally categoric in denying that any notes had been printed or that there was any Soviet intention of a separate currency reform. But the rumors gathered strength.

After the London foreign ministers' meeting of January 1948 broke up without any results, General Clay announced that he was "going to have one more try to get agreement on currency reform." British financial experts had been convinced from the beginning that agreement was possible. Following Clay's announcement, there were special meetings of the Allied Control Council at which only the four commission heads and their financial advisers were present. American and Soviet plans were so similar that a special committee was set up to report back to the Control Council, at the latest by April 10, 1948.

Early in March I had dinner with one of Clay's financial advisers. He was so gloomy and depressed that he could hardly eat. I concluded that everything had broken down again. Not at all. "God knows what was biting Clay when he talked about having another go at currency reform. We're in the devil of a jam. The Russians have agreed to everything, and it's going to be embarrassing as hell to wriggle out of it."

"But I thought that's what you'd been fighting for. It's certainly what the press has been led to believe."

"How can we have a common currency unless we can control their imports?" he replied, referring to an issue which had never been raised publicly. "To do that, we would have to control their zone and they would demand to control ours. Where the hell would we be then?"

By that time the four powers had decided how much money was to be printed and at what rate new notes would be exchanged for old. It was agreed that they would be printed at the Reichsdruckerei ("State Printery") on the borders of the American and Soviet sectors of Berlin, under four-power control. The designs of the notes were approved, and in deference to General Koenig's well-known obsession, they were to be called deutsche marks, not reichmarks. Plates were cut, and printing was actually started.

What seemed strange to the few journalists who bothered to delve into what was really going on in this most vital matter was that there were no press conferences or handouts—a total blackout. On the other hand, the campaign in the U.S.-British licensed press to the effect that the Russians were about to flood their zone with new currency reached its climax. The activity at the Reichsdruckerei was cited among the "proofs."

It was Marshal Sokolovsky's turn to preside over Control Council meetings in that fateful month of March 1948. Normally they were held on the tenth, twentieth, and thirtieth of each month with an agenda fixed beforehand. Since Sokolovsky wanted to discuss the three-power talks which Generals Clay and Robertson had attended in London two weeks earlier, he did not fix an agenda for the March 20 session. The Western generals refused a discussion on the grounds that only "recommendations," not "decisions," had been taken in London, and they were no business of the Control Council. As the main "recommendation" had been to place Bizonia (formed by the fusion of the U.S. and British occupation zones) and the French Zone within the scope of the Marshall Plan, Sokolovsky disagreed. The generals refused to discuss any aspect of the London talks. Sokolovsky insisted a second and third time without response, then rose from his chair, saying, "The session is closed." This was the formal end to four-power government in Germany, two years and nine months after the signing of the Potsdam Agreement.

Two days later Sokolovsky called for a meeting of the Special Finance Committee. Half an hour before it was to meet, the American and British delegates, followed at the last minute by the French, announced they would be unable to attend. Later in the week he twice called for meetings of the Finance Directorate, a permanent body comprising the four Allied chiefs of their respective finance divisions. The Western reply was that since Sokolovsky had "walked out" of the Control Council, their delegates would attend no further committee meetings. Sokolovsky, in my view, made a tactical error by not calling a Control Council meeting on March 30. His Western counterparts were delighted that he did not.

Had the West wanted the Control Council to continue to function, it was simple. General Koenig was chairman for April. But he called no meeting for April 10. Work stopped at the Reichsdruckerei, and the four-power control team was withdrawn. On June 20 Western authorities started issuing bright new banknotes, printed in the United States in the same format as dollar notes. They had been lying in freighters in Bremen Harbor for more than three months. The charge that the Russians had printed separate notes proved false. As an emergency measure when the Western notes were introduced, improvised stamps were pasted on the old marks in the Soviet Zone. Currency reform there was carried out only three months later.

Germany was sliced neatly in two, and introduction of the Western currency into Berlin raised the question of the status of that city. The Western powers declared Berlin was a four-power-run city in which they had equal rights with the Russians. The latter claimed that inasmuch as they had captured the city and invited the three Western powers in specifically to facilitate the four-power administration of Germany as a whole, the Western powers could now return to their respective zones of occupation. Soviet controls on transport raised the question of Western rights of access to Berlin. A search for documented proof of these rights produced only some sketchy notes of a four-power staff meeting at which it was agreed that the Western powers could use the railway and *Autobahn* leading from Helmstedt—on the border of the British and Soviet controlled zones—but that the Russians would be responsible for the "control and maintenance" of the railway and *Autobahn*.

Four days after the Western allies introduced the separate currency, the Soviet authorities imposed customs controls on all nonmilitary traffic moving across their zonal frontiers by closing the Helmstedt road and railway on the grounds of the requirements of "control and maintenance."

This was interpreted as a "blockade of Berlin," and two days later General Clay inaugurated the famous airlift of supplies in and out of Berlin. During this period Clay's plans for an "Allied task force up the Helmstedt Road" were canvassed. Had this started rolling, a shooting war—limited or not— would have been inevitable.

The splitting of Germany and the whipping up of the cold war had reached a point at which I felt further functioning out of Berlin was impossible unless one was prepared to become a propaganda hack for cold-war handouts. After I communicated this view to the *Express*, foreign editor Charles Foley came out to Berlin, and we amicably agreed that on a date of my own choosing I could revert to my preferred free-lance status. I could cover Eastern Europe for the *Express* on a contributor basis, with a reasonable "retainer fee," and I would be free to write for other publications as well as to choose my own base and the timing of ending my services as a staff correspondent.

My feelings on leaving Germany were a mixture of frustration and alarm. I had been witness to a dangerous display of brinkmanship (the word had not yet been coined) and had been able to do nothing about it. Germany had been transformed into a powder keg which I felt could explode at any moment. To what extent were the Russians responsible? Apart from Sokolovsky's walkout and the well-known Soviet suspicions and lack of flexibility, it was impossible to blame the Russians for the parting of the ways. General Clay and his backers within the Truman administration and especially within the Republican party leadership had consciously maneuvered to bring it about. This is not just my opinion, based on watching the process develop with at least as much diligence as any of my colleagues and exerting special efforts to see both sides of what was going on. It was shared by many other newsmen and some well-informed editorial writers. In his two-volume work on the origins of the cold war, D. F. Fleming cites notable examples of this:

Walter Lippmann deplored the extent to which our German policy was being fashioned by our officials in Germany. General Clay was the prime mover, seconded by his advisers in Berlin and by his immediate superiors in the Pentagon, Draper and Royall. . . . The Nashville *Tennessean*, July 26, 1948.

After Clay denied these allegations, Sumner Welles strongly supported the charges. He declared it was "notorious that General Clay had occasionally taken independent action which has shaped policy" and he was still permitted by Washington to retain the initiative in the formulation of policy. This meant control of German policy by army officers and investment bankers who had no real knowledge of European history or of the social and economic forces and national psychologies with which they were dealing. Thus nothing had been done to prevent the rebirth of German nationalism. There had been "no land reforms and no elimination of the persisting concentratios of industrial power." France especially was repeatedly brushed aside, and the decisions made in Germany "provoked the present crisis with Moscow." *Herald Tribune,* August 10, 1948.*

Such opinions coincided exactly with my own and were the gist of numerous background memoranda to the *Daily Express.* But I believed also that if the Attlee-Bevin government in Britain had mustered enough spunk to defend the country's real interests and been backed by a vigilant press with guts to discover and expose what was going on, the split in Germany could have been avoided and friendly relations with the Soviet Union maintained.

What did the Russians want? Above all, security. At the Allied Control Council and at the various foreign ministers' conferences, essentially they sought a united, but defused and neutralized, Germany, under a social and political system chosen by the German people themselves. They wanted a solution similar to that in Austria. With the passage of years it can be seen that the Austrian solution—which also grew out of four-power occupation and four-power Allied authority—was a good one. It was good for the Allies; it was good for the Austrian people. A neutralized Austria—why not a neutralized Germany? Austria today is one of the most peaceful, prosperous, and untroubled countries in Europe—indeed, in the world. It is never the source of troubles or tensions within the international community. Since it is relieved of the burden of maintaining large armed forces, its inflation rate is about the lowest in Europe.

Was an Austrianized Germany a real possibility? It was. The crucial meeting of the foreign ministers of the Big Four in Berlin (February 27– March 6, 1954) was centered on this question. In fact, final approval for Austrian neutrality and the ending of four-power controls came about because Soviet Foreign Minister Molotov insisted on linking the question to a similar four-power treaty for Germany. But the Western powers had already decided to integrate western Germany's economic and military potential into the Common Market and NATO. It was the period when John Foster Dulles, who regarded neutrality as "dangerous and immoral," ran American foreign policy. Molotov's warning of the creation of two hostile blocs facing each other in Europe was ignored. The treaty which made

---

* D. F. Fleming, *The Cold War and Its Origins* (New York: Doubleday, 1961), p. 526.

Austria independent, neutral, and free of Allied occupation was signed on May 15, 1955, and Allied occupation forces were withdrawn within five months.

The nitty-gritty part of Molotov's proposal at Berlin was that the four powers should withdraw their armed forces from East and West Germany, retaining only a small, mutually agreed number "to form protective functions arising out of their control tasks," and the East and West German governments would have police units "whose strength and armaments should be determined by the four Powers," with four-power inspection teams checking to ensure the limits were not exceeded. The implementation of these provisions "should ensure the neutralization of Germany and create conditions for an overall solution of the German problem."

Nothing came of it, and as a result, the Warsaw Pact of eight East European Communist countries came into being in May 1955, as a counter to the NATO Pact, formed by twelve North Atlantic countries in April 1949. The splitting of Germany meant a world split of fearsome implications, as I sensed at the time.

Eventually there will be—at least—a rapprochement between the two halves of Germany, not necessarily by means, or in a form, which Western policy makers conceive as in their interests. Politically conscious Germans— and by no means only on the left—are aware of who was responsible for splitting their country. It is not just the historians who recall that the Soviet Union fought hard against it just as it fought hard—and in that case successfully—against Western plans to carve up Austria. The pretexts used at the time by General Clay have lost their force, along with his strong-arm methods for achieving reunification. German statesmen have turned east before—at Rapallo in 1922, for instance—in seeking support in shaping their country's national destiny. There are signs that the German people—East and West—are tired and scared of indefinite prospects of a powder-keg existence and want to do something about it. There are political leaders— especially in West Germany—who reflect this, and they receive a sympathetic response from the Soviet Union.

14

---◄●►---

Across the Curtain

S COMPENSATION for the bleak years in Berlin I had been given a fair share of extra assignments outside Germany of the type earlier arranged with the *Sunday Express*. Thus, I had driven through Czechoslovakia from Vienna to Prague on the beautiful spring Sunday of May 26, 1946, when voters were going to the polls in the first general elections since 1935. What a contrast with the grim ruins and street-corner black marketeers of Berlin were the smiling Czechs and Slovaks strolling along roads lined with blossoming fruit trees.

Watching the election results being posted that night in Prague's Wenceslaus Square, I was approached by a compatriot and fellow journalist, John Fisher, son of Australia's first Labour prime minister, Andrew Fisher. He insisted on dragging me off to a house party where I would meet some "interesting blokes." First was my idol of ten years earlier, Egon Irwin Kisch, who had survived Spain and a French concentration camp, cheery as ever, filtering Pilsen beer through his ragged mustache. With him were another well-known Czech writer, André Simon, the future Foreign Minister Vladimir Clementis, and the brother of Rudolf Slansky, general secretary of the Czechoslovakian Communist party.

Beer and *slivovice* (plum spirit) were flowing freely, for there was plenty to celebrate. In elections which all observers agreed were held in a democratic, almost gala atmosphere, the left-wing parties had won 152 seats against 148 for the center-right. It was the first exuberant "spring" in Prague, which was later to suffer the fate of the "second spring" in 1968. Almost all those in that room were later executed as "spies" or "traitors."

Just because I was an Australian, Kisch devoted the entire second day of my visit to escorting me around the marvels of his beloved Prague, a museum

133

of Baroque architecture and one of the most beautiful cities of Europe. A passionate, exuberant man, he had never thought to live to see what he then considered a truly liberated Prague. Mutual friends later commented that it was as well that he died a natural death rather than see—and probably share—the humiliation and destruction of some of his closest comrades. Prague and Czechoslovakia as a whole were a badly needed morale booster at that time, compared to Berlin and what I saw of the rest of Germany. There must have been lots of Soviet troops around, but they maintained a low profile and in any case were genuinely regarded as liberators. Eight thousand Czechs had died in an uprising to seize the city from the Nazis and prevent its becoming a battlefield with the inevitable destruction that later happened to Berlin. But the uprising was made possible only by the swift advance of the Soviet Army to the outskirts of the city and the withholding of artillery fire while Czech patriots dealt with the Nazi occupiers.

In another excursion away from Berlin two years later, I was sent to Belgrade to report on the Danube Conference. At Belgrade Airport, in the hotel, and the adjoining sidewalk cafés, people were talking in hushed tones and with drawn faces. My first thought was that the national hero, Josip Broz Tito, had died. It was only after contacting the Reuters correspondent that I learned that earlier in the day the news had burst like a bombshell that Tito and the Yugoslav Communist party had been expelled from the Cominform. Although the Cominform headquarters was in Belgrade, it was in Bucharest that the fateful meeting had taken place, the decision having been announced the previous day, June 28, 1948, in the Czech Communist party paper, *Rude Pravo.* Tito had boycotted the meeting in view of the agenda. The Yugoslav public knew what had happened only through a statement issued earlier in the day by the Central Committee of the Yugoslav League of Communists, refuting the accusations in the Cominform document as "lies" and "wholesale slander." No wonder that people in the streets looked as if their world had fallen in.

The eight-point document of excommunication, according to a translated version available at the British Embassy that evening, called for nothing less than the overthrow of Tito. The main charges related to "anti-Soviet" behavior and wrong economic policies, including the same heresy for which the Soviet Communist party always criticized Mao Tse-tung—overemphasis on the role of the peasantry. The accusation of lack of internal democracy and a "bureaucratic regime" within the Yugoslav Communist party made ironic reading years later after the Khrushchev revelations as to the situation inside the Soviet Communist party at that time, in fact, ever since Stalin had been its leader. "In the Yugoslav Communist party," stated the Stalin-edited document, "the rights of party members are trampled on, the slightest criticism of party procedure is followed by cruel reprisals. Such a shameful Turkish terroristic regime must not be suffered in a Communist party. The very existence of the Yugoslav Communist party demands an end to such a regime."

In almost all eight points of the indictment there were references to "nationalism" and "bourgeois nationalist" tendencies. With hindsight one can find in these words and phrases the key not only to Tito's excommunication but to the political trials which later took place in Eastern Europe. Tito and Georgi Dimitrov of Bulgaria had been carrying on an open flirtation for setting up a Balkan Federation, for a start to unite their own two countries.

In Belgrade, in the days which immediately followed the bombshell, the situation was very tense, and there were rumors of a coup by pro-Soviet Communists. Because I had arrived too early for the Danube Conference but had a valid visa for Bulgaria, I was politely requested to leave and return just in time for the opening session. It was clear the authorities did not want too many foreign journalists around. Nature took a hand on my behalf in the form of heavy floods which washed out a section of the Belgrade–Sofia railway line, so I was forced to stay on a few days. There were reports of demonstrations all over Yugoslavia in favor of Tito, confirmed by travelers arriving in the capital. Three days after the expulsion I witnessed a massive meeting in Belgrade under the auspices of the People's Front. All the evidence was that Tito was immensely popular and would have overwhelming support in any showdown with the Soviet Union.

Although unclear as to the rights and wrongs of the issues raised, I was able to publish a long feature-page article in the *Express* testifying to Tito's undoubted popularity. It earned me numerous reproaches from left-wing friends, whose simplistic reasoning was: How can Tito be right when eight veteran Communist parties—headed by that of the Soviet Union—say he is wrong? I had many friends who were Communists in different parts of the world, but they were wrong in assuming I had abandoned my critical faculties and blindly followed some ideological "line." I had happened to believe that Molotov was more right than Dulles over many key aspects of policy in Germany. That did not imply that I considered Stalin more right than Tito on matters affecting Yugoslavia or international Communist doctrine about which I was woefully ignorant.

The floods subsided, rail services were restored, and I left for Sofia with a return visa for the conference. The Bulgarian capital was animated and relaxed, one of those Balkan cities where the people take over the streets in the evenings, strolling up and down the yellow-tiled main boulevard as they discuss local and world affairs. There was not much in the shops, but the summer-night strollers were decently dressed, especially the young women, who have a tradition of keeping up with what is not too elaborate in the Western fashion world.

At a foreign ministry reception for some visiting dignitary, I was fortunate enough to have an impression, at least, of Georgi Dimitrov, Bulgaria's national hero, who goes down in history as the man who turned the tables on his accusers, including Hermann Göring, at the Reichstag Fire Trial, in December 1933. He turned up at the festivities which marked the end of most official receptions in Bulgaria. A popular orchestra of string and wind instruments struck up, and soon everyone had joined hands in the *khoro*, the group dance of the Balkans. Dimitrov hopped and cavorted as nimbly as the youngest of them. He appeared to be a warm, jovial figure, close to his people and adored by them. It was easy to accept the appreciation of those who had worked with him that he was frank and open, easily approachable, including by those whose ideas were very different from his own. By training he was a printer—traditionally a progressive profession—and lifelong revolutionary. He retained a critical and independent mind, demonstrated, among other occasions, during a visit at the beginning of 1948 to Bucharest, where he signed a Bulgarian-Rumanian friendship treaty. Certainly by then he had learned of negative reactions to a twenty-year treaty of "friendship, collaboration and mutual aid," and accompanying speeches, signed with Tito a couple of months earlier. No one knew better than Dimitrov, founder secretary of the Comintern and a very long-term associate of Stalin, that if the latter hated one thing more than another, it was any threat, imagined or real, to the monolithic unity of the world Communist movement under Stalin's leadership. After signing the Bulgarian-Rumanian treaty, Dimitrov gave a press conference, at which he spoke of a possible federation of Eastern European countries, including those not necessarily within the Communist bloc. It was a projection of his "united front" concepts. Although the idea of federation at that time was "premature," he said, the first step could be a customs union between all the East European socialist countries plus Greece. When the "time was ripe," the countries could decide whether the customs union should become a "federation of states." Such an eventual federation would "cooperate fully with the Soviet Union" but would also seek trade with the West "on the principle of complete equality."

Such ideas were not very different from some of those for which Tito was castigated in the Cominform expulsion document, and they were severely criticized ten days later (January 28, 1948) in a *Pravda* editorial. Here it was clearly Dimitrov who was the target. But it was easier for Stalin to expose Tito's head on a stake than that of Dimitrov, as a warning to other incipient heretics that non-Cominformism would never be tolerated. To imagine that it was possible to pick up all this catalyst type of wisdom in a few days in Sofia would be absurd. But after Belgrade, it was undoubtedly in Sofia where Tito's apparent downfall was most discussed—and with a good deal of sympathy. It was with regret that I left beautiful, friendly, and highly politically conscious Sofia to return to Belgrade.

The Danube Conference was one of the most extraordinary ever, not least by the fact that the majority of the participants were countries the leaders of which three weeks earlier had pronounced anathema on that of the host country and by the fact that of the six countries through which the Danube actually flowed, five now had Communist regimes. The Western powers, which had formerly regarded the Danube as their domain, fought a gallant, but slightly ridiculous, rearguard action to preserve old privileges, defined in a 1921 convention on "Freedom of Danubian Navigation." Soviet Foreign Minister Andrei Vishinsky, with all the cards in his hands, could have been a little more generous. For once the Soviet bloc was in the majority, and Vishinsky made the most of it.

My reporting of the event was cut short by an attack of pneumonia, complicated by renal calculi, or kidney stones, brought on by my not imbibing enough liquid with the sulfa drugs delivered to my hotel room by a Canadian doctor. Whisked off to hospital in a painful condition, I awoke from a deep sleep to find a group of nuns, with enormous triangular hats, doing something very unpleasant to my penis. They were injecting colored liquid into the urinary tracts and watching its course through a catheter thrust up through my main genital organ, prior to tackling the stones. The nuns worked well, and the stones were passed in time for me to attend a memorable reception to mark the end of the conference. (The Western powers deemed it useless to sign the new convention since all their proposals had been rejected.)

The host was Foreign Minister Edvard Kardelj. Until the last moment there was speculation that Tito might turn up. But he was "resting" at his favorite resort on the island of Brioni. East-West diplomats, who had been hurling insults at each other for a full month, and the six foreign ministers of the Communist countries, who had excommunicated their host, ate and drank copiously together under the sharp eyes of journalists and the local diplomatic corps.

Suddenly there was a hush, and everyone started converging on a room away from the banqueting table, where Vishinsky and Kardelj held center stage. Towering over Kardelj, but saying nothing, was Tito's formidable-looking interior minister, Alexander Rankovich. Vishinsky's normally pink face was red, and so was Kardelj's. Ringside standing room was occupied by Rumania's foreign minister, Ana Pauker, her sturdy, impassive face framed in graying bobbed hair; Czechoslovakia's Vladimir Clementis, puffing furiously at his pipe; Hungary's Erik Molnár; and their aides. The main actors were speaking in Russian. Circling that group were the local ambassadors, pretending to be studying paintings on the wall, several of them making urgent gestures for interpreters to hasten to their sides. The most active was the elegant bearded French ambassador, making notes as he circled, ripping pages from his notebook, and sending them back to his embassy with relays of messengers. Interspersed with the diplomats were the journalists who needed to make no secret of their professional eavesdropping.

It was an astonishing spectacle, continuing for a good fifteen to twenty minutes. Central to at least part of the conversation were two sets of documents, surreptitiously distributed during the conference. Translated copies, as was evidently intended, soon fell into the hands of delegates and journalists. The first set, released by the Yugoslavs, was a series of messages to Stalin, signed by Tito and Kardelj, pleading for more help at a critical moment in their struggle against the Germans and their puppets. It included offers to integrate Yugoslavia into the Soviet Union immediately after the common victory. The second, circulated by the Russians, was replies signed by Stalin and Molotov to the appeals. They pointed out the impossibility at that moment, with the Battle of Stalingrad raging to its climax, of sending supplies. They also urged Tito to try to come to terms with the Chetnik guerrilla leader, General Draza Mihailovich (whom Tito had correctly accused of collaborating with the Nazis). Stalin and Molotov characterized the proposal of integration with the Soviet Union as "premature."

At a certain point Vishinsky and Kardelj seemed simultaneously aware that the reception room had been transformed into a diplomatic arena. The dialogue was broken off. With curt nods the two men parted, and everyone drifted back into the milling around and small talk that are routine for official receptions. It marked a fitting end to that particular foray behind the Iron Curtain.

15

Trials Behind the "Curtain"

"**Y**OUR NEWSPAPER rendered great services to Hungary in the past, and we hope you will lead again a crusade for Western, Christian civilization against Jewish Bolshevism, under which we suffer today as we did thirty years ago." It was Jozsef Cardinal Mindszenty, archbishop of Esztergom and prince primate of Hungary, who was speaking, and I wondered what on earth he was talking about. It was in the late summer of 1948, and I was interviewing him in his residence alongside the massive Esztergom Cathedral. He strode to the window of his dark study, opened it, and pointed across the broad stretch of the Danube to the lands beyond.

"All Hungarian territory," he said, "populated by Hungarian people, now subject to Communist oppression and forced to submit to Red ideology, lost to Western civilization, engulfed in the new Slav Empire. It started with the Treaty of Trianon and has ended with this—"

All of a sudden I realized that the pale young priest, Zakar, who had arranged the interview had made a mistake. I knew that he had telephoned the British Legation following my request for an interview to make sure that I was from a "respectable" British newspaper. Now either he or the cardinal had confused Lord Rothermere of the *Daily Mail* with Lord Beaverbrook of the *Daily Express*. The *Mail* lord after World War I had waged such a campaign against the dismembering of Hungary under the Treaty of Trianon that he was offered the Hungarian throne. The cardinal, I could only assume, had been told by Zakar that the Rothermere empire had sent another savior to Hungary. In fact, I had come to get his views on the way land reform had been carried out and what I thought seemed a reasonable attempt—since it was a Communist government in power—to normalize church-state relations.

It was an impossibly negative interview. The new People's Colleges, conceived as a shortcut for children of humble origin to secondary education, were "pagan" institutions. Because they were open to both sexes, they were "immoral" as well. He had ordered the faithful to keep their children away from such places and threatened to excommunicate teachers who taught in them. "The church," he explained, "alone could decide who taught, who was taught, and what was taught." As for land reform, it was "banditry pure and simple, which God will punish." When I returned to his remark about "Jewish Bolshevism," he looked at me warily, perhaps with the first twinge of doubt whether I was a Rothermere crusader after all. A few weeks earlier Bertha Gaster of the London *News Chronicle* had listened to a long tirade against the Jews and then said, "Thank you for the information. . . . May I add that I am the daughter of the rabbi of Whitechapel." The young priest was by now wringing his hands in anguish as if saying, "I've done it again." However, the cardinal knew how to handle my remark. "The Bolshevik Béla Kun after World War One was a Jew," he said. "So is the Communist Mátyás Rákosi after World War Two."

I left, after what was a quite extensive interview, amazed. Mindszenty fell far short of the intellectual stature I had expected of a cardinal. That he championed the most retrograde aspects of a feudal state, I knew, but that he would espouse such anti-Semitic views and archaic ideas on education, slamming the door on any prospects of improved church-state relations, was depressing.

I next saw him and the unfortunate András Zakar five months later charged before a People's Court in Budapest with high treason, conspiracy against the state, and black-marketeering in foreign currency. A worldwide wave of sympathy for him and indignation against the Hungarian government was generated, partly because it was assumed by the world Catholic community and millions of others that he must be innocent of such charges, partly because of the enormity of a Communist government—or any government—putting a cardinal on trial. The facts of the Mindszenty case were buried under distortions and emotional denunciations from the first day. That it was not the Catholic Church which was on trial was lost sight of in the hue and cry over the fact that a trial was taking place at all.

The essence of what it was all about was set forth in Cardinal Mindszenty's opening statement. After giving the date and place of birth and the fact that his father's name was Johann Péhm, he continued:

"I am a Hungarian nobleman. . . . The titles of nobility of the Péhm family date back to 1732. On my mother's side I am a descendant of the Hungarian noble family of Kovacs. In February 1917, I was ordained as a teacher of religion at Zalaegerszeg. In 1919, I was appointed priest of that village, and I continued in that post until March 29, 1944, the date on which I was nominated bishop of Veszprém. I was nominated prince-primate in October 1945. In political affairs I have always been a legitimist. My aim has been the creation of a Federated Kingdom of Central Europe, uniting, under the scepter of Otto of Hapsburg, the states of Hungary and Austria, in a form in which they could be joined eventually by other Catholic states, particularly Bavaria. . . ."

When Mindszenty explained that he was a "legitimist," this meant that he considered himself the legal ruler of Hungary, acting in trust for the Hapsburgs, until the 1,000-year-old Crown of St. Stephen could be placed—by him—on the head of the "legitimate heir." In Mindszenty's view this was Prince Otto von Hapsburg, living in exile in the United States. Elements within the U.S. State Department—or whatever "dirty tricks" operatives were trying to run policy in Hungary—seemed to encourage the cardinal in this fantasy.

Soon after the Communists, headed by Mátyás Rákosi, came to power in Hungary, Mindszenty handed over the historic crown to Selden Chapin, minister at the U.S. Embassy in Budapest. Chapin sent it back to the United States, where it ended up in the gold vaults of Fort Knox for the next thirty years. Not all American officials went along with such nonsense. Chapin's predecessor in Budapest, H. F. Arthur Schoenfeld, had curtly replied to three of the cardinal's letters asking for U.S. support for his conspiracies by stating that U.S. help could not be forthcoming "in altering certain conditions which your Eminence deplores" and reiterating that U.S. official policy was "non-interference in the affairs of other nations." But Schoenfeld was soon replaced by Chapin, who seems to have followed a more "active" policy.

It was Chapin who had arranged for Mindszenty to meet Otto of Hapsburg in the United States in 1947. The crux of the plot was that if a "vacuum" could be created by overthrowing the Communist government, Mindszenty could claim constitutional legality as prince primate and assume the reins of power, assured—as he seems to have believed—of immediate U.S. recognition, followed by the rest of the Western world.

Because of travel and visa difficulties, I missed the first day of the trial, but on the night of my arrival there were numerous messages from the *Express* to the effect that reports from Vienna spoke of heavy censorship and false translations and that Mindszenty was under the influence of a sinister "truth drug" called Aktedron. This accounted for the sensational revelations made by Mindszenty and Zakar on the opening day of the trial. The official Hungarian press service had itself to blame for the easy acceptance that Mindszenty had been drugged. Apparently to deflate the cardinal's image at home, their photographers concentrated on shots from angles to make him look as much like a monster as possible. In fact, when I saw Mindszenty and Zakar in court on the second day of the trial, the only two of the seven accused I had seen before, they looked as they had at Esztergom months earlier.

Before I started to dictate my account of the second day, the assistant foreign editor read me some of the fantastic accounts of the new mind-distortion drug Aktedron. It was on the front pages of most of the papers together with pictures of a punch-drunk-looking Mindszenty. "It's Hungarian Benzedrine," I replied. "After nearly three days' nonstop travel I took it myself today to keep awake in court. It's on open sale in any chemist's shop." Shortly after I dictated my dispatch, there was a call from foreign editor Charles Foley, asking for more details on Aktedron. Since I had a pack in my pocket, I dictated the enormously long chemical formula. Then he asked if I had to submit my story to censorship and if what I had written was my true opinion of the day's proceedings. I was able to assure him that I had returned to my hotel room the moment the day's session was over, placed a call to London, and within five minutes was dictating my story to the foreign desk. It was the first—and only—time that Foley had ever checked in this way, and it obviously reflected pressures on him to accept the Vienna fantasy versions. But he followed the tradition of believing the man on the spot—or sack him!

Apart from the elements of a medieval conspiracy, the trial was a historical event. Cardinal Mindszenty and Prince Paul Esterházy, the two main accused, were the supreme representatives of the feudal church and aristocracy, of everything that was most retrograde and obscurantist in the old Hungarian society. They were the two largest landowning factions, using their influence to block progress in every field. That they defied the new state power for so long was the result of their unshakable belief that the West would come to their rescue.

As a human being Esterházy was the more acceptable. Aloof and seemingly indifferent to his fate, he intervened occasionally to protect his underlings: "He only obeyed my orders as his family has always done." There was an *ancien régime* nobility in his behavior, in contrast with Mindszenty, who was glad to shift blame onto others. Asked why he had bought $15,000 in checks from Mindszenty after his 1947 visit to the United States at more than three times the official rate, Esterházy replied, "I bought them with the intention of helping the chief of the royalists, Cardinal Mindszenty. This was in my interest as a restoration of the Hapsburgs would bring me considerable material gains—in the first place, the return of my estates, which were carved up under land reform." (The reform had confiscated 280,000 acres of Esterházy's estates and about 840,000 acres from the Catholic Church.)

At the end of the six-day trial Mindszenty was sentenced to life imprisonment; Prince Esterházy got fifteen years; Zakar, found guilty of "treason and complicity with the cardinal," was given six years; the others reecived from three to fifteen years.

In view of the worldwide commotion about the trial and the charges of drugging, censorship, faked translation, and others, twenty-eight of the thirty correspondents covering the proceedings issued a statement denying the charges. Among those who signed were staff correspondents of *The Times* of

London, Reuters, Agence France-Presse, *Daily Express*, and local correspondents of the Associated Press, International News Service, the London *Daily Telegraph*, and others. Edward Korry, staff correspondent of United Press (later U.S. ambassador to Chile at the time of the anti-Allende coup), explained that UP staffers were banned from signing such statements, but he cabled the contents to his agency.

Cardinal Mindszenty was released during the uprisings in Hungary in October–November 1956 and later sought refuge in the U.S. Embassy in Budapest, where he remained for fifteen years. He was relieved of his post as primate of Hungary, by Pope Paul VI, in February 1974, thus clearing the way for a normalization of relations between the Vatican and Hungary. He died in Vienna in May 1975.

In April 1949 I transferred my base from Berlin to Budapest with a general brief to cover developments in the East European socialist world, except the Soviet Union. Unfortunately much of my activity for the next year or so was reporting on political or espionage trials. The *Express* was not the paper to be interested in the great social and economic transformations that were taking place. Reporting them did not fit in with Beaverbrook's pet criteria: "Will it go down well with the morning tea and toast?" Was ignoring what was happening on the "other side of the curtain" the best way to make it disappear? I did not think so. A case in point was the funeral of Georgi Dimitrov.

He had died in July 1949, in the Barvikha Sanatorium near Moscow, of diabetes, according to the communiqué announcing his death. His embalmed body was returned by special train to Sofia on July 6 and borne on a gun carriage through streets lined with tens of thousands of weeping people to where it was to lie in state for three days. It is the only time I have seen a city in tears, but it was the only fitting description. Dimitrov was loved and respected for himself, for what he had done and what he symbolized. But tears go ill with morning tea and toast, and my account of Dimitrov's funeral was reduced to a few lines on who was present among visiting Communist party bigwigs. I had hoped to reach across the curtain and remind readers that human emotions were universal, not atrophied by artificial barriers. For the first time in seven years there were some sharp words between Foley and me, the upshot being that I switched to writing for *The Times* (London).

For Stalin, the death of Dimitrov must have provoked mixed feelings. They had worked closely together during the stormiest years of the advance of fascism and had got on well together. But personal loyalty to devoted comrades was not one of Stalin's characteristics. His chief phobia at the time of Dimitrov's death was the development of parallel power centers. Tito had been isolated within the Communist world, and Dimitrov was now dead. A factor which newcomers like I overlooked was that a few days before

Dimitrov left for the Barvikha Sanatorium, a former secretary-general of the Bulgarian Communist party, Traicho Kostov, was removed from the Politburo and from his post as vice-premier and was made director of the National Library! The official reason was that he had pursued an "insincere and unfriendly policy toward the U.S.S.R." during trade negotiations and had displayed signs of a "nationalist deviation." Was he to be punished for Dimitrov's speech in Bucharest a few months earlier?

In October of that somber year of trials I reported on that of László Rajk, member of the Politburo of the Hungarian Communist party, former foreign minister charged with seven co-accused. My feelings on entering the court were very different from those at the Mindszenty-Esterházy trial. The latter proclaimed their sworn hostility to the new regime inside and outside the courtroom. But here were men who had sacrificed much to bring the new regime into power and to defend it. Part of the indictment made sense—that is that Tito was trying to install regimes in neighboring countries more favorable to him. A conspiracy to overthrow the Hungarian government with the aid of Yugoslavia could just make sense after the cavalier way in which old Comrade Tito had been treated.

For nine days, together with other Western journalists, I sat about twelve feet away from László Rajk and listened to his appalling story of how he had been recruited as a police spy at the age of twenty-two; of how he had infiltrated the Rákosi battalion of the International Brigade in Spain in order to betray its members. It was a long, long saga of betrayal and treason, ending with his secret meetings—when he was minister of the interior—with Tito's minister of the interior, Rankovich, to plot the overthrow of the Hungarian regime and the assassination of Mátyás Rákosi and other Hungarian Communist leaders. It all sounded incredible, beyond anything I had ever heard of, but also terribly plausible as related in easy conversational tones by a man who was obviously not under the influence of any drugs. The following is a sample of his testimony:

"During the visit I made to Yugoslavia in 1947 it became clear to me that Trotskyists occupied leading positions; that they are close to the American intelligence service; and that not only are Rankovich, Djilas, and their friends in contact with U.S. intelligence, but also Tito himself. . . . I am of the opinion that Tito was long ago recruited by the Americans and that they have evidently made use of some sort of information compromising him. . . ."

Rajk claimed that in October 1948 he had been escorted to an estate south of the capital for another secret meeting with Rankovich—on Hungarian soil:

"At this meeting, Rankovich explained the methods by which the Soviet Union was to be discredited, saying that Marshal Tito was now certain the plan could only be carried out by armed intervention. At the right time, after leaflets had been distributed and frontier incidents provoked, Hungarians from Yugoslavia, dressed in Hungarian uniforms, would cross the frontier with arms and be joined by Hungarian refugees from the western zones of Austria, transiting through Yugoslavia. All these forces would be incorporated into the Yugoslav Army. Thereafter the Hungarian government would be overthrown . . . its leaders assassinated and a new government formed. . . ."

Another of the accused, former Defense Minister General György Palffy, confirmed Rajk's account. All the accused spoke in a calm, factual way—responding intelligently to questions and in clarifying points. All were found guilty. In a statement before being sentenced, Rajk said, without any particular emotion:

"Everything I have done I did deliberately and as a result of my own resolve. To a certain extent I was influenced by international imperialism and by Tito, but their influences played only a secondary role. To a certain extent, I became the instrument of Tito and his gang. . . . I agree with what the Public Prosecutor has stated, and whatever sentence the court may pass, I shall consider just."

Not a muscle in his face moved as he was sentenced to death by hanging, as were also Dr. Tibor Szönyi, former head of the Personnel Department of the Communist party, and the latter's assistant, András Szalai. The sentences were carried out on October 15, 1949, on a gallows erected for this purpose in the courtyard of Budapest's central prison. I had no doubt of their guilt or of the inevitability of a death sentence for László Rajk, given the gravity of the activities to which he had confessed.

Less than three months after the Rajk trial I was again in Sofia, this time for the trial of Traicho Kostov and nine other former leaders of the Bulgarian Communist party and government. They were charged with plotting an armed coup to be carried out with Yugoslav support, aimed at overthrowing the regime and assassinating its leaders.

At the opening session on the morning of December 7, 1949, everything seemed like a replay of the Rajk trial. All the accused were in court, and the prosecutor started reading a 32,000-word handwritten statement by Kostov, admitting that he had plotted with the Yugoslav government to enable Tito to "absorb" Bulgaria, had betrayed state secrets, had attempted to undermine Dimitrov's leadership of the Communist party, had carried on anti-Soviet activities. . . . At that point, Kostov stood up, and to the stupefaction of all present, denied, for a start, that he had ever engaged in anti-Soviet activities and insisted that whatever negotiations he had undertaken with the Yugoslavs had been with the full knowledge of Dimitrov—and the Soviet government. He denied that he had ever betrayed members of the Communist party's Central Committee.

That was as far as he got. The presiding judge intervened: "But there is a contradiction here between your written and your oral evidence. I adjourn the court." In his own way, Kostov had done what his old comrade Georgi Dimitrov had done sixteen years earlier at the Reichstag Fire Trial. He had knocked the stuffing out of the prosecution.

Because of atrocious flying conditions the previous day, with visibility at near zero point at Sofia Airport, mine was the last plane to land, leaving other journalists stranded at Belgrade. As the only "outside" correspondent covering the trial I used the adjournment period to telephone news of Kostov's denial to the United Press in Belgrade. Within minutes the news went around the world that an accused in a political trial in Eastern Europe had gone back on his written confession.

Kostov's honesty and courage could make no difference to the conduct of the trial or its outcome, but it posed questions in everyone's minds about the methods by which such confessions were produced and the validity of the charges against Tito.

All the accused were found guilty, but before being sentenced Traicho Kostov again denied that he had ever been a police agent, an imperial spy, or had ever taken part in anti-Soviet activities. The sentences were announced on December 14: death by hanging for Kostov, life imprisonment for five others, the rest from eight to fifteen years. The sentence was carried out two days later.

Years later, a *Pravda* correspondent, Babenko, the sole journalist witness of the execution, told me that before Kostov mounted the scaffold, he took off his glasses, handed them to a member of the commission which verified political executions and quietly said: "Give them to 'Bay' Vassil Kolarov. Tell him I die an innocent man." (Kolarov, a lifelong friend and intimate aide of Georgi Dimitrov, had succeeded him as prime minister and general secretary of the Communist party. "Bay" is a respectfully-affectionate equivalent for "uncle" for an admired elder.)

Within a month of Kostov's execution, Kolarov suddenly died—at the age of 72. Next to Dimitrov, he was the country's most popular figure. There were again very emotional scenes during the funeral ceremonies, but friends assured me that a proportion of the tears shed were also for Traicho Kostov. Of immense popularity and a much younger man, he would have been the natural successor to Dimitrov and Kolarov.

I was considerably shaken by the Kostov trial, although it was still possible to believe that, in the tradition of Balkan politics, Tito was doing his best to bring down the leadership which had outlawed him. If Kostov's whole confession was false, what of those of Rajk and the others. On the other hand what madness had seized those who destroyed cadres of the level of those in the Rajk and Kostov trials unless they really represented a threat to the socialist regimes. These were questions which plagued me long after Rajk, Kostov, and the others were posthumously rehabilitated. It was not until a quarter of a century later that I came across a book by Stewart Steven, assistant editor of the *Daily Mail* (London) when he wrote it, which seems to provide the missing link between what happened before the eyes of scores of experienced journalists and the unsatisfactory, official *post facto* explanations.* I was so impressed by certain chapters that I immediately phoned him to ask if he still stood by what he had written. He replied that every new scrap of information acquired on the subject during the more than six years that had elapsed only confirmed what he had written. The astonishing thesis which he defends with a wealth of detail is that although the master hand which ordered and directed the trials was Joseph Stalin, aided and abetted by his diabolical security chief, Lavrenti Beria, an important support role was played by Allen Dulles, then chief of the C.I.A. In a brief introduction, he concedes the weak point in such a book:

> I have employed all of the journalistic techniques I know in establishing the material, operating in an area where facts are spread thinly over a ground covered with half-truths and lies. Necessarily I have had to rely on verbal evidence; documents and files are simply not available. If we believe that contemporary history must be told on the basis of documentary evidence, then we must also accept that everything will either be written with the government's seal of approval or not be written at all. We certainly would have to accept that no book about modern intelligence operations should ever be attempted for no files worth having will ever be disclosed. It is a situation with which I'm accustomed.†

On a related subject, I once asked a highly placed colleague in Rumania why there had been no political show trials in Bucharest, similar to those in Budapest, Sofia, and Prague. His astonishing reply, given in the strictest confidence, was that there had been a serious attempt at one, in which Gheorghe Gheorghiu-Dej, who headed the country's Communist party (and was successively prime minister and president), was to be the chief victim. He had rejected pressures in 1949 to adopt a scenario in which some of his immediate subordinates would come to trial as pro-Tito plotters, but he did carry out a massive purge within the Communist party. But this was no contribution to the outlawing of Tito, so Gheorghiu-Dej and some of his closest colleagues were marked down for elimination. In the spring of 1952, some six months after the Slansky trial, the dreaded head of Stalin's secret police, Lavrenti Beria, arrived secretly in Bucharest to present the scenario for Gheorghiu-Dej's downfall to Ana Pauker and two other top party leaders. Gheorghiu-Dej got wind of it, arrested Pauker and the others, and ordered Beria out of the country immediately—or else. . . .

---

* Stewart Steven, *Operation Splinter Factor*, (Philadelphia and New York: J. B. Lippincott Company, 1974).
† *Ibid.*, p. 10.

How could a Western journalist check out the account? Discreet inquiries in Bucharest and Moscow were met with blank looks and tight lips. The only evidence that "something" went on was that Ana Pauker and two other Politburo members were expelled in May 1952, and Gheorghiu-Dej took over the premiership of the country a month later.

The essence of the narrative part of Stewart Steven's book, which in most cases uses real names, is that in 1947 Captain Michael Sullivan, head of British SIS (Secret Intelligence Service) in Poland, was contacted by a Lieutenant Coloned Jozef Swiatlo, then deputy chief of Department 10 of the Bezpieka (Polish Secret Police), which, controlled directly by Beria, spied on Polish Communist and government leaders. For personal reasons, which Steven gives in detail, Swiatlo wanted to defect. The British were not then interested but passed the offer on to the CIA, where it was brought to the attention of Allen Dulles. Set up only in 1947, the CIA had no agents worthy of the name in Eastern Europe.

Dulles sent one of his top men to contact Swiatlo to arrange a salary, working instructions—to continue exactly what he was doing—method of contact, and arrangements to lift him out of the country if things got too "hot." As if a direct pipeline to Beria over the heads of the Polish Communist party were not enough, Dulles had a second incredible piece of luck. An American, Noel Field, turned up in Warsaw and was on first-name terms with most of the members of the Communist party's Politburo, especially with Swiatlo's personal enemy, Jakub Berman, in charge of party affairs. Swiatlo queried Dulles whether he should denounce Berman to Beria for "actively collaborating with the American agent Noel Field." (He had to check with Dulles in case Field really was an American agent.) Dulles could hardly believe his luck.

When Allen Dulles was running the cloak-and-dagger OSS (Office of Strategic Services) in Switzerland during World War II, Field, a former State Department official, was European director of the United Services Relief Organization. He was a good source of information and passed on to Dulles that which he considered useful in the fight against the Axis powers. At one point Field sold Dulles on a scheme to parachute former International Brigaders back into their own countries and finance them to work to overthrow the Axis powers from within. After all, they had proved themselves militant and competent antifascists. Field sent back into what were to become the People's Democracies hundreds of Communists who later turned up in key positions ". . . able to get their hands on the reins of power long before the non-Communist democratic forces were able to regroup and organize themselves." *

Dulles, as his European counterparts later loved to rub in, had been

---

* *Ibid.*, p. 86.

duped by a well-known Communist. And there was Field in Warsaw and Swiatlo asking Dulles how to dispose of him. As if that were not enough, Berman's secretary, Anna Duracz, had been Noel Field's secretary in Switzerland. She agreed to transmit a letter from Field to Berman asking him to facilitate contacts with Russians that could be "helpful" and said she would vouch for him with Berman, as she did. A copy of the letter fell into Swiatlo's hands. In the spy neurosis atmosphere of Eastern Europe at that time, Swiatlo could use the letter to compromise both Berman and Field.

Anna Duracz advised Field to return to Geneva and wind up his affairs there while awaiting word to come to Warsaw. This he did, leaving behind in Prague a suitcase full of books and other belongings. While Swiatlo was awaiting a reply from Dulles, the latter, according to Steven, was quarreling with other CIA executives, who wanted Swiatlo to be activated in the classical work of a top-level agent, reporting on military and political affairs, on Communist leaders open to Western influence, and so on.

> Dulles brutally brushed aside the notion of some Western diplomatists that nationalist Communists should be given every support, diplomatic and otherwise, representing, as they did, the best hope for restoring some Western influence behind the Iron Curtain. Instead he believed that Communism could be shown for what it was only through the unrestrained practise of Stalinism. . . . Surely all that was holding the French and Italian workers back from voting the Communists into power in their countries was the realization among a majority that a vote for communism was a vote for the Russians. . . .*

Dulles imposed his concept, and Swiatlo was instructed to continue doing the work for which his Polish and Soviet masters paid him: find spies, U.S. agents, Trotskyists everywhere—prove that Titoism was rampant in all the countries of Eastern Europe.

> He would report to Beria himself that the center of that conspiracy, the link man between these traitors and Washington, was a man named Noel Haviland Field, who, Beria was to be told, was the most important American intelligence man in Eastern and Western Europe. . . . He would show, in short, that Noel Field was bent upon the destruction of the entire Soviet bloc and that, moreover, he was perilously close to achieving his aim.
>   . . . Swiatlo did as he was bid, and a report went forward to the Russians, both locally and in Moscow.†

Machinery was set in motion to ensure that Soviet agents got the idea of a super-American agent at large on a monstrous softening-up mission as

---

* *Ibid.*, p. 98.
† *Ibid.*, p. 99.

part of Truman's rollback policy. Dulles made sure that confirmatory bits of information were dropped everywhere. While Field was in Geneva, he got a call from the prestigious Charles University in Prague, offering him a lectureship. He left on May 9 for Prague and booked in at the Palace Hotel, where he was picked up two days later by agents of the Hungarian secret police, who whisked him off to Budapest. Then started the interminable interrogations which paved the way for the Rajk trial.

How could he deny that he had once worked for the State Department; that he had had contacts with Dulles in Geneva, who had paid him large sums for smuggling "selected" Communists back into their home countries; that Yugoslav Communists had been prominent in all the relief camps he ran; that he had once been an intermediary between Tito and the Americans? Within Field's rich experiences were all the necessary ingredients to embellish any scenario the trial fakers intended to stage.

The raw material extracted from Noel Field and passed on to Stalin, via Swiatlo and Beria, led to the physical or political liquidation of scores of leading Communists, especially in Hungary, Bulgaria, and Czechoslovakia. Field's name cropped up several times during the Rajk trial but never attracted much attention. But in the trial of Rudolf Slansky and thirteen other accused, which opened in Prague on November 20, 1952, the accused were often referred to as Fieldists. (Of the fourteen accused at the Slansky trial, by which time I was far away in Korea, eleven were executed.) All of them were loyal Communists, whose devotion to their party, their country, and internationalism had been well tested. They were well equipped to build and maintain a bridge with the West. It was precisely for this that Dulles and Stalin decreed between them—without Stalin's ever knowing that he was a dupe of Dulles—that they be liquidated.

Swiatlo was "lifted out" of Poland two days before Beria was executed. Noel Field and his wife, Nora—arrested while trying to find him—were freed in Budapest in November 1954 and were each paid $40,000 compensation for the years in jail. Noel's brother Hermann, arrested while trying to track his brother down in Warsaw, was released about the same time and also paid $40,000 compensation.

A valid, but not decisive, objection to Stewart Steven's account is that Stalin's paranoia was so great that he did not need any outside help in concocting evidence for the show trials and executions which followed. This is probably true, but it is equally true that the international intelligence community spends great time and effort trying to discover weak points in those they wish to entrap or manipulate. The discovery that the target is a drug addict, a homosexual, an alcoholic, is betraying his wife is a factor to be worked on and exploited. It would be naïve to think that the immense possibilities of feeding Stalin's paranoia would be overlooked by an operator like Dulles when such incredibly rich fare fell into his hands.

16

---◀◆▶▶---

Into Mao's China

ARLY ON THE MORNING of June 26, 1950, the doorbell rang at my Budapest apartment. To my surprise it was the daughter of my landlord, a former chief of staff of Admiral Miklós Horthy de Nagybánya's fascist army. After apologies for disturbing me so early, she said, "Father wants to know when we can have the flat back." I pointed out that we had renewed the contract only two weeks previously. "But now everything's changed," she said. "We want to come back to Budapest immediately. Father says he will refund the money and pay you compensation." To my polite inquiry as to what had changed, she exclaimed, "You who are so well informed! You don't know the war has started? Father expects the Americans to be here in a matter of days and feels he should be on hand to greet them."

Thus, I learned that fighting had broken out in a faraway place called Korea. With the time difference, it had been going on for twelve hours, but I had happened not to listen to the news the previous evening. After assuring my visitor that there would be no Americans "in a matter of days," that I would not be abandoning the flat, but that her father was welcome to come to talk things over, I got rid of her.

Later, strolling over to the office of Agence France-Presse, I was astonished to see the outdoor café of the Bristol (now Duna) Hotel crowded with a clientele rarely seen in Budapest those days. From their polished black legging boots to the cockades in their tweed hats, they were cronies of my landlord and his brother officers, who had sallied forth from their villas on the banks of Lake Balaton. They were obviously discussing the "great news," many with maps spread out on the café tables.

AFP correspondent Georges Heuzé was not yet in, but his elegant Hungarian secretary was. Just as excited as the landlord's daughter, she also had a map out and said, "It's a matter of hours." She was crestfallen when I ex-

151

plained that it was in distant Korea, not Corfu, that the fighting was taking place. This was the state of mind induced by Radio Free Europe which hammered away implicitly on the theme "Get the fighting started—anywhere—and the Free World forces will be at your side." The dispossessed aristocrats and pensioned-off colonels lived in a dreamworld, drinking in every word from Radio Free Europe, heavily staffed with Hungarians, under the direction of a longtime CIA operator, "Captain Bell" (Ladislas Farago to those who knew him).

A couple of weeks earlier I had visited my landlord in his splendid Balaton villa to renew the lease on my apartment. His study walls were covered with illustrations of aircraft carriers, new types of tanks, artillery, and other weapons. Pride of place was given to an artist's concept of an enormous airborne aircraft carrier, with dozens of planes roaring out of the monster's main body. The general asked if I had seen one, and when I said I had not because it did not exist, he smiled and said, "Ah, it's still on the secret list." When I mentioned that I had spent some time on U.S. aircraft carriers during World War II, he pressed me to stay to dine and meet a "few friends."

These turned out to be a dozen counts, generals, and colonels—some with their wives—addressing each other by ranks and titles, with many bows and kissing of hands. After warming up with *barack palinka* (apricot brandy), we sat down at a candlelit table gleaming with silver and crystal. Of the gastronomic part, I remember only the fogas, a trout type of fish caught only in Lake Balaton—rare to find in a Budapest restaurant—accompanied by a vintage Badacsyöni white wine, then roast pheasant, with some unlabeled, but excellent, light red wine. After that I recall only the alacrity with which the males retired to the general's study for coffee and cognac and my tales of World War II. What interested them most were the fantasy-type stories: a night fighter taking off into the blackness from an aircraft carrier, guided to its target by radar; the Japanese kamikaze suicide pilots, diving down through red snowstorms of antiaircraft fire, virtually sitting on a bomb and guiding it to its target or blowing themselves up in the sea if they missed; the sinking of the Japanese fleet in the great Battle of the Philippine Sea. The eyes of those dispossessed nobles shone with hope as I described the island-hopping operations which inexorably led the attackers to their final target. Of the climax at Hiroshima, it was not the sufferings of the victims that impressed them or the implications in case of a third world war, but the enormous destructive power of the A-bomb, then exclusively in American hands.

There was excited chatter when it was all over. Invitations were extended to other dinners at other noble tables. It was obvious that I could dine off war tales in the Lake Balaton villas for months—but once sufficed!

With the UN forces, including those of Britain, involved in the Korean

War, it was difficult to publish anything from Eastern Europe, even in *The Times* (London), which had been far more open to reports on economic and social developments than the *Express*. Suspicions about foreigners, engendered by the Rajk and Kostov trials, were going to make contacts more difficult—and could be dangerous for good friends—so perhaps it was time to think of fresh pastures.

From the day that Mao Tse-tung had proclaimed the setting up of the Chinese People's Republic (October 1, 1949) I had been trying to establish contact with friends there with a view to making a visit. Eventually word had come back from an American journalist friend, Betty Graham. She had reported the final phases of the fighting prior to Mao's takeover in Peking from the Communist side and assured me that old friends—by then in high places—had not forgotten me. The best way in would be by contacting the China Travel Service in Hong Kong. (On January 6, 1950, braving strong opposition from the United States, the British government recognized that of Peking. Since I held a British passport, this would facilitate matters in Hong Kong.)

In the meantime, I had been invited to make a lecture tour in Australia, which I had not visited for five years. But a personal problem was keeping me in Budapest, a problem I shared with my Bulgarian wife, Vesselina Ossikovska, since we married in Sofia on Christmas Eve 1949. Many years of separation from my first wife, Erna, had led to our divorce early in 1948. Vesselina and I had met during my first Sofia visit in the early summer of 1948 and we formed a friendship which deepened during each of my subsequent visits. Her family had been among Bulgaria's first socialists, and she had been an activist of the antifascist youth movement in Bulgaria and later of the resistance struggle in Italy, where she completed doctorates in literature and the history of art at the ancient University of Padua. When we met, Vessa was working in the Press Department of the Ministry of Foreign Affairs, awaiting a posting as a correspondent abroad, for which her journalist's training and expertise in four European languages other than her own qualified her. Our common interests and tastes were multifold, and we seriously contemplated marriage.

The Kostov trial was a catalyst in deciding our future. With the spy psychosis at its height and strong overtones of Western involvement, it was the worst time to contemplate an East-West marriage. It was equally true that it was a now or never situation. We decided to opt for "now" with no illusions as to difficulties ahead. They were more serious than we could have expected, aggravated by some information or opinions given that I was a British intelligence agent (an allegation I learned of only ten years later). Vessa was not permitted to leave the country, and my visa was not extended, so I had to leave, and having returned to Budapest, I was not allowed back in Bulgaria. It was during this waiting period that the invitation from

Australia arrived. After numerous discussions—fortunately the Budapest–
Sofia telephone link worked well—we decided there was no point in my remaining in Budapest since there would be no speedy decision in her case.
Thus, I informed *The Times* that it was about to lose its Budapest correspondent and flew back to Melbourne.

At that time—early 1951—it was considered rather disloyal for an Australian
even to contemplate going to "Red China." As far as the Australia of Robert
Menzies was concerned, People's China was an "outcast" and Australian passports were stamped "Not Valid for Red China." Fortunately I had taken the
precaution of getting a new British passport before leaving Budapest, specially
endorsed as valid for travel to the China of Mao Tse-tung.

After four months of writing and lecturing in Australia, I flew off to
Hong Kong and contacted the China Travel Service, a dingy one-room office
in those days, with two bright young men who immediately understood my
needs. It would take about two weeks to get a reply from Peking. In just
two weeks I was told to take the train to the frontier the following day.

It happened to be the day when the Year of the Tiger gave way to the
Year of the Hare, and the streets to the Kowloon railway station were littered
with debris and burst tubes of millions of firecrackers. The paper I read, as
the train pulled out of the station toward the frontier, quoted Kuomintang
soothsayers as interpreting the year's-end signs and portents as meaning that
the Year of the Hare would be the year of World War III.

Passengers got out of the train on the Kowloon side of the border and,
after British passport and customs controls, walked with their baggage a few
hundred yards to Shumchun on the Chinese side. An Indian officer, with
chrome "Palestine Police" shoulder plates, took my passport, looked at the
name, and started moving swiftly up a slope to a galvanized-iron hut, with me
in pursuit. "The said person has arrived, sir," he was shouting into a telephone
as I caught up with him, and started dictating details of my passport.

Grabbing passport and telephone out of his hands, I asked for an explanation of such conduct. "This is a British passport, endorsed for China, and I
am a journalist on professional assignment," I said in my best *Times* voice.
There were some mumbles about routine controls to ensure the safety of
British nationals, and I was asked to hand the phone back to the security
officer. There was no further trouble, and I walked across the border where
smiling China Travel Service agents took charge of me and my baggage.

Remembering the chaos and filth of China's railways in the past, I found
it impossible not to be impressed by the smoothness of the journey from
Shumchun to Canton. Every ticket had a seat number on it, so there was
no crush or standing. In the old days, even far from the war zones, people
had hurled their baggage in through the windows and clambered in after it.
Each conductor had had an allotment of seat tickets for which he had paid
squeeze to the next highest authority, recovering his investment with in-

terest as he auctioned the tickets to the highest bidders. Compartments had always been thick with coal dust, floors littered with filth, toilets had never worked, nor had there ever been water for washing.

The train to Canton was spotlessly clean. Instead of looking for bribes, the attendants looked after aged people or mothers with babies. If passengers threw peanut shells on the floor, they were gently reproved and shown a large notice asking passengers not to spit or litter the floor. A show train, I thought, to make a good first impression. But the Canton–Peking train was even better, and I was later to find service and cleanliness were equally high everywhere aboard new China's trains.

The Peking-bound compartment was spotlessly clean, and corridors were swabbed down every two hours. Tea, coffee, cocoa, and hot milk were served in the compartment, and excellent meals in the dining car. Beer in one's glass was scarcely ruffled as the train glided along at a steady fifty miles per hour. Freshly built bridges and stone embankments, neat station buildings, and the friendly, efficient service all pointed to something new indeed in Mao's China. It was a first impression but remained valid for most other things I was to see.

My first telephone call after settling into a modest hotel in Peking was to the Hsinhua news agency, the number that Betty Graham had given in her letter six months earlier. There was confusion when I asked to speak with her. After explaining who I was and where, I was told that someone would immediately come to see me. Betty had committed suicide the previous day, and I was invited to the funeral!

She had been very depressed since the death—also by suicide—of one of her closest friends, the American writer Agnes Smedley. Next to Edgar Snow's works, Agnes Smedley's books, *Battle Hymn of China*, *The Great Road*, and others, had done most to popularize the Chinese Revolution. Having been denounced from General MacArthur's Tokyo headquarters early in 1949 as a "Soviet spy," Agnes Smedley found life had become impossible for her in the United States, and she had moved to London, where she took her own life. Betty had been preparing to return home but had second thoughts in view of Joseph McCarthy's denunciations of all associated in his sick mind with the "loss" of China. Betty Graham's front-line reports of Communist battlefield victories in the New York *Herald Tribune* had doubtless won her an honored place on his hate list. To cap it all, a love affair with a Western journalist had just ended in disaster.

At the funeral there were numerous old friends from the Chungking days —including Kung P'eng, Yang Kang, Chiao Kuan-hua, and others of Chou En-lai's entourage. Several of her intimate friends were convinced that part of the reason for her fatal depression was her belief that it would be impossible to publish anything valid about China when she returned. Also, as a good progressive—but definitely non-Communist American—she was shocked and humiliated that her image of a decent, liberal United States, of which she was very proud, could have been submerged under the filth of McCarthyism. She had actually packed her trunks for departure via Hong Kong when the news came—while I was still in Hong Kong—that under United States pressure the UN General Assembly had condemned China as an "aggressor" in the Korean War.

My own intention was to stay in China for about three months to gather material for articles and a book about what was going on in Chairman Mao's China, after which I would return to Australia. Confident letters from Sofia hinted that Vessa's problems were on the way to being settled.

In typical style, Mao was tackling simultaneously all the great scourges and evils which had symbolized China's backwardness from the times when its gates were first opened to foreign visitors. Floods, warlordism, landlordism, illiteracy, disease, the feudal status of women—all were being attacked on a broad front. As far back as history records and legends relate, the greatest and most constant scourges have been the recurring cycles of flood and drought. Of the great waterways the Huang Ho (Yellow River) and the Huai had been the greatest offenders. But in the years immediately preceding Mao's victory, the Huai easily outstripped the Huang as the country's greatest troublemaker. If the people called the Huang Ho the River of Sorrows, however, it was because historically it had been the source of most of the sorrows as far as floods were concerned. It was not only nature, however, that took a hand in flood making. Invaders and warring dynasties played their parts. The Huai is a case in point.

For about 3,000 years, it had been a relatively respectable river, flowing steadily east toward the sea, its water level well below that of the surrounding fields. Then politics took a hand. In 1194 the Chins—of Manchu origin —were exerting pressure on the reigning Sung dynasty, while the Chins themselves were having problems with the Mongols farther north. It was a year of heavy rains, and there was danger that the Yellow River, China's northern frontier at the time, would breach its banks. The Sung government rushed tens of thousands of peasant workers to the danger point at Yun Yu, where the mighty river changes its north-south direction, at the Yellow River Bend, and heads due east toward the sea. The Chins saw the flood potential as an unexpected and unbeatable ally to keep the Sung busy in the south, while they beat off the Mongols to the north. They attacked and drove away the repair workers, and the turbulent Huang Ho breached its banks and poured across the North China plains, taking over the myriad tributaries of the Huai, finally expelling that river from its own bed and taking its place.

Heavy with the yellow sands of Mongolia, the Huang Ho started fouling up the bed of the Huai until the old way to the sea was completely blocked. With nowhere else to go, the surplus waters spilled out to form a series of lakes. Seven centuries later the Huang Ho had so fouled up the middle and lower reaches of the Huai that it was forced to make its way north again via the original Huai tributaries to settle back in its own bed. The Huai returned to a bed which was so silted up that the water level was almost as high as the surrounding countryside, even in normal years. At the slightest flooding it spilled out of its normal course to form a series of shallow lakes on its way to the hospitable Yangtze. Each of these changes of beds was at the cost of millions of lives.

Kuomintang military strategies also played havoc with the Huang Ho. In June 1938 Chiang Kai-shek thought that by diverting the Yellow River waters south again, he could block the advancing Japanese armies while he continued to deal with the Communists. So a breach was blown in the dikes at a point in the Yellow River Bend. Local people who rushed to try to plug the breach were driven off by machine-gun fire. Half a million people, including many of Chiang's own soldiers, were estimated to have drowned in the first twenty-four hours, and another 6 million made homeless. Once again the floodwaters made for the Huai, silting up the middle and lower reaches and raising the water level above that of the surrounding countryside so that restraining dikes had to be built. In 1946 and 1947 U.S. engineers plugged the Yellow River Bend breach to facilitate another unsuccessful Kuomintang offensive against Mao's armies south of the river. But the Huang Ho was at least tucked into its own bed again.

So much for the politics of floods, explained by General Fu Tso-yi, one of Chiang Kai-shek's crack generals, who was made minister of water conservation by Mao as a reward for having surrendered Peking in January 1949 without a shot fired.

The overall plan to tame the Huai, was in three parts: a system of reservoirs in the mountains to control the rate at which the waters rushed toward the middle reaches; smaller reservoirs, dams, and slowdown traps in the middle reaches, combined with gouging out deeper channels in the tributaries and a system of locks and sluice gates to slow down floodwaters rushing to the sea; the building of a new outlet to the sea in the lower reaches and the strengthening of dike walls in those regions. The project would involve shifting twice as much earth as in the building of the Suez Canal.

The work sites provided an awesome demonstration of what can be done by human hands. The first was at Suihsien in North Anhwei Province, where the Sui River, one of the Huai's most important tributaries, had gone on a terrible rampage the previous year, flooding more than 3 million acres of rice-growing land. Work was going on to cut a 21-mile channel to divert the Sui away from the Huai into a lake, as well as to deepen one 110-mile stretch of the river.

From the top of a high dike wall, as far as the eye could see in all directions, were thousands of black and blue dots, digging, carrying, ramming, singing and chanting as they worked. It was tempting to describe them as "human ants" until one got among them and discovered that each had passionately moving tales to tell of families broken up and farms lost in the flood-drought cycles, of the miseries of living under the landlords. Those I was among were digging the last 7-mile section of the main channel, 150 feet wide at the bottom, 660 feet wide at the top, 12 feet down, both banks topped by 15-foot-high dike walls. There were no ditchdiggers or bulldozers —all was done by hoes and hands with little wicker baskets to carry the earth.

Much of the work was done by teams, those doing the ramming being the most spectacular. They stood in groups of ten or twelve around a 250-pound stone, leaning back on ropes which sent it soaring into the air to thud down on the earth as they bowed forward. Back and forward they leaned and bowed, chanting in unison as the huge stone rose and fell and the dike walls were compacted into a solid waterproof mass. The carriers jog-trotted from the channel bed up to the dike bank, each with two baskets of earth swinging from the ends of a shoulder pole, also chanting so their steps would be coordinated with those in front and behind, so closely did each follow behind the other.

"Would it not be more economic to introduce a few laborsaving machines?" I asked engineer Chang Tso-ying. "Pumps, for instance," I said, pointing to bucket brigades and hand-operated water wheels emptying water from the bottom of the new channel.

"We had a few five-and-a-half-horsepower diesel-operated pumps," he said, "but we abandoned them as too costly. For what it costs to shift one cubic meter by diesel pump, we could shift twenty-two with water wheels and fourteen with buckets. It was better to give the money to the peasants than spend it on imported fuel." Financing, he explained, was calculated in terms of rice, not money. The whole investment was in the tens of thousand tons of rice needed to feed the 3 million movers of earth and stone on the overall project.

In the evenings there were literacy classes, the peasant workers laboriously copying an ideograph or two under the tutorship of someone who had mastered twenty or thirty at special on-site courses given by those who knew several hundred and were adding to them rapidly. The flood-control project was a microcosm of everything that was going on in the new China, part of which was taking place before the eyes and under the skilled, work-roughened hands of the flood-control workers. It was not only the shoulder poles and stone rammers that were in movement. Wang Feng-wu, the local county commissioner, stressed another aspect:

"You can see a peasant's outlook changing from day to day. . . . A peasant comes to the river-control work initially to earn some relief grain to feed himself and send some back to his family. At most he accepts the idea that he is working to stop floods in his own village or country, to protect land that will be his, after land reform. He expects to mark out a piece of ground, dig it, and carry it away, measuring to the last cubic centimeter how much he has cut and carried during the working day, and get paid accordingly. Instead, he finds it more convenient to work in a team, and if he is on ramming work, he can work only in a team. He gets the first notions of cooperative labor. He starts exchanging ideas with others and attends meetings where peasants from other villages and even other districts tell of their past sufferings from floods. He feels he is part of a bigger thing —working to save the whole district. Part of the family concept is extended to include his workmates.

"He goes to lectures where the cause of floods is explained with simple charts of the river, its tributaries, and other work sites. He sees his own village and where he is working in relation to the whole vast scheme, with work sites hundreds of miles apart where other peasants like him are building dams to prevent floodwaters from rushing down to his village and county.

". . . he begins to think of the village as well as the family, the district as well as his village, the county and region, and eventually the concept of China. An abstract concept becomes real.

"The only reason he can leave his village to work on river control is that there is organization at home. His wife, children, and aged father have got together with other wives, children, and parents to get the work done. Where there has already been land reform, or they are smallholders, they plow the land, sow the crops, and reap the harvest together, pooling animals and plows if necessary. Here on the riverfront and at home in the villages, the first steps are being taken in cooperative work. They will never fully return to their individualistic ways. Not only are we taming nature here on the Huai, but we are changing human nature as well."

The enormous scale of the work could be appreciated at Shih Man Tan, where most of the streams which made up the Huai originated in the rugged mountains of Honan. One of ten reservoirs was being built there, plus twenty-two weirs and dams. Six hundred thousand peasants were at work, dam building, widening existing river channels, and strengthening dikes.

The Hung, which the new reservoir was intended to bottle up, was in a surly mood. There had been unseasonal rains a few days earlier, and in a last-minute effort to escape encirclement, the river tore through the restraining earthworks in five places, washing away ten days' labor of the 20,000 workers on that particular section. But 10,000 reinforcements were on their way, and the engineers were confident that the reservoir would be finished before the real flood season started.

The main work was to build a sixty-foot-high dam between two red quartz mountains. The only nonmanual aid was locally made black powder for blasting. Eleven hundred quarry workers and miners were attacking the mountains with sledgehammers and cold chisels. The water which, in a few months, would flow through the tunnel would be diverted into channels to irrigate 3,000 acres of land in the first phase and 16,000 acres in the second phase of the project, to be completed the following year. But within a few weeks 10,000 acres of valuable grain lands on each side of the Hung, normally flooded every year, would have complete protection.

Among the recurrent great surprises of a trip to Jen Ho Chih in the spring of 1951, was to find that the engineer in charge of the most ambitious section of the overall project was a striking young woman, Chien Cheng-ying, all of twenty-nine. Articulate and competent at explaining the complexities of the Jen Ho Chih works, she blushed like a schoolgirl in talking about herself. It was false modesty. A quarter of a century later, at China's Fourth National Congress, Chien Cheng-ying was elected minister of water conservancy and power. She was reelected to that position at the Fifth National Congress (November 1977–February 1978).

Her father had been graduated in the United States as a hydraulic engineer, returning full of enthusiasm to work on flood control. But "The Kuomintang only played at it, grabbing extra taxes at every flood, but doing no real work." He became disillusioned and went into building construction in Shanghai. "My childhood games were clambering over the scaffolding of my father's building projects. He was not against my studying engineering, although this was very rare for girls, but he warned me to stay away from hydraulic engineering. 'You'll never get a job, and if you do, you'll never get any work.' " But she did study and was tops in her engineering faculty at Shanghai University. Six months before graduation she ran away from Shanghai—by then occupied by the Japanese—and joined the Communist New Fourth Army.

"I thought I had given up engineering work forever to become a revolutionary." But although the New Fourth was engaged in a life-and-death struggle for survival, it still carried on some flood-prevention works. In her years with the New Fourth she helped destroy highways and bridges; later she helped repair and rebuild them when the fortunes of war changed. Her most famous exploit, as her prompters insisted on extracting from her, was near the mouth of the Yellow River in February 1948. An enormous ice dam had been formed, causing ice and water to back up and spread over several counties. It threatened a catastrophe of major proportions. The twenty-six-year-old engineering student, together with the unit demolitions expert, drilled through the ice and poked clusters of explosive-filled brandy bottles under it over a sizable area. Linked together with fuses and electrically detonated, the bottles tore a big hole in the center of the jam through which the warmer waters at the bottom started gushing up to melt the ice. The whole mass began breaking up and moving toward the sea as the two workers raced across the disintegrating floes to safety. (Later on captured Kuomintang planes were used to bomb such jams, but Chien Cheng-ying was credited with having initiated the idea.)

She had been enjoying a well-earned rest in Shanghai when the call went out for the Huai project. She plunged again into the immensity and crucial importance of what was being done on the Huai project in general and at Jen Ho Chih in particular. She summed it all up in political terms:

"In the past such a project was simply inconceivable. . . . Under the Kuomintang, it was not only impossible to carry out such a project, but even to draw up such plans. The region through which the Huai flows was ruled by warlords, landlords, bureaucratic capitalists, and other despots. . . . Jen Ho Chih was so infested with bandits that we couldn't even dare set foot in such a place—let alone survey it. If we got so far as to drive pegs into the ground, we would certainly go no further. Landlords would complain we were going to expropriate their land, money would change hands, and the matter would be finished. That's what disgusted my father. . . ."

The passion and conviction with which engineer Chien expressed herself symbolized the ardor with which, I was later to find, many intellectuals from well-to-do families identified themselves with the Chinese Revolution (but were poorly repaid in what was termed the Great Proletarian Cultural Revolution).

If I have written much about the Huai River project, it is not only because it was my first and biggest impression of the mighty transformations that were going on in Mao's China, but also because so many of the problems and their solutions were concentrated there. During the next quarter of a century I was to visit many more great work projects in China, but none made the same impact.

Within about six months, after traveling widely and delving deep, I had collected enough material to write a book, apologizing in the introduction for my haste: "because there is as yet no other available record of contemporary developments." * As I was about to leave for Australia with the manuscript, a telegram arrived from the foreign editor of *Ce Soir* (a Paris evening paper linked to the French Communist party). Could I possibly go to Korea, where there were to be negotiations for a cease-fire? Kung P'eng, who headed the Press Department of the Foreign Ministry, agreed that my accreditation could cover the activities of its delegation to the negotiations. Moreover, her husband, my old friend Chiao Kuan-hua, by then also heading a department at the Foreign Ministry, would be a member of that delegation. When I asked him how long the talks might last, he typically wrinkled his nose and blinked his eyes for a few seconds, then said, "I would say about three weeks. Take the minimum of gear, for we must travel very light." Those "three weeks" turned into two and a half of the longest years of my life.

---

* Wilfred Burchett, *China's Feet Unbound* (Melbourne: World Unity Publications, 1952), p. vii.

17

Press War in Korea

I<small>T WAS A BEAUTIFUL</small> midsummer evening on July 13, 1951, when we crossed the much-battered bridge over the Yalu linking Antung on the Chinese side with Sinuiju on the Korean. Sitting on our baggage and sacks of rice in an open Molotova truck were some Chinese journalists and photographers, Alan Winnington of the British Communist party's *Daily Worker*, and I. The mild air and afterglow of a richly colored sunset diverted thoughts from the fact that we were heading for war, a reality which was abruptly obvious as we drove through what U.S. bombers had left of the town of Sinuiju. There were wrecks of passenger and freight cars piled up alongside the railway line. Sinuiju, a city of 200,000, was in ruins, and roadside villages south of it were reduced to a few shells of houses and black patches where others had stood. We were heading for Pyongyang, the North Korean capital, and on to Kaesong, where the cease-fire talks were to start within a few days. First surprise was the number of bridges still intact on that single north-south road which crossed and recrossed dozens of rivers and streams and had been the target, for more than a year, of the world's most powerful air force. Another impression, as night fell and the stars came out, was the simple and effective air-raid warning system. Sentries were spaced one kilometer apart along the length of the road. Each fired a single shot when his ears picked up the approach of a plane. Truck headlights were immediately doused. As soon as the planes were out of hearing range, whistles were blown, and on went the lights again. The convoys hardly slackened speed whether it was shot or whistle. On that first night we passed long columns of rubber-tired carts hauling artillery pieces, their drivers controlling teams of six to eight horses without reins, but with flicks or cracks of their long whips. When planes were announced, they wheeled off the road and became part of the scenery.

We passed what was left of the night after reaching the outskirts of Pyongyang in a small pine grove, sleep made impossible by the fearful din of exploding bombs in the routine nightly bombing of the area around Pyongyang's railway station. After each stick of bombs was dropped, there was a moment of total silence, broken by the jaunty hoot of a locomotive, followed by others in a chorus of "I'm all right, too." Resting up in relative peace and quiet the following day, we were amused to hear some radio reports to the effect that the "Communist press" was on its way and was expected to have strict instructions to avoid any contaminating contact with that of the Free World.

The most dangerous section of the road was a long, straight stretch just south of Pyongyang. We had got about halfway along it when warning shots were fired. Above the sound of our truck, swaying along at a dangerous speed without lights, we could hear the roar of a diving plane and a few seconds later the terrible racket of its machine guns. Where the bullets hit we could not see, but neither our truck nor any other in the convoy was touched. The parachute flares took an interminable time to fall, and before the first reached the ground, they were replaced by others. Huddled together on our baggage in the glare of that dazzling white light, expecting bombs crashing down at any moment, we found it impossible not to admire the steady nerves of the Korean and Chinese drivers who nightly took the supplies down that single lifeline to the front. The drivers took advantage of the flares to press on at full speed with the road clearly illuminated for miles ahead.

At times convoys were held up while peasants and soldiers worked side by side to repair a bridge or fill in a crater gouged out of the road. When truck engines were silenced, one could hear peasants at work in the fields, urging a softly plodding ox in night plowing or the swish of sickles and women's voices as they carried in the sheaves. Convoys of oxcarts drew alongside during those enforced stops, awaiting the signal to proceed or plunging across the fields to tracks which motorized traffic could not use.

By daylight we had the first real impressions of what bombing had done to the North Korean countryside. Not even the smallest hamlet had been spared. Villages could be recognized only as level black patches ready for the plow, a few foundation stones, remnants of stone gateways, or broken chimneys poking up like grotesque plants out of the ashes. Whole villages and—as I saw later, when I traveled the entire Kaesong–Sinuiju road in daylight—whole towns had moved into primitive cave shelters, devoid of any comfort save that of protection. In Pyongyang there were still a few buildings intact when I first passed through. But there was no hospital, school, church, temple, or any public building standing along the entire road from the Yalu to Kaesong.

The last few miles into Kaesong were littered with the wreckage of U.S.

tanks; artillery tenders on their sides; and trucks which seemed only slightly damaged but which had been thrust off the road to make way for others in a healthier state. They marked the line of the U.S. retreat after the Chinese People's "Volunteers" had entered the fray some seven months earlier in November 1950. At the outskirts of the ancient city of Kaesong—immune from air or ground attacks to ensure the safety of the delegations that were soon to meet there—was a British RAF gun carrier on its back.

At first glance the city seemed totally destroyed. The center was a shambles, a few apathetic white-clad citizens sitting at improvised stalls of fruit and vegetables. Remnants of Western-style schools and hospitals poked up out of the ruins of the more lightly built Korean structures. But Kaesong—the center of Korea's world-famed ginseng production—had been a favorite summer resort for the wealthy. Tucked away in the innumerable folds of hills and valleys surrounding the center were still intact isolated villas. It was to one of these that we were driven. Within a few minutes we were splashing under a waterfall, dissolving the encrusted dust and sweat from two nights' journeys, making ourselves presentable for our first meeting with the press of the "other side" at a conference session due to start within a few hours.

The conference site was a typical wealthy Korean's pavilion, built in classical style with a curved tile roof. It bore a few battle scars but was intact and commodious enough for its purpose. It would be an understatement to say that the apparition of Winnington and me created a sensation. After the first rush to film and photograph the two "Caucasian Communists," the press was not quite certain how to proceed with us. They were clearly nonplussed by the fact that we had no shadows, showed no reluctance to mix with them, and behaved in the way journalists normally do on such occasions. Among the U.S. journalists were several who knew me from my war-corresponding days. One thing that impressed me on that first day was that the correspondents accredited to the UN side were convinced that the talks were going to last for a very long time.

Because I had taken Chiao Kuan-hua's advice very seriously and had brought with me just one spare set of light clothes and underwear, I tackled him about his "three weeks" theory that same night. (He had arrived in Kaesong a couple of days ahead of the journalists.) He was still certain of himself, explaining as follows: "It was Dean Acheson who started things off by stating, on June second, that a cease-fire based on the thirty-eighth parallel, where the war started, would be acceptable to the U.S.A. and regarded as a victory for the UN. Our official position—and that of our Korean comrades also—is that the Syngman Rhee regime, backed by the U.S.A., started the war. So a cease-fire based on the thirty-eighth parallel can be regarded as a victory for us. This position was made known to the Soviet Union. On June twenty-third, Jacob Malik replied to Acheson, stating that a cease-fire based on a mutual withdrawal of troops from the thirty-eighth parallel was an acceptable solution. Three days later, specifically referring to Malik's reply, Dean Acheson informed the U.S. Congress that such a solution was acceptable also to the UN. We have come here—in full agreement with our Korean comrades—to implement such a solution: an immediate cease-fire along the thirty-eighth parallel and withdrawal of both sides' forces to create a controlled, demilitarized zone. Why should it take more than three weeks to settle that?" This was one of the rare occasions about which I personally am informed that an analysis of the brilliant Chiao Kuan-hua proved totally wrong.

One of the secrets of the two years of negotiations at Kaesong-Panmunjom was that Chiao Kuan-hua—whose person was never seen nor name mentioned—was a key figure on the Chinese-North Korean negotiating team.

At the opening session on July 10, 1951, General Nam Il for the North Korean-Chinese side proposed a three-point agenda for an immediate cease-fire based on the withdrawal of each side's forces ten kilometers north and south of the thirty-eighth parallel, exchange of POWs, and withdrawal of all foreign troops in the briefest possible time. Vice Admiral C. Turner Joy, head of the UN delegation, refused to stipulate the thirty-eighth parallel as the basis for a cease-fire line or to include withdrawal of foreign troops on the agenda. This was "political," and he was empowered to discuss only military matters. Moreover, he wanted the exchange of POWs to be the first item discussed. It took two weeks to get agreement on a five-point agenda which omitted any mention of the thirty-eighth parallel, placed the exchange of POWs as the fourth item, and dodged the issue of withdrawal of foreign troops by including as the fifth item "recommendations to governments concerned."

From the first day of the substantive talks—the discussion on the cease-fire line which started on July 27, 1951—until a cease-fire agreement was signed on July 27, 1953, Chu Chi-p'ing, Winnington, and I found ourselves in the unsought role of unofficial "briefing officers" for the journalists accredited to the UN Command. This, as the world's leading news agencies and press organs were publicly to state, was the result of the suppression, distortion, and untruthful accounts of conference proceedings given by the official UN spokesmen. Since Winnington's and my reports published in London and Paris were at variance with those distributed by the regular news agencies on some of the most burning issues of the conference, newspapers started "lifting" our versions and publishing them side by side with the others. Because our reports showed that we were more correctly informed on factual matters than the UN journalists, they started turning to us ever more frequently for facts not only about North Korean-Chinese proposals but even about those being advanced by the UN side. Things came to a point at which no responsible journalist accredited to the UN would file a report from the conference site without checking with Winnington, Chu Chi-p'ing, or me.

It started with the discussions of the cease-fire line. Although the talks were held in closed sessions, the UN correspondents were briefed that the North Korean-Chinese side was refusing to accept a line along the thirty-eighth parallel. In fact, Admiral Joy had started by demanding that the Communist forces abandon to a depth of 35 miles the defensive positions they had established along the whole 150-mile front from the Yellow Sea to the Sea of Japan. The argument was that this would "compensate" the UN Command for the fact that it would be ceasing military operations on the sea and in the air, as well as on land, whereas the North Korean-Chinese forces would have to cease fire on land only (they having no air or naval forces worth the name at that stage of the war).

Nam Il argued that the battlefront had been established where it was (the UN forces slightly to the north of the thirty-eighth parallel in the east, the Communists slightly to the south of it in the west) by the employment of the total military force available to each side. The logical thing was to end the war where it had started and where the military balance had roughly been restored.

Regardless of the rights or wrongs of the two positions, the UN press not only was not informed about Admiral Joy's claims but was told that the Communists were holding up the talks by refusing to agree on a cease-fire line along the thirty-eighth parallel. The UN correspondents started getting queries based on Winnington's and my dispatches and started to probe to see if we really stuck to our versions, despite the emphatic denials of the UN press officer, Brigadier General William P. Nuckols.

On one occasion when the UN journalists were puzzled over an obvious discrepancy between what they were *told* and what we *knew*, they invited us to pinpoint on the map being used by their briefing officer the real cease-fire line being demanded by Admiral Joy. It was clear that their map was one specially faked for the press. They confronted Nuckols with our amended version, and finally, he admitted that it was correct. On August 22, Bob Tuckman of the AP quoted a "Communist newsman" (me) as saying that if the UN side really wanted a cease-fire along the actual battlefront—by then Admiral Joy's stated position—it could have it: one along the thirty-eighth parallel or one along the actual battlefront. The same night the North Korean-Chinese delegation headquarters in Kaesong was bombed; the first stick of antipersonnel bombs landed halfway between General Nam Il's residence and the villa where the press was quartered, a few fragments actually falling on Nam Il's jeep.

An investigation carried out by both sides' liaison officers that night was adjourned till the next morning. Meanwhile, the next day's meeting was canceled by Nam Il. The chief UN liaison officer, Colonel Andrew J. Kinney of the U.S. Air Force, reported back that the "Communists" had faked an incident to wreck the cease-fire negotiations. They had broken off the talks! News of this flashed around the world within hours. Winnington's and my reports, published the next morning, stating that only the meetings for August 23 had been canceled, brought another shower of queries to the UN correspondents. But contact between the press of both sides was broken. Kinney, who had promised to continue the investigation next morning and bring journalists with him, claimed that the "Communists" had refused further investigation of the "so-called incident" and had banned UN journalists from Kaesong.

A statement from General Kim Il Sung and the commander of the Chinese "Volunteers" on August 23 protested the bombing but made no mention of breaking off the talks. On the contrary, it said: "We hope that our armistice negotiations may proceed smoothly and reach a fair and reasonable agreement acceptable to both sides. . . ." The UN commander, Mathew B. Ridgway, continued to act as if the talks really were broken off, but the more serious press in the United States, Britain, and France was beginning to ask whether he had not been somewhat hasty in his conclusions. General Nam Il moved to another residence, but on the night of August 31 two 500-pound bombs were dropped within 200 yards of it. The press accompanied Colonel Kinney for the investigation the next day, the fact that they had never been "banned from the Kaesong area" having been duly reported by Winnington and me. Kinney could hardly deny that two large bombs had exploded, but he developed the fable that an "unidentified aircraft" had been picked up on the radar screen that night, so "the attack must have been carried out by your own aircraft." After that, except for General Nam Il, most of the North Korean and Chinese delegation staff, as well as the Chinese journalists, except Chu Chi-p'ing, left for Pyongyang and Peking respectively. Peace prospects seemed blown to smithereens.

General Nam Il moved his residence again—this time into the center of Kaesong. In the small hours of September 10, we were awakened by a diving plane and the roaring clatter of its machine guns as it strafed the area of the new residence. Another investigation—this time by a Colonel Darrow, also of the U.S. Air Force, who advanced the theory that the bullets lodged in the houses alongside Nam Il's residence could have come from a machine gun fired from a nearby roof. He was invited to question the whole population of Kaesong. After the first three testified to hearing the plane and the shooting, he gave up. Reuters reported from Tokyo later in the day that the investigation "appeared to be little more than a formality. The Allied Command had little or no reason to suspect the latest Communist allegation had any more basis than previous similar charges. . . ."

The atmosphere was very tense on the night of September 10. A large part of the remaining population had taken off for the hills to the north, aircraft having been over the city all day in violation of its neutral status. Our press trio, and the North Korean-Chinese liaison officers with whom by then we were quartered, felt it was the night on which peace or a vastly extended war would be decided. We did not bother to undress as B-26 bombers zoomed and dived overhead and we waited for the first bombs to fall. It had been strongly suggested that we return to Peking with the others, but we felt that for history's sake, whatever happened should be witnessed and recorded by professionals. It might be the dreaded start of World War III.

Over the radio at 11:00 P.M. came the electrifying news that Ridgway had admitted and apologized for the incident. This time the radar revealed that a UN aircraft *had* been over Kaesong at the time the attack took place as a result of a "navigational error" and that "disciplinary action" had been taken against the pilot. The apology seemed to prepare the way for the resumption of talks. At liaison meetings it became clear that the UN delegation wanted the conference site to be moved from Kaesong to the three-hut hamlet of Panmunjom, almost astride the thirty-eighth parallel. At a meeting in a tent on the new site on October 11, it was agreed that a circle with a 1,000-yard radius, centered on a conference tent, would constitute a neutral zone. The roads leading from Munsan in the south (where the UN delegation had its forward headquarters) and from Kaesong in the north would also be "attack-free."

Within twenty-four hours three U.S. jets had strafed inside that 1,000-yard circle, killing a small Korean boy, fishing in a stream alongside the road.

By this time the more responsible members of the UN press strongly suspected—as we had from August 22 onward—that the U.S. Air Force was trying to wreck the talks. This suspicion was reinforced when, for the first time, a U.S. Marine officer, Lieutenant Colonel John J. Murray, conducted the investigation. He confirmed the violation, there was another apology, and on October 25 Admiral Joy and General Nam Il faced each other again over a conference table—this time in a large military tent. UN correspondents were there again, having been instructed not to have contact with Chu Chi-p'ing, Winnington, or me, instructions which most of them ostentatiously ignored.

On November 14, 1951, on the eve of negotiations for the exchange of POWs, Colonel James Hanley, judge advocate of General James Van Fleet's Eighth Army, released a report alleging that the "Communists" had killed at least 5,790 UN POWs, including about 5,500 Americans, since the start of the Korean War. The implication was: Why continue the talks when all the POWS have been massacred? It was so blatantly aimed at wrecking the talks that President Truman felt impelled to tell the press the following day that he had never been informed of such massacres. Three days later Ridgway's spokesman expressed "utmost regret" that coordination had not been effected with Washington and that the release of Hanley's state-ment had, "of course, no connection whatsoever with the current armistice negotiations."

Bob Eunson, head of the AP's Tokyo bureau—old friend from the war in the Pacific—turned up at Panmunjom with an original idea. The AP had a photographer, Frank "Pappy" Noel, whose name had turned up on a POW list broadcast over Peking Radio. Why not send him a camera and film and let him take pictures of his fellow POWs? In this way families would see their sons and husbands were alive and start putting on pressure to get a cease-fire signed. Because the POWs were in camps run by the Chinese, I put the proposal to Chiao Kuan-hua. "Why not if the AP wants to risk a camera?" was the reply. A few days later a press camera and generous supply of film were handed over at Panmunjom and were soon on their way to the POW camp on the Yalu where Noel was being held. Ten days or so after that Noel's pictures started filtering in to Panmunjom. They created a sensation.

Ridgway was furious, but there was worse to come. The talks on the POW exchange got under way. On December 18, 1951, a list of 11,559 names of UN prisoners held in the North was handed over to Rear Admiral Ruthven E. Libby of the U.S. Navy, who headed the UN subcommittee on the POW question. At the top of the list of more than 3,000 American POWs was the name of Major General William Dean, commander of the U.S. 24th In-fantry Division, which had been decimated in the first days of the war. His name was pounced upon by press officer Nuckols in informal briefings of selected correspondents to prove that the whole list was a fake. The UN Command had "positive information" that Dean was dead, executed imme-diately after his capture. The press corps had long taken it for granted that Dean was dead.

General Ridgway was not the only one upset about the success of the Noel photos. The UP was suffering badly. "The Noel pictures are killing us," said one of the UP Tokyo chiefs who made a special trip to Panmunjom to salvage something in the photo line for his agency. "The North Koreans say they are holding General Dean. Our people insist he's dead. Can you get us some pictures of Dean to prove he's alive?"

A few days later I was speeding up the Kaesong–Pyongyang road with a Chinese photographer—by chance in the car of General Nam Il, on his way for a conference with Kim Il Sung. The car was strafed, and I still retain the vision of Nam Il, imperturbably smoking his long Russian *papyros* through a much-photographed amber cigarette holder, not even looking back at the bullets kicking up the dust behind us and the white-clad peasants diving into roadside ditches. The driver managed to plunge the car into a cleft in the road cutting, and I again watched the split-second appearance of myriad puffs of sand as bullets pounded along the road from three jets which soared skyward again. After a sleepless few hours, during which bombs came very close in the usual night attacks, the interview with General Dean took place, and the photographer took his pictures.

A couple of days later the official U.S. Army daily, *Stars and Stripes*, carried a double-page spread of General Dean, sleek and trim in a double-breasted suit, playing chess with his guards, eating with chopsticks, shadow-boxing, and walking in the forest. (After his release General Dean told me he had taken advantage of the photographic session to get as much rare exercise as possible. He was the only POW to be held by the North Koreans and had a much harsher regimen than those in the Chinese camps.)

The photos were carried by virtually every newspaper in the United States, together with General Dean's story, as he had told it to me, and I relayed it to the journalists at Panmunjom as soon as I returned. Dean had wandered around for about three months after the disintegration of his 24th Division at Taejon, hiding in the woods and living off wild fruit. Eventually he found an English-speaking South Korean, to whom he paid dollars for guiding him through to Allied lines, but who turned him over to the nearest partisan headquarters. Thus, he became North Korea's most important POW.

In late January 1952, a memorandum was circulated from General Ridgway's headquarters, complaining that it had come to the attention of the Supreme Commander that "certain correspondents were abusing their news coverage facilities for the purpose of fraternization, and were consorting and trafficking with the enemy." The memorandum, issued by Ridgway's personal press officer, stated that the UN Command "viewed with growing apprehension the practice of some reporters of excessive social consorting, including the drinking of alcoholic beverages with Communist journalists." Correspondents were warned that such practices must cease forthwith and, in future, they must comport themselves in such a way as "not to endanger military security."

On the morning after it was issued, the whole UN press corps made an ostentatious display of "fraternization," including some "drinking of alcoholic beverages." They could afford to, many of them having received specific instructions to deny the Ridgway edict. Not so the hapless editor of *Stars and Stripes*. He was sacked and sent home. His replacement ran a nasty attack on the AP, implying a "sellout to the enemy to get a few pictures." The AP protested and demanded the same space for a reply. It was written by Charlie Barnard and reflects part of the public relations stupidities which led Ridgway to paint himself into such an untenable corner:

Why would the Army make such wild charges? The Army doesn't like the newsworthy information and pictures the Communists give out. . . . All correspondents know exactly what kind of guys the Communist correspondents are. They are tough babies from the word go and Communism is the only creed they know. But many's the time they have given hot news stories on what is happening in the armistice tents to Allied correspondents, and the stories have turned out to be correct. A few months ago, the UN Command announced there would be no further briefings while sub-delegate armistice sessions were in progress. But the Communist journalists got briefings and they in turn "briefed" the Allied newsmen. For days that was the only armistice news the newspapers of the free world got.

The Army doesn't like it because pictures of Allied prisoners in North Korea always show the prisoners looking well-fed and comfortable. No adult American would expect a picture from Communist territory to show anything else. . . . But the recognizable faces of the UN boys, published in the newspapers must have meant a great deal to the folk back home. Communist propaganda? Sure, that's what the Reds intended the photos for. . . . Nobody does any bargaining with the Red newspapermen. Pictures and stories from those boys are absolutely free. . . .*

Ridgway and Nuckols suffered a major propaganda defeat of their own making. The reason the UN press did not even get texts of their own side's proposals was that they disclosed the gap between what was being said for consumption by a public urgently demanding an end to the war and the real policy of the military bigwigs who wanted that war to continue. U.S. negotiating strategy was aimed at just that, but it had to be hidden from the public. All journalists who covered the negotiations long enough were well aware of this. In an implicit rebuke to the Ridgway-Nuckols press-suppression policy, the Overseas Press Club awarded its 1951–52 prize for the best photographic work of the year to Pappy Noel. And a well-merited prize it was. In May 1952, General Ridgway left Tokyo to take up his new post as Supreme Allied Commander, Europe, and I do not remember many tears being shed at his departure—at least not by the press.

In the meantime, because my wife's Bulgarian exit visa had been granted and it was clear that the Korean cease-fire talks were going to continue for a long time, I had sounded out the chances of her working as a polisher of French publications at China's Foreign Languages Publishing House. With the right qualifications, there was no problem. She also made arrangements to be accredited as correspondent of *Literaturen Front*, the weekly journal of the Bulgarian Writers' Union. I was visiting the POW camps on the Yalu when a telegram arrived that Vessa was heading for Peking on the Trans-Siberian express. Then followed a quick dash to Antung by jeep, thence by

---

* *Stars and Stripes* (February 10, 1952). Barnard was incorrect on a couple of points: Alan Winnington was a member of the British Communist party, but neither Chu Chi-p'ing nor I had ever been Communist party members. Also, Barnard omits that the initiative for the POW photos was entirely that of the AP.

train to Shenyang (Mukden), where I arrived in a temporary blackout re-
sulting from the U.S. bombing of the Suiho hydroelectric complex on the
Yalu, through which I had passed twelve hours earlier.

A hurried conference with railway officials established that the train was
passing through that night. Help was promised to locate my wife and get
her and her baggage out of the sleeping car during the train's brief stop.
An astonished Vessa—expecting to meet me in Peking—was awakened,
clothes were thrown into bags and bags handed out through compartment
windows. The train puffed off toward Peking, while we headed in the
opposite direction and within a few hours were crossing the incredibly damaged, but still serviceable, Yalu bridge into Korea. It was an unmannerly
fashion to greet a wife of two and a half years of marriage, only the first
month of which had been spent together.

For eighteen months after the major questions of fixing a cease-fire line
and the international policing of an overall agreement had been settled,
the war continued while the delegates wrangled over the POW exchange.
Normally this is the simplest of questions to be solved. Under all existing
conventions the return to their home countries of prisoners of war takes
place as soon as possible after the end of hostilities. U.S. negotiators, however, insisted on the brand-new principle of voluntary repatriation, which
meant in effect that Chiang Kai-shek wanted to get his hands on all Chinese
POWs, South Korea's Syngman Rhee wanted to get his on all North Koreans, and the U.S. negotiator generals, who never wanted a cease-fire
agreement anyway, had the perfect device to block overall agreement indefinitely. The North Korean-Chinese negotiators termed this "forcible detention," and in view of the brutal pressures applied to force Chinese and
North Korean POWs to renounce their rights to repatriation, they were not
far from the mark. But eventually even this question seemed to have been
settled.

It was agreed that all POWs who obviously wanted to go home would
be exchanged as soon as the cease-fire was signed. Others would be brought
to special zones, where they would make up their minds to go home or not
after receiving explanations of the conditions of repatriation. On June 16
and 17, 1953, when an overall agreement had been drafted ready for signing, Syngman Rhee troops—with the complicity of U.S. prison guards, according to on-the-spot reports of the UN press—forced 27,000 North Korean
POWs out of their compounds at gunpoint. Rhee then announced they
would be incorporated into his armed forces. This destroyed the basis of
the agreement which was to be signed on June 25, the third anniversary
of the outbreak of the Korean War.

To placate public opinion and the increasingly restive UN allies with forces in the field, President Dwight D. Eisenhower (who had beaten the Democratic candidate, Adlai E. Stevenson, in the 1952 presidential elections because of his pledge to end the Korean War) sent Undersecretary of State Walter S. Robertson to talk with Rhee. After two weeks of daily meetings between these two notable "hawks," a joint communiqué stated that a "mutual security" pact had been agreed on. Within twenty-four hours Rhee had jubilantly announced that the political talks to be held after the cease-fire (Point 5 of the agenda) would be limited to three months, after which he would be free to go it alone. This wrecked another important provision of the draft agreement.

The North Korean-Chinese forces went into action again and in six days wiped out five ROK divisions and severely crippled two more. What was not known was that Canada had delivered a virtual ultimatum to the United States, revealed by the Canadian diplomat Chester Ronning, who, at the time of which he was writing, headed the American and Far Eastern Division of Canada's Department of External Affairs:

> Canada could not agree to being pinned down to a "final position" which risked a break-off in negotiations. Canada threatened to withdraw from participation in renewed hostilities if the United Nations Command failed to accept United Nations terms for an armistice. *It was a virtual ultimatum in the sense that it was a final statement of terms, the rejection of which would have involved a complete rupture in Canada's relations with the other powers associated with the United Nations' action in Korea. It was this determined position on Canada's part which forced a decision either fully to comply with the General Assembly's terms and sign an armistice or to continue a military solution without Canadian participation.* *

The UN negotiators returned to the conference tent. General Nam Il sought a series of guarantees that there would be no time limit on the armistice; it would include both South Korean and UN forces; the UN Command would not give logistic or other support to any aggressive actions by the South Korean Army; the latter would also cease fire within twelve hours of the armistice agreement's being signed and other assurances. These all were given by Lieut. General William K. Harrison (who had replaced Admiral Joy as the chief UN negotiator), and the last obstacles were removed to signing the cease-fire agreement.

In an imposing Peace Pagoda built in five days by Korean People's Army men at the Panmunjom negotiating site, at 10:00 A.M. on July 27, 1953, Generals Harrison and Nam Il signed the documents which were to end

---

* Chester Ronning, *A Memoir of China in Revolution* (New York: Pantheon Books, 1974), p. 209. Emphasis is Ronning's.

the shooting in Korea twelve hours later. Later in the day these were countersigned by General Mark Clark (who had replaced General Ridgway) in Munsan and by General Kim Il Sung in Pyongyang.

On a personal level an event of considerable importance had taken place ten weeks earlier. The nom de plume invented for me by the *Daily Express* had been legitimized by the birth in Peking and registered naming of Peter, son of Vessa Ossikovska and Wilfred Burchett.

As a footnote to the title of this chapter it should be noted that the "press war" was waged far more vigorously between the journalists accredited to the UN Command and their American press officers than between the journalists of each side. Relations were almost always normal as between professionals, and friendships made at Kaesong-Panmunjom have stood the test of time.

18

The Indochina Attraction

I T SEEMED INCREDIBLE, but there was no doubt. The slight, wispy-bearded figure coming out of the jungle shadows, stick in hand and a windbreaker thrown over his shoulder, was none other than the legendary Ho Chi Minh. Reported dead by the French a score of times, there he was, hand outstretched, fragile, but unmistakable. It was impossible to forget that first meeting, the warmth and wisdom in his dark brown eyes. It was just a week since I had left Kaesong, pausing a couple of days in Peking to say hello to Vessa and young Peter. Ho Chi Minh's first inquiry was about health—not just a formal, polite inquiry, but was I not exhausted after years in Korea and the long journey from Peking?

As I listened to a shortwave radio on the way down, much of the news from French-occupied Hanoi was about a place called Dien Bien Phu. The French had seized it as a base to attack the Vietminh from the rear and wipe out their headquarters. What was going on at Dien Bien Phu was an obvious first question. "Uncle" Ho turned his sun helmet upside down on the table. Running his slim fingers around the rim, he said, "Here are mountains—where our forces are. Down there is the valley of Dien Bien Phu—that's where the French are with the best of their troops. They will never get out—although it may take some time."

"An Indochina Stalingrad?"

"On a modest scale—yes, something like Stalingrad."

As I discovered in many subsequent meetings, this was typical of Ho Chi Minh's capacity to present complicated problems in a few words and graphic images. The image of the cream of the French Expeditionary Corps bottled up in "Uncle" Ho's sun helmet was to remain as the historic Battle of Dien Bien Phu raged to its climax.

175

At the jungle headquarters I met Pham Van Dong, emaciated and with burning, deepset eyes, suffering in those days from chronic malaria and six years' detention in the "Hell Island" of Poulo Condore. He was interested in hearing about the Korean cease-fire talks—especially the political talks which had taken place at Panmunjom after the signing of the cease-fire agreement. Pham Van Dong would shortly be leaving for Geneva to head the Vietminh delegation at the conference aimed at ending the Indochina War.

To brief me on the background to the war and the present situation, and reply to my innumerable questions, was Xuan Thuy, who twenty-three years later was to head the Democratic Republic of Vietnam's delegation to the Paris Conference to settle another war in Vietnam. The only one of the main leaders I did not meet during that first visit was Vo Nguyen Giap, chief of the Vietminh's armed forces. "Giap's busy elsewhere at the moment," Ho Chi Minh explained, almost apologetically. A few days later Giap's forces, under his leadership on the spot, launched their first attacks against the outposts guarding the approaches to the main French positions at Dien Bien Phu. The battle actually started while I was at Ho Chi Minh's headquarters.

I was in Vietnam almost by accident. The political talks at Panmunjom had abruptly ended when the chief of the Chinese delegation, Huang Hua (later to become foreign minister), described as "plain perfidy" the U.S. approach to the negotiations. Arthur Dean, who headed the UN delegation, considered this an insult to his country's honor and stalked out. At the foreign ministers' Berlin Conference, it was agreed to convene a special conference at Geneva to discuss the Korean question. Almost as an afterthought, it was agreed to add an attempt to settle the war in Indochina to the agenda. Alan Winnington was having passport problems at that time, so the London *Daily Worker* asked me to cover the conference for it. Because I knew nothing at all about the war in Indochina, I felt it essential to have some informed background when the talks started in Geneva.

That first visit to Vietnam was necessarily short—two weeks. For days there were meetings with top cadres and discussions on various aspects of the struggle. Neither at that time nor since, neither with the Vietminh in the North nor ten years later with the Vietcong in the South, have I ever found a Vietnamese revolutionary boastful or overoptimistic. If anyone erred, it was usually on the side of the understatement.

It was not only from meetings with top cadres and their very detailed briefings that my impressions were formed, but also from traveling in the countryside, from villages bordering the Red River Delta to those on the main supply route to Dien Bien Phu. Had the French been able to see what went on at night along the roads and trails leading over the mountains to that decisive battleground, their shock at the firepower suddenly unleashed

at them would have been less. The countryside, so quiet and passive—
especially as seen from the air—in daytime, boiled with activity at night.
From trucks to oxcarts, bicycles, and human backs, every imaginable form
of transport hauled supplies through the jungle and up and down the steep
mountains toward Dien Bien Phu.

Munitions from China and some from the Vietminh's own arsenals; rice
smuggled out of the Red River Delta—everything needed to supply and
feed the attackers passed in endless convoys at night. Before dawn and the
inevitable reconnaissance planes, shrubs and trees were planted on those
supply lines, to be removed as the convoys started moving again at dusk.
It was at night that one had the impression of a whole people at war—
at least in the areas I saw during those two weeks. Although we passed
within a mile or two of French positions on several occasions, there was no
feeling of the French presence, except for their planes during the day.

The struggle was not confined to military affairs. It had reached a stage
at which massive support from the peasantry would be decisive in the cli-
mactic battle shaping up at Dien Bien Phu. Ho Chi Minh explained that
to get this, the peasants needed to have a clear vision of their own stake in
victory. Thus, I was present when the peasants at Hung Son village, in
Thai Nguyen Province, where Ho had his headquarters, marked the start
of land reform by making a huge bonfire of the cadastral deeds and records
of debts which enslaved them to the landlords. It was a moving ceremony—
held at night because of planes which ruled the sky by day. A misty rain
could neither dampen the ardor of the peasants squatting around the bonfire nor quench the flames which leaped up every time a fresh bundle of
documents was thrown in. It was one of those solemn moments when I
had chanced upon history on the move.

At Ho Chi Minh's headquarters—a score or so bamboo and thatch buildings scattered in the jungle with enough space between them to ensure
minimum damage from bombs—arrived Prince Souphanouvong. As head of
the Pathet Lao resistance movement in neighboring Laos he had come for
a meeting to coordinate strategy at Geneva. An intense, vital man, exuding
physical and mental vigor, he had long quit the comfort of the royal court
at Luang Prabang for the austere, dangerous life in the jungle. Like Ho Chi
Minh, he was an excellent linguist. He reviewed the situation in Laos,
insisting on close coordination between the struggle in Vietnam and that in
his own country. This would be reflected, he said, in the developing battle
at Dien Bien Phu as well as at the Geneva Conference.

As a parting gift, I was presented with a detailed hand-drawn map of
Vietnam, six feet long by three wide and in three colors: red, for areas solidly
under Vietminh control; yellow, for what were designated as guerrilla zones,
which guerrillas controlled by night but in which the French could operate
by day; green, for territory solidly controlled by the French. It seemed wildly

optimistic—in Vietminh favor—to judge by the few situation maps I had seen published by the French.

At least I left Vietnam much wiser about the affairs of Indochina, the spirit of the people, and the quality of their leadership in Vietnam and Laos than when I arrived. Plenty to ponder about during the long journey back to Peking and the still longer one, with Vessa this time, on the comfortable Trans-Siberian express to Moscow and on, by plane, to Geneva. It was an enjoyable trip, a much-needed rest therapy and change of diet after the austere rice and pickled cabbage of two and a half years in Korea. In those days it took seven days and nights just to cover the Lake Baikal-Urals section of the Trans-Siberian, with only ten minutes at the widely spaced halts.

At Geneva—despite the Panmunjom experience—we sought out Chiao Kuan-hua and asked how long he thought the conference would last. He pursed his lips, blinked his eyes, and said, "Three months." Informing some Panmunjom press colleagues a few days later that we had taken an apartment for three months, they said, "You're crazy!" In fact, this time Chiao Kuan-hua was right. The conference lasted almost exactly three months.

During the abortive discussions on upgrading the Korean cease-fire into a peace treaty, in which all participants in the Korean War took part, John Foster Dulles exerted his main efforts in trying to organize a Korean type of intervention to save the French in Indochina. British Foreign Minister Anthony Eden was later to reveal that at a dinner party three days before the conference was to start, Dulles had taken him aside to demand British support for U.S. air strikes at Dien Bien Phu. Eden wrote that he "went to bed that night a troubled man. . . . We might well find ourselves involved in the wrong war against the wrong man in the wrong place." * On the following day, as Eden reveals in the part of his memoirs entitled *Full Circle,* Dulles, together with the Chairman of the U.S. Joint Chiefs of Staff, Admiral Arthur W. Radford, went further, demanding that the RAF join the USAF in such strikes. Eden rushed back to London to see Churchill and told him that he disagreed with the American belief that such intervention could be effective or even limited to air strikes. He quotes Churchill as summing up the position as: "What we are being asked to do was to assist in misleading Congress into approving a military operation which, in itself would be ineffective, and might well bring the world to the brink of a major war." †

Without knowing such details, journalists during the Korean phase of the conference knew that something very fishy was going on. Dulles distinguished himself on the first day by refusing to shake the hand offered by Chou En-lai, thus defining the style of American participation. The overwhelming majority of the Sixteen—as the UN participants in the Korean

---

* Anthony Eden, *Full Circle* (Boston, Mass.: Houghton Mifflin, 1960), p. 102.
† *Ibid.,* p. 102.

War were known—had twice accepted proposals for a Korean settlement, one by Chou En-lai, the other by Molotov, only to have them rejected by the U.S.-South Korean delegations. General Walter Bedell Smith, who replaced Dulles after the first few days, proposed that the Korean question be referred to the United Nations. And thus exclude China!

Compared to Panmunjom, press representation at Geneva was on a very different level. At the top were the carefully screened State Department and Foreign Office specialists, conditioned never to rock the boat of high diplomacy, pundits like Joe Alsop and other columnists like him, for whom the hawkiest proposals were always too dovelike. But there were other high-quality professionals who were startled at the roughshod methods of Dulles and his team: journalists like Tom Hamilton of *The New York Times*; Richard Harris of *The Times* (London); Sy Frieden of the New York *Herald Tribune*; Geneviève Tabouis, of *L'Information* of Paris, whose courageous exposure of the Nazis and fascists on the eve of World War II made newspaper history; Pierre Courtade, *L'Humanité*'s prestigious daily columnist; and Alberto Giacovello, his opposite number from the Italian Communist party daily *L'Unità*, plus others from the most varied points of the political spectrum.

If only they had been at Panmunjom, I sometimes thought with a sigh, to ask the sort of questions they asked at the Geneva press conferences. It was not only some of the journalists but diplomats also who were shocked. The comments of Chester Ronning, acting leader of the Canadian delegation, were eloquent in this respect:

> I thought I had come to participate in a peace conference along the lines laid down in Berlin. Instead, the emphasis was entirely on preventing a peace settlement from being realized. I was particularly disturbed by statements—especially from the South Koreans and supported by the Americans—giving the impression that the Conference had been called merely to go through the motions of proving that there could be no political solution by negotiation.*

Ronning is also categoric as to why the Korean part of the conference failed. Coming to the Smith proposal—when agreement was already within reach—to refer the question to the UN for settlement, he writes:

> Chou replied that this would mean that China would be excluded from further negotiations, since China was excluded from the United Nations, and would make eventual agreement on Korea impossible.
>
> There were no more speakers, and the Conference ended in failure. Dulles had promised Rhee that the Conference would achieve nothing unacceptable to him. He had kept his promise.†

---

* Ronning, *op. cit.*, p. 220.
† *Ibid.*, p. 235.

With the Korean question disposed of, the decks were cleared for action on Indochina. Pham Van Dong arrived on May 4, 1954, to be welcomed at Geneva Airport by Molotov and Chou En-lai. At a UN debate a few months earlier, French Foreign Minister Georges Bidault had described him as a "non-existent phantom." Despite his fragile health, Pham Van Dong looked quite "substantial" as he stepped out of the plane, but Bidault continued to ignore his existence for the first few days of the Indochina debate, which started on May 8.

Pham Van Dong's old comrade, Vo Nguyen Giap, presented him with the most potent weapon any negotiator could ever wish for to mark the start of such a conference: a total victory at Dien Bien Phu, the day before it opened. Because of Giap's superb timing, the Dulles plan to internationalize the war failed. His offer to give Bidault one or two A-bombs to use at Dien Bien Phu was too late. This little-known incident, which I learned of from a very shocked French journalist at Geneva, was referred to by Bidault in his book *D'une Résistance à l'autre* (Paris: Les Presses du Siècle, 1965), p. 198. At a meeting in Paris among Bidault, Dulles, and Eden, on April 23 and 24 on the eve of the Geneva Conference, Bidault writes, Dulles drew him aside and said, "And if we give you two A-bombs for use at Dien Bien Phu?" Bidault's reaction was that this would "cause more harm to the defenders than the attackers."

Bidault continued to act as if he had the United States and the Western powers as his allies, but he did not. He still had Dulles—but not the United States. And not even majority support in the French Parliament. After a month of sterile discussions the Laniel-Bidault government fell, to be replaced a week later by one headed by Pierre Mendès-France, who pledged to negotiate peace in Indochina by July 20—just one month after taking office—or resign.

From Washington, Dulles was still working hard to prevent a peace settlement and set up an instrument of international intervention. Thus was born the Southeast Asia Treaty Organization (SEATO), which he hoped would rush into action in time to prevent France from "capitulating." A crucial meeting among Dulles, Eden, and Mendès-France was held in Paris on July 12 and 13—a week before the fatal date for peace or breakdown. Good relations had been established between Mendès-France and Chou En-lai (too good for Vietnamese liking, as was disclosed later), but the Russians and Vietnamese were suspicious that Dulles had won the day in Paris and there would be a Korean type of intervention. It was one of the most critical moments of the Indochina conference, as I knew from my contacts with the Chinese and Vietnamese delegations. What deepened their suspicions was that there had been virtually nothing published in the press about the Paris meeting.

Pham Van Dong, as was revealed publicly only many years later, had already made substantial concessions because of Chinese pressures. These were based on assurances which Chou En-lai had obtained through bilateral meetings with Mendès-France. By July 10 Pham Van Dong had agreed to a temporary military demarcation line along the sixteenth parallel, instead of the thirteenth, which he had proposed. He had also agreed to elections in each of the three countries within two years instead of six months, and he withdrew demands for the Khmer Issarak in Cambodia and Pathet Lao in Laos to participate in the conference. But by July 10 it was a thus-far-and-no-farther situation as far as he was concerned, and Molotov backed him on this. So far everything hinged on the validity of the assurances given by Mendès-France to Chou En-lai. The atmosphere around the three Communist delegations—especially the Vietnamese—on the night of July 13, 1954, was a replica of that in Kaesong on the night of September 10, 1951. It was a flash point situation, but perhaps one in which journalistic initiative could play a role.

The following morning I flew to Paris and brashly walked into the Quai d'Orsay (French Foreign Ministry). I got through the main gates but was then stopped by a security guard. Flashing my Geneva Conference press card, I asked to see a press spokesman. "But it's July fourteenth [Bastille Day]," said the security man, something I had entirely overlooked. "There's no one here."

I insisted that there must be someone on duty, and at that moment a tall, elegantly dressed person appeared and asked my needs. When I presented my press card, he gave it a long look and said, "Follow me!" Taking me into a spacious office, he introduced himself as Monsieur Massenet. He asked how he could be of help. Explaining as best I could the importance of my question in relation to the critical stage of the Geneva Conference, I asked what he could tell me of the foreign ministers' meeting. In one of the frankest ever replies at that level, he said in substance: Dulles was very insistent on a SEATO organization now and intervention in Indochina immediately. Mendès-France said no. Dulles banged the table. Mendès-France banged the table. Eden supported Mendès-France firmly. Dulles went away angry. French policy was to do everything reasonable to get a cease-fire by the twentieth.

Regretting greatly that I was not then writing for *The Times*, I telephoned the *Daily Worker*, and the next morning it gave good space to my piece about the failure of Dulles to bully the French and British into agreeing to sabotage the Geneva Conference and create a second Korea in Vietnam. It had already been seen in Geneva by the time I returned next day and contributed to renewed efforts to get a settlement, Pham Van Dong even agreeing to move up to the seventeenth parallel from the sixteenth to facilitate getting an overall agreement signed in time to meet the self-imposed deadline set by Mendès-France.

Contacts within the responsible section of the journalistic fraternity played an important part in getting points across to delegations when diplomacy was too rigid. Such contacts cut across politics and ideology and were facilitated by the fact that Eden and Mendès-France were sincere in wanting to end the fighting, and so—for once—they rejected the dictates of Dulles. An instance was my friendship with Adelbert de Segonzac, then diplomatic correspondent of the French evening paper *France-Soir*. He had been with Mendès-France in De Gaulle's Free French movement from the days when it was headquartered in London. His relations with Mendès-France were approximately those of mine with Chou En-lai, Chiao Kuan-hua, and Pham Van Dong, so views exchanged at journalistic level quickly got back to ministerial level.

However, the Panmunjom type of fraternization with U.S. journalists died away. McCarthy was still riding high (he fell just nine days after the Geneva Conference ended), and most of the U.S. journalists ate and drank in groups apart. My meetings with Sy Frieden of the New York *Herald Tribune*, for instance, always had to be arranged in some obscure restaurant far away from the conference press center. The official U.S. view was that the Geneva Conference would end in a spectacular failure and that an expanded war in Indochina was inevitable. U.S. press officials seemed intent on insulating the journalists from what was really going on but adopted a less spectacular method of achieving their aim than that of the Ridgway type of ukase.

Throughout July 20 there was intense diplomatic activity, with draft agreements being exchanged between delegations. Precious time was lost because Walter Bedell Smith refused to associate himself with any of the work, remaining in his hotel room, to which all drafts had to be sent. Far from helping, he was busy with the delegates of the Ngo Dinh Diem regime, which the United States had installed in Saigon just fifteen days earlier, and those of Laos and Cambodia, to provide as many last-minute hitches as possible so as to avoid at all cost the signing of an agreement by midnight on July 20.

A final session was announced for 8:00 P.M., then adjourned hour by hour till midnight. Cars and drafting experts moved back and forth between the villas of Eden and Molotov, as the two cochairmen and their staffs worked on acceptable drafts, a task made difficult by last-minute retractions and provisos dictated by Smith to his protégés.

Correspondents, including myself, were telephoning their newspapers every few minutes. But midnight came, then one o'clock, two o'clock—too late to catch the editions of most European papers. Technically Mendès-France had lost his race with time. But the cars were still dashing to and fro, while the press corps stayed on at the Maison de la Presse, where information and transmission facilities were centered, until at 3:50 A.M. on July

21, came the announcement that the cessation of hostilities agreement had just been signed for Vietnam and Laos. (A similar agreement for Cambodia was signed at 11:30 A.M. the same day.) A final declaration of the conference would be released later on the afternoon of the twenty-first.

For spectators, the last act of that historic conference took place on the afternoon of the twenty-first, when the delegates emerged after approving the final documents. Photographers, professional and amateurs, jostled for best positions to snap the foreign ministers as they emerged for the last time, with secretariat personnel, typists, drivers mixed up with the journalists—anyone who had a pretext to be there that day.

The foreign ministers, accompanied by one or two staff members, came out one at a time to step into their delegation cars. What was extraordinary was that the crowd cheered and clapped according to their estimate of performance. For Eden and Molotov, there were big ovations for their tireless work as cochairmen. There was generous applause for Mendès-France, perhaps for having won his wager with himself. A few handclaps for the rarity value of the delegates from the kingdoms of Laos and Cambodia. For Chou En-lai and Pham Van Dong, there were ovations, justified by Chou En-lai's statesmanship at his first appearance on the world diplomatic stage, for Pham Van Dong for his obviously generous and conciliatory role. The last to emerge was Walter Bedell Smith, and he was received in silence. He was the only one to emerge without a smile on his face, and there was not a handclap or cheer: the sort of silence of respect for the bereaved. His final contribution had been to disassociate his government from the agreements reached but he had pledged that the United States "will refrain from the threat or the use of force to disturb them." (In fact, as I was reporting from the spot within a few months, and as the *Pentagon Papers* confirmed seventeen years later, the United States was engaged in the "use of force" to sabotage the agreements before the ink was dry on the signatures.)

Later that day selected journalists were told in off the record briefings by U.S. and British delegation spokesmen that the provisional demarcation line along the seventeenth parallel, to facilitate the separation and regrouping of combatant forces, would become a line of permanent political division. Asked about this, Pham Van Dong said, "The Americans came to Geneva with their plans, and we with ours. They intended that there would be no Geneva Conference. Instead of a cease-fire, they wanted an extended war with U.S. intervention. But as you see, we have a cease-fire. And you will see that we will reunify our country. No government can be maintained in the South—even with massive American aid—that stands openly against the unification of the country."

History proved he was right. But a tremendous amount of Vietnamese—and American—blood was spilled in the jungles and rice fields of Vietnam before that prophecy came true. And in the light of what later happened in their own country and the hostilities with China and Kampuchea, many Vietnamese twenty-five years later were publicly voicing the doubts expressed privately at the time: Were the sacrifices made at Geneva justified? Would it not have been better to have unified Vietnam by force of arms and aided the revolutionary forces in Cambodia and Laos to come to power? As far as the military balance between the Vietminh and its allies and the French Expeditionary Corps was concerned, it would have been simple to sweep the French completely out of Indochina. But the unknown, which weighed heavily on Chinese and Soviet thinking at Geneva, was the extent to which the brinkmanship of Dulles was bluff or reality. So the full fruits of victory were not harvested. In his comments after the signing, a deeply moved Pham Van Dong had told us, "I don't know how we are going to explain this to our comrades in the South!"

That it was Vietnam, the undisputable, but generous, victor, which made the most concessions at Geneva is implicit in Chester Ronning's assessment, twenty years later:

> It was the concessions Chou [En-lai] made and those he induced Ho Chi Minh to make that helped Mendès-France to reach agreement in Vietnam, Laos and Cambodia. Despite General Giap's victory over French military forces in Vietnam, Pham Van Dong made the most important concession when he accepted the temporary division of Vietnam for a period of two years. That concession ultimately prevented reunification. . . .*

Villages had already moved back to the roadsides and peasants were working their fields in daylight by the time I followed the road from the Chinese border to catch up with the vanguard Vietminh unit designated as the first to enter Hanoi on October 9, 1954. Children were playing in the streets; newly built houses were decorated with red flags and banners; women, children, and shopkeepers lined the village streets; and peasants came running across the fields to cheer us as we passed. For most, our little convoy of foreign journalists was the first tangible evidence that peace had ended Vietnam's isolation from the outside world. If we stopped for a moment, people came running with tea, fruits, and flowers, pressing around to touch us.

The road led through the ruins of what had once been substantial colonial towns and new villages built on the ashes of the old. People's sufferings were written on their wasted faces and pitifully thin bodies, their patched and tattered clothing. From the border to within about twelve miles of Hanoi, not one bridge was standing. Four major streams had to be crossed by ferry; dozens of smaller ones, by deep fords. Thousands of acres of terraced rice

* *Ibid.*, pp. 240–41.

fields were bare, the earth cracked and dry, in one area where the French had bombed the reservoir on which the irrigation channels depended.

Our group—two Soviet, one Czech, Polish, Austrian, Italian journalists, and I—passed the night at a small VPA (Vietnam People's Army) advance post, twelve miles from Hanoi. (Bulgaria's representative was in Peking doing a crash course in Chinese in order to converse with young Peter, who had started to talk—in Chinese—during our six-month absence at Geneva and a rest in Bulgaria following the conference.) Early the next morning we drove to a rendezvous with a French officer. He was to escort us through territory not yet evacuated into Hanoi itself, to observe the stage-by-stage transfer of power. The asphalt road was lined with barbed wire, French forts, and bunkers—the latter covered with closely woven nets of barbed wire that looked like gigantic spiders' webs from the distance.

At a bridge straddling a small branch of the Red River, the escort officer was waiting, along with the VPA vanguard unit. Trim in their spotlessly clean khaki uniforms and rubber-tire sandals, very boyish-looking and smiling, they gave an impression of effortless discipline as they lined up, awaiting the signal to move. The first sign of the Expeditionary Corps was a dispirited African soldier, squatting on the bridge, uniform stiff with sweat and dust, rifle between his knees, and head on his chest—a caricature of misery and demoralization. He was typical of the rest. As we neared Gia Lam—just the other side of the Red River from Hanoi—we passed some of the might of the French Army: heavy tanks, armored cars, artillery, steel-helmeted troops piling into ten-wheel troop carriers getting ready to move out as the youngsters —or so they seemed—with their carbines, homemade grenades, and rubber sandals, waited to move in.

The gray and seemingly deserted city sprang into life as they moved. The transfer was block by block, sector by sector until the whole city was freed. Sometimes one side of a boulevard and a section of street blocks behind it was freed while the other side remained occupied for another hour or so. They provided a dramatic contrast: one side with gold-starred red flags hanging from every window, the population packed on the footpath between curb and shop- or housefronts, cheering and weeping, embracing soldiers, who also wept; on the other side, bulky French military police, bayoneted rifles at the ready, jabbing at anyone trying to move into the street or hang a flag a moment before the transfer. Their zeal symbolized the reluctance with which the French were abandoning their colony of eighty years.

Along the footpaths the people moved level with the foremost VPA soldier, stopping when he stopped, moving as he advanced, the flood swelling in volume as the liberators penetrated ever deeper into the city. The VPA Command had appealed for calm and order—above all, no provocations. And so it was. But block by block the city blossomed into life. Within hours there were flags, solid welcoming arches covered with peace doves, portraits of

"Uncle" Ho, slogans, banners, streamers, lanterns, everything that symbolized peace, victory, liberation, and jubilation.

The ceremonial entry of the VPA took place the following day, residents working all night to erect welcoming arches along the entry route. Apart from a handful of collaborators who were withdrawing with the French, the whole population turned out to see the liberators arrive in American trucks and jeeps, manning American artillery and antiaircraft guns, carrying American bazookas and machine guns—booty from Dien Bien Phu and a dozen other battlefields. (Some of it had been captured in Korea and passed by the Chinese to the Vietminh.) The excitement reached its peak when word spread like wildfire—from relatives who recognized them—that the conquering heroes were from Hanoi's own regiment. It had been formed from mainly workers and students who had defended the capital against the French invaders almost eight years earlier. After two months of heroic barricade and house-to-house fighting, they had left in rags and tatters, armed with a few aging rifles and carrying their wounded with them. It was an unforgettable day of tears and cheers, of brief emotional reunions and abrupt partings.

The ceremonial entry ended at midday, and before it was over, the first garlanded trams were moving through the streets—thanks to the vigilance of local staff in defending the electric power station from French attempts to dismantle it. Truckloads of rice and other provisions moved into the city behind the troop convoys. In the afternoon groups of soldiers and civilians were working together in a general cleanup, loading heaps of refuse into army trucks; sweeping streets, footpaths, and gutters—troops and people exchanging experiences of the eight years during which they had been separated.

There were rumors of sabotage, and certainly acts of sabotage, from the first day of the takeover, but the new authorities were discreet in talking about them. The main impression of the journalists who came in with the VPA and those accredited to the French who stayed on a few days was how smoothly order was restored and the city started to function normally. In reading seventeen years later the revelations of the Saigon Military Mission (SMM), set up during the Geneva Conference by the CIA, to wage sabotage and paramilitary operations, among other activities in the North, one can only marvel at the efficiency with which the Vietminh cadres got things running again and thwarted the saboteurs.

> The Saigon Military Mission started on June 1, 1954 [when the Geneva talks were three weeks old], when its chief, Colonel Edward G. Lansdale (USAF), arrived in Saigon with a small box of files and clothes and a borrowed typewriter. . . .
> The northern SMM team left with the last French troops. . . .

The northern team had spent the last days in Hanoi in contaminating the oil supply of the bus company for a gradual wreckage of engines in the buses, in taking the first actions for delayed sabotage of the railroad (which required teamwork with a special CIA special technical team in Japan, who performed their part brilliantly) and in detailed notes of potential targets for future paramilitary operations. . . .*

When former State Department employee Dr. Daniel Ellsberg was indicted in 1971 for having released a copy of the Pentagon Papers to *The New York Times*, the committee set up for his defense invited me to become an "honorary expert consultant." My very easy task was to provide documentary evidence that what was regarded as top secret for the U.S. public was public knowledge to those on the receiving end of U.S. policies in Vietnam. A case in point is the reference to the CIA's "delayed sabotage of the railroad." In Volume 5 of the Gravel edition of *The Pentagon Papers*, I contributed a chapter "The Receiving End," in which is described how most of Lansdale's agents deserted the moment they set foot in the North, as he admits. The Vietnamese were well aware of Lansdale's activities and those of his psywar, espionage, and sabotage teams. By accident I stumbled across the story of attempted railroad sabotage when I was doing a story on the Hongay-Campha coal mines, shortly after the French had withdrawn. Someone had noticed a nocturnal prowler around the stacks of coal briquettes at the Campha storage area. It was thought he was a petty pilferer until it was noticed that he was putting briquettes into the stacks. A watch was kept, he was arrested, and the "briquettes" were found to contain powerful explosives—doubtless the work of the "brilliant" CIA team from Japan. Fed into locomotive or powerhouse and factory furnaces, they could have caused tremendous damage with no way of tracing the source. While I was at Campha, teams were still combing through the mountains of briquettes to discover the "hot" ones—recognizable because they were slightly less shiny than the others. The Vietnamese authorities, after explaining the whole story—how the culprit was a former French undercover agent taken over by the CIA, given a crash course in espionage-sabotage techniques, and infiltrated into the North—asked me not to write about it because they did not want Lansdale to know how much they already knew of his activities.

When life in the North was restored to normal, I went to Peking and returned with Vessa and Peter, giving him—at the age of two—the chance to switch from fluent Chinese to fluent Vietnamese, with a halting French in between. There was plenty to report on about the great changes taking place—land reform, a new deal for the minorities, the beginnings of cooperative agriculture—with the exception of any progress toward fulfilling the

* *The Pentagon Papers*, Senator Gravel ed. (Boston: Beacon Press, 1971–72), vol. 1, pp. 574–75, 579.

key provision of the Geneva Agreement: elections within two years to re-unify the country. Newspapers soon started to lose interest in Vietnam after the killing stopped—or seemed to have—so I concentrated on gathering material for a book which was published in several countries and languages under the title *North of the 17th Parallel*. It was first published in 1956, and on the flyleaf of the English-language edition it is noted: "The author expresses the conviction that no force can prevent the Vietnam people from joining hands across this artificial barrier [the Seventeenth Parallel] to sweep it away."

In mid-May I was in Haiphong to watch the French Tricolor being lowered for the first time north of the seventeenth parallel and the last military and administrative officials embarking on a warship for Saigon. Vessa marked this historic event by giving birth to George in a Hanoi hospital.

There were visits to Laos to renew my acquaintanceship with Prince Souphanouvong in his jungle headquarters in Sam Neua Province and to Cambodia to make the acquaintance of Prince Norodom Sihanouk in his royal palace at Phnom Penh. July 1956 came and went, without the elections provided for as an essential part of the Geneva Agreement. By then it was perfectly clear that as long as any government dependent on the United States remained in power in Saigon, there would never be elections or any other form of political solution for Vietnam. And what happened in Vietnam was bound to decide the fate of Laos and Cambodia.

By early 1957 I had written and published a second book, *Mekong Upstream*, dealing with the situation in Laos and Cambodia. There were not likely to be new developments in the area for the foreseeable future, so I began to look around for fresh pastures. The choice was bound to be limited because, in the meantime, I had lost my passport.

19

---◄◆►---

Eastern Europe - 1956

E VER SINCE WORLD WAR II I had been reporting on perimeter
problems. The key to the solutions of several—if not all—of these
problems lay in the capitals of the two superpowers. Journalistically the idea
of being inside, looking out for a change, made sense. Without a travel document acceptable to the Western world, it could be only Moscow. (I had by
this time lost my British passport, as explained earlier. The British government said it was a matter for the Australian government to give me a new
one; the latter under Robert Menzies refused.)

The problem was posed when I received an invitation to attend a congress
of the International Organization of Journalists to be held in Helsinki in
June 1956 and talk about press reporting on the Korean War. How to travel
without a passport? The Vietnamese Foreign Ministry could issue a one-trip
laissez-passer with a return visa stamped in it. With my invitation telegram,
the Finnish authorities would give me an entry visa, the Soviet authorities
a two-way transit visa. Attending the journalists' congress was the British
journalist-writer Cedric Belfrage, whom I had long admired but never met.
We had much in common, apart from the fact that he also had worked six
years for Lord Beaverbrook's press empire and had worked in the U.S. zone
of West Germany when I was in Berlin.

In August 1948 Belfrage, together with two American friends, James
Aronson and John McManus, founded the *National Guardian*, an "independent, radical newsweekly," as it proclaimed on its masthead. It was
formed primarily to provide "other side" information and views to offset the
Establishment view of things. An admirable nonconformist, at the time we
met in Helsinki, Belfrage had been less than a year out of a U.S. jail, released on condition that he accept deportation from the country as a "sub-

versive." On a "Contempt of Congress" charge McCarthy had had him thrown into prison indefinitely, and this ended only when McManus and Aronson decided by "majority vote" that Cedric should transfer his "office" from the Federal Detention Center on West Street, New York, to London, where he would function as the paper's editor-in-exile. It was in that capacity that I met him in Helsinki. There had been an amicable arrangement dating back to the Korean War—anything of mine that *National Guardian* saw fit to print it could have.

Discussing the impasse in Indochina, including my journalistic impasse and vague ideas of a new base, Cedric said, "Why not formalize our relations and become the *Guardian* correspondent in Moscow? The post-Stalin era is of tremendous interest to our readers." Would the Soviet authorities agree? Accreditation for Western correspondents in those days was still very rare. How would we finance it? The *Guardian* could make only a very modest contribution, but we both had large amounts of uncollected rubles which had piled up from books published in the Soviet Union.

After the Helsinki congress we both would be transiting through Moscow, Belfrage returning to London, I visiting Poland for a few days, then on to Yugoslavia, where Tito, Nasser, and Nehru were due to hold a three-party meeting at Brioni to lay the foundations for the nonaligned movement. It was agreed that I prospect the possibilities of accreditation during my transit through Moscow to Warsaw and check on the results during my return transit to Hanoi.

The morning (June 28, 1956) in Warsaw, where, together with a few other journalists, I was the guest of the Polish Journalists' Association, was devoted to visiting the huge combine which printed the Communist party daily, *Tribyna Ludu*, and a few other publications, the sort of protocol visit that bores most journalists stiff—including me. But not this one, as things turned out. Our guides and interpreters were nonplussed that the presses were not turning. At one point a wedge-shaped group of workers came forward, and one fingered my Chinese silk shirt and—in German—asked, "How much did that cost?" Surprised, I made a rapid calculation and gave him the modest price in the dollar equivalent of Chinese currency. "That would cost us over a month's wages," he said, launched into a passionate attack on the poor living conditions, and concluded, "We are on strike."

Everybody was embarrassed, and we were hastened out to a luncheon with our hosts. The president of the Journalists' Association was in the middle of proposing the first welcoming toast when someone came in and handed him a piece of paper. Still on his feet, he read it, then said slowly, "As it is our policy to keep you and the public informed, I have to announce with deep regret that there have been serious riots in Poznan this morning. There has been shooting in which at least twenty people have been killed, numbers of others are wounded. The troubles are continuing."

Our host sat down, and the luncheon continued in silence but for the clatter of knives and forks and the occasional clinking of glasses. The workers at the printing combine had obviously been informed and were staging a sympathy strike.

In East Berlin, Prague, and Budapest in short stopovers on my itinerary to Belgrade and then Brioni, there were tensions which old friends in these places conceded but found difficult to define. Stefan Heym, a popular novelist in East Germany, said there was considerable discontent there, not so much because of economic conditions, which had greatly improved since the Poznan type of riots there three years earlier, but because of bureaucratic idiocies, which he philosophically attributed to the "growing pains" of a socialist system. Although he and his American wife could easily have "gone West," where his books were best-sellers, they had decided to stay and fight to improve things from within. (In 1979 Heym was expelled from the Writers' Union of the GDR, apparently because he pushed his criticisms too vigorously.)

At the Tito-Nehru-Nasser meeting of July 18 and 19, 1956, on the island of Brioni, journalists were kept on the mainland opposite—ostensibly for security reasons. It was more a sixth-sense feeling of the shape of things to come than any idea of an important news story that took me there. Tito had not found an orbit in which to place his country after his expulsion from the world Communist movement eight years earlier. The Bandung Conference, however, had projected a new element into the international firmament. Countries whose links had been severed during the heyday of colonialism, or who had freshly thrown off the yokes of colonialism, had met together and affirmed their collective identity and enunciated new principles which would govern their relations. Above all, they had affirmed their independence from the superpowers, even though that term was not then in use. If Tito could hitch Yugoslavia to that new star, he could find the lacking orbit, and since Yugoslavia was a European state, relatively developed in comparison to the Afro-Asia countries which met at Bandung, he could even have a leading role. I had noted that Tito had announced his support for the ten major decisions of the Bandung Conference. Through careful reading of the Brioni communiqué, one could see the germs of what later became known as the nonaligned movement. It was no great surprise to anyone who followed this important new trend that the founding conference took place in Belgrade.

During a short stop in Belgrade I found that a friend, Srdja Price, editor of a trade union paper during my first visit to Belgrade in 1946, was now undersecretary of state for foreign affairs—and as accessible as formerly. When I apologized for some of my own confused writings during the period immediately after Tito's expulsion, Price laughed and said, "Don't worry. Many of our best friends did the same, so you were in good company." He went on to give a detailed exposé of the way Stalin's attempt to isolate Yugoslavia from the outside world had forced the country to become more self-reliant and explained the importance that Tito attached to developing a "third force" movement, capable of resisting the sort of pressures to which Yugoslavia had been subjected.

Back in Budapest it was clear—as in Warsaw two months earlier—that there was an abnormally tense situation. The vibrations this time were not coming from the counts and generals and their Lake Balaton villas. The normally impeccable Váci Útca, a fashionable shopping street in the very heart of the city—a minute's walk from my hotel—stank from uncollected garbage. Shopwindows were filthy, and the displays neglected for months. The situation was worse in the less fashionable streets. The city—even from its visual aspect—reflected a breakdown in civilian morale. What was going on? It was a question I put to Miklós Gimes, as I met him striding along Petöfi Street. I had met him during the Geneva Conference, where he represented the Communist party organ *Szabad Nep*, of which he was editor. To my question, Gimes gave me an address where he would be at a dinner party that evening, to which I was cordially invited and would find "highly interesting."

I went, and it was scary, to say the least. In the spacious garden of a villa in the outskirts of Buda—the posh residential half of Budapest—there were beautiful women with long cigarette holders clustered around Gimes, all talking loudly about "revolution." As I entered, Gimes wheeled on me. "When will the Americans liberate us from the Russians?" he asked. When I said I thought the chances were nil, and even the attempt could lead to World War III, Gimes replied dramatically, "Then we will do it ourselves, and to hell with World War Three." The only guest who expressed abhorrence at contemplating a new world war with such frivolity was Ivan Boldizsar, whom I had last met as an assistant minister of foreign affairs. He had been downgraded for suspected "right-wing tendencies." We had remained good friends, and I could feel he shared my repugnance at having been drawn into a conspiratorial meeting to discuss an armed uprising.

Hungarian workers at the time had good reasons to be in a rebellious mood. Rákosi had seen as the main internal danger not the officially proclaimed plot of Belgrade, which he knew was nonsense, but the former landlord gentry and absentee landlords, who had dominated Hungarian political life for centuries. So the regime bestowed special favors on the newly liberated peasants and former landless laborers, at the expense of the working class, to insulate the peasants against the blandishments of the feudal landowner for a return to the "good old days." The presence of large numbers of Soviet troops—despite their low profile—was an easy target for discontent. It was a situation ripe to be exploited by Radio Free Europe and other such agencies. As at the time of the Mindszenty conspiracy, the line was: "Get the first shots fired, and we'll do the rest!" This was the sense of the question Gimes (who thought I was American) dramatically put to me as I arrived at the dinner party.

Apart from the rights and wrongs of the situation and genuine grievances, it was adventurism for drawing-room revolutionaries to push Hungarian workers into what could only be a hopeless enterprise. When I voiced my displeasure at having been present at such a gathering to the Hungarian journalist who had originally introduced me to Gimes, and who escorted me to my hotel from the dinner party, his only response was: "Miklós Gimes is one of our foremost intellectuals, our greatest Greek scholar." What credentials Greek scholarship bestowed on anyone to lead the risky, bloody business of an armed uprising—as Gimes did a few weeks later—I was unable to grasp.

In sharp contrast with Budapest, Prague was spick-and-span. When I remarked on the contrast in the living standards in a talk with the editor of *Rude Pravo*, the Czech Communist party daily, he maintained that the duty of his party's leadership was to ensure that Czechs ate, dressed, and lived better than anyone else in Europe. How "proletarian internationalism" came to mean that the Czechs must outmatch the West Germans car for car, refrigerator for refrigerator, TV set for TV set, and so on down the line to Pilsen lager for Munich lager, I was unable to grasp. But I was beginning to wonder what criteria were used for picking the editors of Communist party organs.

I returned to Moscow a wiser and somewhat saddened man.

The question of getting accredited for the *National Guardian* in Moscow required several days to settle. There was a reciprocal quota system in force between the United States and the Soviet Union on accrediting journalists, and all places had been taken up. That was overcome by the fact that although the newspaper was American, I was Australian, and none of my compatriot colleagues was then in Moscow. Then came the question of my Vietnamese *laissez-passer* instead of an Australian passport. That could be settled if the Vietnamese agreed to regular renewals—as they did. The last question was that of accommodation for a family of at least four. A housing unit to be reserved for journalists was under construction and would be completed within six months.

On to Peking for a rendezvous with Vessa and work for both of us in reporting on the Chinese Communist party's Eighth Congress. Almost everyone I knew in China was at Peking Airport—to welcome Khrushchev and Bulganin as the star foreign delegates.

The Eighth Congress, the first since 1945, was the counterpart of the Soviet party's Twentieth Congress as far as the post-Stalin liberalization overtones were concerned. Chairman Mao made the opening report and set the tone for what followed. Chinese-Soviet relations were still good. "We must be good at studying," said Mao, "good at learning from the Soviet Union, from the People's Democracies, from fraternal parties in other parts of the world, as well as peoples from the world over. We must never adopt the conceited attitude of great-nation chauvinism and become arrogant and complacent because of the victory of the revolution, and some successes in the construction of our country. . . ."

In his overall report, General Secretary Teng Hsiao-p'ing—whose name was almost unknown abroad at that time—backed the Soviet line in denouncing the "cult of the personality" (the euphemism used to cover up the crimes and aberrations of Stalin). An important aspect of the new party constitution, adopted after discussion and revision, was the strengthening of the right to hold minority views and protection for those who espoused them. "If the truth turns out in the end to be on the side of the minority," said Teng Hsiao-p'ing, "then the protection of the rights to minority views will help the party discover the truth." (He was later to be one of the most notable beneficiaries of this provision.)

It was a congress which reflected China's close relations with the Soviet Union, the modesty which prevailed at that time, and the prevailing wind of national reconciliation which had been a feature of the Soviet party's Twentieth Congress.

By then we had to weigh up the pros and cons of moving our base to Moscow. Among the con factors—Peter and George were now fluent in monosyllabic Vietnamese. How would they adjust to superpolysyllabic Russian? Not to mention the near-Arctic winters after the tropics. Also, Vietnam, from its ordinary citizens to the leaders, had captured our hearts. It would be an emotional wrench to leave. Among the pro factors were that there would be great, newsworthy changes in the post-Stalin era while we were running out of themes to write about with any certainty of publication in Vietnam. For Vessa there was the attraction of moving to a country nearer her own, with a language which presented no problems.

Shortly after we returned to Hanoi, the insurrection broke out in Hungary. As I had been certain, there was no "liberation force" to rush to the rescue of those who had taken to arms. The Soviet Union, strongly supported by China, intervened in a decisive way. Miklós Gimes, one of the leaders of the uprising, was captured *flagrante* distributing arms in the streets and was one of the first to be executed. A significant aspect was that the insurrection had no support from the peasantry, traditionally a strongly revolutionary force in Hungary but by then the most satisfied sector of the population. Instinctively they knew what Gimes and those at higher levels in the insurrection ignored: that Western intervention would inevitably put the Esterházys and Mindszentys on their backs again. A lot of heroism was uselessly expended in that uprising, with many of those who fomented it—

like the journalist who had introduced me to Gimes—fleeing as soon as the first shots were fired.

In April 1957, after a brief visit to Laos and Cambodia, we reluctantly packed our bags and made our farewells. Our visas for the Soviet Union had been granted, my *laissez-passer* renewed, so we left Hanoi to spend May Day in Peking, then on to Moscow.

20

Getting Used to Moscow

Moscow, 1957, was a great place for news stories, and there were few newspapermen to report them. It was the year of an international youth festival, preparations for which were in full swing as we arrived; the year of the purge of the old guard leadership; and the year of the greatest ever conference of world Communist leaders—with Mao Tse-tung present at such an event for the first and only time. Above all, it was the year of the fortieth anniversary of the Bolshevik Revolution, accompanied by the launching of the first two sputniks and a whole family of jet passenger aircraft which startled the world's air transport community.

Other aspects were not so satisfactory. The journalists' apartments were not completed, so we had to be content with two rooms in the Savoy (now Berlin) Hotel. The young monsters slept and woke at the wrong times, rarely deigned to speak anything but Vietnamese, of which we understood not a word. They boycotted food until discovering a certain "jam," which they wolfed by large spoonfuls, innocent of the fact that its true name was caviar, partaken of with reverence by well-heeled gourmets. Much of their waking time—until they were exiled to Bulgaria—was spent in kicking the testicles of an enormous stuffed Siberian bear propped up on one of the hotel staircases, putting a strain on the well-known Russian affection for small children.

An early recompense for the trials of nostalgia for Vietnam was the arrival, a few weeks after our own, of Ho Chi Minh on a state visit. There was a twenty-gun salute, national anthems of both countries, a goose-stepping march-past by the guard of honor, presentation to the diplomatic corps, on to the press corps. . . . He spotted us standing among journalists in the third row, and to the horror of security and protocol personnel and the stupefaction of the diplomatic corps, he left the solemn line of welcomers and strode over to place the huge bouquet of flowers presented as he stepped down from the plane into Vessa's arms. The members of his delegation broke line and did the same: piling their bouquets into our arms and embracing us while security and protocol looked on with almost open mouths.

Spontaneity and loyalty to old friends always took precedence over protocol with Ho Chi Minh. A few days later—after a couple of telephone calls —a huge black limousine whisked us off to what had been Stalin's dacha in the forests outside Moscow. And there we had breakfast with Ho Chi Minh. It was a simple enough brick building—certain of the walls of which lay down at the touch of a button to enable guards to rush out and deal with intruders. After inquiries about our health and that of the monsters, "Uncle" Ho filled us in about developments in Vietnam since we had left. The breakfast was just a renewal of a close friendship, with Ho Chi Minh his usual simple and cordial self. His special marks of attention almost certainly helped us with one of our major problems.

Housing for diplomats and journalists was allocated by the Service Bureau for the diplomatic corps, and until "Uncle" Ho's visit, I was met with blank looks on the weekly visits of inquiry about housing. The special unit for journalists had been completed, but it was decided to break down separating walls and convert two standard large-family apartments for Soviet residents into one for foreign journalists. That would take a few more months. But suddenly space was available in the posh Vissotni Dom (skyscraper) overlooking the Moskva River, half a mile downstream from the Kremlin. As fellow residents we had such celebrities as ballerina Galina Ulanova and writer-editor Alexander Tvardovsky. Stalin himself, it was said, had chosen the original list of occupants.

A few weeks after our arrival I had attended my first diplomatic reception, at the Burmese Embassy. I was surprised at the grim, unsmiling looks of the guests of honor—almost the entire Soviet leadership, squat, plumpish figures in uniformly dark, padded-shouldered suits, who arrived and left together, with a minimum of protocol courtesies for their hosts. It was the last time they were seen together in public. On July 3, 1957, it was announced that Vyachaslav Molotov and Georgi Malenkov, among others, had been removed from the party leadership. That evening I got a call from an old friend—Russell Spurr—then with the *Daily Express*. He asked me about the atmosphere in Moscow; how were the press and public reacting to the sensational news and so on? I had to remind him that there were special procedures for journalists talking to newspapers. (In those days and for several years that followed, telephoned or cabled stories had to be cleared by censors at the Gorky Street Central Telegraph Office.) An hour later there was another call from Spurr. Could I become the *Daily Express* correspondent in Moscow? The Press Department had no objection when I raised the matter next day; my general accreditation was sufficient to cover several papers. Since my dispatches were appearing regularly in the *National Guardian*—a paper of a very different political color—it suited Spurr and me that I write for the *Express* under another name. We settled on Andrew Wilson.

From the first days in the Soviet Union I had been fascinated by articles in scientific journals dealing with space and rocket research. I offered a feature article on this subject to the *Sunday Express*, accepted despite great reservations from its scientific editor. The next thing was a call from the foreign editor: "What great timing, old boy! You are really on the inside track." Soviet space scientists had established my "expertise" in space matters by sending aloft their first sputnik on the Saturday (October 4, 1957) before my article was due to appear. It was moved from the feature page to lead news story on page one. The bigwigs of the *Express* empire believed I was omniscient on space affairs when the next day—without violating censorship—I could permit the editor to hear the sputnik's crisp bleep-bleeps, as monitored by Moscow Radio and heard in our flat, as well as tell them when to have a man in position to photograph the sputnik streak across the sky.

World reactions were extraordinary. Within twenty-four hours, I was queried by a New York weekly specializing in aviation affairs if I had not made a mistake—was it not *eight* kilograms, not *eighty*? Among noteworthy comments was one from former President Truman, who was sure the event had never happened and the "bleeps" were Communist propaganda. Senator Stuart Symington, former U.S. secretary of the air force, demanded an immediate investigation into the delays of the U.S. space program. Overnight I had been propelled into Fleet Street headlines via outer space.

Six days before the fortieth anniversary up went another sputnik—508 kilograms and with a female dog, Laika, aboard. Among the almost universal acclaim for such a fantastic scientific feat were also some demented reactions. The British League Against Cruel Sports expressed "horror, disgust and contempt" at such an experiment with a dog, which "put scientists, whether Russian or otherwise, outside the pale of decent people," and expressed the hope that the United Nations would "outlaw such foul experiments and those who perpetrate them." Senator Symington described the event as a "technological Pearl Harbor." President Eisenhower addressed the United States on the fifth day of Laika's flight and explained that the nation had "thirty-eight different types [of missiles] either in operation or under development."

Meanwhile, Laika continued to yap her way around the world. On the twelfth day it was announced that the oxygen regeneration plant aboard Sputnik II had stopped working and that Laika had "died a painless death." At the Moscow press conference at which one of the Soviet's leading space scientists announced the death, there was a "moment of silence" for the demise of the world's first traveler in outer space. It was the sacrifice of Laika which ensured the safe return of Yuri Gagarin from a similar flight three and a half years later.

Between those flights I spent a lot of time delving into the history of Russian space and rocket research, which had started long before the Bolshevik Revolution. There were many visits to observatories and museums, including that installed at Kaluga in the home of Konstantin Tsiolkovsky, the great world pioneer in the working out of the fundamental problems of interplanetary travel, including the three cosmic speeds that had to be attained. Solutions for problems from dealing with weightlessness to designing an enormous outer-space "lifeboat" with a capacity for 200,000 people (in case some cataclysmic event made it necessary to ensure human survival by quitting our planet), were plastered around the walls of the Kaluga home of this humble teacher of mathematics.

Many specialists in the West considered the Soviet success due to the collaboration of German scientists who had worked with Wernher von Braun at Peenemünde in developing World War II guided missiles. It was a question I put to Professor Evgenyi Fyodorov, in overall charge of the Soviet space program, just after the first U.S. attempt to launch a three-and-a-half-pound satellite failed when a Vanguard rocket blew up on the launching pad at Cape Canaveral. Fyodorov's reply was:

It's true that many German rocket experts worked here after the war, but their work was restricted to showing us how the V2 worked, and its principles. But even at that time we were operating along entirely different lines. We were soon convinced that we had little or nothing to learn from them. . . . No one expects us to give away our secrets, but it must be understood that we had certain ideas which differed in important points of principle from those the Germans were proposing. We turned their schemes down: the Americans accepted them. It's as simple as that. . . .

Our scientists from the earliest days of the revolution have had the stars as their goal. . . .

Tsiolkovsky was convinced that man would conquer outer space and his works are still guiding us in our research. We had done a good deal of work on this subject long before World War II, and we were well ahead of any other country, including the United States, in rocketry. After the war our progress was faster, still with the aim of eventually constructing space-ships that would take us first to the Moon, then to other planets.*

Together with President Brezhnev, Prime Minister Khrushchev, and half a million Russians, our family was in Moscow's Red Square on April 14,

---

* Wilfred Burchett and Anthony Purdy, *Gagarin: First Man into Space* (London: Panther Books, August 1961), pp. 29–30.

1961, to welcome back to earth Yuri Gagarin, who, forty-eight hours earlier, had made history by circling the globe in 108 minutes at about 18,000 mph and guided his good spaceship *Vostok* safely back to earth. He, his wife, Valya, and Khrushchev had driven in an open flower-bedecked car through a million or so Muscovites packing the last ten miles of the route with flowers, banners, flags, and red silhouettes of rockets. "Glory to Columbus of the Cosmos," "Now to the Moon," "On to the Planets" read the slogans. Khrushchev was beaming—happier than anyone had seen him. Gagarin wore his typical, easy smile. Nothing in his space training had prepared him for this ordeal—being presented to the entire diplomatic corps at the airport reception, for instance. Everybody of importance in the Soviet Union who could be there was there. Both at the airport and at Red Square our family was at full strength, reinforced by Anna Wilfredovna, born in a Moscow hospital three years earlier; George and Peter with their eighty-nine-year-old grandfather George, who had arrived from Australia a few days earlier.

Gagarin's speech was brief, cheered madly at every sentence, especially at his conclusion: "I am sure that all my fellow space pilots are ready to fly around our planet at any time. We can state confidently that we shall fly our Soviet spaceships on more distant routes." Khrushchev took over, and Gagarin listened with the awe of one who suddenly realized he had done something really big.

> Now, when Soviet science and technique have demonstrated the highest achievement of scientific and technical progress, we cannot help looking back to the history of our country. In our mind's eye we cannot help seeing the years that have passed. . . . We have defended our state in the fire of civil war even though we were often barefooted and half naked. . . . It is with special respect that we recall the name of Konstantin Edouardovich Tsiolkovsky, scientist, dreamer and theoretician of space flights. . . .*

Khrushchev went on to mock at "some not very clever people on the other side of the ocean" who had disbelieved the announcement of the first sputnik launching, adding, "Now we can actually touch a person who has returned from the sky." After the speeches there was a monster parade. A mighty river of people with flags and banners flowed through Red Square—all eyes on the trim uniformed hero on the tribune. Later that evening, the culmination of the day's rejoicing, there was a fabulous Kremlin reception. While some 2,000 people feasted and drank inside, hundreds of thousands more thronged the streets and squares and packed the bridges to admire the floodlit Kremlin towers. Soon they were etched against a sky exploding with myriad colored showers of fireworks, all reflected in the calm waters of the Moskva River. After the speeches and toasts, the Kremlin banquet climaxed with a concert

---

* *Ibid.,* pp. 14–15.

in which the country's greatest singers, musicians, and dancers paid their homage to the first hero of outer space.

Back at the apartment the telephone was ringing. A London literary agent and old friend! Panther Books, London, wanted a book on the first man into space and everything connected with him getting there. If it sent a writer on space affairs to Moscow to help, could I turn out a book within a month? The reception had been a heady affair, and I agreed. My shelves by then were bulging with everything I had been able to collect on the subject. A few days later Anthony Purdy arrived. We divided our tasks—mainly to reduce into orderly and connected form the vast amount of background material I had filed away. Within less than four months of Yuri Gagarin's being blasted off into outer space, the book telling all about it was in the windows of England's leading bookshops and being translated into a dozen different languages.

Like a thousand or so other journalists around the world, I had applied for an interview as soon as he went into orbit. By that time extracts of my space reports in the *Daily Express* had often been reported back to the Soviet press. But until the last moment it was not certain that an interview would be possible.

Even after it was set up, as we waited in the old-fashioned reception room of the State Committee for Cultural Relations, Vladimir Kozhin, deputy head of the Press Department, who had helped arrange the meeting and was to act as interpreter, said, "I never thought this would happen. . . . It is rare enough for our own journalists to talk with him. We have had applications from all parts of the world. They have all been turned down." However, the door opened.

Gagarin entered briskly, alone and smiling. The first impression was of his good-natured personality: big smile—a grin, really—light step and an air of sunny friendliness. He is short, stocky and powerfully built. But the key to his character, perhaps, lay in two other points: his handshake and his eyes. His hands are incredibly hard: his eyes an almost luminous blue. . . .

Gagarin had not asked for questions in advance, and his replies were very rapid—the translator had difficulty in keeping up.

Words tumbled out, facts and jokes and interjections, with pauses only to refresh his memory. He gestured with his hands constantly, trying to draw pictures in the air. "My worst moment?" His right arm shot up: "The first minute." The hand swooped down—"and the re-entry." He tapped the table with his finger. "But 'worst' is a comparative word. There wasn't one 'bad' moment. Everything worked, everything was organized properly, nothing went wrong. . . ."

Before he left our interview, the young major collected another memento of his historic trip. Burchett's father, at 89, the oldest working journalist in Australia, was on holiday in Moscow at the time. In his luggage was a hunting boomerang and he walked into the room with it just as Gagarin was leaving. "Please take this," he said, holding it out, "as a symbol of safe return. It always comes back and I hope you and your colleagues do too." Gagarin, delighted, examined the precision-carved weapon closely, while one of the interpreters rapidly explained its use, and how experts could actually catch it on its return. "I shall treasure it," said Gagarin, swishing it a few inches in the air. "It's a nice sort of symbol to have." *

Unfortunately the talisman did not work. In March 1968 Colonel Yuri Gagarin was killed while testing a new type of jet plane. His ashes were buried in the Kremlin wall, and the country observed one minute of silence. Apart from all his other merits, he was a warm, lovable human being who never failed to greet our family members when our paths crossed.

The book was an immediate best-seller, but there was a curious incident with a publishing firm in the United States. It had bought North American rights from Panther Books for a considerable sum but later refused to publish on the grounds that it was "Soviet propaganda." Panther Books sued and, in an action which was settled only five years later, extracted a large sum for breach of contract. The publisher received a drubbing down from the judge who heard the case. If the flight itself was undoubtedly splendid propaganda for the Soviet Union, it would have been strange had the book not reflected this, observed the judge quite properly in his summing-up.

On almost the same day the Gagarin book appeared, Gherman Stepanovich Titov was projected into outer space. Instead of 1 orbit in 108 minutes, he performed 17 orbits and stayed aloft for 25 hours. Another request from the same publishing house. Purdy came out again, and we had a much longer interview with Titov than with Gagarin. He had the training of a scientist as well as a cosmonaut and was very articulate, but in layman's language, as to the scientific aspects of his flight. After three weeks Purdy returned with the bulk of the manuscript, while I went into the depths of Siberia to spend a memorable weekend with Titov's family. Father Stepan epitomized everything that is good, romantic, and generous in the Russian character. He lived near Barnaul, on the southeastern fringes of the Siberian lowlands. It was only midautumn, but the country was already deep under snow; I stayed in the home of the manager of a collective farm, the lands of which included the village where Stepan was the local schoolteacher. I was driven to and from his home through a magnificent birch forest in a one-horse sleigh with tinkling bells. The reason for the visit was to get not only something of the family background of Gherman Stepanovich but also a feeling of how people lived in remote Siberia.

---

* *Ibid.*, pp. 119–23.

At our first meeting Stepan, a lithe, energetic man with a limp, apologized for not having had room to accommodate me in his log cabin. As we drove back that night, the farm manager explained that Stepan had returned from World War II to find that a large family, whose breadwinner had been killed at the front, had been evacuated to the village but was lodged in very crowded conditions. As the schoolmaster Stepan had a spacious house awaiting him. After family discussions, he and the future cosmonaut built a log cabin big enough for the parents, younger sister, and Gherman. The schoolmaster's house was turned over to the fatherless family. It is the sort of thing that could have happened in the pioneering days of my native Gippsland.

When the farm manager learned that I was Australian, he asked if I knew anything about rabbits, explaining that as a new sideline the farm was breeding them for their pelts. He had a feeling that it was wasteful just to feed the carcasses to the pigs. Were they edible for humans? "Try roasting them like chickens," I advised. The next evening at the Titov home, where as many people as could be accommodated were crammed into the dining room, there was a mountain of roast rabbit on the table—at least three per head. Since vodka flowed in the same proportions, it was a merry evening. Stepan played the violin; the guests sang all the old favorites; toasts were drunk to Gherman Stepanovich and spacemen in general, to peace and international friendship, and a special one to me for having introduced roast rabbit into the local diet.

The Titov book had an unhappy ending as far as I was concerned. While production was under way, I discovered it was being published under the title *My Flight into Outer Space*, by Gherman Titov, as told to Wilfred Burchett and Anthony Purdy. The clear understanding when my coauthor left with the manuscript was that it was to be *Gherman Titov's Flight into Outer Space*, by Wilfred Burchett and Anthony Purdy. How could Titov be held responsible for what we had written about his flight when only about one-fifth of the contents had come directly from him? The covers for the first edition had already been printed by the time I telephoned the publishers to demand that the original title—as agreed with Titov—be retained. This was done, and I was billed with the costs, which turned out to be more than my share of the royalties.

21

Icebreaking

CAREFULLY ADJUSTING a cream-colored *shapka*—for full photographic effect—as he stepped from the plane's hatchway at Moscow's snow-covered airport, the tall figure stepped down the gangway to be effusively greeted by Nikita Khrushchev, his face wreathed in smiles. After the welcoming formalities, the visitor walked to the microphone:

"Until today, the only British prime minister to visit the Soviet Union has been Sir Winston Churchill. I am content to follow the example set by the greatest living Englishmen. At the same time I can claim to be making history. When Sir Winston came as the guest of Marshal Stalin, our two countries were joined together in a common alliance; we were both resolved to spend the last drop of our blood and treasure to prevent the triumph of tyranny. This is the first time a British prime minister has visited the Soviet Union in time of peace. . . ."

At the Kremlin reception that night George Hutchinson, diplomatic correspondent of the *Evening Standard*, the evening member of the Beaverbrook empire, shook my hand and said, "You know we arranged Macmillan's visit. He took your story in the *Sunday Express* as an official invitation." On a Saturday afternoon a few weeks earlier the *Sunday Express* had telephoned to say that on the previous Friday, Hutchinson had reported in the *Standard* that in reply to a question whether he had any plans to visit the Soviet Union, Harold Macmillan had replied that there was no invitation for such a visit. Could I check the Soviet attitude? On a Saturday afternoon! Moreover, the Soviet Foreign Ministry never commented on newspaper speculation. It so happened that sitting alongside me was an old colleague of Molotov's who occasionally dropped in on a Saturday. He was in retirement, but I knew he still had some contacts at the Foreign Office. He knew enough

English—and about politics—to grasp the importance of my query and offered his "very personal" and "absolutely nonofficial" opinion that ever since the Bulganin-Khrushchev visit to England in April 1956, there was an outstanding invitation for a return visit. The Soviet Union always favored such top-level contacts.

Knowing that I could be expelled, with practically nowhere to go in view of my no-passport situation, I phoned the *Sunday Express* from my office—three rooms away from my Soviet friend—to the effect that a Macmillan visit, "according to well-informed sources," would be welcome. It made the headlines next day. Having committed a most flagrant breach of censorship, I spent a few uneasy days, while Hutchinson and the other diplomatic correspondents in London speculated about the implications of what was taken as an official reaction.

Fortunately, in a surprisingly short time, Macmillan announced to the House of Commons that he had "instructed Her Majesty's ambassador in Moscow" to suggest a visit, and "I am glad to tell the House that the Soviet Chargé d'Affaires in London informed us that his Government welcomed this proposal. . . ." Five days later, on February 10, 1959, Macmillan arrived. Happily the visit was a success—a major breakthrough, in fact—in East-West relations, the beginning of the era of détente.

The name of Andrew Wilson was appearing on too many important exclusives to please the hearts and minds of some of the back-bench powers at the *Daily Express*. It was decided to send a staff correpondent, Christopher Dobson, to whom I would play the role of an anonymous second fiddle. Andrew Wilson dropped dead on the day he arrived. (At the time the pseudonym was agreed on I was unaware of the existence of an authentic Andrew Wilson, writing for the *Observer*. My sudden disappearance from Moscow must have confused those who followed Fleet Street affairs.)

If Macmillan's arrival at Moscow Airport was an exercise in "antifreeze," I was to witness another airport reception later that year, in which Khrushchev also starred, which was a study in "deep freeze." I had gone to Peking to cover the celebrations of the tenth anniversary of the founding of the Chinese People's Republic. The most notable of the guests was Nikita, arriving after only one day's stopover in Moscow from his famous Camp David talks with President Eisenhower. When he walked down the gangway, he clearly expected to be embraced by Mao. Instead, there was a handshake, and with a wave of his hand, Mao directed the Soviet leader to an improvised tribune and microphone. Fumbling in his pocket, Khrushchev pulled out a bit of paper and started to speak. The message was that American capitalist society was very strong and not to be trifled with. Khrushchev was convinced that Eisenhower wanted peace, and the "Camp David spirit" was a new foremost element in international affairs.

Stuffing his speech back into his pocket, Khrushchev looked up at Mao, awaiting the applause. Like a bandleader conducting a very slow fox-trot, Mao clapped his plump hands about five times, and the rest of the front-rank welcomers followed suit. Right in front of the tribune clapping in rhythm with Mao were Chou En-lai, Defense Minister Lin Piao, Vice-President Tung P'i-wu, and other party and government leaders. Clap-clap-clap-clap-clap! Khrushchev looked up again at Mao for the return speech. All he got was a look of cold contempt as Mao waved to the steps leading down from the tribune. Red in the face and looking like a schoolboy who had been spanked in front of the class, Khrushchev stepped down and got into the waiting limousine.

It was the first visual signal that something had gone wrong in Chinese-Soviet relations. There were other signs that same evening—September 30, 1959. Five thousand people were at the great banquet to celebrate the tenth anniversary and honor the chief guest. Unprecedentedly the foreign press were seated in such a position that they could hear—but not see or photograph—the main participants. While interpreters were on hand for Chou En-lai's welcoming speech, there were none for Khrushchev's reply. Nor was there a text, except for a few copies distributed by a *Tass* correspondent. For most of the foreign correspondents Khrushchev, straight from his meeting with Eisenhower, was the main attraction, but he had carefully been relegated to the role of a sideshow.

Chou En-lai, always the impeccable diplomat, congratulated him on the "success of his mission to the United States as an envoy of peace." Khrushchev gave an extended version of his airport remarks.

He got about the same sort of reaction as at the airport. When I asked Chiao Kuan-hua and a few other friends what had gone wrong, I was told that Mikhail Suslov, chief Soviet ideologist, who had arrived in Peking three days ahead of Khrushchev, had revealed that in order to give the "spirit of Camp David" a good start, Khrushchev had promised Eisenhower that he was going back on an earlier pledge to help China develop a nuclear capacity. (Later versions claimed that he had also revealed the site at which China was preparing its nuclear installations.)

Unofficially the abnormal atmosphere at the airport and banquet was explained away as caused by the Chinese official concern not to let Khrushchev steal the thunder from the tenth anniversary celebrations. The real truth, which few of us outsiders grasped at the time, was that a historic rift, bound to widen and deepen, had started. Sino-Soviet relations were to be put into the deep freeze, "for ten thousand years—give or take a thousand or two years," as Mao was later to express it. Who could have predicted that within less than a year of the scene between the glowering Mao and the sulking Khrushchev at Peking Airport all Soviet aid projects in China would have been halted, all technicians withdrawn together with the blueprints of the enterprises under construction?

Another cause of dissension was the tacit support given by the Soviet Union to India in its frontier dispute with China—the first time a socialist state had ever sided with a nonsocialist state in such a situation. China, correctly in my view, took umbrage and interpreted it as an unprincipled attempt by Khrushchev to take an important trick at China's expense.

The core of the problem was China's assertion of authority over Tibet, where the India of Jawaharlal Nehru considered it had inherited the "special interests" that Britain had carved out for itself at the end of the nineteenth century. China had built a motorable highway providing access to Tibet from Sinkiang. It passed through Aksai Chin in Ladakh, which Nehru claimed as part of the Indian territory of Jammu-Kashmir. India did not discover this highway until it had been functioning for two years, but this did not deter Nehru from pushing his claims and demanding a Chinese withdrawal. As each side dug in and reinforced its military positions, border clashes occurred. Aksai Chin in the west and Longju—a disputed mountain peak in the east—became two big names in the world press as the hot spots along the Sino-Indian frontier which could spark off a major conflagration. I knew from contacts with Chou En-lai and Chiao Kuan-hua during the Khrushchev visit that China was not looking for trouble on its southern borders. But there was no question of abandoning the strategic and only all-weather highway linking the two provinces of Sinkiang and Tibet.

It was a situation in which some diplomatic-journalistic therapy might be useful. At least this was the opinion of K. P. S. Menon, the Indian ambassador to Moscow, who persuaded me to look into the situation. "You know the Peking end," he said. "You are a friend to both our countries. Why not get the New Delhi view?" Early in March 1960 I flew from Moscow to New Delhi.

One of the first persons I met was General Brij Mohan Kaul, who had just been promoted Chief of the General Staff of the Indian Army. An old friend, he was his frank and amicable self. In the map room at General Headquarters, he unrolled a map showing Longju and the McMahon Line (the British-Indian version of the frontier). It was an inch thick on the map, and Longju was in the middle of it. "It looks big in the newspaper headlines," he said. "In fact, it's nothing. It was a deserted peak until we occupied it a few months ago. But the Chinese knocked us off it, and now there's bloody hell to pay."

He rolled down another map of the Aksai Chin area which showed part of the Sinkiang–Tibet highway passing through it. "We say it's ours. They say it's theirs," General Kaul said. "We didn't even know there was a road until we sent in a reconnaissance patrol after a Chinese newspaper had published a map showing the road on it. They grabbed our patrol." When I asked what the solution was, he said, "Simple. We give them Aksai Chin; they give us Longju and recognize the McMahon Line." When I remarked that I thought that was what the Chinese had been proposing, General Kaul said, "Maybe they should propose it again."

I found Defense Minister Krishna Menon in a very gloomy mood. 'The Chinese are out to humiliate us," he said. "Nehru has got such a shock that he'll never get over it."

To my surprise, I found that Chester Ronning, the Canadian high commissioner, and Walter Crocker, the Australian high commissioner—whom I met separately—considered India in the wrong, at both Longju and Aksai Chin. "Nehru has not a leg to stand on," said Ronning, "and my opinion is based on extensive research." Crocker, who turned out to be an old friend of Sir Frederick Eggleston, Australia's first ambassador to China, said, "I have had to do a lot of research and look up a lot of historical records to prepare a report for my government. I have come to the conclusion that Nehru is very much in the wrong."

The Western press had automatically swung to Nehru's defense, but here were two senior Commonwealth diplomats saying that a senior Commonwealth prime minister was in the wrong and Communist China was in the right. Crocker, moreover, was highly critical of Nehru's inflexibility in refusing to respond to conciliatory approaches from Chou En-lai. Both Ronning and Crocker expressed the hope that Nehru would be in a more reasonable frame of mind when Chou En-lai arrived for talks the following week.

At the initiative of P. N. Menon, head of the Press Department, I had a talk with Nehru. Menon wanted me to get the point across that having been in China only five months earlier, I had found no trace of hostility toward Nehru in top-level circles.

Nehru was ill at ease, looking everywhere except at me, as I expressed my regrets at the situation developing between two countries and leaderships that I admired and told of my Peking conversations. When I expressed the hope that the negotiations with Chou En-lai would be positive, he looked up sharply and said, "Talks, not negotiations." He would not be drawn into any discussion, except to reiterate that it was a clear-cut case of Chinese aggression and that China would have to withdraw or would be forced to do so. It was the only meeting at such a level which I felt was a total loss of time. The impression was that Nehru's hurt pride had become the major factor. But there were other factors, more cogent than hurt pride.

From the first hints of serious Sino-Indian differences both the United States and the USSR had been assiduously wooing Nehru. President Eisenhower had visited New Delhi in December 1959, and in a very different tone from that in which John Foster Dulles had railed at Indian-type neutralism as "dangerous and immoral" Eisenhower told the Indian Parliament that India "speaks to other nations of the world with the greatness of conviction and is heard with greatness of respect. India is a triumph that offsets the world failures of the past decade, a triumph that . . . a century from now may offset them all." This was heady stuff for a nation that had been berated for having a begging-bowl approach to its economic problems and had been rapped over the knuckles every time it proffered an opinion on world problems. The material rewards for a tough attitude toward "Red China" were also not to be niggled at. U.S. economic aid to India in the twelve years preceding mid-1959 averaged $16 million. In the four following years, it increased to an annual average of $1 billion. This was the type of almost irresistible bait that Eisenhower was able to offer Nehru.

To maintain "balance," Khrushchev also arrived in New Delhi in February 1960, and agreement was reached on greatly expanding Soviet economic aid—including the development of nuclear power—and the supply of special military equipment suitable for use in mountainous areas. It was only after the arrival of Khrushchev in New Delhi that Nehru accepted the third of Chou En-lai's proposals for a meeting to settle the frontier and any other problems between the two countries.

I was back in Moscow when the Chou En-lai visit took place and he proposed in great detail a formula suggested by many of my highly placed Indian friends and contacts. Nehru rejected the lot. It seems that after Eisenhower's assurances of active support and Khrushchev's benevolent neutrality, Nehru had invited Chou En-lai to humiliate him in revenge for what he considered his own humilitation. Chou En-lai returned to Peking empty-handed.

Nehru adopted what was called the forward policy of military tactics, a provocative concept of what he described as establishing a "crisscross of military posts" in between and sometimes behind Chinese positions in the eastern sector. After repeated warnings from Peking, the Chinese struck back at the end of October 1962, hurling the Indians out of all the positions they had occupied, chasing them well south of the McMahon Line before withdrawing to their original positions. Krishna Menon was sacked, Kaul resigned, and Nehru this time tasted the real bitterness of humiliation. After Nehru several times refused to discuss the return of Indian prisoners (he having none to offer in exchange), the Chinese returned them without negotiations. Indian-Chinese relations went into the deep freeze. Nehru died two years later, but this changed nothing.

Years later, when India began to have second thoughts about the whole question, it was China that played hard to get. At the fourth summit conference of nonaligned nations in Algiers in September 1973, I was approached by P. N. Haksar. By then he was in semiretirement but was at Algiers as principal secretary to Prime Minister Indira Gandhi. After inquiries on my relations with the Chinese—which were still good—he speculated whether the time was not ripe to settle India's relations with China. Peking's suspicions (strong at the time) that India was going to grant naval bases to the Soviet Union were absolutely unfounded. India would remain faithful to its nonaligned and anti-imperialist positions. He would be glad to go to China in an official or a private capacity to sound out the possibility of an overall settlement. Haksar made clear that he was talking to me with the approval of Indira Gandhi.

It was a good idea, and since India and China were still not talking to each other, I transmitted it to my old friend Chiao Kuan-hua, then deputy foreign minister. There was no reply, meaning that a serious peace offer had been passed by.

This venture into quasi-diplomatic activity was unsuccessful, and there is a viewpoint that it is unprofessional for a journalist to step in "where angels fear to tread." Obviously I do not subscribe to this. Those who are responsible and discreet can be icebreakers and bridgebuilders without violating any ethics of the profession or contractual arrangements with their editors and publishers.

In disputes between states there are more than reasons of face involved in a leader's taking the initiative in proposing a solution. There are plenty of examples for the side that takes the initiative to be considered by the other side as weakening and so the pressures should be increased to make him crack. But for either side to reply to a journalist's well-placed questions involves neither loss of face nor a weakening of a bargaining position. Also, for a journalist to use his unique position to transmit discreetly a bit of information from one side or the other to get clogged machinery moving (without making newspaper headlines out of it) is a useful and honorable thing to do. I have no apologies for having acted as a "drop of oil" on such occasions.

22

Vietnam Burns Again

AFTER FIVE YEARS in Moscow my thoughts were turning more
and more to Asia, specifically to Vietnam. Occasional travelers from
Vietnam brought alarming reports of renewed fighting and the possibility of
full-scale war. In Moscow the *Daily Express* had a staff correspondent, soon
joined by others from the *Daily Mail*, the *Daily Telegraph*, and the BBC.
As far as the British press and media were concerned, my trailblazer role was
finished. After the *Express* no longer needed my services, I transferred to the
Financial Times, whose investor readers needed objective information about
Soviet economic developments and market research reporting. This was interesting as a new field of activity, but remote from my real interests. My
conviction that I was never cut out to be a headquarters reporter was reinforced. Even at the most exhilarating moments in reporting on outer-space
conquests, my interests were firmly anchored in the problems of our ter-
restrial globe. It was there that the future of humanity was to be decided.

In the spring of 1962 I revisited the former states of Indochina, for a
much-needed touchdown with reality. In talks with Ho Chi Minh in Hanoi;
with the Laotian half brother princes, Souphanouvong on the Plain of Jars
and Souvanna Phouma in Vientiane, with Prince Norodom Sihanouk in
Phnom Penh; and with scores of refugees along the borders of Cambodia,
Laos, and trickling across the seventeenth parallel into North Vietnam, I
became convinced that the United States was already engaged in a secret
war in South Vietnam and Laos and that intolerable pressures were being
brought to bear on Sihanouk to abandon his policy of neutrality in Cambodia.

I found Ho Chi Minh deeply distressed at the increasing hostility between
the Soviet Union and China and at the violence of Khrushchev's attacks
against Stalin and the Albanian Communist leadership at the Soviet's
twenty-second Party Congress in October of the previous year. It was the

211

congress at which support for Khrushchev's denunciations of the Albanians was the touchstone of loyalty to the Soviet or Chinese party leadership. The Vietnamese delegation, like many others, had refused to join the routine attacks, expected from every delegate as his message of greetings to the Congress. But Ho Chi Minh, representing a country performing a prodigious balancing act between the two Communist giants, resented the surrogate role allotted to Albania.

"I am very angry at the attacks against Albania," said Ho Chi Minh at a typical early-morning breakfast. "I am also angry at the nature of the Albanian attacks against the Soviet leadership after the congress. Words and expressions were used which will leave irreparable scars." As an expression of confidence in my discretion, he revealed that he had written to Khrushchev, making three main points: Stalin belonged to the international Communist movement as well as to the Soviet Union, and his image should not have been destroyed without consultations with other fraternal parties; Albania must still be considered part of the socialist bloc; Vietnam rejoiced at each Soviet success in building socialism and each victory in the conquest of outer space as its own success and victory. "Uncle" Ho was very concerned about the effects of the Sino-Soviet split on Vietnam's own struggle. "We consider," he said, "that in fulfilling our duty to our comrades in the South, we are also fulfilling our international duty. In the long run, we hope this will contribute to healing the rift between our Soviet and Chinese comrades." Historically the Vietnamese party, through its links with the French Communist party, of which Ho Chi Minh was a founder member, had closer links with the Soviet than the Chinese Communist party.

When I changed the subject by suggesting that I have a look at the situation in the South, Ho Chi Minh advised me first to visit the frontier areas and I proceeded to do so in the following weeks.

All along the frontiers the story was the same, from the Vietnamese and from the minority peoples, especially along Vietnam's borders with Laos and Cambodia. A great drive was on to herd the peasantry and tribespeople into the glorified concentration camps known as strategic hamlets. Along Cambodia's southern frontier, which bordered Vietnam's Mekong Delta provinces, the smoke and smell of battle lay heavy in the air as Operation Sunrise raged to its climax. It was the first big one of its kind directed by American advisers and supported by U.S. air power. At that time I could only see and hear what was going on and listen to the tales of refugees fleeing the horrors of napalm and antipersonnel bombs and the "pacification teams" which came to drag the survivors off to the strategic hamlets.

It was along the seventeenth parallel that I ran into Nguyen Van Hieu, general secretary of the South Vietnamese Liberation Front, on his way to Hanoi to report on the First Congress of the National Liberation Front, held in Tay Ninh Province between February 16 and March 3, 1962. He was the first leading Vietcong cadre I had met, an impressive person, with a calm, reflective face and a brilliant, analytical mind. (After Vietnam's re-unification he became the Socialist Republic's minister of culture.) To my first question on what stage the struggle had reached, he replied: "By and large, Ngo Dinh Diem controls the towns and most—but not all—of the strategic highways. We hold the countryside. But if Diem and their U.S. military advisers want to move outside Saigon, they can do so only by mounting a military operation. They dare not move even ten or fifteen miles north of the capital. Terror and brutal repression are driving everyone into the arms of the resistance." When I asked where the NLF was getting its arms from, Nguyen Van Hieu said, "At this stage we use captured U.S. arms in all major actions, also those brought over from deserters from the Saigon forces —often whole units. The Americans claim we get our arms from North Vietnam. That would be stupid even if it were possible. Think of the transport problem—especially when our most important actions take place in the southernmost regions. The Americans deliver them right where we need them. Obviously it's better to have the type of arms for the type of ammunition we can capture—or buy on the black market."

It became clear that the Vietcong war in the South was following a similar pattern to that which had been waged by the Vietminh against the French. I returned to Moscow convinced that the war would become of major dimensions. Once having engaged in such a venture, the United States would keep doubling its stakes—but it would be defeated. By that time I knew something of Vietnamese history and the way in which rulers and people had stood up to every invader and occupier for more than 2,000 years—and in the end defeated them. Thus, in a book which I wrote immediately after that lengthy visit, there were some prophetic remarks which successive U.S. Presidents would have done well to have heeded:

> France sent its most illustrious generals and marshals to the Indochina war. One after another they lost their reputations or their lives, sometimes both. . . .
> The Pentagon generals seem bent on following the same road. They seem to think they can do better with Dictator Diem than the French did with Emperor Bao Dai, plus US support. The debris of US planes, tanks and artillery pieces in Dien Bien Phu valley should be sufficient warning as to what lies at the end of the road. America may have more generals than the French, whose lives or reputations—or both—are expendable. The end result will be the same. They do not have enough to force the Vietnamese to their knees.*

Clearly the White House could be excused for not changing its policies

* Wilfred Burchett, *The Furtive War* (New York: International Publishers, 1963), pp. 138–39.

because of the opinions of a foreign, radical journalist like myself. But there were prestigious, homegrown, nonradical American journalistic experts who were saying the same sort of thing. They found, as I did, that there are few enterprises as difficult and hazardous as trying to take a war away from the warmakers once they have sunk their fangs into it. If any reader thinks I got satisfaction at being one of the first to warn about what the United States was heading for in Vietnam, this was not the case. To the contrary. I was so depressed by the certainty of what was going to happen in Vietnam and frustrated with the widespread official indifference that I spent four months on my back—three of them in a Moscow hospital—starting shortly after my return from Indochina. Medically my trouble was diagnosed as radiculitis, an inflammation of a nerve root in the back. Western psychiatric friends later told me I was more likely suffering from "radicalitis," which in my case took a psychosomatic form brought on by worrying too much. I was in bad shape for a while, so much so that the Australian writer Frank Hardy, after visiting me in the hospital, reported back to mutual friends that "Burchett will never walk again—probably he will never even leave the hospital." I, however, had other plans—mainly to get into South Vietnam as soon as possible and see things for myself.

In the waiting room at Vientiane Airport in early November 1963, awaiting the courier plane of the International Control Commission to continue its flight from Hanoi to Phnom Penh, I suddenly noticed that in the vacant chair alongside me was a Hermès baby typewriter. Moving discreetly to another seat in the shadows farthest from the entry, I watched with horror as the bulky form and well-known face of Ted Howe sat down to share the seat with the typewriter. We had worked together in the Berlin days, when he was correspondent for Lord Kemsley's *Daily Sketch*. His wife, Robin—author of numerous books on international cuisine—and Ted had been my hosts at a splendid luncheon in New Delhi some three years previously. His eyes traveled vaguely around the waiting room, dwelt momentarily on my face, then passed on. My disguise—a Hemingway type of graying black beard and dark glasses—had worked. Had he checked the passenger list, he would have found an Austrian, named Burckardt, businessman, booked to Phnom Penh. Ted's eyes roamed back and started to give me a fixed, puzzled look when, mercifully, his flight to Bangkok was announced. He grabbed his typewriter and hastened to the exit.

I was engaged in my most important journalistic enterprise since Hiroshima, and my deepest desire was not to encounter any colleagues at that stage. The beard was a real one, acquired during more than a month's sojourn with NLF guerrillas just south of the seventeenth parallel, across the frontier from Laos. Cadres from the northern provinces of South Vietnam and from the Central Highlands came to various rendezvous points to brief me on what was going on in their areas, mainly on exactly how the first shots were fired and on the up-to-date situation. Obviously I needed to get closer to the heart of things—nearer to Saigon, where the NLF leadership was located. So I returned to Hanoi to make elaborate plans to get into Cambodia and from there into the NLF headquarters area without any risk of compromising Sihanouk's policy of neutrality. He would have had no option but to refuse if I had asked legal permission. If it were done without his knowledge, it would be just one more of the hundreds of daily illegal crossings, over which he had no control. Thus, the slight alteration to my face, name, and nationality. The North Vietnamese and the NLF attached great importance to not compromising Sihanouk's position, and so did I.

There were no problems at the airport, where the identities of travelers on the ICC plane were virtually never checked. But an hour after I settled into my hotel, there was a knock at the door, and there was a tall sandy-haired individual, with outstretched hand and an American voice, saying, "Hi! You're Wilfred Burchett? I'm Russ Johnson of the American Friends Service Committee. I saw your name on the list downstairs and couldn't believe my luck. I've been reading your articles in the *Guardian* and thought you were probably still in the jungles of Quang Nam."

What to do? The carefully laid plans were blown sky high. He had a decent face, and his organization a good name. I decided to throw myself on his integrity. "I've just come from Quang Nam," I said, "and you will read about it in my articles. But please do me one favor. You've stumbled across me by accident. Don't reveal my presence to journalist colleagues, or they'll be pestering me every moment. I need a rest, which is why I chose this rather obscure hotel." He promised total discretion and kept his pledge. This was the basis of a solid friendship, renewed at meetings in many parts of the globe.

Later I found out that my local friend who had made the preliminary arrangements had booked me into a hotel off the beaten tourist tracks, as requested, but had forgotten about my changed identity. It was one of the few hotels which listed its guests on an illuminated panel alongside the reception desk. The usual hotel accommodations were all booked up for the celebrations of the tenth anniversary of independence, the reason why Russ Johnson had discovered my modest hideout.

Early the next morning I was whisked off by car toward the border with South Vietnam's Tay Ninh Province. That night, after we had crossed the Mekong by ferry at Kompong Cham and rested up in a rubber plantation during the heat of the afternoon and early evening, the driver made several approaches to a point where the road most closely paralleled the frontier. On the fourth or fifth run—when there were no followers—the driver slowed down and blinked his lights three times. There were three answering points of light. We braked to a halt, and I jumped out. Body and haversack were seized by faceless hands and propelled into a reed-filled ditch just as three truckloads of Cambodian troops, arms at the ready, trundled slowly by, spotlights sweeping our side of the road. Then there were handshakes, but no words, and it was indicated that I should cling to the rifle barrel of the guerrilla ahead of me as we moved off. We walked as fast and noiselessly as the crackling dried leaves under rubber sandals permitted. After about an hour we sat down on a log, and signs were made indicating extra caution. A few minutes later a guerrilla turned up to indicate that all was well. We continued for another two hours, the most difficult moments for me—as in my travels farther north—being when we had to shuffle across "bridges" made of a single, perfectly round tree trunk.

Finally, we halted, and haversacks were dumped on the ground. Now there were broad smiles, more vigorous handshakes, and the words *Nam Bo* ("the South") were pronounced. Cigarettes were lit, and everyone relaxed. Conversation was limited only by language difficulties—my too few words of Vietnamese and their too few words of French.

While we were resting, two guerrillas hacked down a small sapling, trimmed the branches, and attached the cords of my hammock to each end. I was invited to lie in what was by now a palanquin suspended between the shoulders of two stocky guerrillas. With some indignation I invited them to test the steely quality of my leg muscles. There were smiles and appreciative murmurs, as a result of which the hammock was untied and folded and the pole thrown away. When we met up with an interpreter next day, he explained that the guerrillas had been informed that I was "old and not used to walking." This was a slander on my fifty-two years and previous months' activities, including a stiff training program. But it was rare that I found the guerrillas to be misinformed.

In those days, only those southerners who had been evacuated to the North in accordance with the Geneva Agreement were permitted to return. They had gone north by boat but would return on foot. Many were too old or not fit enough to make it, so the training program in North Vietnam's mountainous Hoa Binh Province was, in fact, an elimination test. It included high-speed forced marches, mountain climbing, eating rice or manioc exclusively for days on end, shooting with rifle and pistol. (In fact, I never carried a weapon during my four subsequent visits to the war zones.) But just as my hosts did not want to risk my life because of an inability to survive the rigors and pace of People's War, neither did I want to risk the lives of traveling companions by failure to match their pace. Thus, I insisted—and succeeded in proving—I could meet their standards, thanking my lucky stars for those years of tramping around Australia during the Depression years.

On the second day after I crossed the frontier, bicycles were produced. Dashing across clearings, fording streams, and clambering up dried riverbeds on pony back had been included in the training—but not bicycle riding. My impressions, noted down at the time, deal with some of the hazards:

A narrow, winding trail, never more than three or four yards straight, with roots and snags everywhere; tiny stumps where undergrowth had been slashed close to—but not level with—the earth, jabbing at your pedal and ankles; overhead creepers waiting to strangle you while you are looking down to avoid a stump; trellises of bamboo banging at your head no matter how low you bent over the handle-bars: a multitude of spikes reaching out to rip your shirts and flesh to shreds; a combination of traps, snags, loops and spikes trying to trip you up and unseat you at every turn. . . .

Worst of all, added to the previous terror of the single-log bridges, was that the bike as well now had to be manoeuvred across, usually on one's shoulders. But when we emerged after a few hours of snag-ridden, serpentine trail on to what still bore resemblance to a hard-toppd highway, I began to appreciate being on wheels again. The old sense of balance soon returned and the miles began to whizz by. It was better than a jeep because with the silence of bike travel we always had plenty of warning of approaching planes and could pull into the undergrowth.

My first Nam Bo bike was a Mavic, and although it was French-made, the frame and both wheels were stamped with clasped US-Vietnamese hands and the legend that it was a gift of the people of the USA. Just like the bombs and napalm! The same with the haversacks of the guerillas and troops we passed on the road. Haversacks were almost invariably white flour sacks, stamped in big letters: THIS IS A GIFT OF THE PEOPLE OF THE USA. NOT TO BE SOLD OR EXCHANGED. . . . Apart from the captured weapons themselves, almost every other bit of equipment I came across, from generators to spot-welding machines and X-ray equipment, bore the clasped hands and the standard legend. . . .*

On the third day after crossing the frontier, our group was expanded to include an interpreter, a doctor, a cook, a cadre in charge of security, another from the NLF press service, and a personal bodyguard. For almost three months we traveled together, supplemented by guides who were changed from region to region. We were almost continually on the move, setting forth immediately after dawn and traveling until midday, with a ten-minute break for each hour of cycling. After lunch there was a siesta, and in the late afternoon and evenings, visits to army units, villages, jungle arsenals, clinics, interviews, cultural performances. The temperature, hot and humid by day, was always tolerable at night, and except when artillery and mortar shells were exploding too close, I slept wonderfully well in a hammock slung between two trees, under a mosquito net topped by a nylon fly to keep off leaves and insects.

It was before U.S. chemical warfare had stripped the trees of their leaves and killed off bird and animal life, before rubber plantations and virgin jungle had been gouged out of existence by "Roman plows," and one felt

---

* Wilfred Burchett, *Vietnam: Inside Story of the Guerilla War* (New York: International Publishers, 1965), pp. 25–27.

wonderfully secure traveling and resting under a thick canopy of jungle green. Having set forth the sort of things I wanted to see and photograph, the type of people I wanted to meet, everything which could illustrate how People's War was being conducted in South Vietnam, I was happy to leave all the arrangements in the hands of my hosts.

Our itinerary was often changed from one hour to another, according to the contents of little notes—of a size easy to swallow—covered with minuscule writing, brought every few hours by cycle-borne messengers. The bane of our life when we were in relatively open country was what my companions called the *mademoiselles*, French-built Morane reconnaissance planes. Once they spotted something, the fighter-bombers and helicopter gunships would soon be on the job.

One late afternoon, having been spotted by a *mademoiselle* and having had to do some very fast pedaling through a rubber plantation, while it was still very hot, I was astonished at being escorted into a hut and seeing a bottle of John Haig whisky on the bamboo table. My elderly host, introduced as a "veteran revolutionary from the 1940 My Tho uprising," asked whether I took it neat or with soda. Within seconds, another miracle—a bucket of ice with the soda. When I expressed my wonderment, he said, "But you are in Saigon now!" We were, in fact, about six miles from the center of Saigon, near a large village, An Thanh Tay, solidly in NLF hands. As I was to see next morning, it could be approached only on foot. There had obviously been recent fighting there; some houses were destroyed, but it was a lively village covered with NLF flags and banners.

One of the major exploits of my "programmers" was to escort me inside a strategic hamlet, theoretically under the control of Saigon. It was in Saigon's Hoc Mon District. A small unit of guerrillas had accompanied us, and the inmates rushed out to embrace them, thinking they were being liberated. A skinny old man with a frame like an Auschwitz victim's acted as spokesman for a group that quickly gathered around as soon as my guides assured them that I was a "foreign friend."

"This is no life at all," he said. "Just when we should be going to the fields in the cool of the evening, we have to come back. We have to be inside the gates half an hour before sunset, or we'll be beaten up. No trees for shade—they cut everything down. No chance of raising pigs or chickens with houses on top of each other like this. Not even a fishpond!"

A guerrilla came with the news that we should leave. Four enemy troops happened to be inside the hamlet near our entry point and had raced back to their post about 1,000 yards away. They might start shelling. So we walked away briskly until the security expert said we were out of danger, whereupon we rested on a rice field terrace, drank some beer, and watched bombers roaring down the runway of Saigon's Tan Son Nhut Airfield.

Another highlight of the ten days spent in the Saigon area was a meeting with twelve of the sixteen members of the Executive Committee of the Saigon-Gia Dinh branch of the NLF. Acting as interpreter was its chairman, Huynh Tan Phat, a former Saigon architect, concurrently general secretary of the NLF's Central committee, later prime minister of the Provisional Revolutionary Government of South Vietnam, set up in June 1969, and still later deputy prime minister, charged with urban and rural reconstruction, in the Socialist Republic.

Sitting at a table in a typical peasant's cabin as committee members talked of the activities of their respective organizations, I found it more and more difficult to catch Huynh Tan Phat's translations because of the increasing noise of exploding bombs and shells and mortar and machine-gun fire. During a pause we went outside to sit under a trellised porch, with acrid battlefield smoke drifting over to make breathing uncomfortable. I tried to sound unconcerned in remarking, "It sounds like quite a battle going on there."

"Didn't anyone tell you about that?" said Huynh Tan Phat apologetically. "That's the U.S. Parachutist Training Center at Quang Trung, a couple of kilometers down the road. The trainees can't do parachute jumps anymore because too many fall into our areas. Now they give them infantry training under simulated battle conditions. By the noise, it means that a class is about to graduate."

"Two kilometers? Isn't that a bit close for comfort?"

"Not really." This smiling, trim man, who looked as if he had just stepped out of his Saigon architect's office, pulled out a map and proceeded to give me a lesson in what it meant to live "integrated with the enemy," as the NLF cadres often expressed it, an essential ingredient of People's War as they practiced it. "If you look at the map, it seems that our liberated villages are encircled everywhere. But it is the enemy's posts which are, in fact, encircled by our guerrillas." He showed me the hamlet in Binh Chanh District just three miles southwest of Saigon, where I had stayed a few days previously to celebrate the transition of the Year of the Cat into the Year of the Dragon. According to the map, we had spent that night and most of the next day a few hundred yards from an enemy post. "Actually that one doesn't exist now," said Phat, who put a red cross through it. "It was taken out a couple of months ago, but I forgot to cross it off. For months previous to the withdrawal it was encircled day and night. They feared our attack at any moment, so it was abandoned."

If I had heard this in Hanoi or Moscow, despite the many examples I had experienced of the veracity of Vietnamese revolutionaries, I would have had difficulty in swallowing that one. But I was living the reality of such situations week after week, month after month. An ambition to get close to the reality of People's War had rarely been so completely satisfied as during that period around Saigon in the first half of February 1964.

Early one morning, as the Saigon papers were being delivered to Ba Tu, my French-speaking interpreter, a messenger arrived with a tiny note. It was for the Saigon area military chief, who remained anonymous, but who had happened to spend the night with us in a corner of a rubber plantation. A brisk, cheerful man, he showed the note to my companions, together with his rapidly scribbled reply, buckled on his belt and Colt, and, with a few terse words and sunny smile, strode off. Ba Tu, who later turned up as a translater at the Paris Conference on Vietnam—and still later as my guide-interpreter in liberated Saigon—explained that a company of parachutists had moved into the perimeter of the plantation just after midnight and, under Vietcong observation, was slowly moving our way. "We had better put you in the tunnel system," said Ba Tu (whom I referred to as Huynh in my writings at the time). I noticed that everything was being packed up with more than usual speed. "They're still about half a mile from here," he continued, "but we also have some troops around. The bullets will soon be flying, so we'd better not dawdle." Because I did not favor an unnecessary plunge into tunnels which would obviously not be tailored for my girth, I was installed in a well-camouflaged circular trench, with communications trenches leading deep into the rear.

The parachutists, in mottled green camouflage uniforms, advanced cautiously, in two groups: about fifty in front with ordinary infantry arms, about thirty with mortars slightly to the rear. With the first group were three American advisers. Sighting two trenches with some NLF troops in them, the parachutists flopped down and opened up with heavy machine guns from both groups. The NLF replied with two short bursts—also from heavy machine guns—wounding three. The Americans were gesticulating and shouting, obviously ordering an advance. The troops wavered a moment, then swept up the machine guns and the mortars which they had just been setting up and retreated into the trees. It was over as quickly as that. Guerrillas followed along the trench system, and soon little notes started arriving. The parachutists had withdrawn back to their Quang Trung training base.

A local guerrilla leader complained that if the NLF heavy machine gunner had held his fire, the parachutists would have walked right into a trap and the lot could have been wiped out. The area commander had to explain that his job was to protect a "foreign friend" with the minimum of military action.

As we were about to head back from the Saigon area, the arrival of a little note produced grave looks. "In two days' time," explained the area commander, never far away at critical moments, "the enemy will start a big operation with five battalions, about four thousand men, sweeping through the very area you have to traverse. It will last four days, and we propose you stay here, where we can protect you."

On the first morning of that operation there was nothing for it, at a certain moment, but to obey instructions and, with arms extended high above my head, drop feetfirst through a manhole-sized entry into a tunnel system, followed by some of my companions. The others had to get ready for "military affairs." As predicted, five battalions, spearheaded by twenty-three M-113 amphibious tanks, were on the move. Some units had occupied a road junction half a mile away; artillery and mortar shells were bursting alarmingly close, but it was a deafening rattle of machine-gun fire that prompted the order to drop through the manhole. Once our reduced group was inside, the entrance was covered with earth and leaves and all traces were erased. Where the others could crouch and walk, I could only sink to my knees and crawl. Even breathing was difficult because of the abnormal consumption of oxygen following the exertions of getting us and our baggage into the tunnel.

Once the rest of the party had moved on, the air got better, but I still had a claustrophobic impulse to burst out and face the machine-gun music. While I was still breathing heavily and firing seemed to be coming from all directions, Ba Tu appeared to assure me that "we will certainly get you out of this." I explained that among my worries were my notes and films and the fact that I'd not been able to send word for weeks past to my family in Moscow. He shuffled off and returned within a few minutes to say, "If you want to send a very short message, three or four words, we can send it. But you must do it immediately." I wrote down "BURPRESS MOSCOW PERFECT HEALTH GREETINGS" and tore the page out of my notebook. Ba Tu shuffled back to report that it had been sent and that my bag, with films and notes (over more than 300 pages of single-spaced typed notes by then), had been sealed up in a hole in the tunnel wall. He then guided me to a place where there was a tiny ventilation duct. With my face pressed close to a marvelous flow of fresh air, I dozed off.

The tunnel system was very extensive even then. The one we were in was linked with several villages and was later extended into Saigon, with an exit under the Presidential Palace. On another occasion I got stuck passing from one tunnel section to another. In what seemed a dead end, a rectangular plug was pulled out from the other side, and, with some ahead pulling my arms and some pushing my buttocks from behind, I managed to get through. But the edges of the slot had crumbled, and it was explained to my mortification that the tunnel entrance would have to be sealed up and abandoned, the neat fitting of the earth plug between sections being essential to maintain security. I was transferred to another tunnel entrance built especially to accommodate a bulky unit cook, of approximately my girth.

This hide-and-seek with death was taking place in Cu Chi, one of Saigon's northern administrative districts. On one occasion we moved to the Saigon River separating us from the famous Iron Triangle in Ben Cat District, which remained the hottest spot throughout the war. No sooner had we arrived at the riverbank than we heard the drone of the engine of some heavy river craft. Notes converged from all directions, the contents of several reporting that a large American landing craft was moored about a mile downstream, its engine running and only the crew aboard. The assessment was that it was waiting to embark troops for our intended bivouac area, so we had better decamp forthwith.

It was a fine moonlight night, and for the first half hour we marched quickly over freshly harvested rice fields. We could hear the landing craft heading for the direction we had just left, and almost immediately salvos of shells started coming our way. This time it was hide-and-seek with the shells, with brisk orders, based on the sound of the firing, when to throw ourselves on the ground and when to resume the march. This continued for three hours before we reached a thick belt of forest where we could sling our hammocks in comparative safety.

On the evening of the fourth day the operation ended, the five battalions pulled back, and we headed for our next target area in Binh Duong Province to the northwest. In the meantime, I had caught a bad cold and was slightly below par. Because of the information contained in the notes, we set out in the heat of the day—about 104°—this time on bicycles again. Deep sand in the middle of the biggest clearing forced us to dismount halfway across. Almost immediately came the sound of fighter-bombers heading our way. Heaving the loaded bicycles onto our shoulders, we ran for it, reaching a thicket as the planes circled, looking for a target. After a few circles they roared off again. When I tried to stand up, my legs gave way; trees and sky were suddenly mixed up with the sandy track. Two husky guerrillas who had noted my plight came over. A young sapling was cut down, and my hammock attached to it. I could not refuse a palanquin this time because the security of the whole group was at stake. But then the miracle-working cook started toward me with a large bottle of Saigon's Larue beer, white foam oozing from its neck. The doctor urged me to drink it slowly. My trouble was dehydration, the sweat having poured out of me especially during the final dash across the sandy clearing. Within half an hour we all were bike-borne again, pedaling toward a "safe" bivouac area.

It was the nearest I have ever come to fainting. How the bottle came to be there—and the beer inside cold—was one of the constantly recurring mysteries of NLF organization which never failed to astonish me. That narrow escape marked a fitting end to that most highly instructive phase of my journey. The rich experiences in the Saigon area reinforced my conviction that the NLF had its roots deep among the people of the South; if it remained a question of a straight fight against the Saigon regime—despite the massive U.S. support for the latter—the NLF would undoubtedly win. The imponderable was whether direct U.S. military intervention—which I was certain would take place—would tip the scales in the other direction.

23

---◄◆►---

Into the Quagmire

AFTER FURTHER ADVENTURES, I returned to Phnom Penh and arranged to see the head of state, Prince Norodom Sihanouk. I was not at all certain how I would be received. I had entered his country with false identity papers and had illegally crossed its frontiers to and from South Vietnam.

As I entered his reception room at the Chamcar Mon Palace, he grasped my hand in both of his and said, "Monsieur Burchett, I have learned that you have achieved an extraordinary exploit. Congratulations!" A bottle of champagne appeared at the same time as a photographer to snap the clinking of glasses.

·I had a present for Sihanouk from Nguyen Huu Tho, the former Saigon lawyer and the president of the NLF. A few days after my arrival in the South, NLF guerrillas had overrun a Special Forces training camp at Hiep Hoa, about twenty miles northwest of Saigon. Among documents captured were those relating to the training and operational plans of the CIA-backed Khmer Serei ("Free Khmer") traitors, aimed at overthrowing Sihanouk's neutralist regime. Sihanouk was highly appreciative, also very interested in a map showing that most of the border areas were solidly Vietcong on the South Vietnamese side. His eyes grew round with astonishment as he spread the map out on a table and exclaimed, "Now I see with whom I have to discuss frontier problems."

Sihanouk asked intelligent questions about the situation, and when I apologized if anything I had done had embarrassed Cambodia's position, he replied, "We are neutral, but we are also independent and thus have the right to choose our own friends." We parted on more cordial terms than ever.

From Phnom Penh to an incredible reception in Hanoi, first to see Ho

Chi Minh and give him my impressions, then to Le Duan, general secretary of the Lao Dong ("Workers") party to tell it all over again and reply to his searching questions, then to Vo Nguyen Giap, who gave me a copy of his *People's War, People's Army,* with an autographed dedication referring to my "heroic" journey, and asked even more searching questions. Finally, there was, for a foreigner, an unprecedented reception by the entire Politburo—and more questions. They all were interested in the evaluation of an outsider, one with some grounding in military and political affairs.

The most numerous and searching questions came with my return to home and family in Moscow. The children were then six, nine, and eleven respectively. Vessa had performed marvels—helped out by a few romantic campfire photos—in explaining my prolonged absence. This had whetted their appetite for more.

Vietnam had become for me an obsession. So at the turn of the year 1964–65 I was there again. For me, it was more of the same, except that it was interesting to note that in the intervening year companies had developed into battalions and battalions into regiments and that there had been a considerable standardization of weapons.

For the visit I had taken a 16 mm camera, trying my hand at filming for the first time. With the aid of an NLF cameraman, who insisted on snatching the camera and himself filming in moments of great danger, I returned with enough footage for a French TV producer, Roger Pic, to put together a forty-two-minute documentary. It was the first on the Vietnam War as seen from the "other side" and was shown all around the world—except in Australia. (A filmed interview subsequently made by the Australian Broadcasting Commission's Tony Ferguson not only was not used but was actually burned —apparently to avoid polluting the archives.)

In February 1965, while I was still in the South, the United States started the systematic bombing of North Vietnam, and the following month U.S. marines were landed at Danang, thus committing the United States to what was bound to be another long and costly war on the Asiatic mainland. In April I was in Djakarta for the tenth anniversary of the Afro-Asian (Bandung) Conference. At the reception given by President Sukarno, Chou En-lai spotted me and immediately drew me aside to a corner of the banqueting hall, which was discreetly cordoned off by some of his aides. "You've recently been in South Vietnam again," he said. "Tell me how things are going. I can't say I've read your articles, but my wife [Teng Ying-chao] sees them regularly and reads bits out to me."

I gave him a summary of my impressions with illustrations of the identification of the people with the armed struggle and my conviction—based on the second visit—that even massive U.S. intervention could not change the situation. He posed a few questions and then said, "It's remarkable. We thought we had taken guerrilla warfare to a certain level of perfection, but our Vietnamese comrades have raised it to heights that we never dreamed of. Come to Peking, and talk to our generals. They'll be fascinated."

Taking advantage of the encounter, I asked if he would agree to a filmed interview on China's attitude toward U.S. intervention in Vietnam. It took place a few days later—April 25, 1965. For weeks before hand there had been threatening noises from Washington as to the dire consequences of any Chinese attempts to interfere with U.S. activities in Vietnam. Chou En-lai addressed himself to these:

> The United States has sunk into a most wretched position in Vietnam. Like all aggressors in history, U.S. imperialism is doomed to utter defeat in South Vietnam. Even statesmen of France, which is an ally of the United States, are pointing out that there is no way out for the United States in its war in South Vietnam. . . .
>
> Mutual assistance among the Vietnamese people to resist foreign aggression is their inalienable sacred right. The Chinese people resolutely support this firm and unyielding stand of the Vietnamese people. Like the Vietnamese people, the Chinese people will never accept the U.S. gangsters' logic. If the United States can be allowed to take the North Vietnamese people's support and assistance to the South Vietnamese people as a pretext for bombing North Vietnam, can it not take a similar pretext of China giving support and assistance to the Vietnamese people to bomb China? This is a matter of principle towards which there should be no ambiguity. The Chinese Government and people will not yield an inch before the U.S. threats. . . .
>
> We have firmly responded to the March 22 appeal of the South Vietnam National Front of Liberation [for former Vietnam troops and cadres in the North to return to the south and for all socialist countries to support the struggle in South Vietnam] *and are ready to send our men to fight shoulder to shoulder with the South Vietnamese people when they so require.* [Emphasis added.] We also fully support the stand of the Head of State of Cambodia, His Royal Highness, Prince Sihanouk, that is, a new Geneva Conference on the Cambodian question must not touch upon the Vietnamese question. To settle the Vietnamese question the United States must stop its aggression against Vietnam and withdraw all its armed forces from South Vietnam. The South Vietnamese question can only be settled by the Vietnamese people themselves. The independence, unity and territorial integrity of Vietnam must be assured. Do what it may, the United States cannot save itself from certain defeat in South Vietnam.*

Immediately after the Chou En-lai interview I had one with Pham Van Dong, who confirmed that North Vietnam had only "to lift a finger" and Chinese troops would be at its side. "In fact, we do not foresee such a situation," he added, "as we have no shortage of manpower."

---

* The text of this interview is from the official Chinese English translation.

With hindsight there was another revealing episode relating to the Chou En-lai interview. It had been agreed that it would be released, together with those of Pham Van Dong, Souphanouvong, Prince Sihanouk, and Nguyen Van Hieu—all on the same subject—in the prestigious French TV monthly program *Cinq Colonnes à la Une* ("Five Columns on Page One") on Friday, March 4. But while I was still in Djakarta, I received a telegram from Chou En-lai, who had interrupted his return flight at Canton, urging that his interview be released immediately. (This was impossible because it was too late to revise the program.) Did Chou En-lai want to get it out before Mao—who would know all about it within minutes of the plane's reaching Peking and who had already indicated he did not want China involved in Vietnam—could intervene to stop it? It is a tantalizing thought, as is the question of whose view, Chou's or Mao's, won out?

By documents released by the Vietnamese in 1979, it is clear that it was Mao's. There had been a secret military agreement, for example, under which China was to send fighter pilots to Vietnam in June 1965. But on July 16, 1965, Peking cabled Hanoi that "the moment is not yet opportune" and that there was no way "of preventing the enemy from intensifying the bombings." In discussions between the two sides in August 1966, the Vietnamese were told that "China has no air power available for the defense of Hanoi." *

As early as December 1964 Vietnamese were later to reveal that Teng Hsiao-ping, as general secretary of the Chinese Communist party, had conveyed a message from Chairman Mao to Ho Chi Minh offering all necessary military and other aid—on condition that Vietnam refuse any aid at all from the Soviet Union. Naturally this was rejected.

I was unable to take up Chou En-lai's invitation to meet the generals in Peking, but later he told me that he had been greatly interested in what I had written and had told him in Djakarta, adding, "Of course, People's War is taken to a higher level during struggle. If we had had the experiences of the South Vietnamese comrades at the time, perhaps there would have been no Long March!"

Transiting through Hanoi on the way back to Moscow from Djakarta, I asked Ho Chi Minh what he thought about speculation in the U.S. press that the swift buildup of U.S. forces at Danang foreshadowed a U.S. invasion of the North. He smiled and said, "You'd better speak to Giap about that. But the idea reminds me of a fox with one foot in a trap. He starts leaping about trying to get out, and—pouf—he gets a second one in another trap." I did ask Vo Nguyen Giap, reading him some quotes from the U.S. press deriding him as an apostle of People's War with an army equipped

---

* *La Vertité sur les relations Vietnamo-Chinoises durant les Trente dernières années* (Ministry of Foreign Affairs of the Socialist Republic of Vietnam, 1979), p. 53. Translation from the French is the author's.

with old weapons captured at Dien Bien Phu. With his usual ironical smile, he said:

"Let them try! We would welcome them where we can get at them with modern weapons which our comrades in the South don't have. . . . But they will also find themselves caught up in People's War. The whole people are united as they were under our ancestors and invaders will find every village a hornets' nest. Whenever and wherever we fight, it will always be People's War."

In talks with Sihanouk in Phnom Penh on my way to Djakarta, I had raised the possibility of moving my base to Cambodia, to follow what we agreed would be a long, dangerous military confrontation in the area. He already knew that I supported his brand of neutrality unreservedly. "Come with your family whenever you like," he said.

The problem was to persuade the children to reconcile themselves to another move halfway across the globe. They had good friends at all levels, from school classmates to "uncles" such as Kornei Chukovsky, eminent Soviet literary figure. Many a weekend was spent at Peredelkino, the writers' colony in the forests outside Moscow, where Chukovsky and other amiable writer "uncles" had their dachas. We had to conjure up visions of "jungle uncles," as we had decided to designate any guerrillas who might (and subsequently did) turn up at our Phnom Penh home; of monkeys and other house pets; of fishing in the warm, open sea instead of through holes bored through the ice over the Volga—as we often did in winter—to break down the children's resistance to yet another change.

Impending departure after more than eight years' living and working in the Soviet Union caused me to examine my own feelings. The Soviet government had been friendly and tolerant toward me, a bit puzzled as to where I stood, but the Foreign Ministry and its Press Department could have no reason to doubt that I was a genuine supporter of such proclaimed pillars of Soviet policy as peace, peaceful coexistence, détente, and an opening to the West. So I did not share the fears of many colleagues of whether my phone was tapped or letters opened. Nor did I have the problems of attempts to compromise me with a ballerina or choirboy or to catch me in the act of receiving state secrets. All my "errors" were in print.

My basic criticism was the almost totally negative attitude, and lack of respect, toward foreign journalists. The hard-line attitude was: All foreign correspondents are spies. The more enlightened attitude was: Foreign correspondents are a necessary evil that we have to put up with, but let's limit to the maximum the harm they can do. I was never able to make the slightest dent in those positions, although Lord knows I tried hard enough. The hard cutting edge of suspicions of the outside world came to bear on the unfortunate foreign correspondents, who—especially in my early years in Moscow—were unnecessarily harassed. Censorship of news dispatches, for instance, was maintained far longer than any security interests could justify.

It seemed to me that the Soviet Union stood only to gain by a more tolerant and positive attitude toward the foreign press corps. Even the hardline Chinese position was far better: Foreign correspondents are a necessary evil, but they exist. Let's get maximum benefit from their presence. If the Chinese considered all foreign newsmen spies, they did not usually let them feel it.

An example of lack of respect toward the profession in general and me in particular occurred not long after I arrived in Moscow. As I was about to leave the apartment for a Khrushchev press conference, a Soviet journalist dropped in and said, "If you want to provoke an interesting reply from Khrushchev, ask him what he thinks of Adenauer's recent statement on Soviet relations. I've got it written down and was going to ask the question myself, but Khrushchev will take it more seriously if it comes from the *Daily Express*."

I took the note and asked the question, and it was obvious that Khrushchev had his long reply already prepared. It was a major policy statement, and I realized that I had been used. The journalist came to me after it was over with a smirk and said, "You made a major hit."

But the correspondent of the *Frankfurter Allgemeine Zeitung* also came up and said, "Where did you get that quote from Adenauer? He never said anything like that."

When I tackled the Soviet journalist later with having given me false information, he retorted, "What was important was not what Adenauer said, but what Khrushchev said."

The frivolous way in which my reputation was imperiled left its mark, and I never fell into that type of trap again. It was an early example of disrespect for journalistic integrity which I could not forget. It rankled in my mind even up to the moment of the farewall party we gave at the Prague restaurant on the night before our departure. The press corps turned out in force, as did officials from the Press Department and the State Committee for Relations with Foreign Countries. Rubles, accumulated from book royalties, but unexportable, were invested in caviar and smoked salmon—with plenty of vodka and champagne to wash them down—in a splendid final contribution to friendly coexistence between press people and the officials with whom they dealt.

As the last bags were zipped and straps tightened that night, we thought of the many warm friendships formed, especially among journalists, writers like Boris Pasternak and Ilya Ehrenburg, the scientific community, with whom we had plenty of contacts as a result of my interests in outer space. Because Vessa was Bulgarian and our children also had many school friends whose parents became our friends, we had wider contacts than most other correspondents. We had good reason to remember the warmth and spon-

taneous generosity of the Soviet people, especially once the long-instilled
fears of foreign contacts had begun to disappear.

In early September 1965, we left our Vissotni Dom apartment for Cairo,
on the first stage of a new migration to Cambodia. By then the two boys
were fluent in French (the family language) and were starting to speak
some English learned in the specialized Russian-English school which they
attended; all three were fluent in Russian from school and kindergarten
and in Bulgarian as their "summer language" from holidays spent with
Vessa's family.

We kept our promises to them. Their first excursion out of Phnom Penh
was to the famous Angkor temples, where shrieking monkeys abounded in
the majestic jungle surrounding the famous monuments and there were even
elephants to ride. At home, there was always an affectionate gibbon ape
waiting to wrap his long arms around some child's neck, a dog, and a cat
and, after the first few months, a sociable black bear with a cream collar.
A round handful of fur when we acquired him, Mishka grew at an alarming
rate. If sea-fishing expeditions were not very successful, there were frequent
visits to the splendid beaches at Sihanoukville (Kompong Som) on the Gulf
of Thailand and the older tourist resort of Kep—only a few miles from the
Vietnam frontier. There was a steady trickle of "jungle uncles," who informed me about the state of the war and told the children wondrous tales
of life in the jungle with minimum mention of war.

The branches of Mishka's favorite tree reached into the garden of our
neighbor—the residence and office of the Japanese Embassy. On one occasion he fell into an incinerator under the tree in which the Japanese were
burning papers. Roaring with rage and singed sides, he charged into an
embassy garden party, causing diplomatic guests to seek sanctuary in the
nearby French Embassy as he took over. Anna enticed him home by dangling a bottle of Pepsi-Cola (of which he had become an addict) in front
of his nose. The Japanese burned no more papers under his tree.

During a weekend away from home we left Youpi, the gibbon, with the
family of the Bulgarian chargé d'affaires. No sooner had we returned than
the chargé was at our house declaring his eternal love for the little ape, but
begging to be excused from further Youpi watching. In his invariably joyous
mood, Youpi had bounded out of the chargé's office window with a batch
of confidential telegrams, casting them to the four winds as he leaped from
tree to tree in the neighboring Laotian Embassy garden.

Two months after settling down in Phnom Penh, I was back in South
Vietnam. The main purpose was to see how the NLF was coping with the
fast-increasing scale of U.S. intervention and how its leadership saw future
developments. From the frontier crossing point, where a small escort was
waiting, we pedaled for eleven hours—with the standard hourly breaks of
ten minutes—straight to a NLF headquarters area. In two days and nights

of talks with President Nguyen Huu Tho and a senior NLF staff officer, Nguyen Van Chau, there emerged a clear and realistically optimistic perspective. Inevitably my mind went back to the briefings presided over by Ho Chi Minh at his jungle headquarters more than eleven years earlier. But the personalities were very different. Ho Chi Minh was a self-taught peasant revolutionary who dressed and acted like one. Nguyen Huu Tho was a French-educated city intellectual who had given up a lucrative law practice in Saigon to throw his talents and patriotism into the first resistance war against the French. He dressed—even in khaki—with elegance; his speech and manners were those of a sophisticated intellectual. But the problems were the same. Could the revolutionary forces hold out against overwhelming superiority in military technique and economic resources? How did the NLF count on tackling the world's mightiest military machine? To this question of questions, Nguyen Huu Tho gave an image which remained with me throughout the war, as had Ho Chi Minh's sun-helmet image of Dien Bien Phu:

> Warfare is sometimes compared to a game of chess. But war in South Vietnam is certainly not a game of chess. When the Pentagon decided to commit US troops, this is because they had already lost "special war" [that is, warfare in which the United States supplies everything but the combat troops]. Whoever loses in a game of chess, the board is swept clean, each side redeploys his men and you start again. Not so in war. When the Americans shifted to "limited war" [nonnuclear and geographically limited], they moved into a situation in which our men were already in winning positions on the chessboard. In military terms—we hold the strategic initiative. The Americans only have limited freedom of choice of where they can place their pawns and generals. They could not draw a line and say: "South of the line is yours, north of it is ours—let's fight and see who wins!" . . .
> One of the decisive factors will be on whose terms the war will be waged. If the Americans could impose their terms, our armed forces would soon be finished. We have no planes, naval vessels, tanks or heavy artillery. But since we are masters of the situation—we have the mountains and the people— we shall impose our terms. It is we who will decide where, when and how the decisive battles take place. . . .
> We will force them to fight our way, giving them no choice whether to concentrate or disperse. If they want to disperse, we will force them to concentrate. If it suits them better to concentrate we will force them to disperse. . . .*

This fundamental analysis, by a man with no training in military affairs, remained valid throughout the war. To invalidate it, the U.S. war planners

---

* Wilfred Burchett, *Vietnam Will Win* (New York: Guardian Book distributed by Monthly Review Press, 1968), pp. 66–67.

would have to do two fundamental things: physically occupy the Central Highlands and make it their territory, and ideologically occupy the hearts and minds of the South Vietnamese people. Successive U.S. military commanders made no progress in either direction, so defeat was inevitable. Henry Kissinger, when he was a private citizen, had sensed this. But when he became Richard Nixon's national security adviser, he cast aside reason and encouraged Nixon to believe he could succeed where other Presidents failed. He closed his eyes to his own logic, expressed perceptively when he wrote: ". . . we lost sight of one of the cardinal maxims of guerrilla war: the guerrilla wins if he does not lose; the conventional army loses if it does not win." *

After the first year of U.S. direct engagement in the war had produced no dramatic results, the air attack against the North was stepped up, and there was theorizing in Washington and Saigon about "winning the war in the South by bombing the North." On April 24, 1966, a few days after B-52s had been used for the first time against the North, I asked General Vo Nguyen Giap how he viewed this thesis. In an interview recorded for French television, he gave a scornful laugh and said:

"The American strategists are not lacking in theses. There are the theses that you speak about, but there are other, more reasonable ones, which affirm that it is in South Vietnam itself that the outcome of the war will be decided.

"The only correct thesis, in fact, is this: The war which the U.S. government is waging in South Vietnam is an aggressive war, a neocolonial war of aggression. As for our people in the South, they are fighting in legitimate defense, to safeguard their national rights. . . .

"By their air raids against the DRV, the Americans have carried the war to the whole of Vietnam. In such circumstances we will resist American aggression, arms in hand, for our national salvation. This is the most sacred duty of every Vietnamese patriot, of the entire Vietnamese people. Our people are determined to fight to defend the North, to liberate the South and to achieve the peaceful reunification of the motherland. . . ."

Giap was saying what no other Vietnamese had said till then: that by carrying the air war to the North, the United States had brought about a de facto military reunification of Vietnam. If U.S. bombers could treat Vietnam as a single entity, why could Giap's ground troops not do the same? Washington, however, made a point of ignoring that type of explicit warning.

While an interview on the same subject was being filmed a few days later with Pham Van Dong in the Presidential Palace, Ho Chi Minh strolled in to say hello to Vessa and me. With the camera all set up I could not resist saying, "The Americans are saying they will win the war in the South by bombing the North. What do you say?"

---

* Henry A. Kissinger, *American Foreign Policy, Three Essays* (New York: W. W. Norton, 1969), p. 104.

"Never. We will fight ten, fifteen, twenty, or more years. Our cause is just. We have the support of the people of the world. We will win." That very simple statement, the only one recorded by "Uncle" Ho in a TV interview, very quickly went around the world.

Three months later I was back at Nguyen Huu Tho's headquarters. U.S. forces had by then been built up to 300,000, although the original estimate of Defense Secretary Robert S. McNamara was that even if North Vietnam *and China* entered the war, the maximum number of U.S. ground troops needed would be 205,000.* There were rumors of 500,000. How did the NLF view this? It was a question I put to Nguyen Huu Tho in late August 1966. "Will you be able to stand up to such staggering military strength? The most optimistic friends of yours abroad say, 'Granted the Americans can't win, but neither can the NLF!' The less optimistic say, 'It's all over for the NLF!' Many of my own friends—including some editors —think I'm crazy in insisting that you can hang on and eventually win. How do you see things now?"

Nguyen Huu Tho, whose crew-cut hair was beginning to show a sprinkling of gray which had not been there three years earlier, replied:

We believe the strength of an army in time of war is composed of a great number of factors of which the determinant ones are political and moral. We have absolute supremacy over the Americans on the political and moral fronts. Our entire people wage this war and do not shrink from any difficulty or sacrifice. We are also stronger than the Americans in other fundamental aspects of the struggle, such as our strategic position, our rear areas, our actual conduct of the war. Our ground forces are superior to theirs; these are factors that decide the outcome on the battlefield. Although the Americans are strong in material and equipment, they also have fundamental weaknesses, politically and materially, strategically and tactically. . . .

We can successfully stand up to new American reinforcements and militarily defeat the American aggressors in any situation whatsoever. In fact, just as it is obviously true that the Americans cannot bring off a military victory in South Vietnam, it is also obvious to *us* that the South Vietnamese people and their armed forces *can* bring off the final victory, despite US military and economic strength.†

---

* On November 8, 1961, the Defense Secretary submitted a memorandum to the President to the effect that chances were "probably sharply against" preventing the "fall of South Vietnam" without a U.S. troop commitment, but that even with a major troop deployment (205,000 was the maximum number of ground forces estimated necessary to deal with a large overt invasion from the DRV [Democratic Republic of Vietnam] and/or China, the U.S. would still be at the mercy of external forces . . .) An earlier assessment (October 1961), was that 40,000 U.S. troops would be needed "to clean up the Viet Cong threat" and another 128,000 to oppose DRV/CHICOM intervention. (See Gravel Edition, *The Pentagon Papers*, Vol. 2, pp. 13, 16.)

† *Ibid.*, pp. 66–67.

Another of Nguyen Huu Tho's staff officers, Truong Ky, explained that because of the necessity to enlarge its supply bases and thus increase the numbers of troops to guard the expanded perimeters, the U.S. Command would have fewer fighting troops with 500,000 men than it had had with the 250,000 at its disposal for the 1965–66 dry-season campaigns. "We will continue to encircle and hug their bases wherever they establish them," said Truong Ky. "Our forces are also increasing in quantity and quality. As we get stronger, they will need proportionately more to defend those bases. . . . Doubling the number of troops under such conditions means more than doubling the problems. . . . Their mobile forces will get progressively smaller, not bigger."

Since the Saigon regime of Nguyen Van Thieu at that time was making territorial claims on Cambodia and stating that the frontiers had never been defined, I asked questions on this point, and Nguyen Huu Tho replied that the NLF "recognized the independence and sovereignty of the kingdom of Cambodia within the confines of its present frontiers." This was to become a historically important formula.

I returned to Phnom Penh a few minutes after midnight on August 30, 1966; President de Gaulle arrived on a state visit some hours later. By that evening the text of the Nguyen Huu Tho interview—much more detailed than that quoted in these pages—was in the hands of Prince Norodom Sihanouk and President Charles de Gaulle. I was assured that both studied it with great interest and that as a result, De Gaulle amended the draft of the historic speech he made two days later at a mass meeting in Phnom Penh's Olympic Sports Stadium. The parts which particularly offended U.S. President Lyndon Johnson, taken from the official English version of that speech, distributed as it was being made, are:

On the morrow of the 1954 Geneva Agreements, Cambodia, with courage and clearsightedness, chose the policy of neutrality which resulted from those agreements and which, as the responsibility of France was no longer in force, alone could spare Indochina from becoming a field of confrontation between rival dominations and ideologies, and an incitation for American intervention. That is why, while your country succeeded in salvaging its body and soul, because it remained master in its own house, the political and military authority of the United States installed itself in its turn in South Vietnam and, as a result, war was rekindled there in the form of national resistance. . . .

I hereby declare that France entirely approves the efforts of Cambodia to keep out of the conflict, and to this end will extend its support and backing. . . . Yes! France has taken its position. It has shown this by its condemnation of the present events. . . .

And so on, in the same vein. In this audacious speech De Gaulle defined the cause of the war, U.S. attempts to replace the French in Indochina;

its nature, U.S. aggression and national resistance to that aggression; its solution, negotiations based on a U.S. withdrawal. He also stressed France's refusal to burn its fingers in trying to pull U.S. chestnuts out of the Indochina fire. No wonder U.S. policy makers were dumbfounded!

On the Sunday following De Gaulle's departure, Sihanouk gave a luncheon for the members of the foreign press still in Phnom Penh. Expressing himself as eminently satisfied with the visit, especially with a passage in the communiqué stating, "France, for her part, reaffirms her respect for the territorial integrity of Cambodia within the limits of its present borders," Sihanouk raised a glass to me and said, "I have to thank Mr. Burchett, who brought this formulation from Maître Nguyen Huu Tho, president of the National Liberation Front of South Vietnam. From now on its acceptance will become the criteria for any country wishing to establish diplomatic relations with the kingdom of Cambodia and even for those countries wishing to maintain relations already established." It was a solemn declaration, and within the next few months—starting with the Democratic Republic of Vietnam—there was a flood of assurances of "respect for the territorial integrity of Cambodia within the limits of its present borders." It was the formula which Washington had to swallow in reestablishing diplomatic relations three years later.

24

---◄●►---

Risks for Peace

T HE PENTAGON, with McNamara in the lead, continued to be obsessed with the certitude that once the correct dosage of bombs was found for the North, the war would be won in the South. The Pentagon could carry public opinion along when McNamara predicted after each of his numerous visits to Saigon that the war was about to end. In fact, the war was growing fiercer; intensified "dosage" of bombs had no effects on the North–South flow of supplies, and the morality of the bombing policy started to trouble religious leaders, writers, and other intellectuals who deal with matters of public conscience. An attempt was made to quiet their misgivings by repeated and solemn declarations from the White House and Pentagon that only "steel and concrete," as President Johnson once expressed it, "strictly military targets," as the Pentagon specified in the daily communiqués, were being bombed. It took someone with the courage, integrity, and prestige of Harrison Salisbury of *The New York Times* to tear the veil away from this pack of official lies.

Owing to a shortage of transport and English-language interpreters, we happened to visit the textile city of Nam Dinh—about fifty miles due south of Hanoi—together on Christmas Day 1966. We shared an interview with the city's diminutive woman mayor and inspected part of the city together. After a good look around, Salisbury said, "I'm going to have words about this with Arthur Sylvester [then chief Pentagon spokesman] when I get back to New York." Nam Dinh became the issue on which Salisbury took on the whole American Establishment as far as the policy on bombings and press relations was concerned. His reactions are expressed in the following passage from a book he wrote after his return:

Before Christmas Day 1966, I had never heard of Nam Dinh. . . . But after Christmas Day, 1966, I would never forget Nam Dinh. Nor, I think, would many other Americans. Nam Dinh became a catalyst, a kind of prism through which the United States bombing offensive in North Vietnam took on human dimensions. For the first time we began to see through the barrier of meaningless military terminology, the banal vocabulary that turns reality into a kind of etymological stew. . . .

We came into Nam Dinh from the north and almost all the streets we drove through bore signs of bomb damage. Two local officials briefed me about Nam Dinh, and from them I learned that it was a textile city of about 90,000 people, before most of them had been evacuated. They said Nam Dinh had been repeatedly subjected to United States attack—fifty-one or fifty-two up to that moment, including four on December 23. There had been, I was told, American reconnaissance planes over the city during the night, and thus far on Christmas morning, the alert had sounded twice. . . . The officials, including the mayor, a petite woman named Tran Thi Doan, who had been a textile worker herself, insisted that as far as they were aware, the city possessed no military objectives whatever.

Of course, definitions of military objectives are apt to differ between the civilians who live in a town and the men in the planes dropping the bombs. The residents of Nam Dinh reinforced their contention that the city could not be considered an important target area by insisting that it had never been mentioned as a target in a United States communiqué. The question whether Nam Dinh possessed significant military objectives and whether it had been mentioned in a communiqué later became the focus of a brush-fire controversy touched off in Washington by the Pentagon. . . .

Salisbury relates that after diligent research, it was found that Nam Dinh had been mentioned three times in communiqués in the spring of 1966, but in such unimportant terms that these did not find space in The New York Times.

This was hardly surprising. Like most of the "military objectives" which I was to see in North Vietnam, Nam Dinh seemed much more imposing in the language of a Pentagon spokesman than when viewed with the naked eye. . . .

After my dispatches began appearing in The Times, Arthur Sylvester urged that I walk down the main street of Nam Dinh, where, he said, I would find a large antiaircraft installation. I only wished I could have taken him with me on that stroll. My car had passed down the main street and turned at an intersection. No antiaircraft installation was in sight that day. . . . The nearest thing to a military installation which I saw on Nam Dinh's main street was a rather pretty militia woman, or traffic officer. She had a small revolver on her hip, but I doubted that it would have been effective against a supersonic attack bomber. . . .

I put my thoughts down on paper when I returned to Hanoi on Christmas evening and sent a dispatch off to The New York Times which shocked the Pentagon and produced a rash of denials, assaults on my personal reliability and hastily fabricated explanations. But after all the statements and all the verbal brickbats had been hurled, the mystery of Nam Dinh remained. For even by the Pentagon's least strict definition there were no very remarkable targets in Nam Dinh. True, materials going south passed through the city. True, there was a railroad, a (small) freight yard, an area along the river bank where boat and barge cargo was sorted out and reshipped. But it didn't amount to much. This, I was to come to find, was one of the tragedies of the Vietnam war, and perhaps the total fallacy in our whole bombing policy.*

The Salisbury series caused a very great sensation not only in the United States but throughout the world. Public pressures to end the bombings of the North were intensified. President Johnson and Secretary of State Dean Rusk, in an effort to divert attention, made a series of statements that the most ardent desire of the U.S. government was to end the war, bombings and all, by negotiated settlement. One or the other was willing to "go anywhere, anytime" to bring this about. So I sought and fought for an interview in Hanoi with someone with the necessary authority to define the North Vietnamese position on negotiations.

There is an occasion of which most journalists dream—an exclusive interview with the right man at the right time and place on the most burning question of the day. For me this came true on January 28, 1967, when I interviewed the DRV's foreign minister, Nguyen Duy Trinh, in Hanoi about the prospects for negotiations.

Nguyen Duy Trinh, a short, stocky man with a very stubborn face, devoted most of his replies to my questions to hammering at the United States for the air war of destruction against the North and stressing the determination of his people and government never to yield to force. The real message came in his reply to my last question: "The United States has spoken of the need for dialogue between itself and the DRV. Would you comment on this?" He said:

"The United States has made such statements, but in its deeds it has shown the utmost obduracy and perfidy and continues the escalation, stepping up and expanding the aggressive war. If it really wants talks, it must first unconditionally halt the bombing raids and all other acts of war against the DRV. It is only after the unconditional cessation of bombing and all other acts of war against the DRV that there could be talks between the DRV and the United States."

This was interpreted throughout the world as the clear signal President Johnson had said he was awaiting from Hanoi. To make it quite clear, Mai Van Bo, head of the DRV's diplomatic mission in Paris, informed Etienne M. Manac'h of the French Foreign Office that his government wanted Washington to understand that the interview was very important and that talks could

---

* Harrison Salisbury, *Behind the Lines: Hanoi* (New York: Bantam Books, 1967), pp. 84–92.

really follow an unconditional end to the bombings. Manac'h relayed the message to John Dean, first secretary at the U.S. Embassy in Paris, in the presence of Robert Kennedy.

When Kosygin arrived in London ten days later, Vietnam was an important subject of conversation between the two prime ministers. In his memoirs, Harold Wilson describes how Kosygin "directed the conversation straight to Vietnam."

> Basing himself on public statements, and particularly the Burchett interview I had cited, he [Kosygin] could see similar phrases in public utterances by President Johnson and Mr. Dean Rusk. Warming to his subject, he said that if we, he and I, could take the North Vietnamese [the DRV Foreign Minister's] statement in the press interview as a basis and say to the President—together or separately, privately or publicly in the communiqué or in a special message—that the statement was an acceptable basis for discussion, then this was the best move for us to take, leading to bilateral talks. He specifically agreed that because of Tet, the present time was the most appropriate one.

Kosygin was able to transmit a secret assurance, which could be passed on to Washington, that if the bombings were halted, no new troops from the North would be infiltrated into the South on condition that the Americans also stopped reinforcing their troops there. A letter in this sense was prepared and authenticated by the U.S. Embassy. Wilson quotes the U.S. ambassador to London, David Bruce, as exclaiming enthusiastically, "Prime Minister. I think you've made it. This is going to be the biggest diplomatic coup of this century."

It was not. The State Department had second thoughts when confronted with the specter of the acceptance of proposals which it had advanced as an exercise in public relations only. The response to the Wilson letter was a new text from Washington, drafted by Walter W. Rostow, posing new conditions which Wilson described as "a total reversal on the policy the United States had put forward for transmission to the Soviet prime minister."

The "diplomatic coup of this century" disappeared into thin air. A disillusioned Wilson, musing over the possible reasons, wrote: "One which I was reluctant to believe, was that the White House had taken me—and hence Mr. Kosygin—for a ride. Two, the most likely, that the Washington hawks had staged a successful takeover. . . ." *

By the time Kosygin was flying back to Moscow U.S. bombers were over North Vietnam again and hopes for peace had been blasted to bits. The

---

* Harold Wilson, *The Labour Government: 1964–70. A Personal Record* (Penguin Books, pp. 444–46).

least surprised were North Vietnam's leaders. Wilson and Kosygin got the customary snub reserved for all those—no matter how high their status—who tried to take a war away from the Pentagon. If Harrison Salisbury of *The New York Times* could be officially vilified for having revealed the truth about U.S. bombing policy, the full wrath was bound to fall on my head for having revealed that Hanoi was prepared to give Johnson what he said he wanted: peace talks. My reward for putting the specter of peace onstage took the form of attempts to destroy my credentials and to cast doubt on whether I was capable of interpreting what Nguyen Duy Trinh really meant. In their first issues after the interview, *Time* and *Newsweek* carried identical photos of me in Vietcong black pajamas and conical straw hat. *Time* referred to some "change in the air" based on predictions by Senator Robert Kennedy —who was privy to the serious nature of Nguyen Duy Trinh's offer—and to testimony given by Harrison Salisbury before the Senate Foreign Relations Committee. It continued:

> If the optimism had any visible attachment to fact, it was by a frail thread of innuendo spun by Hanoi's Foreign Minister, Nguyen Duy Trinh, in an interview with newsman Wilfred Burchett, an Australian-born Communist, who has long been a mouthpiece for Asian Reds, but has been more attuned to the Moscow line than to that of Peking. The key to Trinh's position was his well-hedged sentence: "It is only after the unconditional cessation of U.S. bombing and all other acts of war against the DRV that there could be talks between the DRV and the U.S."
>
> Though the words were carefully conditional and hardly conciliatory, several governments with consulates in Hanoi were advised by the Communists that it was a "semaphoric" statement. Accordingly, they relayed to Washington the implication that an American bombing halt might result in peace talks. . . .*

The fact that the foreign minister had said there "could be" talks, not "would be" or "will be," was seized on by the State Department and press semantic experts as proof that he was not proposing anything definite. *Newsweek* in two full pages developed this theme:

> Two points in the statement intrigued State Department officials: first was Hanoi's use of the subjunctive word "could" (which may be stretched to mean "might"); second was Hanoi's failure to emphasize its "four points" (which include U.S. withdrawal from Vietnam and recognition of the Viet Cong as the "only" representatives in South Vietnam) as a prerequisite to any peace talks.
>
> Publicily, State carefully declined to characterize Hanoi's statement as a "change of position." . . . Although Mr. Johnson steadfastly insisted that

---

* *Time* (February 10, 1967).

he was "not aware of any serious effort" by North Vietnam to stop the war, his tone was studiedly moderate and conciliatory.*

These were more or less reasonable reactions clearly based on the same State Department briefing. But the pretended puzzlement over the use of "could" was ominous. It quickly became clear that the mood in Washington, not that of the verb, was the stumbling block. Not all the U.S. press maintained the *Time-Newsweek* pose of innocent inquiry into Hanoi's intentions or my own motivations.

> Burchett is a man seemingly bedevilled, firm in his conviction he has chosen wisely in adopting Communism, but not yet at peace with himself over the choice, and tugged still, though increasingly less so—toward the West. He is a man of great and intense Communist feeling for Asia, with wide experience in the Communist Far East.
>
> But above all, Burchett is a man of malevolence toward the West, endeared toward Asians as subjects for communism, bitterly anti-American and possibly the most significant Communist political agent in the Orient in the past 20 years. It was Burchett at Panmunjom during the Korean truce negotiations who probably helped fashion and then tried diligently to push on Western reporters the Communist party line in those discussions, aimed at ousting the United States from Asia.
>
> It is Burchett now, in Hanoi or Cambodia, who is trying with equal diligence to initiate Vietnam peace negotiations on the Communist pattern, again trying to expel the United States from the Far East. . . .

The writer, whom I had known about thirteen years earlier as a very junior cog in the public relations machinery of the U.S. Pacific Fleet, goes on to deal with my nefarious activities at Panmunjom and "skillfully written" articles from Hanoi suggesting that North Vietnam's peace demands were "eminently reasonable" and then comes to his main point:

> The political or diplomatic journalist has long been a fixture in the newspaper world, the man whose subject is diplomacy, the relations, interplay and exchanges between nations. But with the inception of communism, and its deliberate subjection of journalism to ideology, a new type of reporter came into being in modern history—the journalist political agent. As such, Burchett is one of the most valuable in the Communist world. His contacts and abilities also make him one of the most suspect, perhaps one of the most dangerous. Burchett's eminence in his field is manifest in various ways, in both the Communist and free worlds. . . .†

Really! The attacks against me were in the sense that I had behaved improperly—even treacherously—in enabling Nguyen Duy Trinh to call President Johnson's bluff. I, at least, should have been loyal enough to the West,

---

* *Newsweek* (February 13, 1967).
† Tom Lambert, Los Angeles *Times* (Feebruary 26, 1967).

and sophisticated enough, to accept that Johnson and Rusk were bluffing in the best interests of humanity and not do anything to upset this. In fact, I had been naïve enough to think that they probably were really interested in finding a face-saving way out in the sense of the repeated "anywhere, any-time" proclamations. If Prime Minister Wilson and U.S. Ambassador David Bruce felt that the "diplomatic coup of this century" had resulted, I would have been justified in thinking that in my flashing a light at the "end of the tunnel," a word of praise might have come my way for a positive bit of journalistic initiative.

What alarmed and disgusted me was to find that I was also in trouble in Peking for the same reason, but at a level that I was unable to define at the time because the country was in the convulsions of the Cultural Revolution. In April 1967 I had to rub my eyes to realize that I really was in Peking. The great east-west boulevard which runs in front of the Peking Hotel and tra-verses Tien An Men (Gate of Heavenly Peace) Square was jam-packed with milling crowds of blue-clad peasants, through whom loudspeaker trucks gradually edged their way, exhorting people to support or denounce one or another of the warring factions. Every building, from footpath to top story, was entirely plastered with *da tze pao* (big letter posters) also exhorting and denouncing. From the window of my hotel room on the morning after ar-riving, I watched an extraordinary Peking Opera type of spectacle, with the flat roof of a big department store in Wang Fu Chieh (formerly Morrison Street) as the stage.

Two groups, each with leaders waving poles topped by huge red flags and hundreds of their supporters massed behind, were fighting it out for posses-sion of the roof. Poles were dipped and raised, flags dancing in the wind. The crowds swayed back and forth until one side slowly forced the other to retreat by the fire escape. Fortunately I had the telephone number of an old friend, the former American Dr. George Haitem, now the Chinese Dr. Ma Hai-teh. He came to the hotel, and clad in peasant-blue boilermaker clothes like the others, he escorted me to the department store for a frontline view. With his perfect command of the colloquial language, the crowd opened up and closed in behind us. Someone pressed a leaflet into his hand; someone else promptly did the same. He perused them, cocked his ears at the loudspeakers, and explained that the "East is Red" and "Red Flag" factions, hurling *Little Red Book* quotes from Mao at each other, were fight-ing for control of the store. Each faction, claiming to be the only true champion of the "Great Proletarian Cultural Revolution," had called in its supporters from the industrial areas and villages in the outskirts to drop their tools and hoes and join in the battle. In other areas—inside the universities, until they were closed, and in the factories—the struggles took on a far more violent form, explained Ma Hai-teh.

On my return journey, in mid-May, I dropped in to see the American writer—and staunch supporter of revolutionary struggles—Anna Louise Strong. At eighty-one years, she still radiated vitality and intelligence, pecking away at her typewriter, as usual, when I walked in.

I asked her what was going on. "Mao has let the genie out of the bottle, and I'm not sure he's going to be able to get it back in," she said.

"How is Chou En-lai getting on?"

"Terrible. He's wearing himself out. Doesn't eat, doesn't sleep—on the go twenty-four hours a day. Stamping out fires. He's killing himself." At that she got up from her typewriter, stomped stiffly around the room, stopped, and said, "At this stage of affairs it's more important that Chou survives than Mao," and abruptly sat down, having uttered what for her was probably the greatest heresy of her life. She went on to describe an incident a couple of weeks previously, when students from the Foreign Languages Institute marched to the Foreign Ministry, where they swarmed over the walls after the massive gates were slammed in their faces. Demanding the "skin" of Foreign Minister Chen Yi, they had swept into the offices, seizing files and records, shouting for Chen Yi to present himself for their questioning.

"It was Chou En-lai who came out to face them and said he had forbidden Chen Yi to appear. He would come later to their institute to answer their questions. 'If you have any questions now, you can put them to me,' Chou said, 'but I warn you I'll be a bad listener. I haven't slept for twenty-four hours.' They started dispersing and shouting, 'No, No. . . . Please get some rest, Comrade Premier.' He told them to go back to their institute. 'But before you go, I want you to understand that you've behaved disgracefully,' he called after them as they started to break up."

The previous day some of the students rather sheepishly had told Anna Louise all about it and that when Chen Yi came to the institute, Chou En-lai was at his side.

Anna Louise questioned me much about Vietnam—North and South— then asked if I would give a talk in her apartment that evening to a group of "progressives in the foreign community." I agreed, and it was a lively affair. The subject was Vietnam, and after my introductory remarks the questions came thick and fast. They all were based on the premise that the leadership in the North had "gone soft on revolution" and that the real revolutionary forces were in the South, "battling away on their own" and about to be betrayed. In truth, there was one single revolutionary strategy for the military, political, and diplomatic fronts of Vietnam and one united leadership of that strategy, but that was still secret. Just as I was explaining that the struggle might soon be extended to the diplomatic field by negotiations in stalked Sidney Rittenberg, the American chief English-language adviser at Peking Radio. His brown shirt and Red Guard armband took me back to Berlin in 1939. Wagging his finger at me, he shouted, "You don't negotiate with imperialism—you destroy it!" He then put an insulting question as to my "guilt" in having produced the Nguyen Duy Trinh formula on negotiations. To my request that he rephrase it according to what he really had in mind— that is, "Is Ho Chi Minh betraying the Vietnamese Revolution?"—he exclaimed, "I won't have you putting words in my mouth." I replied that this was the essence of every question so far. "Where does it come from? Is this official Chinese policy?" At that moment Ma Hai-teh touched my arm and suggested that it was perhaps time I returned to the hotel.

The next day I sought out Chiao Kuan-hua, assistant foreign minister by then, and we dined that night together with Kung Peng, who still headed the ministry's Information Department. At an appropriate moment, I asked if "with the passage of years it is now considered that the Korean cease-fire negotiations had been a mistake."

"No," replied Chiao Kuan-hua. "It was the only thing to do."

"Then why is it considered near treachery for the Vietnamese leadership to contemplate negotiations to end their war?"

"It's up to the Vietnamese to decide," he said. "All we hope is that they will be cautious and not have their pockets picked by the West, as has so often happened in the past."

More than a year later, when negotiations finally started, I was given to understand in no uncertain terms at the Chinese Embassy in Paris that the talks were indeed regarded as a "betrayal." The "progressives" within the foreign community had the "line" right, although a number of them were later jailed for pushing it too vigorously and too soon.

While passing through Hanoi on my way back to Phnom Penh, I asked Nguyen Duy Trinh for another interview aimed at "correcting the mood of the verb," but he declined. "The Americans still think they can break us with their bombs," he said. "Let them do their worst. Only when they realize they've failed will it be worthwhile having another try." Meanwhile, the daily tonnage of bombs had steadily increased under the Pentagon's escalation policy.

With my experience in Peking in mind, I asked a contact at the Foreign Ministry if there was any reflection of this hostility toward negotiations at official levels. "At the top levels—specifically with Chou En-lai—we have no problems; at lower levels, plenty." I learned that returning Vietnamese diplomats had been hauled out of their train at Nanning—the last railway stop before entering Vietnam—and made to stand with bowed heads on a public platform as penance for Hanoi's "capitulationist" policies and that sections of the railway carrying Soviet, Chinese, and other supplies to Vietnam were ripped up by ultraleftists to punish Hanoi for its "revisionist" line.

Despite Peking's secret hostility toward negotiations and Washington's continuing illusions about cracking Hanoi by escalated bombings, I found the leadership there well pleased with its ability to cope with the air war in the North and with the battlefield successes in the South.

25

Travels Without Passport

WITH MY NUMEROUS TRAVELS the lack of a passport was becoming a problem. My *laissez-passer* was getting bulky and dilapidated. Pages had been added on numerous occasions. Each was the size of a school exercise book and was folded in four—four visas per page. It was no problem in traveling in what were then the friendly socialist or neutral countries in the corner of Asia I most frequently visited. But when I ventured farther West the passport control officer would invariably open the folded document with a snap, tearing a page or two at the creases, with an accompanying "What is *that?*" At a journalists' congress in Berlin it was temporarily lost. After frantic inquiries at the reception desk, it was produced with the explanation that because of its green paper cover, someone had mistaken it for an old exercise book, screwed it up, and thrown it into a wastepaper basket, from which it was miraculously retrieved. An entire evening was spent with friends in East Berlin repairing torn creases with scissors and tape and finally ironing it, page by page. It was a solid repair job but could no longer be folded.

Something drastic had to be done. During a visit to Paris in transit to Cuba, I had the document, reinforced by another fifty blank pages, bound into a black Moroccan-leather cover of the full, unfolded size of the pages. In a dingy atelier on the rue du Cherche-Midi, there is a craftsman who specializes in gold embossing. To avoid the wearisome "What is that?" every time I crossed a frontier, I asked him to emboss in large golden letters across the top half of the splendid cover LAISSEZ-PASSER TENANT LIEU DE PASSEPORT and in smaller letters across the bottom *Livré par la République Democratique du Vietnam.*

Thanks to accumulated Czech royalties from TV films and books and a

Czech air service Phnom Penh–Prague–Paris, we traveled, for once, as a whole family to Paris. A little Parisian French would be good for the children; a little Paris air, for their parents.

For Anna Wilfredovna, starting her educational career in the French-run Lycée Descartes, together with little Cambodian, Vietnamese, and Chinese non-French-speaking Phnom Penhites, there was no takeoff problem. By the time she was about eight I was able to converse with her freely for the first time, my Russian being vastly inferior to hers and my Bulgarian useful only for reading newspapers. Peter and George had sat with folded arms when they were given a "dictation test" for entry into the same *lycée* and were turned down. After three months' intensive tutorship, they were admitted during the second term of our first year in Phnom Penh. George and Anna were to spend a few weeks in a children's holiday camp in the south of France. Peter was to return to his "summer mother" in Bulgaria while the parents continued to Havana to cover the conference of OLAS (Organization of Latin American States).

My new-bound travel document created a sensation at Havana Airport. It was too big and rigid to slip into the slots for the passport control officers. One of them had to come around and take it. When he returned, his colleagues gathered to inspect this rare object. Despite its size and originality, it had two great merits. If it was not a forgery, it was issued by Cuba's most honored friend, the Democratic Republic of Vietnam. And if the visa was not a forgery, it was signed by Cuba's most honored contemporary writer, Alejo Carpentier y Valmont. (At that time he combined the functions of consul and cultural attaché at the Cuban diplomatic mission in Paris.) Vessa's clearly authentic Bulgarian passport was sufficient to get us into the VIP lounge and benefit from some frosted daiquiris, while the authenticity of my outsize document was checked. It took three daiquiris to get my credentials established.

By the time we had lunch with Fidel Castro on the Isla de Pinos (Isle of Pines in those days, but now Youth Island), the enormousness of my travel document had reached his ears. He asked to see it, but I had to explain that it was not of a size that I could slip into a pocket, so I had left it back at the hotel in Havana. I needed a special briefcase to carry it around! After a marvelous day with him, he interrupted a discussion on Australian techniques in sugarcane farming and experiences in crossbreeding of cattle to say, "I've been thinking of your passport problem. It must be very inconvenient to travel around the world with a document like that. If it would help your work, you can have a Cuban passport. At least it will fit into your pocket. One for each of you if you want them," he added. When the time came to leave for the Paris Conference on Vietnam, May 1968, I recalled Fidel's offer. With a Cuban passport I needed no visa for France. I discovered that one had been awaiting my signature at Cuba's Phnom Penh

Embassy for several months. Over the next four years, until a change of government in Australia led to the immediate restoration of my Australian passport, it was mostly on that offered me by Fidel Castro that I traveled— especially in Europe.

The OLAS Conference took place within the framework of Che Guevara's plea for "one, two, three, or more Vietnams in Latin America"—a well-intentioned, but impractical, slogan born out of Che's passionate idealism, impractical because it violated a well-tested principle that you cannot stop a people from making revolution if they have decided to go ahead, but you cannot force people to make revolution if they are not ready for it. The conference was a Mecca for revolutionary leaders from all over Latin America, and I was astonished to find the extent to which my works on Vietnam were known to them. Extracts in Spanish-language editions published in Mexico had been duplicated and passed from hand to hand everywhere from the Andes Mountains in the eastern states to the Banana Republics in the center—wherever there was a militant activity against dictatorial regimes. Cuba had also published Spanish translations, and these had made their way to the remotest corners of the Spanish-reading countries. This was the most highly appreciated form of recognition—to have readers avid for the information you have to impart, particularly those who are certain to make good use of it.

Everyone had expected that Che would appear at the conference, but he had already embarked on the tragic enterprise of "one more Vietnam" in Bolivia, which was to end in his death.

The highlight of our visit was the greater part of a day spent with Fidel on the Isla de Pinos. (That we had been on the original Treasure Island, renowned as a hideout for the buried loot of pirates who reigned supreme there in the sixteenth and seventeenth centuries and supposedly the setting for Robert Louis Stevenson's novel, won us far more prestige in the eyes of the children than the fact that we had lunched with Fidel.) There was a memorable drive around the island in a jeep, Fidel at the wheel, the security guards following in despair. "He hates driving in our dust," one of them explained during the first of many impromptu stops. They occurred whenever a plantation worker waved him to a halt to discuss some problem or another. There was always someone on the side of the road with a pretext to flag down the easily distinguishable chauffeur with a cloud of cigar smoke in the cabin and a cloud of dust behind.

Crammed in the back of the jeep were Vessa, Rossana Rossanda, well known in Italy as the head of the very leftist Manifesto movement, the Polish-born journalist-writer K. S. Karol, and I. Alongside Fidel was Comandante Réné Vallejo, one of his closest aides and Spanish-English interpreter. In jeeps following behind were various ministers concerned with economic affairs. Fidel was on one of his frequent reconnaissance trips aimed at transforming the island by an ambitious development program into the Isle of Youth, with model educational facilities and a massive increase in the production of citrus fruits for which the soil and climate were especially propitious. The tour lasted several hours, during which we discussed everything from the "fast-breeder" habits of Australian rabbits for potential meat production to the tardiness of the arms industries in the socialist countries in producing specific weapons for guerrilla warfare—especially shoulder-carried arms to deal with helicopters and amphibious tanks, the main innovations in counterguerrilla operations.

At one point, I could not refrain from asking Fidel to relate something about the Bay of Pigs invasion—what was the most dramatic moment, for instance? His reply, punctuated by puffs at a foot-long cigar and the frequent roadside halts, was as follows:

"It started on April 17 [1961] after attacks on our air bases a couple of days earlier. The plan to wipe out our small air force failed. The main landing was at Girón at the approaches to the narrow inlet of the Bahía de Cochinos [Bay of Pigs]. A secondary landing was at Playa Larga [Long Beach] at the tip of the inlet. The invaders were immediately engaged by our local defense forces and could not attain their objectives.

"Early on the morning of the third day, word came that a second invasion fleet had anchored off Girón. We had some Czech artillery in a training school, but the Czech instructors considered our trainees not yet qualified to fire the big guns. Unbeknown to the instructors I ordered guns and trainees to be put in position overlooking the invasion fleet, while I rushed to the spot. There was a lot of troop movement around the beaches, but I suddenly realized the invaders were moving out of the swamps toward the beaches. It was a Dunkirk—not a second invasion! The boats had come to pick up the remnants of the original invasion force. But we had to stop them getting away.

"We had some tanks nearby. Jumping into the first one, I said, 'Follow me,' and the whole column raced at full speed toward the beaches to cut off the retreaters. Just as we got onto the beaches, our artillery opened up—but at us! They thought the enemy was already on the beaches—with tanks. How awful, I thought. At the moment of victory we're going to be wiped out by our own guns.

"In those days we had no walkie-talkies, no radio communications at all. I commandeered a jeep and drove at full speed to the artillery positions, escaping by a miracle an ambush set up by our militia to stop the invaders. Fortunately someone recognized me in time. Then I ordered the artillerymen to raise their sights and sink the 'Dunkirk' ships—which they did very well."

Over a preluncheon drink at the guesthouse where Castro had his temporary headquarters, I learned from an indiscreet aide—while Fidel was washing up—that it was his fortieth birthday. Thinking that I was doing the right thing, I raised my glass as he reappeared for a "many happy returns" drink. My spirits were somewhat dashed when he responded, "I've never understood why the adding of another year to one's life should be a matter for celebration." But he downed a glass of home-brewed coffee liqueur and did not seem to be too upset. (Later I learned that he was sensitive on the question of age and felt that time was passing too quickly for the various projects, national and international, which he had in mind.)

In the luncheon which followed, the vigor and down-to-earth quality of the morning dialogue were lost, I felt—and I think Fidel did also—by the insistence of Karol and Rossana in diverting the conversation to the history of the world revolutionary movement: Lenin's "error" in signing the Treaty of Brest-Litovsk, the unjust treatment of Trotsky, and such matters. Fidel was clearly more interested in discussing current world problems—above all, Vietnam. At the slightest pause in the conversation Karol dragged it back to one or another of Trotsky's "correct positions" at vital stages of the Bolshevik Revolution. It ended with Fidel yawning and indicating the need for a break.

Among our strongest impressions, as we flew back to Havana, were Fidel's simplicity and straightforwardness, his casual and friendly relations with the people, evidenced during our drive around the island. His attention to detail and thoughtfulness, illustrated by his concern about my passport, left an indelible impression. That he had special magic for his own people was evident from the rapt attention with which hundreds of thousands stood and listened—under a blazing sun—to a six-hour speech by Fidel at Santiago de Cuba, to commemorate his abortive attack against the Moncada barracks fourteen years before. Food conditions in Cuba were tough, but the crowd roared their approval when Fidel appealed for a tightening of belts to help Vietnam.

Devotion to the struggle of the Vietnamese people, we found, was very deep-rooted. "To the Last Drop of Blood" was a much-repeated theme in posters all over Havana and along the roads in whichever direction one traveled. It was a central subject of discussion wherever we went, and more space was taken up in the press by reports from Vietnam than by any other international subject.

We gradually collected the children, speaking better French in the one case and better Bulgarian in the other, and escorted them back to Phnom Penh. Shortly afterward I visited Hanoi again. It was the period when Operation Rolling Thunder was in full force, aimed at destroying every man-made structure north of the seventeenth parallel—except in Hanoi and Haiphong. In a breakfast conversation with Ho Chi Minh, I asked whether there had been any fresh moves toward getting talks started. "How can one negotiate with a gangster?" he asked, referring to a speech which President

Johnson had made a few days before at San Antonio, Texas. He was particularly incensed at what he considered the hypocrisy of Johnson's closing words:

> "Why not negotiate now?" so many ask me. The answer is that we and our South Vietnamese allies are wholly prepared to negotiate tonight.
>
> I am ready to talk with Ho Chi Minh and other chiefs of state concerned, tomorrow.
>
> I am ready to have Secretary Rusk meet with their Foreign Minister tomorrow.
>
> I am ready to send a trusted representative of America to any spot on the earth to talk in public or private with a spokesman of Hanoi. . . .
>
> The United States is willing to stop all aerial and naval bombardment of North Vietnam when this will lead promptly to productive discussions. We, of course, assume that while discussions proceed, North Vietnam would not take advantage of this bombing cessation or limitation.*

Ho Chi Minh described this as "throwing dust in the eyes of the public" and said that all that a few behind-the-scenes diplomatic probes had revealed was that Johnson and Rusk were demanding "total capitulation" as the price for ending the bombings and that their conception of talks was that of "dictating surrender terms." After further talks with Pham Van Dong and Nguyen Duy Trinh I wrote an article for the Associated Press in which I said, "Hanoi is in no mood for concessions or bargaining. There is an absolute refusal to offer anything—except talks—for a cessation of the bombardment. . . . One difficulty that foreign diplomats have in persuading Hanoi to make any new peace gesture is what one of the leaders referred to as the 'credibility gap' between what President Johnson says and does. . . ."

In the first week of December 1967, as I returned through Paris from a session in Roskilde, Denmark, of the Bertrand Russell War Crimes Tribunal, my services as a "dangerous political agent" were sought by John Dean, first secretary at the U.S. Embassy in Paris. Out of the blue came an invitation to lunch in his apartment. Dean, a short, affable man, introduced me to another guest, Heyward Isham, a tall academic type, who explained that he was a member of the State Department's task force on Vietnam and that his particular specialty was following up any leads on peace or negotiations. The lunch was clearly set up to probe further into the Nguyen Duy Trinh interview and into the basis of some of my Associated Press articles.

It seemed to me that this was the most serious effort yet to discover a basis for negotiations. The fact that it had taken more than ten months since the Nguyen Duy Trinh interview to put such questions indicated to me that the truth was beginning to sink in at least in some quarters in Washington that

---

* *The New York Times* (September 30, 1967).

neither North Vietnam nor the NLF was at its "last gasp." It was clear that
the contents of our protracted luncheon conversation would be going directly back to Averell Harriman, who headed the Vietnam task force.

The luncheon reinforced my conviction that there were more reasonable
and lucid voices in Washington than those which made the most noise and
featured largest in the newspaper headlines and that there were those who
had a different opinion about my activities and purposes from that of the
hack pack which had taken after me following the famous interview. Messrs.
Dean and Isham, for instance, must have been convinced they could count
on my discretion—it was a matter they did not even raise.

That there were more lucid voices in Washington—and I suspected that
Harriman was one of them—was a view I hammered away at with my Vietnamese friends—with understandable difficulties, in view of what was being
hurled at them day and night in ever-increasing tonnage of bombs. If I had
some faint hopes of voices of reason in Washington, my hopes of a superior
intelligence in Hanoi were far greater—and justified. Shortly after the Paris
meeting, at a reception for some visiting Mongols in Hanoi, Nguyen Duy
Trinh changed "could" to "will" in repeating almost verbatim the essential
part of the interview. But as a concession to Isham's probe about an agenda,
Nguyen Duy Trinh added, "talks on all questions concerned."

My consistent interest in all that I had done and written—and would
continue to do and write—regarding the Vietnam War was to encourage the
doves on both sides to impose their views on their respective hawks, keeping
in mind that it was Washington hawks that were operating in Vietnamese
skies and on Vietnamese soil—not vice versa. Objectivity is great as far as
collecting and passing on real facts are concerned, but cannot be stretched
to placing those who were defending their country and those who were
attacking it on the same level.

Increasingly this was being understood in Washington and other parts of
the United States and abroad, especially as far as public opinion was concerned.

26

——◄◆►——

Vietcong in Paris

AFTER MY AUGUST 1966 visit, I had not been in the NLF areas of South Vietnam again for the good reason that it had a well-informed diplomatic mission in Phnom Penh, headed by Nguyen Van Hieu, my first Vietcong contact in 1962. Apart from that, "jungle uncles," many of them Cambodian-born Vietnamese on "home leave," arrived quite frequently. Ba Tu, valiant interpreter during the first visits, had turned up in Phnom Penh as correspondent for the NLF's Liberation News Service. So I was kept well informed of the situation on the ground and could afford a hearty laugh at the predictions of the prestigious U.S. commander, General William C. Westmoreland, at the end of 1967. Small wonder that Washington was still not interested in peace talks when "Westy" assured the world that the Vietcong had been driven into the frontier area with Cambodia and no longer presented a problem. The military outlook had never been better! Since the maps his staff officers prepared for him in Saigon must have looked very different from those I was seeing in Phnom Penh, it was he—not I—who was stupefied when the Tet offensive blew up on the night of January 30–31, 1968. In his excellently documented book on the Tet offensive, Washington *Post* correspondent Don Oberdorfer relates that as the first flash reached the State Department, four of his *Post* colleagues were being briefed on how well the war was going, with the usual collection of "captured Communist documents" to prove that the Vietcong were at their "last gasp." After a few slips of paper had been passed to him, the briefing officer "with a thin smile" announced, "It appears the 'Vietcong' are attacking the Embassy in Saigon." * Probably at about the same hour

---

* Don Oberdorfer, *Tet, the Story of a Battle and Its Historic Aftermath* (New York: Doubleday, 1971), p. 18.

I was getting a sober, factual briefing on what was going on by Nguyen Van Hieu in Phnom Penh. "It is a 'generalized,' but not a final 'general,' offensive," he warned, adding, "Don't forget that we gauge the results of military action by their political effects."

The political effect was felt two months later in my room at Hanoi's Thong Nhat (Reunification) Hotel on the night of March 31, 1968. Present was—for Hanoi—a rare gathering of American writing, editing, and journalistic talent: writers Mary McCarthy and Franz Schurmann, journalist-editors Harry Ashmore and William Baggs, and the chief foreign correspondent of CBS News, Charles Collingwood. They were there because I had a good shortwave radio, and President Johnson was about to make a major speech on the Vietnam War. The essential bit about the Vietnam War was as follows:

"There is no need to delay the talks that could bring an end to this long and bloody war. Tonight I renew the offer I made in August—to stop the bombardment of North Vietnam. We ask that talks begin promptly, and that they be serious on the substance of peace. We assume that during these talks Hanoi would not take advantage of our restraint. . . .

"Tonight I have ordered our aircraft and naval vessels to make no attacks on North Vietnam, except in the area north of the demilitarized zone where the continuing enemy buildup directly threatens allied forward positions and where movements of troops and supplies are clearly related to that threat. . . .

"Now, as in the past, the United States is ready to send its representatives to any forum at any time, to discuss the means of bringing this war to an end. I am designating one of our most distinguished Americans, Ambassador Averell Harriman, as my personal representative for such talks. . . ."

He went on to talk about economic affairs, and because Ashmore and Baggs had come in late, there were shouts to turn off the radio and compare notes to make sure we had correctly taken down this most dramatic statement by any President about the Vietnam War. We rushed down to the bar to celebrate. It was only after about the third round that a Vietnamese friend came to ask what we thought about Johnson's decision not to run again for President. We looked at him blankly, having missed the supreme political effect by turning off the radio too soon.

Within a couple of days Nguyen Duy Trinh proposed that talks start in Phnom Penh, at ambassadorial level; despite "any forum at any time" Johnson rejected the Cambodian capital on grounds of lack of communication facilities and the fact that the United States had no diplomatic relations there. Hanoi proposed Warsaw, where both sides had diplomatic relations and the United States had been negotiating with the Chinese—off and on—for almost ten years; this was refused. Dean Rusk then proceeded to make an ass of himself by laying down the criteria for an acceptable site and then proposing places which violated his own criteria. "It must be neutral, where

both sides had diplomatic relations and adequate communications existed."
He proposed six countries in Asia and four in Europe with which North
Vietnam had no diplomatic relations and in some of which—Afghanistan and
Nepal, for instance—the availability of adequate communications was ques-
tionable. Hanoi proposed Paris; Rusk countered by accepting an Indonesian
offer of a cruiser and passenger ship anchored in "neutral waters." It looked
as if he were intent on holding the talks some place where there would be
a minimum of press coverage. Eventually Rusk accepted Paris. Editorials in
several U.S. papers complained that France—after De Gaulle's Phnom Penh
speech—could not be considered "neutral" regarding the Vietnam War. The
first full conference session was scheduled for May 13, 1968.

I arrived in Paris a few days earlier as consultant to the high-powered
CBS team covering the conference—a discreet arrangement which did not
interfere with my weekly dispatchs to the *Guardian*. I was booked into the
Hôtel Lutetia in the boulevard Raspail, where former Foreign Minister
Xuan Thuy, who headed the DRV delegation, and his colleagues were
staying. As previously agreed, I dined on the night of arrival with Charles
Collingwood and his wife in the Lutetia restaurant. We ate and conversed
as best we could, in view of the tear gas drifting in through the smashed
plate glass windows, while students battled with riot police a few blocks
away down the boulevard St.-Germain.

After the Collingwoods retired, I headed in the direction of exploding
tear gas grenades and flames lighting up the sky. At the corner of the boulevard St.-Germain and the rue de l'Ancienne Comédie, I ran into the first
barricade, rapidly being reinforced by cobblestones and logs from trees being
cut down with electric saws a bit farther along the boulevard. I was stopped
by two stern, well-muscled young men. There ensued the following dialogue:

"What *is* going on?"

"You can read the papers and listen to the radio!"

"I've just arrived tonight in Paris. This is like Vietnam—not Paris."

"Who are you?"

"A journalist—here for the conference on Vietnam."

"Hang on a minute."

They returned with someone wearing an armband who obviously had
leadership functions.

"Who are you? What do you want?"

I produced a press card.

"You're Burchett? The one who writes about Vietnam?" I nodded. "Well,
it's the same situation. We're the Vietcong, and they"—jerking his head to
where the firing was going on—"are the Yanks. Come with me."

He guided me around the end of that barricade to a second, where we
had to make way for two teams of stretcher-bearers racing for the École de

Médicine, a few hundred yards away. On each stretcher was a young man, hands over his head and blood oozing between the fingers. We came to a third barricade, by which time tears were streaming down my cheeks and there were sharp, pricking pains in my eyeballs. Here automobiles turned on their side formed part of the barricade together with steel tree guards, metal shutters ripped from shopwindows, and even traffic light standards uprooted from the intersections. The fiercest action was going on a bit farther ahead, where the boulevard St.-Germain and St.-Michel met, and up and down St.-Michel. "No farther," said my guide. "It's really rough up ahead."

Handkerchief pressed to my burning, streaming eyes, I staggered back, my guide holding one of my arms as he escorted me to the first barricade. He took over command again, leaving me to grope my way along, bumping into shattered shopwindows and lampposts until I left the "combat area" to lean against the Drug Store, on the corner of the rue de Rennes. There I witnessed a curious scene. There was a huge pile of garbage stacked on the corner—garbage workers, like almost everyone else, having been on strike for the previous few days. A group of young people were fiercely arguing whether or not to set fire to it. As the argument reached its height, I watched a mournful-looking man set fire to the garbage with his cigarette lighter, methodically choosing the most combustible spots for his miniature flame-thrower. It was only when the flames were soaring up that those debating the issue realized it had been settled. The mournful one had already moved off; the others also started moving, still shouting at each other—but this time about some matter of doctrine. It was an unimportant incident, but it symbolized the confusion, the lack of leadership or clear aims as to what the May Events, as they became known, were all about.

The following morning it was announced that 60 barricades had been erected during the night of violence; 188 cars had been destroyed or damaged; 367 people—mainly students—had been injured, and 460, arrested. The head of the Paris police accused the students of waging "real guerrilla warfare," but public sympathy was with the students. It was generally agreed that there had been excessive brutality by the police. To complicate the situation still further, the country's two largest trade unions joined in calling for a twenty-four-hour strike, which coincided with the opening of the conference. France that day was at a standstill. Ten million workers went on strike—and stayed on strike, most of them having occupied the mines, factories, offices, department stores, and other places of work. The Paris police were also on strike; students were directing traffic at "hot" intersections.

For those interested in belittling the fact that the United States was again sitting down with Asian peasants—from a relatively small country this time—to negotiate a way out of a failure, the May Events were a fabulous gift of the gods. That an explosive situation had developed within the student ranks was no secret, nor was the massive discontent among the workers. But the timing, which took political leaders and those of the trade unions— from Communists to Gaullists—completely by surprise, was uncannily propitious as an irresistible and compulsive counterattraction to the conference on Vietnam. The hundreds of journalists and scores of TV teams who had converged on Paris for the conference were covering the nightly street battles in the Quartier Latin, which made far more dramatic images and copy.

Walter Cronkite and his CBS team held the view that journalism had its part to play in bringing about a settlement and that my role would be to ensure that CBS would have as complete coverage as possible on DRV views of the questions to be discussed. That they had their own means to have fullest coverage of U.S. views went without saying. Journalistic diplomacy, of which Walter Cronkite was no mean exponent, would go on parallel to conference-table diplomacy. This corresponded to my notion of creative journalism and was the basis of my cooperation with the CBS team throughout the first year or so of the conference.

Within this framework of the responsibilities of a journalist involved in covering the most solemn of all subjects—that of peace or war—I found myself just two weeks after the Paris talks started at a luncheon table with Averell Harriman, who headed the U.S. delegation, in his suite at Paris's most illustrious and expensive Crillon Hotel. The other guests were Charles Collingwood and one of Harriman's chief aides, Daniel Davidson. It was all very informal, a typical, relaxed Sunday luncheon atmosphere, Harriman in shirt sleeves and suspenders serving drinks and getting things off to a good start by thanking me for having secured the release of some American POWs at a time when he had been designated by Johnson to "do something" in this field. My first impression was of a warm man with whom it would be easy to talk, and this proved to be the case. Collingwood, an intimate friend of Harriman, had arranged the meeting because, in a moment of confidence, I had once told him of the useful outcome of the friendship between *France-Soir's* De Segonzac and me during the 1954 Geneva Conference. Collingwood mentioned that Harriman would like to crown a long and distinguished career by negotiating the United States out of its most controversial and unpopular war. This was a laudable ambition, worthy of support.

Harriman was understandably interested in having my views on the negotiating aims of the North Vietnamese and the realistic areas of agreement.

Some journalists had already started referring to me as a "spokesman for the North Vietnamese Reds," and I made it clear from the start that I had no official or organic connection with the North Vietnamese whatsoever and that whatever I had to say was my personal opinion. But it would be a well-informed opinion because I had been following Vietnamese affairs closely for many years. Harriman accepted that. He listened attentively as I briefly ran through the long history of Vietnamese resistance to foreign invaders. Because of their having been cheated of the fruits of their victory against the French, it was understandable that they would be supercautious of not being tricked aagin. Even if he came with goodwill and sincerity, Vietnamese suspicions—based on past experiences—might cloud the atmosphere for a while. The minimum they would want was what had been promised in the 1954 Geneva Agreement—independence as a single, united state.

It was normal that the Vietnamese would suspect that the United States was just the most recently arrived great power to try to convert Vietnam into its colony. Harriman insisted, however, that it would be a mistake for the North Vietnamese to see the United States as a new colonizing power. The aim of U.S. intervention was limited to prevent the North from taking the South by force. "We have no intention of digging in."

When I remarked that the size and permanent appearance of U.S. bases in the South would fuel Vietnamese suspicions that the United States *had* come to stay, Davidson intervened for the only time to make a valid point: "You only have to look at the sort of bases we abandoned here in France, with grass growing out of runways three feet thick, to understand that the size of bases has no relationship to permanence of stay."

Harriman said, "When our military move into any part of the world, they insist on the most and best of everything."

At one point he laughed and said, "If the North Vietnamese can persuade us that they don't intend to invade the South and we can persuade them that we don't intend to hang on in the South, then we've got the basis of an agreement."

This was the most important point made in four hours of conversation which ranged over the whole map of Asia and during which I criticized the United States for always pinning its hopes on the most reactionary, antipopular forces. Toward the end Harriman remarked that Xuan Thuy's refusal to admit that there were troops from the North in the South made negotiations difficult. I explained that the Hanoi leadership was flexible and that if there were prospects for a good agreement, there would be no northern troops in the South by the time it was signed.

It was an agreeable, stimulating, and useful conversation. Obviously matters of such import were not to be decided by such conversations. But from the moment that Xuan Thuy and Ha Van Lau, deputy head of the DRV delegation, became convinced of the sincerity of Harriman—and his deputy, Cyrus Vance—they began to make things easier for them. If Harriman, quite admirably, wanted to end his diplomatic career as the man who brought peace to Vietnam, Johnson was determined not to end his political career as the President who had "lost Vietnam." Enough mud had been flung at those held responsible for "losing China" for him not to risk that sort of inglorious exit from the White House. And the shadow of McCarthyism still loomed large—if not directly over the Paris negotiators, at least over those who pulled the strings in Washington. Harriman and Vance did, in fact, successfully execute their negotiations brief and got the type of agreement Johnson had instructed them to get. But Johnson pulled the rug out from under them, repudiating his own guidelines and thus facilitating the victory of Richard Nixon in the November 1968 presidential elections.

With Nixon waiting to take over in the White House, the chance for a quick end to the war on the most favorable conditions the United States could ever hope to obtain was frittered away. In diplomatic language, Harriman hints at what happened:

> There seems to be no doubt that, through one channel or another, Thieu [Nguyen Van Thieu] the U.S.-backed dictator in Saigon was counseled to wait until after the American election.
> He was evidently told Nixon would be much harder-lined than Humphrey, and he was warned that if negotiations began, Humphrey might be elected.
> I don't in any way suggest that President Nixon knew anything about this. . . . But some believe that if we had started actual negotiations during the week before election day, it might well have made that small, but vital difference in the outcome of the election. If Hubert Humphrey had been elected President, we would have been well out of Vietnam by now. . . .*

Chances for an early end to the war disappeared from the day the election results were announced. Everything positive that had been achieved was wiped out. When progress was achieved in the talks, the North Vietnamese, as part of their policy of "making things easy" for Harriman, started a massive pullout of troops from the South in the quiet way I had predicted. They continued, even though the American military on the spot was taking advantage of this. It was within the overall Ho Chi Minh concept that military activity could be judged only in terms of its political consequences, and this applied to withdrawals as well as advances. Harriman and Vance were aware that Hanoi was leaning over backward to get agreement, especially during the period between Nixon's electoral victory and his actual takeover at the White House. Harriman makes this clear:

> I am not very good at making a case for the enemy, but the North Vietnamese did disengage in the two northern provinces of I Corps. That had been an area of some of the bloodiest fighting involving Americans—Khesanh and the like. The North Vietnamese had a large force there. They took 90 percent of their troops out, and half of them were withdrawn to above the 20th parallel some 200 miles to the North. This was almost complete disengagement. . . .†

---

* W. Averell Harriman, *America and Russia in a Changing World* (New York: Doubleday, 1971), p. 136.
† *Ibid.*, p. 137.

As soon as Nixon took over at the White House, Harriman resigned and was replaced by Henry Cabot Lodge. For many of us covering the conference, the arrival of Lodge symbolized the end of attempts to get a negotiated settlement. His lack of interest and boredom in pretending to have to negotiate took the form of ostentatiously yawning and actually dozing off at the conference table. The Paris negotiations had been relegated to the deep freeze. Nixon's election-winning pledge of a "peace plan" turned out to be one of continuing the war by other means, by "changing the color of the corpses," as Ellsworth Bunker, his ambassador to Saigon, expressed it. It was called the Vietnamization of the war—pulling out U.S. troops and replacing them by Vietnamese units formed in their image.

27

Prodigal's Return

WHILE THE PARIS TALKS were in the doldrums and the war raged on in Vietnam, I was invited to a symposium in Australia to lecture on "The War in Vietnam in Its Historical Perspectives." Some months earlier I had created a sensation at London's Heathrow Airport by presenting my Moroccan-leather-bound monstrosity as a valid travel document. It created as much a stir as at Havana, but with less friendly interest. Because I was coming at the invitation of a committee which included several well-known MPs, I was eventually allowed in. This earned a paragraph in *The Times* (London) under the headline "Man Enters Without Passport" and a picture in the *Guardian* of me holding the famous document. I took advantage of the visit to make an official application for a passport at Australia House. The matter had to be referred to Canberra, I was told. When the lecture invitation arrived, I sent a copy to the migration officer at Australia House, suggesting that if there had not been a reply about my passport, a temporary "entry certificate" could be issued.

A brief reply came three weeks later. "I am directed to inform you that you will not be granted an Australian passport or the alternative document which you have requested." Thus, I could not attend the symposium, but I recorded my contribution, adding that I would have preferred to be present to take part in the discussions, but unfortunately . . . and mailed it off. Thus, some of Australia's leading intellectuals and political personalities learned—to their indignation—of my passport difficulties. (Since I had been without an Australian passport for fourteen years by that time, I was astonished at the reaction to this sudden and accidental revelation.) The upshot was the formation in my home state of Victoria of a Burchett Passport Committee, one of the main functions of which was to draw up a petition on the matter for submission to the Federal Parliament. Chairman was the Right Honorable Arthur Augustus Calwell, former chairman of the

Labour party, national vice-president of the Winston Churchill Memorial Trust, and Knight Commander of the Order of St. Gregory the Great (a rare and distinguished decoration of the Vatican). Among prominent members were Frank Galbally, Australia's most eminent criminal lawyer (who offered to take up the passport fight free of charge), Labour party MPs, trade union leaders, writers, journalists, and others active in the field of democratic rights.

The activities of this committee aroused the ire of certain right-wing groups known for their affiliation with the John Birch Society in the United States and kindred bodies. Their counteractivities aroused international interest in the case, starting with the press in England and the United States and spreading to the various organizations which champion human rights and to outstanding writers, scientists, film stars, and others, who signed the petition.

Support from within the profession in which I had been engaged for about thirty years was highly encouraging. The chairmen and general secretaries of both world organizations of journalists (International Federation of Journalists, based in Brussels, and the International Organization of Journalists, based in Prague), which, between them, represent nearly all organized journalists in the world, were among the signatories. The National Union of Journalists (of Britain, my *own* union), the Australian Journalists' Association (AJA), and journalists' associations from India in Asia to Chile in Latin America—and many others in between—signed the petition. So did philosophers and humanists of the quality of Bertrand Russell and Jean-Paul Sartre. Among the signatories were twenty-eight members of the two houses of the British Parliament—Conservatives, Liberals, and Labour—and eight Nobel prizewinners (two of them American). The PEN Club, the British National Council of Civil Liberties League, the International League for the Rights of Man, and many similar organizations specializing on democratic rights lent their support. With Jane Fonda, Vanessa Redgrave, Melina Mercouri among the film stars; Graham Greene, Norman Mailer, and Arthur Miller among the writers; the world's greatest scientists and philosophers; and lords and ladies from Westminster pleading for me—how could I fail? It was a proud and solemn Right Honorable Arthur Calwell who stood up in the House of Representatives in Canberra to present the petition. It demonstrated that by depriving me of my passport, the Australian government had violated Articles 13, 16, and 19 of the Universal Declaration of Human Rights and concluded:

Your petitioners most humbly pray that the House of Representatives in Parliament should act immediately to:

(1) assure Wilfred Burchett and his family of their freedom to enter and leave Australia in accordance with the rights of Australian citizenship:

(2) restore the Australian passport to Wilfred Burchett:

(3) ask the Honorable the Attorney General whether it is alleged that Mr. Burchett has contravened any law of this country, and if so, what law. And your petitioners, as in duty bound, will ever pray.

Prime Minister John Grey Gorton and the members of his right-wing Cabinet were not impressed. The ban would remain. The Australian Journalists' Association pursued the matter vigorously and appealed to the Human Rights Commission of the United Nations, accusing the Australian government of violating the Human Rights Charter over the question of my passport. (Years later I received a letter from that notoriously impotent commission, stating that it was never able to do anything about individual cases of human rights!)

Prayers, petitions, and appeals were of no avail. The government remained adamant: neither passport nor any official definition of my "misdeeds." This latter was something which the AJA pressed for very strongly, as can be seen from the following extract of a letter, published in the Australian press in April 1969:

. . . My association has been trying since 1965 to influence the Government through the Minister for Immigration to grant Mr. Burchett an Australian passport and some weeks ago we asked Mr. Snedden to meet a deputation from the association. He has refused and he will not set out the Government's reason for denying Burchett a passport.

If, in the Government's view, Mr. Burchett is guilty of treason, or had breached the Crimes Act, the Government has its powers to prosecute him, but it should not deprive him of his fundamental human rights to return and, if he desires, leave his own country at his will.*

Old Father George, at the time the petition was presented, was ninety-six—old even by traditional Burchett nonagenarian standards. We obviously wanted to meet before he passed on but had agreed that my demand to return to Australia should be based on the principle of my democratic rights, not on a plea for a "humanitarian gesture." But others raised the question—directly with the government and in the press—of at least the right of a limited sojourn for humanitarian considerations. To no avail. He died in September 1969, two months short of his ninety-seventh year, Australia's "youngest old man," as one obituary notice described him. He made a valiant effort toward the end to hang on, in case I arrived. His death coincided within a few days with that of Ho Chi Minh.

Five months later, a few hours before I was to leave Paris for Phnom Penh, on the first stage of a visit to Hanoi, my brother Winston telephoned from Melbourne to inform me that our elder brother Clive was dying—it was a matter of hours. Only my two brothers and lawyer Frank Galbally had been

---

* Sydney *Morning Herald* (April 18, 1969).

informed for weeks before that I had set a date and flight number for arrival in Sydney to defy the ban on my entry. I took a snap decision, after a brief conversation with Galbally, to continue from Phnom Penh to Australia, taking in Hanoi on the return trip. There was to be a memorial service for Clive—a highly popular figure in his community—and I was determined to attend it.

Earlier having made known my intention to force the government's hand, Frank Galbally had advised me to present a copy of my birth certificate to the immigration authorities on arrival, and one of my brothers would be on hand to identify me as the person described in the birth certificate. Galbally was now advised discreetly of my change of plans. Success depended on perfect functioning of air schedules.

Had anyone asked me what went wrong, I would have to have replied, "Everything!"

Timetables had been changed, and an hour's waiting between planes at Colombo turned into an overnight stop, with control of passports on leaving the transit lounge and the discovery that I was equipped with a birth certificate instead of a passport. Quoting international air regulations which stated that "Australian nationals" did not require transit visas for Sri Lanka got me nowhere, nor did the production of press cards, a driving license, and other documents describing me as Australian make any impression. "To prove you are an Australian national, you must produce an Australian passport," was the wearisomely repeated reply. The final judgment was that I definitely could not transit through Colombo Airport and must return whence I had come.

An agent from the UTA (Union des Transports Aériens) Airline, whose ticket I held, appeared beaming, with a copy of a telex he had just sent off to Singapore. Until then, because of a fortunate error of the girl in the Paris booking office who had taken my name over the telephone, my ticket was in the name of Burnett, which I had to explain when producing my identity documents. The telex to Singapore spelled out my name in full, described me as a "famous journalist," gave full details of my *laissez-passer*, explaining that I had no passport and required twenty-four hour transit facilities for a connecting UTA flight to Sydney. My elaborate arrangements for a discreet entry into Australia were blown sky high. Singapore was noted for its supertough security. The reply was prompt and negative. By this time my name was being Ping-Ponged back and forth. The UTA agent booked me on a Colombo–Phnom Penh–Nouméa (New Caledonia) flight, leaving in a few hours, with a connecting UTA Nouméa–Sydney flight. Nouméa gave passengers up to ten days' stay without a transit visa, provided they had tickets and confirmed onward bookings. More telexes featuring my name yielded confirmation of the Sydney flight.

Six hours after arriving in Colombo, I was heading back for Phnom Penh, hoping to get some sleep for the first time in forty-eight hours. The air hostess gave the flight itinerary as Phnom Penh—*Saigon*—Singapore—Nouméa. Sleep prospects faded as I wrestled with the problem of my fate in Saigon were it known that I was aboard. Apart from the telex messages, doubtless monitored by various intelligence services, my correct name was now on the manifest—plus the fact that I was traveling on a North Vietnamese *laissez-passer*. The air hostess assured me that it was only a refueling stop and that passengers usually stayed aboard. I decided to risk it and pretend deep sleep when we arrived. At Phnom Penh, leaving my hand baggage aboard, I went into the transit lounge with the other passengers. About twenty minutes later an old friend from Royal Cambodia Airlines came running into the lounge. "Monsieur Burchett, you must leave the plane. They are waiting for you in Saigon. We have intercepted messages. . . ." This was repeated a few seconds later by the representative of Air France—also an old friend—who came bustling in just as my name was being announced over the loudspeaker asking me to report to the information desk. There was the Bulgarian chargé d'affaires, whose diplomatic cables Youpi had distributed from the treetops. He had been on the same plane from Singapore and noticed two gangsterish-looking Vietnamese pointing at me and muttering my name. There was nothing to do but hand in my ticket and baggage checks. There would be another plane for Nouméa in six days, and the friendly Cambodian immigration officials gave me a ten-day transit visa.

In the meantime, the news that I was homeward-bound and had run into trouble in Colombo and Singapore was making headlines in the Australian press. Frank Galbally made a request to Prime Minister Gorton for facilities for at least a short visit to attend the memorial service for my brother. Gorton responded with his usual "no passport, no facilities" formula, from which he could not be shaken in the weeks that followed.

At Nouméa the passport control officer viewed with bulging eyes the dimensions of my *laissez-passer*, but he turned the pages with near reverence, doubtless impressed by the numerous French visas. After checking my tickets and the date of my confirmed onward flight to Sydney, he stamped my document with a standard ten-day entry permit. First thing was a telephone call to my brother—and it was agreed that he and Galbally would be on hand for my arrival in Sydney on February 18, 1970.

I was checked in normally at Nouméa's Tontouta Airport, baggage weighed, airport tax paid, name checked on the passenger list, coupon detached from the ticket. Then someone emerged from an inside office and asked to see my Australian passport. There ensued the same scene as at Colombo.

A senior UTA official asked me to step into his office, where he showed me a telex from his company's Australian headquarters. UTA had been warned that it would face a "very heavy fine" if it carried me unless I could produce an Australian passport or visa. Who had issued this warning? "The Australian authorities, of course," he replied. I offered to buy a return ticket to Nouméa so that I could return on the same plane if there were difficulties in Sydney. "Normally we would accept your assurances," he said. "After all, you have a through ticket to Paris. But UTA has only very tenuous landing rights in Australia, which is why we are very vulnerable to threats. In view of this telex we simply cannot carry you." I pointed out that his airline would be involved in an international scandal when it became known that it had yielded to governmental pressure to violate its contract—which is what an airline ticket represents. He shrugged and "regretted." My baggage and airport tax were returned, and I drove back through New Caledonia's beautiful nickel-filled mountains to Nouméa.

Among the journalists waiting with Frank Galbally and Winston at Sydney Airport were some who had passports with them, so they embarked for Nouméa on the UTA return flight. They included a TV team from the Australian Broadcasting Commission and half a dozen other journalists. Films, tapes, and words by the thousands and tens of thousands started flowing back. The cartoonists—especially in my native Melbourne—started having a field day. The government at first tried to deny having applied pressure on the UTA. But the airline's traffic manager in Sydney said he had been threatened by the Immigration Department. The minister of immigration said that he had only repeated the prime minister's statement after the Colombo incident, that the government "would do nothing to grant a passport to Burchett or facilitate his travel in any way." By this time the government was actively hindering my travel and lying about it. Gorton started to get a bad press.

At the Australian government-owned airline Qantas office in Nouméa the local agent said he had been instructed by the Australian consul, David Wilson, not to issue me with a ticket. With me at the airline office was a Reuters correspondent, who promptly reported this. Later in the day Wilson issued a ridiculous one-and-a-half-line communiqué, denying he had issued any such instruction. Other reporters checked with the Qantas man, who stuck to what he had told me.

Telegrams started pouring in from trade unions, student organizations, personalities, some of them known to me, others not, pledging support and urging me to continue the fight. My mind could not but go back to Egon Irwin Kisch and his fight thirty-six years earlier. But travel methods had changed. I could not jump out of a plane somewhere over Australia! Galbally published a letter he had written to Gorton pointing out that the government had gone far beyond its decision on the nonissue of a passport. With my concurrence he requested an official inquiry:

for the purpose of determining whether or not he, Burchett, has, in fact, by his conduct renounced his citizenship. . . . Our client will undertake to abide by any reasonable conditions your government would impose on his return. He would enter into any bond to leave the country at the expiration of such an enquiry, and would present himself for evidence and examination before any tribunal you set up for this purpose. Indeed Mr. Burchett is quite prepared under conditions set down by your government to present himself in Australia for questioning by the relevant Department's officials.

Had there been any basis for the allegations the government was leaking to certain journalists against me, here was the chance to prove them. Gorton turned it down. In numerous daily interviews on TV and radio and with the daily press, I hammered away at the theme. "If I am guilty of such heinous offenses that the government has taken the unprecedented step of refusing me a passport, Gorton should be glad to get his hands on me. But I am the one fighting to get in, while the government fights to keep me out."

There were several offers of private planes to fly me in; someone offered to pay the "heavy fine" with which UTA had been threatened; there was a scheme to smuggle me in on a collier from Nouméa to Newcastle. The most serious proposal came from Gordon Barton, then proprietor of the Melbourne *Sunday Observer* (later the *Nation-Review*), who had been negotiating with a private charter company to fly me in. The editorialists and, above all, the country's leading cartoonists had supported Galbally and forced the government to adopt a "neither help nor hinder" formula, which represented a marked retreat. Under this formula Barton and Galbally obtained a clearance from the Department of Civil Aviation for the specific mission of flying to New Caledonia and bringing me back to Brisbane (several hundred miles closer to Nouméa than Sydney).

Meanwhile, the Nouméa authorities were beginning to wonder what sort of "international desperado" they had on their hands to tie up all cable and telephone facilities between the island and Australia. I was "invited" to appear at the local security headquarters. The officials were polite, but severe. It had been discovered that my *laissez-passer* was not an appropriate document in which to stamp a ten-day visa-free entry permit. My press card to cover the Paris Conference and the facts that I had written the only contemporary book in English on New Caledonia and that my family was installed in Paris counted in my favor. But most important of all was the fact that I had an okay confirmation for my return flight to Paris. "Don't exceed the ten days," they said. Consul Wilson was stepping up his pressure to have me expelled.

Barton, who by then was paying my hotel expenses, urged me to hang on, cancel my return to Paris; Galbally was coming to Nouméa, and the private plane a few days after. The government had slightly changed its position. I returned to explain to the security authorities that I might be exceeding by one or two days the ten-day visa limit. I was asked to wait a few minutes. Then the chief security officer returned and said, "I have just phoned the

Australian consul, and there is no change at all. You are not to be allowed into Australia. And you cannot stay here after the ten days are up."

"I have an idea which I think solves both our problems," I said, "and which is in conformity with international practice. Why not deport me to my country of origin?"

They looked puzzled for a moment, then roared with laughter. I no longer felt the cold touch of handcuffs. "We have no intention of deporting you anywhere, Monsieur Burchett. You have committed no wrong on our *territoire*. But it would be better not to exceed the ten days."

Frank Galbally arrived, along with his lawyer-nephew Peter, and we had a glacial session with Consul Wilson, which ended by the filing of a request for a certificate of identity (an acceptable travel document for Australian residents returning from abroad in unusual circumstances—lost passports et cetera). The matter would have to be referred to Canberra. Later that afternoon Wilson phoned me and with obvious satisfaction read the reply from Canberra. No certificate of identity: "Any further requests should be made directly to the Department of Immigration."

The Galballys returned, the ten days passed, and I made another visit to the security people. By that time a twin-engine six-seater Piper Navajo aircraft was parked for me at Tontouta Airport. It suited Gordon Barton to have me wait a couple of days in order to arrive on a Saturday so that whatever news story there was would break first in his *Sunday Observer*. (This led to a cartoon of me Scotch-taped to a cross, with a photographer saying, "Could you hold it like that, Mr. Burchett, until the first edition?") The Nouméa police agreed that a couple of extra days would not worry them now that there was tangible evidence that I would soon be leaving.

It was a strange turn of the wheel that I should be returning to Australia by more or less the same route as that by which I had left thirty-three years earlier. Except that instead of four days on the *Pierre Loti*, it was to take me four hours, on the Piper Navajo—the call sign for which was "Victor Bravo Yankee"! Within minutes of takeoff, we were over the water. The advantage of a small plane is the sense of movement, lost with the big jets. We were never out of sight of lines and whorls of coral reefs. After almost four hours of flight, a gray smudge of land was visible, and *Sunday Observer* journalist Bill Greene, who had flown in with the plane, opened a bottle of champagne to celebrate landfall.

The only evidences of human activity, as the plane taxied to the passenger terminal, were placards—"Burchett Back to Hanoi," "Burchett Traitor"—and, as I stepped from the plane, there were boos with a few cheers. In a small enclosure, rival groups were jammed together, some shaking fists, others waving welcoming hands. Among the hand wavers, I was relieved to see Winston and Frank Galbally. The fist shakers and booers had been organized by the ultrarightist Citizens for Freedom movement. The hand-wavers were from trade union, student, and peace groups, and even though it was a midsummer Saturday afternoon, their numbers were greatly reinforced as word got back about the activities of the ultrarightists.

At the terminal I was asked for my health card, which was in order. Then I was handed a blue card to fill in for immigration. In the space marked for passport details, I gave the data from my birth certificate. This was checked against the photocopy I was holding, and I was passed on to customs. After carefully studying the form, I said there was nothing to declare. A cursory glance at my transistor radio and typewriter—my suitcase was not even opened—and the formalities were over.

A few moments to greet Winston and Galbally and then on to the lowest form of press conference I have ever attended, before or since. The journalists, if that was who they were, interrupted each other's questions and my replies —no matter how brief—with their own shouted absurdities. Tripods for TV cameras and cables got mixed up with their feet, and there was such a pushing and shoving that tempers got very frayed. "Now you're in, how are you going to get out?" was one of the final, jeering questions. Nothing about the Paris peace talks or anything of real import.

From the press conference to another plane. A stop at Sydney Airport and a brief interview with a group of normal professional journalists, who *were* interested in the Paris peace talks. On to Melbourne. Lots of police and lots of people at Melbourne Airport, including many journalists. Professionals! The police closed in on me, herding me toward a car and telling me not to speak to the press. I insisted on saying a few words to the journalists and to the large crowd—all welcomers. With lots of pushing and manhandling I was edged toward a police car. I was confused about what was going on—but suspected I was being taken into custody. As the door of the police car swung open, I asked Frank Galbally, who had never left my side, what to do. "Jump in," he said. Winston and Bill Greene jumped in, too.

A police officer in the front seat turned around and said, quite amiably, "Where to, Wilfred?" My brother gave his address in East Melbourne, and with welcomers swarming around the car, we drove off. The only time in my life I had used a police car as a taxi! "Too many longhairs around here for my liking," mumbled the police officer as we drove off.

There, after phoning his paper, Bill Greene informed me that somebody had telephoned in that afternoon to say that he had resigned from the Victoria Freedom Australia Committee (a kindred body to that which had organized the Brisbane "reception") when $500 were paid out by the committee "to kill Burchett." Winston had also found a note stuffed into his letter box that morning to say that I was to be "executed." Galbally warned me to be careful in walking around on my own. Money had changed hands for various incidents to be staged. One of them was to be a street scene— with photographer on hand—of an "enraged father" of a Korean or Vietnam

War veteran striking me with his walking stick. Galbally's specialty as a criminal lawyer resulted in several "tips" of the "enraged father" type, none of which eventuated.

There was no "quiet Sunday at home" in that first day in Australia for nineteen years. Relays of TV teams were setting up and dismantling their gear from breakfast till lunch, with newspaper interviews sandwiched in between. Tom Prior, of the *Sun News-Pictorial*, who had been most assiduous in his attentions at Nouméa, turned up with a collection of cartoons for my comments.

By the time cousins, nieces, and nephews and their offspring arrived for the first family reunion at midday, I had given about a dozen TV, radio, and press interviews. More, including a live TV round-table discussion, were scheduled for the evening. The next morning I was off to Canberra for a televised press conference at the National Press Club.

It was only on the fourth day, Wednesday, March 4, 1970, that I was able to get out into the countryside—what was intended to be a long, relaxing drive into the Dandenong Mountains. In the depths of the bush with its gorgeous early-autumn colors, I felt I was back in Australia. Melbourne could have been almost anywhere else in the world—with all the new building it was almost unrecognizable. The Dandenongs, bordering on my native Gippsland, were the Australia I knew. Winston switched on the car radio, and relaxation was over. It was a live broadcast of question time on the second day after the opening of the 1970 session of Parliament. And the lawmakers were discussing my fate. First was a question to Gorton, from a member of his own Liberal party:

> I desire to ask the Prime Minister a question concerning the entry into this country of a journalist who is alleged to have assisted two Asian countries whose soldiers were fighting Australian soldiers. Has the Government records which would show that this person did assist the enemies of Australia? If so, has he broken any of our laws? If he did assist the enemies of our country, but by so doing did not break Australian law, is it the intention of the Government to alter our laws so as to make future actions of this sort, an offence?
>
> *Gorton:* . . . In relation to the man of whom the honorable member is speaking, there is no doubt, and it is a matter of public record, that he lived with the enemy behind the enemy lines in wartime on an occasion when Australian troops were engaged in that war. There in no question but that he engaged in propaganda activities which were designed to be, and which were, helpful to the enemy in that time of war, and there is no question that he visited prisoner of war camps, run in many cases under the most barbarous conditions by the enemy, in which Australian troops were incarcerated. I believe there is evidence that on these visits he engaged in discussions with Australian troops which would be calculated to lower their morale and their belief in the cause for which they were fighting. That is sufficient for

this Government to say that we do not believe that man should be provided with a passport, asking Australian posts to assist him, and I see no prospect whatever of that approach being changed.*

After repeated attempts by the speaker to silence him, Dr. J. F. "Jim" Cairns, deputy leader of the Labour party, managed to get in a question on whether or not I had asked for a court of inquiry to investigate the reasons for the denial of my passport.

> *Gorton:* . . . Mr. Burchett has asked for a court of inquiry to establish some charges against him. There is no need whatever for a court of inquiry to examine whether Mr. Burchett was living behind enemy lines in the course of two wars. . . .
>
> *E. G. Whitlam, Leader of the Opposition:* I ask the Attorney-General a question. Is it thought that Mr. Burchett has broken any law of the Commonwealth? Alternatively, now that he is in Australia, is any investigation being undertaken to ascertain whether he has broken any law of the Commonwealth?
>
> *Attorney-General Hughes:* . . . I do not propose to give any opinion as to whether Mr. Burchett has broken any law of the Commonwealth. What I will say, however, is that I, as the principal law adviser of the Crown, do not propose, as at present advised, to bring any charge against him in respect of. . . .
>
> *Dr. Cairns:* Oh!
>
> *Mr. Hughes:* . . . I do not propose to bring any charges. . . .

Our car glided from gullies of giant tree ferns to eucalyptus and sassafras-covered hilltops, but there was too much twitching at my entrails to enjoy it all. For fifteen years I had been outlawed, my name dragged through the mud by official innuendos and leaks to the press; my professional activities gravely hampered; my children denied their natural birthright—all for reasons that the prime minister and attorney general admitted they dared not submit to a test of law. What could I do further? I invited Gorton to repeat the charges he had made outside the privilege of Parliament. This he also refused. What was clear was that I was not going to get a passport—this was confirmed by a negative reply to my formal application a few days later.

If the United States, Australia's chief ally, were to have applied the same criteria as Mr. Gorton, they would have had to revoke the passports of Harrison Salisbury; Charles Collingwood; Daniel Deluce, the assistant general manager of the Associated Press and his wife, Alma; author Mary McCarthy; and dozens of other Americans who had visited Hanoi during the Vietnam

---

* Although I made copious notes as we rolled through the Dandenongs, the quotes are from the proof copy of *Hansard,* the official record of parliamentary debates, of March 4, 1970.

War, including a dozen or so who went specifically to gather evidence of U.S. war crimes against Vietnam. If holding "discussions with Australian troops . . . calculated to lower their morale and their belief in the cause for which they were fighting" were to be considered a crime, the passports of most Labour Members of Parliament, of members of the Labour party itself, and of the editorial writers of many newspapers would have had to be withdrawn.

Mr. Gorton and his ministers were entitled to have their opinions about me, as I was to have mine about them. The difference was that they used their powers and privileges to punish me without trial for reasons which the attorney general had to admit were groundless. There were other opinions about my role: that, for instance, expressed in *The Times* (London). In an editorial entitled "An Australian Asks for Justice," after noting that Gorton had "compounded the Australian Government's earlier mistake over Mr. Wilfred Burchett in announcing that he will be refused a passport now he is back in his native land," *The Times* continued:

> Few western journalists who have witnessed Mr. Burchett's conduct in the East would think him anything but misguided in his enthusiasms. He sympa-thised with China, reported the Korean war from the Pyongyang side and in due course went to Hanoi—but his writings show him to be an advocate of détente rather than a tough, committed enemy of the West. . . . His dis-approval of Australian support for the United States in Vietnam was shared by a considerable minority of Australians at home, if less articulately and actively. . . .*

Within two weeks—short of getting a passport—my aims had been ac-complished. Most important I had confronted my accusers and come off best. My case had been put to the public in scores of press and media interviews. I had addressed a packed public meeting in the Melbourne Town Hall and was given the signal honor of being first to sign a document in the launching that night of what became known as the moratorium movement to bring Australian troops back from Vietnam. (It was successful beyond all expec-tations.)

Fifteen days after arriving in Australia, I presented my birth certificate at the passport control office at Sydney Airport and, after a farewell press con-ference, I left for Nouméa on the first leg of my return to Paris via Phnom Penh. Awaiting me at the hotel was the editor of a local paper, who asked if it was true that I was, in fact, a top official of the Australian security services. How on earth could he have such an idea? He swore this is what he had been told by Consul Wilson, also that the Piper Navajo which had

---

* *The Times* (London), (March 5, 1970). (I reported not on the Korean War, but on the cease-fire negotiations. I was not a war correspondent in Korea.)

flown me to Brisbane was an unmarked plane of the Royal Australian Air Force. David Wilson had certainly not counted on my returning via Nouméa. He was reassigned shortly afterward.

At the airport the next morning, passengers were informed that there had been a last-minute change of schedule: The plane would not be stopping at Phnom Penh. This upset me because I was counting on picking up my cameras and other gear and my biographical notes on Ho Chi Minh. (The time consumed by the Australian visit had erased any possibility of my continuing on to Hanoi.)

As I finally walked through the door of our Paris apartment, the phone was ringing. It was the BBC asking if I could rush to its Paris studio and do a TV interview on the latest events in Cambodia. "What events?" I asked. There was a gasp from the London end. "You, the great expert on Cambodia, don't even know that Sihanouk was deposed today?" My reputation was saved only when I explained that I had spent the previous thirty hours on a plane from Nouméa. A quick embrace for Vessa and the children, and without having removed my overcoat, I was on the way to the studio. The interviewer tried very hard to shake me, but I stuck to three points: Sihanouk would fight back; Sihanouk would have the support of the people; in the end he would win.

Fortune, which had played so many dirty tricks on me during that Australian odyssey, for once had intervened in my favor. Had the UTA plane not excluded Phnom Penh from its flight, I would have stopped off on the day of the coup to collect my belongings. My friendship with Sihanouk being well known, I would have been in trouble with the plotters who formed the new regime, especially since I was traveling on my North Vietnamese *laissez-passer.*

What had I accomplished by forcing the back door into Australia? I had demonstrated that traveling without a passport is not the simple matter that some of the pundits in the press—notably the Sydney *Morning Herald*—had claimed. More important, while it was generally assumed that an Australian could enter his country by producing a birth certificate once he got there, I had created a useful precedent that one can also leave Australia by producing a birth certificate. Thus, a passport is not necessary as a permission to travel abroad. This precedent was created, I learned later, because the Gorton government was terrified that I was going on a nationwide campaign to end Australian participation in the Vietnam War. They were so glad to see me go I believe I could have left with a visiting card. The main gain, however, was that six months after I left Sydney, Peter, George, and Anna received Australian passports. This was a sop to public opinion, which could not see why the unsubstantiated "sins" of the father should be visited on the children.

28

———◄◆►———

Tête-à-tête With
Henry Kissenger

I N P A R I S T H E T A L K S to end the Vietnam War churned on without any progress or possibility of progress. As Nixon tried in 1969 to win in the South by bombing the North, so he tried in 1970, after the overthrow of Sihanouk, by invading Cambodia to wipe out the "Vietcong sanctuaries" there and destroy their "Pentagon." In 1971 the war-winning formula was the invasion of southern Laos "to cut the Ho Chi Minh Trail." The yawning, dozing Cabot Lodge had resigned in November 1969, and as if to emphasize the downgrading of the Paris talks, Nixon did not even bother to replace him for several months.

Only after the nationwide uproar in the United States over the invasion of Cambodia, reaching its climax with the killing of four students at Kent State University by national guardsmen on May 4, 1970, did Nixon appoint David Bruce to head the delegation in Paris. A career diplomat, at seventy-two years, Bruce was rumored to have the same laudable ambition as Averell Harriman to cap his long diplomatic career by extricating the United States from the Vietnamese quagmire. It was not the charming and intelligent Madame Nguyen Thi Binh, foreign minister of the Provisional Revolutionary Government (PRG) of South Vietnam, who would discourage such an aspiration. At the first plenary session in ten months, she proposed an eight-point peace plan, the essence of which was that a simple declaration of intention by the United States to withdraw its troops from South Vietnam by June 30, 1971, would be sufficient to end further NLF attacks on U.S. troops. There could then be talks between the PRG and the Saigon regime aimed at a cease-fire and general elections to a new national assembly. It was one of the many occasions on which the U.S. delegation summarily rejected the best possible terms, judged by Washington's own declared interests, that could be had at that particular moment. The options grew inexorably less attractive the longer the fighting continued.

The invasion of southern Laos to cut the trail was the greatest U.S.-Saigon military disaster until that time. Sihanouk was later to tell me how Vo Nguyen Giap regarded the campaign from the beginning. He happened to be visiting Hanoi at the time it was launched on February 8, 1971. Before setting out to dine with Giap, he had heard Nguyen Cao Ky, South Vietnam's fiery vice-president, boast that the invasion forces would remain in Laos "until the dry season finishes at the end of May" and that "we may even launch ground attacks against North Vietnam." Sihanouk, with Ky's boasts still ringing in his ears, was feeling uneasy.

"At one point," he said, "I could contain myself no longer. 'I feel very guilty, *mon général*. I have taken up so much of your time when such a tremendous battle is going on in South Laos.' 'Oh, that!' replied Giap with a smile. 'That's been prepared long ago. Our comrades on the spot have everything necessary to deal with the situation. There's no need for me to bother. . . . According to today's radio, Thieu says his troops will remain in Laos until May or June. In fact, what's left of them will be out by the end of March at the latest.'

"And they were," Sihanouk said, his eyes wide in admiration. "The last had left by March twenty-fifth. Giap is a military genius, undoubtedly the greatest strategist of our time and one of the greatest of all times."

The Laos debacle ended any illusions of military victory by the U.S.-Saigon forces in South Vietnam. On July 1 Madame Nguyen Thi Binh put forward a new seven-point plan which met the main requirements of what David Bruce had been proposing at the weekly meetings. It provided for a three-party provisional government in South Vietnam, composed of the existing Saigon regime, the PRG (which had been set up in June 1969), and neutralist third force elements which would organize elections to a national assembly. South Vietnam would be pledged to a foreign policy of "peace and neutrality establishing diplomatic relations with all countries regardless of their political and social regime, in accordance with the five principles of peaceful coexistence." There were high hopes that this was the major breakthrough which would make an agreement possible. Bruce had every reason to congratulate himself.

Then Kissinger arrived in Paris on his way home after his sensational "secret" visit to Peking, and there was rumored to have been a great row between himself and Bruce. At the end of his short visit Kissinger announced that Bruce was resigning because of "ill health." Bruce immediately informed a group of American journalists that his health was "excellent." But he left for Rome, and Nixon was able to announce two weeks later that he had in his hands a letter of resignation from Ambassador Bruce. There were no farewell parties, no trip to Washington to make a final report.

Bruce had found with Nixon, as had Harriman with Johnson, that the terms for ending the war, as stated for public opinion, and the instructions given to the chief negotiators had little in common with real policy aims, as —in this case—dictated by Henry Kissinger. Bruce was replaced by William Porter, who had been for a long time the number two man in the U.S. Embassy in Saigon, and the Paris talks were again relegated to the deep freeze.

In September of that year I went to the United Nations to cover the China debate for the Paris fortnightly *Afrique-Asie*, the Australian *Sunday Review* (successor to the *Sunday Observer*), and the New York *Guardian*. There is a widespread impression that the United States by adroit offstage maneuvering facilitated China's entry into the UN that year. Nothing could be further from the truth. The United States and its closest allies in obstruction, above all, Japan and Australia, fought a bitter, arm-twisting battle to prevent China's entry. The United States was waging its annual campaign with lavish use of bribes and threats to keep China out. To the best of my knowledge the only two correspondents to have predicted China's entry that year were Henry Tanner of *The New York Times* and I—because we kept a careful tab on the changing mood of delegates.

A few days before the voting was to start—precisely on October 8—I received a telephone call in the New York apartment which a friend had placed at my disposal.

"I'm one of Dr. Kissinger's aides. Dr. Kissinger heard you were in town and wonders whether you would care to have breakfast with him next Tuesday."

"In principle—yes."

"Then at nine-thirty in the West Wing of the White House."

"I have a bit of a problem."

"Oh"—very coldly—"what is that?"

"My movements are restricted to within twenty-five miles of the UN Headquarters."

"In that case, I don't know what to say. I don't know anything about this."

"Under the circumstances, for such a purpose, I propose to ignore the restriction."

"I propose to ignore the fact that you have raised the matter. So you will come?"

"Yes. At nine-thirty on Tuesday in the West Wing?"

Since the weather was foggy that Monday, I went by train rather than risk a canceled plane flight to Washington, pondering what Kissinger wanted to talk about—China or Vietnam? At the time, like all journalists covering the Paris talks, I knew nothing about the secret meetings between Kissinger and the North Vietnamese Politburo member Le Duc Tho, "senior adviser" to the DRV delegation. Also, as the train sped toward the capital, I was wondering what would happen were a check made and I was discovered violating the restriction on my travels. In order to eliminate the risk of a marine guard's running his bayonet through a "Cuban" trying to enter the White House, I was carrying only my UN press credentials. At nine-thirty Tuesday morning I presented these to a marine guard in a sentry box, and within seconds another marine escorted me the few score yards to the West Wing, where a woman receptionist asked me to wait a few moments. Who should appear but smiling Kissinger himself.

At first sight, Kissinger reminded me of an indulgent headmaster of my schooldays. As he accompanied me into his office adjoining the reception hall, he expressed himself as being glad to meet me, and the conversation continued, with Kissinger leading.

"I've been reading your writings for some time."

"I've read some of yours also. And found them interesting."

"What, for instance?"

"In the January 1969 issue of *Foreign Affairs* on Vietnam. Also the essays on foreign affairs where you deal with the multipolar concept in international relations. I find this interesting in relation to the emergence of Japan as a potentially strong force. I imagine the Chinese find it interesting also."

"Ah, yes. I'd forgotten you also have a Chinese background. Japan is already a strong force and starting to make her weight felt. Have you been in China recently?"

At this point someone came in with a tray and served breakfast. While we dealt with it, Kissinger said that he assumed our conversation was "off the record." I replied that I did not intend mentioning that it had taken place. "It won't break my heart if the fact that we have met becomes known," he said. I then answered his earlier question:

"Yes. I was in China at the beginning of Ping-Pong diplomacy when the U.S. and other table tennis teams arrived. I was present when Chou En-lai received them."

"What is your impression of Chou En-lai?"

". . . I have always found him straightforward and frank, saying what he means and meaning what he says."

"That was my impression. I was greatly impressed with him and those around him. Of course, I don't know what are his long-range aims. He's a revolutionary, but I can admire men who have devoted their whole lives to an aim—even if it's a revolutionary one. But I really wanted to talk to you about Vietnam. Have you been in Hanoi recently?"

"The last time was in May 1970. But just before I left for New York, I had dinner with Xuan Thuy, who heads the DRV delegation at the Paris talks."

"How does he view things these days?"

"Relaxed and confident—very pleased with the strong support from both the Soviet Union and China for Madame Binh's seven-point peace plan. It's the first time the Soviet Union and China have agreed on anything relating to the negotiations. Xuan Thuy was also convinced that China was not going to make any deals over the head of Hanoi during President Nixon's visit to Peking."

"Anyone who thinks China would make such a deal against her friends in Hanoi needs to have his head examined. We have no such illusions. But does Hanoi really want a negotiated settlement?"

"Yes, and they believe that the seven-point plan contains all the elements for a solution."

"I admire the North Vietnamese. I wish they were on *our* side. They are a tenacious and disciplined people—even a heroic people. They have great qualities, but they are bad negotiators. They should stop saying, 'You must. . . .' Even if they said, 'You should . . .' it would be better."

"Perhaps it would be better if they said, 'Let us. . . .'"

"[Laughing] That would be real progress. You see, there is a certain language that can't be used with a great power like the U.S.A. if obstacles are to be overcome."

"What is the greatest obstacle to be overcome?"

"Hanoi wants everything to happen at once. They want their people to take over in the South right away. They want us to accept everything they propose without making any concessions themselves."

"They—and the NLF—believe they made the biggest concession right at the beginning, when they renounced immediate reunification. It is clear there is to be no reunification in the foreseeable future. The seven-point plan makes this clear, especially Point Five."

"About neutrality?"

"Not only neutrality. Acceptance of economic and technical aid from both sides. Offers to take part in schemes for regional economic cooperation. Future relations with the U.S.A. These are points that should make a settlement easy for you to accept."

"Frankly the seven-point plan, even with the linking of U.S. troop withdrawals with the release of POWs, is a bore."

"Being stuck with the sort of regime you have in Saigon must be an even greater bore!"

"I won't comment on that, but the North Vietnamese don't come up with any realistic way of changing it. They can't expect us just to dump it. They have produced no realistic scheme as to how to bring about their coalition regime."

"They think that you do nothing to bring about a change of regime and that you could have stopped doing a few things that you do to maintain it in power."

"If we wanted to retain permanent political power in Saigon, which, fortunately for Hanoi, we do not, Hanoi's tactics would facilitate our task. They are so suspicious. They don't believe us when we say we are pulling out."

"History justifies their suspicions."

"I agree with you that they have every right to be suspicious. But they should understand that it is 1971, not 1954. That was the time when Dulles deliberately engaged us in Southeast Asia. . . . Our policy is the opposite —to disengage. But we can't do it all at once. Hanoi does nothing to help. They want everything right now. We are pulling out. They think we want to keep bases. When we are setting out to normalize our relations with China, we can't have a war going on in the perimeter areas. If they think we intend to hang onto bases, they are wrong. What would we want them for? We also don't want a North Vietnam weakened economically or politically by continuing war—a tempting prey to an expansionist-minded Japan. We have learned that it is possible to have good relations with Communist countries—now that they are no longer a monolithic bloc."

"The Communist world is also multipolar!"

"We have no real quarrel with Vietnam. We don't think the leaders there are bad, immoral, and have to be punished. It's a question of finding a realistic basis for settlement."

"They think the seven points provide such a realistic framework, and that private talks on these between the PRG and the U.S.A., at which full details could be discussed and negotiated, would provide an honorable and realistic way out."

"I'm not sure that this is the best, or only, way to solve the problem. The trouble is that Hanoi is not willing to wait for the political processes to work themselves out after we have completed our disengagement."

"They are willing to have the future settled by democratic processes that conform to the strictest U.S. concepts of democracy. But as you saw, even Duong Van Minh or Nguyen Cao Ky could not stand against Thieu, and you backed the farce of a one-man election."

"Hanoi spoiled that possibility, too. They do everything wrong."

"I mentioned Duong Van Minh because I think it's possible to find personalities and a regime acceptable to all sides."

"What about Le Duc Tho? Is he really more important than Xuan Thuy?"

"Yes. He's one of the half dozen top personalities in the Hanoi leadership. He's a member of the Political Bureau, Xuan Thuy of the Central Committee."

"I have been very impressed by Pham Van Dong. . . ."

"He is very impressive. An intellectual and dedicated patriot, straightforward, frank, and sincere. In fact, similar in a Vietnamese way to Chou En-lai."

"Like Chou En-lai! Really! Chou En-lai is tremendous."

"Xuan Thuy had hoped that the arrival of Mr. Porter might mean something new. . . . But when Xuan Thuy proposed that he sit down and discuss details of the seven points with Madame Nguyen Thi Binh, Porter repeated the old counterproposals that the four parties meet in restricted sessions. Neither Xuan Thuy nor Madame Binh can see any point in restricted sessions with the Saigon delegation present."

"They should at least sit down with them and see what is Saigon's negotiating position."

"It is well known. Thieu openly states he wants only a military solution. The sort of secrecy necessary if real negotiating is to be done would be impossible were the Saigon delegates present. Xuan Thuy also told me that the question of releasing more pilots as a gesture was now a closed book. . . . In any case the procedure for prisoner release is also set out in the seven-point plan."

"We want to get it all over with. You can communicate my views to your Vietnamese friends. I don't know if you know, but I worked on the problem of getting talks started under President Johnson, in 1967. It is ridiculous to think that I would be less interested in getting the war ended in my present situation. The very fact that I receive you, just one week before another trip to Peking, should convince your Vietnamese friends of this."

While we were talking, there was a call from President Nixon about a communiqué which Kissinger was to draft announcing that Nixon would be visiting the Soviet Union in May 1972.

Kissinger asked me who, in the unlikely chance of Peking's taking China's seat at the UN that year, would head its delegation. To test his reatcion, I said, "Probably Chou En-lai." He almost jumped.

"No," he said. "He wouldn't do that. He wouldn't come to the United States before President Nixon visits China!"

Comforting him by recalling Chou En-lai's statement in my presence a few months earlier that he would probably not be making any more long voyages abroad, I said that it would probably be Chiao Kuan-hua, whom I described as a "very brilliant man with whom Western diplomats should find it easy to establish contact." On that note the encounter ended.*

I learned from a mutual acquaintance within a few hours that Kissinger considered our exchange "fruitful." Much of what I felt had been achieved in clarifying Hanoi's viewpoints, as I understood them, was devalued when I learned—through Nixon's dramatic TV announcement on January 25, 1972

---

* Readers of my book *Grasshoppers and Elephants* will note discrepancies between the briefer account given there of the Kissinger encounter and that given above. When that book was written, I was certain that notes made immediately afterward were "lost and gone forever." They surfaced years later. I have a well-trained memory, but the reconstruction of a dialogue five years after the event obviously suffers in comparison with notes made thirty minutes after that event.

—that Kissinger had had twelve secret meetings, seven with Le Duc Tho and Xuan Thuy together and five with Xuan Thuy alone, in Paris between August 4, 1969, and September 13, 1971. Kissinger took the initiative on breaking them off on that date, and the message he clearly wanted me to pass on to Xuan Thuy was that he was still interested in a negotiated settlement and that the United States did intend pulling out completely from South Vietnam.

I left the White House with three scoops in my pocket: Kissinger was off to Peking on a second visit; Nixon was to visit Moscow (both events were announced the following day); Burchett had had a long breakfast discussion with Kissinger. What had Kissinger got out of it? By the innocence of my questions and suggestions (private talks, for instance) he had confirmation that Le Duc Tho and Xuan Thuy were observing the pact on total secrecy for the private talks, and he had opened up a pipeline, other than diplomatic, to the "other side." Years later, when I read the book of CIA operator Frank Snepp, I was haunted by the thought that when Kissinger was probing as to the relative importance of Le Duc Tho and Xuan Thuy and asking about Pham Van Dong, he knew of, and was almost certainly responsible for, plans to kill or kidnap North Vietnamese leaders of that category. Snepp reveals:

> Meanwhile, Kissinger requested contingency studies from the intelligence community to determine if there might be some way to jog the Vietnamese off dead center. One proposal drawn up jointly by the CIA and the Pentagon called for the assassination and/or kidnapping of one or more of North Vietnam's leaders, on the theory this might precipitate such turmoil in Hanoi the survivors would be obliged to bow to U.S. demands. When my colleagues and I were asked to evaluate the scheme we could hardly contain our amusement. As the American raid on the Son Tay prison camp outside Hanoi had proved so painfully in 1970, our intelligence on the life and times of the North Vietnamese was something less than perfect. If we couldn't accurately pinpoint the whereabouts of a large group of American prisoners in the North Vietnamese capital, how could we possibly expect to locate and snatch select members of the party leadership? *

This shocking admission of intent to murder sheds a new light on Nixon's promise of further such raids of the abortive Son Tay type. One has to go far back in history to find murder or kidnapping of one's partners in negotiations as an acceptable method of diplomacy. Kissinger as head of the 40 Committee, which directed the "dirty tricks" aspect of US foreign policy, was certainly deeply involved in this odious business. The image of the "indulgent headmaster" had faded long before I read the Snepp book, but such revelations further confirmed the infamous nature of his methods.

---

* Frank Snepp, *Decent Interval* (New York: Random House, 1977), pp. 21–22.

Schemes such as the immorality and savagery of the B-52 "Christmas bomb-ings" of Hanoi in December 1972, the predilection for duplicity over diplo-macy, and the inability to see solutions when they were within his grasp led one of his biographers—and a former colleague in the National Security Council—Roger Morris, to describe the Kissinger moves to end the Vietnam War as "barbaric as well as subtle, often absurd, craven, and inept while historic. In the end, no other policy, no other record in his long and contro-versial service, so stained Henry Kissinger's claim to greatness." *

My main impression of Kissinger's personality was his overwhelming sat-isfaction with himself and the steely, cold eyes which took the warmth out of his smile. I was shocked at his flippant rejection of Madame Binh's seven-point plan as a "bore." It was the best solution the United States could ever expect in protection of its own interests and to achieve a peaceful end "with honor" to the Vietnam War. From the moment Kissinger threw the word "bore" into the conversation I doubted his sincerity in getting a realistic settlement.

Once aboard the shuttle plane to New York, I congratulated myself that my violation of travel restrictions had passed unnoticed. A bulky late arrival hastened in and flopped down beside me. "Burchett," he roared. "What are *you* doing here?" It was Harry Ashmore of the Center for the Study of Demo-cratic Institutions. With many eyes directed toward us because of his effu-sive greeting, I had to explain quietly that I was covering the China debate, with restricted travel facilities, but could not resist a swift visit to Washing-ton at the pressing invitation of old friends. It would not be good if word of this got around. He promised discretion and kept his word. It was not his fault or mine that word of the meeting, but not the contents, leaked out and quickly got back to Australia. Thus, under the title "What Did Dr. Kissinger Tell Wilfred Burchett" the Melbourne *Age* carried a report from its diplomatic correspondent, Bruce Grant, some extracts of which ran as follows:

> On October 19, the Australian journalist Wilfred Burchett, who is an outlaw in the eyes of the Australian Government, met secretly with the architect of American foreign policy, Henry Kissinger. The meeting took place at Dr. Kissinger's invitation. . . .
> Although he is officially an outcast in Australia, Wilfred Burchett's re-porting from Indochina has given him an international reputation as an intelligent and well-informed man, despite his political prejudices. . . .
> This is the kind of political intelligence from which the Australian Gov-ernment has been excluded for many years. We have relied on the siftings of our powerful friends, which are subject on occasion to a fine screen. . . .

* Roger Morris, *Uncertain Greatness, Henry Kissinger & American Foreign Policy* (London: Quartet Books, 1977), p. 150.

Accounts of the meeting, although varied, concentrate on one topic: a political settlement in Vietnam. October 19 was the day before Kissinger left for his second visit to Peking. He was concerned to hear Burchett's opinions why Hanoi had not responded to Washington's overtures for a settlement.*

The long, dreary, and infinitely painful road to the signing in Paris, on January 27, 1973, of an Agreement on Ending the War and Restoration of Peace in Vietnam, the continuing war in the South, and the lightning offensive which wiped out the Saigon regime, leading to the rapid reunification of the country, I have described elsewhere.† It is historically correct to say that had Kissinger acted as the real statesman-diplomat that he is sometimes portrayed to be, the lives of hundreds of thousands of soldiers and ordinary people would have been spared, the United States would have retained a respectable position in Indochina, the tragedies of the "boat people" and of Kampuchea would have been avoided, and peace and stability in that corner of the world would have been preserved.

---

* Melbourne *Age* (November 24, 1971). Bruce Grant, although close to the mark on a number of points, had the date wrong by eight days, and there were a number of other unimportant inaccuracies.

† Wilfred Burchett, *Grasshoppers and Elephants* (New York: Urizen Books, 1977).

29

---◄●►---

Peking and the Nixon Visit

HAVING BEEN ON HAND on November 10, 1971, to welcome Chiao Kuan-hua as he crossed the UN threshold to present his credentials to Secretary-General U Thant, and having been present when, to the accompaniment of tumultuous applause, he led the People's China's delegation to assume its rightful seat, soon after I was on my way to Peking. There I had a rendezvous with Prince Norodom Sihanouk, Cambodia's deposed head of state, former monarch, and by then founder-president of FUNK (Kampuchean National United Front). We were to cooperate on writing a book in which Sihanouk would describe the events leading up to his overthrow and the nature and perspectives of the resistance struggle which, by the time I arrived in Peking, was being waged with great vigor.

Sihanouk was burning to present his case to the world and to rally public opinion to his side. We quickly agreed on what the book should contain and broke it up into chapters and the aspects that each would deal with, establishing a working routine which fitted in with his duties as head of state-in-exile. These were many. All high-ranking visitors of countries which had recognized the resistance government made protocol visits. Mao Tse-tung had given personal instructions that Sihanouk was to be given all facilities to function as a real head of state. The compound of the former Chinese Foreign Ministry (and before that the French Embassy) was formally declared Cambodian territory.

For convenience sake, I was lodged in the residence of the prime minister of GRUNK (Royal Government of National Union)—elder statesman Samdech Penn-Nouth—who had migrated to the warmer south of China. We quickly settled into a work routine. At a preluncheon session I would tape Sihanouk's answers to questions relating to the contents of a chapter to be drafted that night. We spoke in French, but the next morning he would have the draft of the chapter in English, returning it to me in the evening with his comments neatly written in red in the margin. From that—while working on the next chapter—I would provide a near final draft, again submitted for his approval. Once the material was "in the pipeline," we produced a chapter a day.

For three weeks I was totally integrated with the Sihanouk family, lunching and supping with them, the tape recorder always on the dining table. The group included Sihanouk's beautiful and intelligent wife, Monique, and her mother; a son and daughter from one of Sihanouk's earlier wives; his favorite aunt, who supervised the culinary arrangements; and his personal secretary.

He worked off his own incredible energy—and kept members of his government and family fit—with nightly bouts of his own variant of badminton, three players a side to ensure maximum participation. I occasionally took time off from my nocturnal writing and transcription of notes to watch the perpetual badminton tournament, departments pitted against departments, ministries against ministries with Sihanouk always in the middle, bouncing up and down like a rubber ball, dominating any round in which he played.

Mao Tse-tung had insisted that hospitality was to be extended any Cambodians who wanted to come to Peking for temporary exile, so the community was in a state of constant expansion. They represented varying political viewpoints of students, intellectuals, and middle- to upper-class Cambodians who happened to be outside the country when Sihanouk was deposed, including a large number of diplomats who had rallied to the FUNK-GRUNK banner. Newcomers, who had managed to slip out of the country, would be invited to a meal with the Sihanouk family to relate their experiences and the situation inside the country.

Monique acted as Sihanouk's press secretary. In Phnom Penh she had been regarded as just a very decorative element of the prince's entourage, who stood at his side at official receptions, murmuring a few conventional words of welcome and farewell to arriving and departing guests. Now she worked long hours, going through dozens of daily newspapers that came in from New York, London, Paris, and Hong Kong, clipping out all references to Kampuchea and other elements of the international situation which could have any bearing on the situation there. When I congratulated her on the very professional judgment she had shown in compiling her newspaper clippings, she replied:

"I never had any interest in politics until my husband was deposed. On the plane from Moscow to Peking, when he informed me what had happened, I tried to persuade him that after our Peking visit we should return to France and live quietly there. But when he said we should fight back, I agreed and resolved to support him. He asked me to read the newspapers for him and cut out the interesting bits. Since then I have become passionately interested in all aspects of international affairs."

As for the book, the aim was set forth in my introduction, obviously written with Sihanouk's approval, which set the guidelines. In part, it says:

> The account is classic for its description of the total nature of the means employed by the world's mightiest economic-military power to force a small country away from its chosen policy, and to get rid of the architect and executant of that policy. At Sihanouk's first meeting with the brothers Dulles, there was ominous insistence that he should abandon his neutralist ideas. When diplomatic, political and economic pressures—accompanied by military threats—failed, there was a period of plots and assassination attempts. When they in turn failed, it was finally, with well-financed treason at the top, a military coup and armed intervention by the United States and its Saigon satellite to maintain the usurpers in power, that the deed was done. The U.S.A., by the Lon Nol coup of March 1970, had succeeded in exporting to Indochina, the well-tried methods of Latin America. . . .
>
> The present work is viewed by the author as a weapon in the struggle to regain his own country's independence, and as a warning to other countries marked down as future victims.*

In his own short preface, Sihanouk insisted on including the following passage which pleased me greatly: "I have chosen to relate this story to one of a small group of writers who have consistently shown sympathy, comprehension, and respect for our national dignity, for the aspirations of my people, and for my own part in defending those aspirations." †

In little more than three weeks after arriving in Peking, I was back in Paris to type a clean copy of the manuscript and send off a first draft to the literary agent. Then I returned to Peking—this time with the well-known French TV documentary-film producer Roger Pic. We were one of the CBS teams assigned to cover President Nixon's visit to China, starting on February 21, 1972.

If Mao Tse-tung had already decided, as many specialist observers now believe, in a 180-degree *volte-face* in Chinese foreign policy, he had to dose it, at least superficially, for what remained of the Chinese Communist party after the Cultural Revolution and for the Chinese masses. How short a time before the Nixon visit was U.S. imperialism China's greatest enemy! But how wonderfully well was that visit stage-managed in an awesome display of how the masses, down to the last man in the street, could swing behind whatever was the latest line!

No visitor had ever had a colder initial reception. Chou En-lai was there

* *My War with the CIA, The Memoirs of Prince Norodom Sihanouk,* as related to Wilfred Burchett (New York: Pantheon Books, 1973), p. 15.
† *Ibid.,* p. 20.

to welcome President Nixon and his wife, Pat, at the airport, but there were no speeches, no welcoming dance groups, no crowds lining the road from the airport.This was much more than no public welcome. It was a disciplined populace turning its back on Nixon. Peking streets are never deserted except at dead of night, but this was broad daylight. As the streets through which the cavalcade passed were normally some of the liveliest, it was clear that the local street committees had done an exceptional job. So much for the public part of it. The official part was very different.

A few hours after his arrival Chou En-lai escorted Nixon to see Mao, at his residence in the Western Wing of the Forbidden City. There were held what presidential press secretary Ron Ziegler described as "serious and frank" talks, which lasted one hour.

On the eve of that first day Chou En-lai gave a fabulous banquet in the Great Hall of the People, in Peking's famed Tien An Men Square. The highlight was not so much the fabulous food and fiery mao tai spirit (half as potent again as the strongest American bourbon whiskey or Russian vodka), but the rendering of "Home on the Range," by a Chinese military brass band. After a few glasses of mao tai and renderings of "Home on the Range," even the most glacial hearts started to melt. Resident and visiting journalists were seated at large round tables, together with Chinese journalists, officials, and interpreters from the Press Department. I found myself sitting opposite one of the visitors. At one point introductions were made, and hands shaken. Noticing that the outstretched hand opposite me started dropping, I grasped and shook it before it fell. "Something the matter with your arm?" I asked. The hand, I found, belonged to columnist William F. Buckley, one of the most articulate of my self-appointed enemies. Even he mellowed later under the combined influence of the finest food in the world, persuasive mao tai, and the music.

By the time Roger Pic—to whom as "sound engineer" I was physically linked by various umbilical cords, leaping nimbly from one filmworthy scene to another—and I could relax and return to our table, the newcomers were groaning in gastronomic ecstasy. There was no reflection of the carefully staged public rebuke in Chou En-lai's welcoming toast. After noting that Nixon's visit provided a forum for discussing normalizing relations between the two countries and discussing "matters of mutual concern," he continued:

"The American people are a great people. The Chinese people are a great people. The peoples of our two countries have always been friendly to each other, but owing to reasons known to all, the contacts between the two peoples were suspended for more than twenty years. Now, through the common effort of China and the United States, the gates to friendly contact have been finally opened.

"At the present time there is a strong desire on the part of the Chinese and American people to work for the relaxation of tensions. The people and the people alone are the most important motive force in making world history, and the day will come when this common desire of our two peoples will be realized."

He went on to say that although the social systems of the two countries were fundamentally different, relations could be established on the basis of the five principles of peaceful coexistence. In his reply Nixon quickly came to the real point of his visit, although he did not say it explicitly:

"At this very moment, through the wonder of telecommunications, more people are hearing and seeing what we say than on any other occasion in the whole history of the world. What we say here will not long be remembered. What we do here can change the world. . . .

"The world watches, the world listens, the world waits to see what we will do. What is the world? In a personal sense, I think of my eldest daughter, whose birthday it is today. And as I think of her, I think of all the children in the world, in Asia, in Africa, in the Americas. Most were born since the date of the foundation of the People's Republic of China. What legacy shall we leave our children? . . ."

The key to Nixon's enthusiasm for the trip lay in the reference to the "wonders of telecommunications" and the "world watches, the world listens. . . ." That world included several scores of millions of Americans who would go to the polls in less than nine months to elect a President. Between February 21 and 28, he was going to get more free TV and radio time than any candidate could ever dream of—far less, pay for. The 1972 electoral campaign was on from the moment he stepped out of Air Force 1 at Peking Airport. He wore TV makeup night *and day* throughout. The American public saw Nixon in a new superstar role—traveling to the ends of the earth as a peacemaker, the hero who was going to make the world safe for American voters and generations of their children. Never did a presidential campaigner have such backdrops—the Forbidden City, the Imperial Palace, the Summer Palace, the Great Wall, and the Ming Tombs! Richard Milhous and Pat Nixon, accompanied by Chiang Ching (not then the vilified head of the Gang of Four, but the prestigious Madame Mao Tse-tung), at the opera watching the *Red Detachment of Women* ballet (conceived and produced under Chiang Ching's very personal direction). Except for the moon walks, this was the greatest ever TV show. But it was on earth and went on and on.

If Nixon regarded it all as an election-winning device, Kissinger saw it as a war winner, a sure means of driving a wedge between China and Vietnam. Nixon brought with him some tempting betrayal bait, including the proposal to exchange trade missions. It was made clear that there would be huge premiums in dollar credits if China would halt its aid to Vietnam.

Always the impeccable diplomat, Sihanouk had withdrawn to Canton during the presidential visit so as not to embarrass Chairman Mao by having a hostile head of state in the capital while Mao was playing host to his adversary. But there was more to it than that. Kissinger had rebuffed an earlier chance of contact with Sihanouk which could have reduced the influence of the Khmer Rouge and avoided the tragedy which followed. He admits as much in his memoirs and confirms the devious game which Peking was playing at Hanoi's expense. Kissinger reveals that on the evening before Chiao Kuan-hua led his delegation into the UN General Assembly (and Taiwan's Foreign Minister Chow Shu-kai led his delegation out) he had a private dinner with Chiao Kuan-hua at New York's exclusive Century Club:

> Chiao's line was an even softer version of what we had come to recognize as the standard Chinese position: sympathy for Hanoi, but no expenditure of capital on its ally's behalf. . . .
> In appealing again for a ceasefire in Cambodia, I emphasized that American and Chinese interests in Cambodia were congruent because we both wanted a neutral, independent Cambodia free of the domination of any one country. He did not dispute this. Instead, he asked if I would be prepared to meet Sihanouk on my next visit to China (then scheduled for January 1973). I evaded the specific question but replied in general terms that we were not opposed to Sihanouk provided he was able to establish an independent country.

Kissinger then quotes Chiao Kuan-hua as saying:

> I can tell you on a confidential basis it would be possible to arrive at an understanding with the Prime Minister [Chou En-lai] that does justice to the concerns of Prince Sihanouk. If the war continues in Cambodia, then we have to maintain our present position. But what we want in Cambodia, to be very blunt, is . . . to preserve it from becoming an appendage of Hanoi. . . .
> The next day, when I reported the conversation to Nixon, I repeated my view that after there was a ceasefire in Cambodia, Sihanouk would become a factor again and "could come back at the right moment." . . .
> I would have been interested in a meeting with Sihanouk to arrange a ceasefire, but negotiations with him could not succeed so long as he was titular head of the Communist forces insisting on total victory.
> My next trip to Peking, which eventually took place in February 1973, was the earliest occasion for such a meeting. (As it turned out, Sihanouk was not there at that time.) As an indication of our attitude and the Chinese perception of it, Chou En-lai asked us to look after Sihanouk's security in view of rumored plots against the Prince on his foreign travels. We readily agreed. (We also arranged later for the safe departure of Sihanouk's mother from Phnom Penh for Peking.)*

---

* Henry Kissinger, *The White House Years* (London: Weidenfeld and Nicolson & Michael Joseph, 1979), pp. 1413–14.

Kissinger's reference to Sihanouk as "titular head of the Communist forces" reflected the anticommunist bigotry which clouded his judgment rather than the real state of affairs. And Sihanouk correctly interpreted Kissinger's sudden interest in a meeting to "arrange a ceasefire" as an acknowledgment that (a) the U.S.-backed Lon Nol was losing, and that (b) Sihanouk should sell out those who were doing the fighting in order to retain his own privileged position. Kissinger badly misjudged his man, another of the reasons why Sihanouk "was not there at that time."

On the fourth day of the Peking part of his visit, with lengthy daily talks with Chou En-lai sandwiched in between his sight-seeing activities, Nixon gave a return banquet in the same huge hall as that used by his host. At each guest's place at the tables was an autographed visiting card from President Nixon, enclosed in a Lucite block, as well as presidential champagne glasses which guests were supposed to pocket as souvenirs.

The food, fortunately, was again Chinese, and the mao tai and beer were reinforced by good California champagne. The band was the same, as was the music. But something had gone awfully wrong. The atmosphere at the presidential table was glacial. None—apart from the participants—were better placed than Roger Pic and I to observe this. Our CBS assignment that night was to be right up front when the kleig lights went up for Nixon's speech and Chou En-lai's reply. There was nothing special about Nixon's speech, but there was about the *ambience* at the table. Kissinger was glowering; Marshall Green, Assistant Secretary of State for East Asian and Pacific Affairs, was red of face and staring at his plate. Only Secretary of State William Rogers maintained a half smile, but everyone knew he had been excluded from the real discussions. Nobody was speaking to anybody else, although each American had his Chinese counterpart alongside him and there was no lack of competent interpreters.

While Nixon spoke, Chou En-lai sat nonchalantly, using a toothpick behind his hand. Foreign Minister Chi Peng-fei, who had kept Rogers busy with some meaningless exchanges while Chiao Kuan-hua and Kissinger did the real work, sat impassive. Chiao Kuan-hua, once he recognized me despite headphones and umbilical cords, wrinkled his eyes in a faint grin.

As the lights went down and we withdrew to our table, a cameraman from another network whispered to me, "Did you see what I saw? When Nixon spotted me—I cover White House affairs—he tried to smile, straight into the camera—at three feet. But only one-half of his mouth worked."

Many of the newsmen hastened back from the banquet, Lucite oblongs and champagne glasses in their pockets, to report to their editors that to judge from the frigid atmosphere at the banquet and the glum expressions of Nixon and Kissinger, the talks had ended in disaster. They were chided for this the next day by Ron Ziegler.

What we did not know was that Chairman Mao had presented the bill that day for all the "incomparable hospitality" and free TV spectacles. It was in the form of the joint communiqué, over which Kissinger and Chiao Kuan-hua had been wrangling until half an hour before the banquet started. When the contents were made public at Shanghai a couple of days later, it was clear that Chiao Kuan-hua had won. It was a masterly document which set forth their differing positions on most subjects of contention. But among the subjects on which there was common agreement was that both countries agreed to base their relations on the Panch Sila, a term which became known internationally as a Hindi abbreviation for the famous five principles of peaceful coexistence, adopted at the 1955 Bandung Conference, as the ideal basis for relations between states of differing political and social systems.

Even if the term "Panch Sila" was not mentioned, the five principles were set out. More astonishing, and certainly the reason for the glum expressions on the American side of the banquet table, was the roundabout turn—at least on paper—of the U.S. position regarding Taiwan. On this, the communiqué stated:

> The U.S. side declared: The United States acknowledges that all Chinese on either side of the Taiwan Strait maintain there is but one China and that Taiwan is part of China. The United States Government does not challenge that position. It reaffirms its interest in a peaceful settlement of the Taiwan question by the Chinese themselves. With this prospect in mind, it affirms the ultimate objective of the withdrawal of all U.S. forces and military installations from Taiwan. In the meantime, it will progressively reduce its forces and military installations on Taiwan as the tension in the area diminishes. . . .

The next to last of the social events was a banquet given for the presidential party at Hangchow by the Chekiang Provincial Revolutionary Committee. Chou En-lai in the afternoon had attended a cocktail party at which the President introduced members of the press corps who had accompanied him: "My friend Stanley Karnow of the Washington *Post*, my friend Walter Cronkite of CBS . . ." and so on. When the evening banquet was over, Chou En-lai spotted me and abruptly came over to shake my hand. Nixon, perplexed, followed him. "*My* friend Mr. Burchett," said Chou En-lai, turning to Nixon.

"Ah, yes," said Nixon, holding out his hand. "You're the Australian journalist. Yes, I know about you." We exchanged a few banalities with me expressing hopes for the success of the visit and Nixon beaming as if we were the best of friends.

Some of the journalists closed in on me and said, "But how would Nixon know your name and that you're an Australian?" My reply was that I did not find it all that surprising since I had been attacking his policies almost every week in a New York paper ever since he took over at the White House.

It was typical of Chou En-lai's loyalty to an old friendship—also his sense of humor—that he should have bothered.

The farewell banquet was at Shanghai the following evening, when Nixon's hosts represented half of those who later became known as the Gang of Four: Chang Chun-chiao, chairman of the Shanghai Municipal Revolutionary Committee, and Wang Hung-wen, its vice-chairman. On the following morning—February 28—Air Force 1 took off again.

My Vietnamese friends in Peking were very unhappy about the visit, and although I could understand the difficulties of explaining to the Vietnamese public how it was possible that their worst enemy and one of their two best friends could suddenly be wining and dining together in an increasingly convivial atmosphere and that the process was soon to be repeated with their other best friend (Nixon was to be in Moscow in three months), I could not share their pessimism on the results of the visit. As far as I was concerned, it was a historic landmark along the road of the sort of East-West peaceful coexistence and contacts for which I had always worked. The door that Nixon had kicked open was soon bound to be entered by many countries—Japan and West Germany, for instance—glad to take advantage of the cover of respectability provided by the Nixon initiative.

When I tried to press my Vietnamese friends on the reason for their disquiet, they referred to the passage in the communiqué which referred to the U.S. pledge to "progressively reduce its forces and military installations on Taiwan as the tension in the area diminishes." "That means that our capitulation is to be the price of the Americans restoring Taiwan to China," one Vietnamese diplomat explained gloomily. I sharply disagreed because I could not conceive that China would abandon Vietnam under any circumstances.

No sooner had Chou En-lai escorted Nixon to his home-bound plane and waved a symbolic good-bye than he flew down to Canton to brief Sihanouk on the conversations and assure him that Chinese aid to Cambodia—far from being diminished, as Nixon wanted—would be increased. He then flew on to Hanoi to brief the Vietnamese Politburo on the conversations. Sihanouk's impression—wrong according to subsequent Vietnamese revelations—was that Chou En-lai had refused to discuss either the Cambodia or the Vietnam questions, advising Nixon that the discussions should be limited to matters of "bilateral interest," but that he could facilitate direct contacts with Sihanouk or the Vietnamese leadership.

At our Shanghai meeting Sihanouk made some minor revisions to my final draft of the manuscript, which we then regarded as complete. After joining some daylong tours for the visiting journalists, I returned to Paris. It had been a strenuous two weeks.

Apart from the TV work, I had provided daily dispatches on the President's visit for *Yomiuri Shimbun*, in Tokyo, whose foreign editor had the unnerving habit of telephoning me several times after midnight to read me the discrepancies between my dispatches and those of the paper's closest rivals, just appearing in the first editions. The following night he would phone to congratulate me on having been correct and hours ahead of the rivals. So it alternated every night between doubts and congratulations. (Nothing seems to worry an editor so much as to have a good scoop too far ahead of his rivals on a well-covered story.) *Yomiuri*, with a good liberal editorial policy, was keenly interested in the Nixon visit. Each of my dispatches was a grain of salt rubbed into the wounds of the injured pride of the militarist-inclined ruling Sato faction of Japan's Liberal Democratic party. The combination of his government's ill-advised association with the U.S. defeat over China's admission to the UN and Nixon's failure to advise Tokyo beforehand of his impending visit to Peking brought about the downfall of the Sato government and its replacement by one much more amenable to détente and a normalization of relations with Peking. I felt at the time that the Japanese reaction was a major reason for Nixon's invitation. Once having established the contact, Mao even had a vested interest in Nixon's continuing as President. It was in the Chinese tradition—revolutionary or not—to appreciate continuity of relations with the "barbarians" of the outside world.

After having seen the Sihanouk book through the various stages of production—galley proofs, page proofs, and final proofs—I accepted another commission from Penguin Books, London, to write a book about China, in collaboration with my old friend Rewi Alley. Some reserves in undertaking this were hinted at in my introduction to the book which resulted. After referring to a book, *China's Feet Unbound*, which I had written twenty years earlier with a promise that there would be a follow-up when I knew more about the subject, I continued:

> If I felt diffident in writing that first book and waited another twenty-odd years before tackling the follow-up, and if Rewi Alley waited almost a quarter of a century after setting foot in China to write his first book, *Yo Banfa* (We have a Way!), it is because we were both conscious of our responsibilities in presenting a valid, authentic picture of revolutionary changes that embrace one quarter of humanity. . . .
>
> What follows represents a synthesis of results of independent travels and investigations carried out in a planned and coordinated way by Rewi Alley and myself in the summer of 1973. This is grafted on to the unique experience of Rewi Alley in forty-six years of almost unbroken residence, work and travels in China, as well as intermittent residence and frequent travels by myself for over thirty years.
>
> The idea of pooling our experiences in book form was born some twenty years ago. Concrete projects were postponed several times. . . . Finally we have got down to it. . . . Paris, January 15, 1974.*

---

* Wilfred Burchett with Rewi Alley, *China: The Quality of Life* (London: Penguin Books, 1976), pp. 9–10.

I think we achieved the limited task that we set ourselves, which was "to measure the changes that have occurred in recent years in China and to set them in perspective against what we knew of old China" and to try to understand, by using Chinese—not Western—weights and measures how these changes had affected the "quality of life" of ordinary Chinese. Gathering the material to "top off" our accumulated previous experiences involved two months of separate travels to the remotest parts of China, excluding Tibet, followed by a couple of weeks spent together in comparing notes, drafting the outline of the book, and deciding who wrote which chapters. After I returned to Paris, chapters whizzed back and forth between Paris and Peking for each to comment on the other's work until we got an agreed-on version. With hindsight, we were lucky to have caught China in a period of relative calm after the storms of the Cultural Revolution and before the convulsions which occurred after the deaths of Chou En-lai and Mao Tse-tung and the denunciation of the Gang of Four.

30

A Change of Scene

SHAKING HANDS with Chiao Kuan-hua on his arrival at the head of his country's delegation at UN headquarters on November 14, 1972, I felt that there was one problem with which I had been associated for a long time finally solved. People's China had won its rightful place in the United Nations. And when in April–May 1975, in the incredibly short space of three weeks, the revolutionary forces in Kampuchea, Vietnam, and Laos—in that order—won their long struggles and peace descended on Indochina, I was certain that there were three more problems, with which I had been intimately linked, solved for the foreseeable future. The militant friendships among the three peoples of Indochina, forged in common struggle against the same enemies, the close relations which each had developed with People's China—there was the guarantee for "peace in our time" in that corner of the world.

Never had I made a greater mistake, but it was how things looked at the time, not only to me but to many Asia watchers and, above all, to Asia well-wishers. It was natural that my thoughts should turn toward southern Africa, where the people of several countries were struggling for independence. There was an Angola, Mozambique, and Guinea-Bissau to match a Vietnam, Cambodia, and Laos—all struggling against a common enemy: Portuguese colonialism. Within three days of the "captains' coup" in Portugal, I was in Lisbon with a special interest in finding out whether the "captains" were sincere in implementing that part of their program which called for the decolonialization of their African territories. After long discussions with the key officers behind the coup—they were not all captains—Major Melo Antunes, its political architect; Captain Otelo Saraiva de Carvalho, his military counterpart; and Colonel Vasco dos Santos Gonçalves, who had helped guide military-political planning from behind the scenes, I was convinced that they were sincere. Indeed, the coup had been carried out because of the refusal of the fascist regime to consider any but military solutions to the national liberation struggles in the colonies. But there were other forces, personified by General António de Spinola, president of the military junta which replaced the fascist regime—discreetly supported in the shadows by the Socialist leader Mário Soares—who, having played no role in the coup, favored hanging onto the colonies under some formula or another—especially onto Angola, rich in oil, diamonds, and coffee.

To my surprise, there was no problem in contacting these officers, although they remained aloof from most journalists. The reason was even more astonishing. Some of my books on Vietnam had been published by an enterprising publishing house which had found a way of beating the censors. But on the demand of the U.S. Embassy, *Vietnam: Inside Story of the Guerilla War* had been seized—all except copies which had already been distributed by mail and a few hundred, which had been bought by the Portuguese Military Academy, where the future "captains" were studying. It was a textbook, required reading for all students, including those called in for refresher courses. The premise was that the tactics being used by the Vietcong today would be used by other guerrillas tomorrow. When I asked the artillery captain who informed me of this what the reaction was, he said, "Even the dumbest right-winger could grasp the fact that if a country like the United States, with its unlimited military and economic resources, could not win against a small, backward country like Vietnam, how could small, backward Portugal win in the African territories, twenty times as big as Portugal, with twice the population?"

For Melo Antunes and Otelo de Carvalho, the three tours of military service that each had done in the colonies were crucial in convincing them that the colonies had to have their independence, and the only way this would come about was by overthrow of the regime.

One month to the day after the coup the first "decolonization" conference —on Guinea-Bissau—opened in London. It got nowhere because all Foreign Minister Mário Soares offered was a military cease-fire and self-determination to be decided by a Portuguese-run referendum. Major Pedro Pires, who headed the Guinea-Bissau-Cape Verde delegation, told me, "In 1945, 'self-determination' would have sounded wonderful, but not in 1974. We have been recognized as an independent state by nearly ninety countries. We have observer status at the United Nations. Over two-thirds of our country is solidly liberated. Why should we discuss about Portugal supervising our 'self-determination'? Our people have already 'determined' what they want: full and total independence with no strings attached."

The talks broke down after four days of useless exchanges. The same thing happened over Mozambique, but more rapidly. Despite the well-photographed emotional first meeting between Soares and the Frelimo leader Samora Machel, the talks were immediately bogged down and adjourned the following day. It was not until Spinola was removed as the de facto head of state and negotiations were entrusted to Antunes—who later replaced Soares as foreign minister—that progress was possible. Full independence for Guinea-Bissau and the Cape Verde islands was quickly negotiated, as well as for Mozambique.

Angola was more complicated, not only because of the rich prize that is represented but because there were three rival independence movements: the MPLA (headed by Agostinho Neto), FNLA (with Holden Roberto as president), and UNITA (under Jonas Savimbi). The Soviet Union backed the MPLA; the United States and China, the FNLA; right-wing groups in Portugal and the South African government, UNITA. The CIA bestowed its favors on both the FNLA and UNITA.

Owing to the good offices of the OAU (Organization of African Unity) and several African leaders, the three movements sent delegations to Alvor, on the southern coast of Portugal, in January 1975, to negotiate an agreement with the Portuguese on the total independence of Angola.

The three leaders were a study in contrasts as they appeared at the closing session of the Alvor Conference on January 17, 1975, to affix their signatures to the document by which Portugal accorded full independence: Agostinho Neto in a Western business suit, belying his character by a rather timid appearance; Holden Roberto in a blue Mao suit, grim and unsmiling behind his smoked glasses; Jonas Savimbi, tall with black beard and rolling eyes, clad in jungle greens. Neto, considered by many Portuguese the finest contemporary poet in their language, was chosen to speak on behalf of the three liberation movements following the signing formalities.

With the Atlantic rollers crashing on the beach outside, Neto referred to the nearby Ponta da Sagres, from which the fleets of Portuguese caravels had set out on their hazardous voyages of discovery from the fifteenth century onward. "Here, relatively close to the Ponta da Sagres," he said, "we have put an end to the unjust relations which were later to besmirch the brilliant feats of the Portuguese navigators. Here the ambitions of the colonialists have been buried forever." The faces of the Portuguese—especially Melo Antunes, Prime Minister Gonçalves, and the "Red" Admiral António Rosa Coutinho—lit up when Neto spoke of the "fourth national liberation movement—that is, the armed forces movement which catalyzed people's aspirations here by overthrowing fascism in Portugal, thus establishing a solid base for ending colonial exploitation." These were sensitively chosen words to warm the hearts of Vasco Gonçalves, Antunes, and Rosa Coutinho, each of whom in his own way greatly contributed to a historic document that—despite shortcomings which unhappily were soon to become apparent—ended almost 500 years of Portuguese rule in Africa.

As soon as the ceremony was over, I asked Neto what he thought were the prospects of the agreement's being implemented. With his typical shy smile, he said, "The agreement is good. But it is on paper only. As for the MPLA, we will do everything possible for the rigorously strict fulfillment of every clause and paragraph. Why don't you come have a look for yourself?" This suggestion was heartily endorsed by the MPLA representative in Cuba, Paolo Jorge, standing at his side.

The next time I saw Paolo Jorge, his face could not have been more welcome. He had spotted me being marched off a plane at Luanda Airport between armed guards. It was at the time that the black racist Nito Alves (later shot for treason) was minister of the interior. Because of decisive battles raging, I wanted to get to Luanda quickly. Despite the efforts of Portuguese airport officials to dissuade me, I had left without a visa. The only document I had was a telex from the Ministry of Information agreeing to my visit and informing me that a visa would be awaiting me at the office of its honorary consul in Lisbon. But he was away in Luanda when I called. Kept on the plane until all passengers had disembarked, I was confronted with a sullen officer who was not interested in my telex, but very much in the fact that there was no visa in my passport. As I marched off between two guards, I longed for my Cuban passport or even my *laissez-passer*. The Labour government in Australia had restored my Australian passport on its first day in office, but it was worse than useless in Luanda without a visa. Feeling was understandably running high against suspicious-seeming foreigners, a group of white mercenaries having been wiped out in the northern frontier areas a few days previously. As I was being marched past the VIP reception lounge, Paolo Jorge spotted me through the window, and my deliverance was immediate. He guided me into the lounge he had just left, where there was great jollification and clinking of glasses. Paolo Jorge pressed a glass into my hand and said, "Two good news. You've arrived, and we've just taken Huambo." It was about midnight of Sunday, February 8, 1976. A few hours earlier Neto's forces and their Cuban allies had won their most decisive victory against the FNLA-UNITA forces and their South African allies, Huambo being their joint capital.

When I arrived in Huambo a few days later, small groups were straggling into the city with fearsome tales of wholesale massacres in the preceding days, many with untended bullet wounds to substantiate their stories. The UNITA-FNLA forces had withdrawn 100 miles west to Bié, Savimbi's stronghold among the Ovimbundu, his own tribal grouping. From Bié, Savimbi had broadcast orders that the Huambo residents should evacuate the city. He threatened to send planes to raze it to the ground and warned that any survivors would be massacred by the MPLA. Savimbi had certainly done his own share of massacring! Within twenty-four hours of the fall of Bié, I joined an official search team trying to track down MPLA cadres who had been arrested some months earlier, when UNITA took over what until then had been a three-party-administered city. It was known that the missing had been transferred to Bié, but the prisons there were empty when MPLA-Cuban forces entered the city on February 12. As I reported at the time, what we found was:

> After an hour's fruitless digging in the Komarko prison in the city outskirts, the search team found nine freshly-dug pits in loose, sandy soil behind the squat, white-walled prison on the edge of a field of young maize. A human foot was sticking out of one of these. The grass around the pits was trampled flat and stained with blood. Lying on the ground were a half-dozen bloodstained iron bars, some with bits of human hair sticking to them.
>
> As exhumation started, it quickly became clear that in the pits were the bodies of some hundred MPLA cadres known to have been detained in the Komarko prison. The still fresh bodies had been thrown pell-mell into the pits, the sandy soil shoveled in on top of them. Toilet bowls in the washroom were covered with blood where the executioners had apparently tried to wash off the traces of what they had done before joining the headlong flight of UNITA forces from the city. When the body to which the foot belonged turned out to be that of a young woman whose face had been battered out of recognition, one of the search team muttered bitterly: "There is the true face of Savimbi." . . .
>
> On the main street of Bié, an emaciated group of some twenty-five people were straggling along with a banner: "Welcome the glorious FAPLA! We are the survivors of the Bié Angola Police Corps Training School." *

The Bié school, according to Domingo Antonio Neto, a skeleton in rags and one of the pitiful group under the banner welcoming the MPLA armed forces, had altogether 720 trainees. When the UNITA-FNLA alliance took over Huambo, it drafted about 100 each of its own nominees into its respective armed forces and threw the rest into a former Portuguese concentration camp. As the MPLA-Cuban forces closed in on Bié, they were taken out in batches of 10 and 20 and shot, their bodies falling—or being thrown into—the nearby Quequema River. The firing squads were unable to finish off their work, and Domingo Neto and his band were among an estimated 75 survivors from more than 500 prisoners.

Later, after all reports were collated, it was estimated that about 10,000 people had been executed in the Huambo-Bié area, most of them just prior to the panic flight of the UNITA-FNLA forces. My own total, compiled from survivor accounts, during a forty-eight-hour stay, was more than 2,000. This could have been done only on direct orders from Savimbi, who reigned supreme in the area.

---

* Wilfred Burchett, *Southern Africa Stands Up* (New York: Urizen Books, Inc., 1979), p. 32.

It was a harsh introduction to the problem of tribal and racial hatreds superimposed on the deadly struggle for political power. Savimbi's power base was among the Ovimbundu people in the center-south, the largest single tribal grouping, about 2 million strong. Although UNITA was allied at the top with the FNLA, the Ovimbundu had no tender feelings toward the 750,000 Bakongo people of the north, among whom Holden Roberto had his power base. If one could speak of a natural power base for the MPLA, it would be among the 1.5 million Mbundu people of the center-north, but also in virtually all the urban centers. Neto had strongly discouraged any polarization around tribal groupings; the MPLA was the only one of the three movements organized on an all-Angolan basis, and this was a principal source of its strength.

Driving back from Bié to Huambo, at a point where a main road led south toward the border with Namibia, our small party of journalists came across an armored unit with Soviet tanks and heavy artillery. A Tass correspondent, camera at the ready, who leaped out of the jeep and rushed to find a Soviet adviser came back somewhat crestfallen. The best he could find was a Russian-speaking Cuban, who promptly told him to put his camera away. It was a mixed Cuban-FAPLA (MPLA armed force) unit, resting up prior to chasing the South Africans across the Namibian frontier. As they lounged around smoking and drinking coffee, it was difficult to tell Cubans from Angolans, especially because a large proportion of the Cuban troops were black; they all wore the same green uniforms, and there was a fair sprinkling of "white Angolans" (Portuguese born in the country) who had rallied to the FAPLA from the early days and were strongly represented in the technical branches. Thus, the first "Cuban" officer I addressed in Spanish replied in Portuguese. (Many of the FAPLA *comandantes* I met later, especially farther south, were either white Angolans or mulattoes, for the simple reason that they were the only ones with educational levels sufficient to master the handling of modern arms.)

The first impression of the free and easy relations between officers and men in the Cuban Army, and between Angolans and Cubans in the mixed units, was confirmed during the rest of that first visit and two subsequent ones.

One of my main interests in three visits to Angola and two to Mozambique during 1976 was to find out how everything had suddenly blown up after half a millennium of Portuguese rule. And why, historically speaking, almost simultaneously in the sixties? Was there organized coordination? As distinct from Vietnam, Cambodia, and Laos, there were no common frontiers between Angola, Mozambique, and Guinea-Bissau. Where was the linkage, and what was the detonator?

One obvious point of linkage was the upsurge of African nationalism after World War II, less strongly expressed in the colonies of fascist Portugal than in those of the parliamentary democracies, Britain, France, and Belgium, where there were far greater facilities for education and at least some contact with the outside world, and where there were pressure groups within the home parliaments of countries which had also been relatively far more exhausted economically by World War II than Portugal. They could not sustain new colonial wars, and when they tried—as was the case of France in Indochina and Algeria and of Britain in Malaya and Kenya—the cost was prohibitive. In the spirit of "enlightened self-interest," they began granting independence by constitutional means. The 1950s thus became the decade in which twenty-six British, French, and Belgian colonies achieved their independence (Ghana having got its in 1957), the eleven French colonies all getting theirs in 1960.

"If them, why not us?" said Mendes de Carvalho, the tiny, vivacious mayor of Luanda at the time I met him, who, unwittingly, had sparked off armed resistance in Angola. There were special problems in the Portuguese colonies apart from that of a fascist regime in Portugal. Among the worst of these, one which continues to have delayed-action-bomb repercussions in the former Portuguese colonies, was that of the mulattoes and *assimilados.* He explained:

> The old "divide and rule" device had been developed in a more subtle fashion. A white was considered superior to a mulatto, a mulatto superior to a black, and even blacks were divided into two categories, *assimilados,* who had to renounce their Africanism to get a minimum of education and escape what was virtually slave status, and inferior, ordinary blacks—natives. . . . In some areas the *assimilados* had to live separated by a few hundred meters from the "native quarters" to prove they had acquired "civilized status." Under such conditions how could we develop the sense of unity vital for a national struggle? *

This diabolical system, among other things, meant that the only blacks to have access to education, on the one hand, were bound to have leadership positions within the liberation movement and, on the other, were bound to be suspect by their less privileged brothers. The linkage between Portugal's widely separated African colonies was the heady wind of independence blowing in from neighboring lands. The detonator was the invariable savage repression by the Portuguese of the slightest display of any hankering after what their neighbors were getting.

The events following the arrest, in his Luanda consulting room in June 1960 of Dr. Agostinho Neto, suspected of harboring ideas about independence, were typical. Residents of his home village of Bengo and the neighboring one of Icolo demonstrated against the arrest outside the district center

---

* *Ibid.,* pp. 3–4.

of Catete. Portuguese troops opened fire, killing 30 and wounding 200 out of a crowd of about 1,000. The following day troops burned down the two villages and killed or arrested anyone on whom they could lay hands. What became known as the Catete massacre was the fuse which fired the powder keg of the Angolan revolution. The arrest of Neto—he was later shipped off to the notorious Tarrafal concentration camp on the Cape Verde Island —was the climax to the wholesale arrest of suspected nationalist leaders from early 1959 to mid-1960. Mendes de Carvalho was one of the earliest to be arrested—and sentenced to thirteen years—for nationalist propaganda. Owing to the misreading of a message he had smuggled out of prison, his friends understood that he and members of his group were to be transferred to Lisbon—considered a death sentence. The leader of those preparing for armed struggle—Imperial Santana—decided the time had come for armed action. He related this episode to me fifteen years later:

> Altogether we were 3,128 men pledged to launch the attack. Our method was to buy the same sort of trousers, shirts, and shoes so it would be easy to recognize friends from foes. But we didn't have enough money left over for everyone to spend twenty-five escudos (roughly one U.S. dollar) for a machete. Those who could bought them; others armed themselves with axes, clubs, and even stones.
>
> Once we had the arms, we started training in the offensive and defensive use of machetes, axes, etc. We went on foot and in small groups to Cacuaco, twenty-two kilometers from Luanda, and trained there for eight days. On February 3, we heard some disturbing reports and decided our attack must be made the following day—so we returned to Luanda.*

They attacked not only the prison housing Carvalho and his comrades but the PIDE † headquarters, military barracks, naval facilities, radio station, and other buildings at midnight on February 3. The guards fled from the prison, taking the keys to the cells with them. The valiant attackers could do nothing with their axes and machetes against solid steel doors. They withdrew at 5:00 A.M., leaving seven Portuguese dead without a single wounded of their own. They repeated the attack, better equipped to deal with the cell doors, a week later, but the Portuguese were ready. Caught between regular troops ahead and the PIDE behind, the attackers suffered heavy losses. The Portuguese then launched a ferocious campaign of repression, not only in Luanda but throughout the country. February 4, 1961, is now celebrated as the day on which armed struggle was launched in Angola. And it was Comandante Imperial Santana, having miraculously sur-

---

* *Ibid.*, p. 7.
† International Police for State Security, the Portuguese equivalent of the Nazi Gestapo, a secret police organization active in Portugal and the overseas territories.

vived a hundred battles, who was awarded the signal honor of hauling up
the flag of Angolan independence in a solemn ceremony in Luanda at one
minute past midnight on November 11, 1975.

In Mozambique armed struggle started nearly three years later, but the
detonator—savage repression—was the same. The Portuguese governor of
the country's northernmost province of Cabo Delgado had arranged to meet
a two-man delegation from a Tanzania-based nationalist group of exiles at
the district center of Mueda. They were to present a petition requesting an
end of arbitrary arrest, forced labor, unemployment, and the precarious living conditions which caused so many to flee abroad. A schoolteacher, twenty-
two years old at the time, gave me this eyewitness account of what happened
at Mueda on June 16, 1960:

> The delegates arrived early on the morning of the 16th. . . . The gov-
> ernor arrived . . . at about 3 P.M. Thousands of people applauded when
> the delegates were invited into the secretariat. Soon they came out again.
> Then the governor came out and started to walk down the steps, escorted
> by the *cipaios* (local police). Everyone was ordered to stand to attention while
> the flag was hoisted. People started shouting: "We haven't come to salute the
> flag, but to learn how you're going to solve our problems." The governor
> stopped and said: "I've come to examine the situation in this province. The
> government thinks you can do much to solve the problems yourselves by
> working harder, by intensifying the cultivation of peanuts and the harvesting
> of cashew nuts."

The governor went back into the secretariat, and the next thing the people
heard were the sounds of scuffles and blows, following which the delegates
were pushed out and handcuffed in front of the crowd. At the governor's
invitation some spokesmen from the crowd also went into the secretariat and
came out handcuffed. The police pushed them toward some Land-Rovers
which the governor had summoned:

> The people—I also—started advancing towards the Land Rovers shouting:
> "Why have they been arrested? You can't take them to prison. What have
> they done? You invited us to come. We won't leave until our demands are
> met." The *cipaios* started hitting people with rifle butts and bayonets and the
> people struck back with stones. The *cipaios* then started firing and troops,
> who had been hidden among shrubs and trees, started advancing and firing
> from behind with automatic weapons. As the people fled, troops and police
> fired into the crowd. People were just mowed down—women, children, old
> people—there were piles of dead and wounded everywhere. Over six hundred
> people were killed. That was Mueda! *

---

* *Ibid.*, pp. 130–31.

The former young schoolteacher who told me all this and much more was Alberto-Joaquim Chipande, at the time of the telling minister of defense of the People's Republic of Angola. Like another young schoolteacher, Vo Nguyen Giap, he had drawn the only possible conclusions from such repeated acts of colonialist savagery—and reached for a gun. Also like Giap, he had personally commanded the first armed action. On September 25, 1964, he led a guerrilla band in attacking two Portuguese military posts in Cabo Delgado Province and thus, under the leadership of Frelimo's first president, Eduardo Mondlane, initiated armed struggle in Mozambique.

Mozambique was the last of the three Portuguese colonies to take to arms. In Guinea-Bissau the massacre of dockworkers at Bissau's Pdgiguiti docks in August 1959 started the process leading to the outbreak of armed struggle in January 1963.

Thus, although the main linking factor of generalized armed struggle in Portugal's African colonies starting between 1961 and 1964 was the infectious breeze blowing all over Africa, a crucial subsidiary link was the unbridled savagery with which the first sparks of independence movements were trampled out in one colony after another. And if Portuguese colonial rule was particularly abominable, the manner of the Portuguese departure was even more revolting.

Traveling very widely by road, as I did in Angola and Mozambique, I found it impossible not to be conscious of the cruel, senseless destruction of everything the settlers could not take with them: trucks, tractors, bulldozers driven over ravines; essential parts smashed or removed from coffee-drying urns; sugar mills; everything down to dentists' chairs and school desks in rural centers.

The greatest sabotage was in the wholesale flight of the Portuguese themselves, motivated essentially by the fact that overnight they would lose the privileges they had enjoyed exclusively because of the color of their skins. The underprivileged at home had become the superprivileged in the colonies. Since apart from the handful of *assimilados*, blacks were denied any education or even the acquisition of technical or administrative skills, the country was run by the Portuguese at all levels.

With independence, the vast majority of these Portuguese could not face up to the prospects of racial equality, including the fact that at some future point they would have to compete for jobs on the basis of competence, not of skin pigmentation. Airport waiting rooms at the time of my visits to Angola and Mozambique were crowded with those caught up in the great exodus, preferring an uncertain future in a land where skills, not skin color, were determinant in the job market to the specter of losing their built-in privileges. Most of those to whom I put the question of why they were leaving replied vaguely, "All my friends are leaving, so I might as well go, too." But one middle-aged woman at Maputo Airport touched on the core of the problem when she replied, "We even have to carry identity cards, and blacks in uniform can order us to produce them." In the past only blacks carried identity cards and any white—official or not—could demand of any black, at any time, that he show his identity card. To be black, in other words, was to be a suspected criminal. Now whites were to be considered "suspected criminals"—at least this was the absurd notion that stuck like fishbones in the gullets of many of those who left.

With the massive departures, Angola and Mozambique were left without all those who staffed the trades and professions which had been the exclusive domain of the Portuguese. Having plundered the countries of their human resources—slaves were the main export item from Angola for several centuries—and of their natural resources—oil, diamonds, and coffee in the case of Angola; coal, hydroelectric power, and agricultural produce from Mozambique—the Portuguese left behind wrecked economies and societies almost totally bankrupt in the skills and experience needed to build a new life.

The African visits marked a watershed in my relations with Peking. Like many other old friends of Mao's China, I had been perplexed, to say the least, at the twists and turns in foreign affairs. Support for Augusto Pinochet in Chile was impossible to swallow. Even more so was China's support for the CIA's paid agent Holden Roberto and the FNLA which he headed and the substantial support also accorded to Savimbi. Many of my left-wing friends in Paris, London, and elsewhere did their best to persuade me that Savimbi was the only true nationalist leader, and China's support was used as one of the most persuasive arguments.

If I had reservations in criticizing China then, it was because I had not been to Angola, and I rationalized that since Africa was so remote from China's problems, the leadership was perhaps ill informed about the true roles of Roberto and Savimbi. My reservations disappeared after what I had seen on the spot and, above all, after a most revealing conversation with Lucio Lara, general secretary of the MPLA. A mulatto veteran from the earliest days of armed struggle, he produced a yellowed and heavily marked copy of my *North of the 17th Parallel* at our first meeting and asked for an autograph.

He had been with Neto in China in July 1974. The delegation was very well received by Chou En-lai, to whom Neto gave a briefing on the general situation. When he mentioned the role of Holden Roberto, Chou En-lai interrupted him to say, "No need to go further. We know Roberto as a self-declared agent of American imperialism!" When Neto spoke of the role of Savimbi as an agent of Portugal and South Africa, Chou En-lai said, "We are not so well informed about Savimbi. If you can provide proof of his treason, we will drop him." The outcome was a pledge to step up aid to the MPLA; to cut relations with the FNLA, including further military aid; to maintain low-level relations with UNITA pending further information.

Lucio Lara was again in Peking in May 1975. Chou En-lai was in the hospital, and the delegation that Lara headed was received by the same deputy prime minister (not Teng Hsiao-ping) and deputy foreign minister who had been present at the previous meeting. Lara read back his notes from the previous meeting and expressed surprise that China's support for the FNLA was stronger than ever, as well as for UNITA, despite the documentary proof of Savimbi's treachery supplied in the meantime.

"The atmosphere had completely changed," Lara said. "We were told very coldly that all we had to do was to abide strictly by the terms of the Alvor Agreement. We produced documentary evidence of the atrocities committed by the FNLA in Luanda. To no avail. A few months later Chinese military advisers were supporting FNLA and Zaire troops in their operations against the MPLA."

Thus, I learned that China was not "ill informed" about Angolan affairs. In a series of articles after my first visit I had no scruples in criticizing Peking's role. Soon afterward I was to become convinced that it was not only in faraway Africa that China's foreign policy had taken an inglorious turn.

31

---◄◄◊►►---

Khmer Rouge and the
Great Madness

I T W A S E A R L Y M A Y 1979, and I was heading from Ho Chi Minhville for Phnom Penh for the first time since the diverted Paris-bound
flight from Nouméa in March 1970. Lush crops and bustling markets escorted our Ford minibus right up to what was left of the former pleasant
frontier town of Ba Vet, in the northern corner of the "Parrot's Beak,"
where maps show Kampuchean territory extending to within about sixty
miles of the former South Vietnamese capital. Ba Vet had been the object
of many a Sunday excursion in the "old days," its chief attraction being the
"open sky" market, a sort of peaceful oasis just inside the Vietnamese side
of the frontier, where Cambodians and South Vietnamese came to exchange,
under official tolerance, whatever contraband goods the one had and the
others had not.

Ba Vet was reduced to chunks of grass-covered rubble with only the
crumbled walls of the former South Vietnamese frontier police headquarters
still partly extant. Life halted at the frontier. Svay Rieng Province on the
other side was ghost country. Even the sugar palms which used to line the
last couple of miles leading to the frontier had disappeared. For nearly
twenty-five miles we drove through a countryside from which all traces of
life had disappeared—no villages, no houses, only overgrown tracings of terraces to recall that it was once an area of rich paddy fields. A projection of
what one could see by standing on the hood of the minibus (and confirmed
later by flying over the area) meant that hundreds of thousands of acres of
Kampuchea's richest food-producing lands in the Mekong Delta had been
taken out of production. We were driving through part of the no-man's-land
which the Khmer Rouge leadership had decreed to prevent "contamination"
of the people of Kampuchea by those of Vietnam.

A few miles before reaching Svay Rieng, the provincial capital, we saw the first signs of the commune type of agriculture introduced by the *Angkar* ("Organization," in the name of which everything from digging ditches and burning books to cutting throats and bashing skulls was carried out). These were big, rectangular fields 1,000 or so yards long by half as many wide, with enclosing walls three or four feet high and a large irrigation channel linking one with another. Within the periphery walls of packed earth, the rectangles were subdivided into squares of 100 yards each way, separated by paddy field terraces and watered by a gravitational irrigation system. It was a rational system, lacking, as we discovered later, an overall source of water supply to keep the main channels supplied at a sufficient level to feed the channels inside the enclosures or solidly compacted dike walls.

Beyond Svay Rieng, the most typical scene was that of little groups— mainly women and children—hauling homemade carts. Teenage boys and very young children were scarce. Boys over twelve had been taken into the armed forces, rarely to be seen again by their families. Malnutrition, over- work, and psychological stress had drastically reduced childbirth and height- ened infant mortality. The first group with which I spoke was squatting around a coffin-shaped cart with wooden disk wheels. As a substitute for tires, strips of rubber had been nailed around the rim of each wheel. They were seven survivors of a family of twenty-five and had been four months on the road, heading back to their home village in Svay Rieng from one to which they had been forcibly evacuated in Pursat Province near the Thai border. Burned black from exposure, reduced to skin and bone by over- working and undereating, they nevertheless raised smiles because they were nearing journey's end. Their pitifully few belongings included a few bundles of clothes, a couple of hoes, a dozen cuttings of manioc cane (which they had only to poke into the ground to start it growing), and—most pre- cious of all—a blackened cooking pot without which they could never have set out.

At a small crossroads before traversing the Mekong at Neak Luong we spoke with a group of twenty-one emaciated family members: one adult male; a wrinkled grandmother; a boy of fifteen years who looked about ten; the rest women and younger children. They had push-pulled their home- made cart from Prey Slay village in Svay Rieng for eight days and reckoned they had another eight days' march to their home village in Kandal Province, of which Phnom Penh is the capital. The movement was in both directions, with about three or four carts heading east for every one west. One lone woman, her belongings in two small bundles suspended from each end of a shoulder pole, was a nurse from Svay Rieng who had been transported with her husband and four children to malaria-infested mountains near the Thai border. Her husband and two of the children had been killed "by Pol Pot" (the customary synonym for the regime); the other two children had died of malaria. She hoped to find her father alive in Svay Rieng and would live with him "or some of the neighbors." A brave little woman, alone in the world with a little better than 50 percent chance of finding her father or any neighbors alive.

While awaiting the ferry to cross the Mekong at Neak Luong, I had a look at the most original market I had ever seen. Stall holders were squatting on the ground with a few baskets of fish and fruit, thick with flies, bargaining with customers over the worth—in rice—of half a dozen fish, a bunch of bananas, or a length of colored cloth. Markets and money had been abolished "by Pol Pot," and the wearing of anything except standard black had been punishable by death. Legal tender was now rice, the standard measure a round condensed milk can full.

In his book written some six months after he was freed from "house arrest," Sihanouk characterizes Pol Pot and Ieng Sary as madmen. It needed only a few hours inside the country and a few conversations with some of the tens of thousands of survivors moving back and forth across the face of the country to realize how exactly right he was.

Who but madmen would have uprooted an entire people, transferring them from east to west and south to north and vice versa, in order to break contacts established for centuries with their Vietnamese neighbors? Who but madmen would have ordered the destruction of plows and fishing nets, cooking pots and household utensils because these smacked of individualistic methods of producing and living, to be execrated by the *Angkar* order of "instant communism"? Who but homicidal maniacs could have massacred 40 percent—up to 3 million—of their compatriots and deliberately conditioned a whole generation of children to regard the most barbarous forms of torture and murder as a great joke? It was this picture which emerged from the conversations with the "road people"—as with those interviewed months earlier—who had sought refuge in Vietnam. It was confirmed by everyone with whom one spoke and by everything which Sihanouk wrote.

At the Monivong Bridge which spans the Tônlé Sap River and leads into Phnom Penh, the westward-moving groups were queuing up to be screened. They were of two categories: those who needed to cross the city to continue on to home villages farther west or south, who were given bits of paper to transit the city with sufficient time to rest up and draw some supplies, and former Phnom Penh residents hoping to return to their homes. To these it was explained that the city was still without electricity, running water, or sewerage. Food was very short, and there were no jobs. They were told to settle down for a while at designated villages a few miles from the city, start growing vegetables for themselves, and even supply the city. Their names and qualifications were registered, and as soon as work became available for even one family member, they all could move into the city, to be housed and fed by the municipality. Once they had settled into the new village, they could go into Phnom Penh with their carts, visit their homes, and take away anything left of their former possessions.

If the first impression of Svay Rieng was of entering into a ghost country, Phnom Penh was a phantom city. Driving down the broad boulevard Norodom, its former elegant embassy villas deserted and dilapidated and scarcely a soul in sight, we entered the commercial district, an incredible sight with its gutted, frontless shops, like empty boxes spewing rubble and garbage onto the footpaths. Apart from a few sentries at street corners, directing an occasional truck or two trundling by, and some children scrabbling at a hillock of garbage, there was nobody to be seen until we pulled up around sunset at the former Hotel Royal. It looked more or less the same, except there were some pigs snuffling around in the formerly well-kept garden. The big fan-shaped travelers' palm remained in front of the entrance; opposite was the Lycée Descartes, where our children had attended school; off to the left was the famous *phnom* of Madame Penh, from which the city took its name, but to the right, as I stood outside the hotel entrance, something was missing. Scarcely able to believe my eyes, and wondering for a split second whether I had lost my bearings, I realized the cathedral was gone! There was no sign even of a foundation stone of the nineteenth-century French colonial-style edifice, the chief social center for the French community on Sundays. It had been removed stone by stone—no one was ever able to tell me where the stones ended up.

One of my first visits was to the former Tuol Sleng secondary school, which had been transformed into an extermination center where thousands of the country's best intellectuals, scientists, doctors, and patriots had been fiendishly tortured before having their throats cut, their heads bashed in or chopped off, or being done to death by disembowelment or other atrocious means. A set of three-story gray buildings, arranged around three sides of a square, was surrounded by a ten-foot wall of cemented-over bricks, topped by coils of electrified barbed wire.

The first room a victim entered was equipped with a camera for numbered identification pictures; alongside was another for electric torture in case the victim was slow in coming forth with his family details. After identification procedures were over, the prisoners were led away to their "accommodation," which varied according to standards established by Pol Pot. Very important prisoners—those who had been his comrades in the Khmer Rouge leadership, former diplomats, and others—had individual leg shackles in individual cells; the next most important prisoners were shackled two at a time in doorless concrete cells six feet long by three wide; ordinary prisoners were held in collective leg irons, ten or twelve together. When their time came for interrogation, victims were led to one of sixteen classrooms on the second floor. The "furnishings" were spartan in the extreme: an iron bedstead without a mattress, but with wrist and ankle irons; a table with a typewriter and two chairs, one for the interrogator, the other for the typist to record the "confessions." Ranged around the walls were hatchets, machetes, kitchen knives with serrated blades, wooden mallets, iron tongs, and pliers.

Daily records of those tortured and killed were kept, written in neat handwriting with special annotations in red giving details of the method of death of prominent personalities, including photographs of the corpses attached to their "confessions." In charge of Tuol Sleng at the time of my visit was a former Phnom Penh secondary schoolteacher, Madame Ing Sarin. With three assistants she was trying to classify the lists of victims into categories. Thus, I learned that one of my good friends, Huot Sambath, Sihanouk's ambassador to the UN and Pol Pot's ambassador to Belgrade, had been killed within a few days of his arrival from Yugoslavia in September 1976 to take part in a conference to define the country's foreign policy. Among the incomplete list of diplomats invited back under the same pretext and killed at Tuol Sleng were those from the Soviet Union, Egypt, Algeria, and other countries.

I selected a few dates at random, to have some idea of the daily toll. The results were as follows:

August 21, 1976	191
August 31, "	92
October 7, "	66
December 6, "	104
June 20, 1977	266
August 3, "	186

Within one six-day period, 147 students and other intellectuals, almost all of them students or graduates in economics, planning, engineering, and medicine, invited to return from France and take part in the country's reconstruction, were tortured and executed.

The daily torture-death rate appears to have depended entirely on the time it took to extract what were considered satisfactory confessions. Madame Ing Sarin showed me a "black book" of directives for "processing" which she said was in Pol Pot's own handwriting. Under a subheading "How to Interrogate" she translated the following: "Each prisoner must know that whatever happens, he is going to be killed, so he might as well confess quickly. But no one should be killed until a full confession is extracted." The importance of not killing victims until the maximum "confession" was extracted is stressed in a document, summing up the experiences in interrogating at a study session by the Khmer Rouge's Group 21, which ran the Tuol Sleng center. Dated July 23, 1977, at the very height of the nationwide extermination campaign, it states:

During the interrogation we make an analysis of the *curriculum vitae* of each enemy in order to profoundly understand his political tendency, his center of activities, his relations, his profession, and his family. We study those influences to which he was progressively subjected, from a quantitative as well as a qualitative viewpoint, which in the end turned him into a CIA agent.

. . . Concerning the torture methods, we must absolutely draw the correct conclusions and always avoid methods which result in death.

. . . Errors! We do not work really well, we make no progress. That is to say we make no real leap ahead. We're not all that good! *

When the Pol Pot forces collapsed on January 7, 1979, and headed south from Phnom Penh in panic-stricken flight, fourteen of the sixteen bedsteads at Tuol Sleng were occupied with corpses, several decapitated, some disemboweled, others with gashes sawn across their throats. Records, photos and all, were abandoned. Also left behind were four adult males and four children, aged eleven, eight, and four years, whose parents had been killed there. The males were artists, whose lives were prolonged by being forced to work sixteen hours per day turning out portraits and busts of Pol Pot. They made him look astonishingly like Hua Kuo-feng, Chinese head of state. These were the only people—apart from the Group 21 staff—who had ever left Tuol Sleng once having passed through its portals.

In my subsequent travels I found that every province visited—Siem Reap, Kompong Speu, Prey Veng, Svay Rieng, and Kompong Cham—had similar centers specializing in the extermination of intellectuals. Ordinary "malcontents," who protested at the slave labor conditions and starvation diet, were dealt with on the spot.

The sadism practiced in the torture centers and the manner of execution were paralleled in the savagery with which everyone—old people, women, and small children—was butchered in the attacks against Vietnamese frontier villages. In general, reports of these were largely discounted in the West as "Vietnamese propaganda." But the same treatment was meted out to Thai villagers, as the following extract from a protest note, made public by the Thai Ministry of Foreign Affairs, on January 31, 1977, makes clear:

At 2300 hours on Friday night of January 28, 1977, large units of the armed forces of Democratic Kampuchea, numbering approximately 300 Khmer Rouge soldiers, armed with powerful and deadly weapons, intruded into Thai territory and, without any warning, launched three-pronged attacks on three Thai villages. . . . The said Khmer Rouge soldiers fired their guns at the innocent Thai villagers and burnt all houses to the ground. These murderers did not only gun down everybody in sight, including helpless women, they also disfigured the bodies and slashed the throats of children

---

* Document 2/5/27, submitted at the Phnom Penh trial *in absentia* of Pol Pot and Ieng Sary on charges of genocide, August 15–17, 1979. The "no death during torture" injunction was clearly aimed at avoiding a premature cutoff of the victim's "confession."

and babies. Before they were driven back across the border, the Khmer Rouge murder squad managed to set fire to the crops and slaughtered animals to complete their bloodthirsty mission. . . .

The protest note goes on to quote reports from journalists of *Asiaweek*, *Time* magazine, *Newsweek*, and others for horrifying details. Such accounts tally almost word for word with those of similar attacks against Vietnamese villages along the whole length of the Kampuchea frontier, starting in May 1975. Eyewitness accounts also agree on the extreme youth of the attackers. The Thai protest note pointed out that in its reply the Pol Pot–Ieng Sary regime did not deny the atrocities, but claimed the three villages belonged to Kampuchea, which had "every right to rearrange its internal affairs."

In his book mentioned earlier, Sihanouk has some pertinent remarks about this generalized sadism of the Khmer Rouge troops and the psychopathic cruelty of the regime in general. How could the "gentle Khmers," as we used to regard them, suddenly be at the throats of their compatriots and their neighbors, killing, maiming, and torturing with a zeal which can only come from perverted minds? Sihanouk lists three main factors:

> *Method of Recruiting*: They recruited only the "poor peasants," the *montagnards*, those living in the jungle and the most remote areas, the most "neglected" under previous regimes. The aim was to promote an unquench- able hatred against urban dwellers and all members of the "upper classes," against anyone who had a decent lodging, was well dressed and well fed, against those who could send their children to school. . . .
>
> *Use of Children*: Once enrolled in the revolutionary forces, these chil- dren are separated from their families, removed from their native villages, and regrouped in the mold of Pol Pot indoctrination. They start their military career at the age of 12 years. . . .
>
> *The Cult of Cruelty*: Pol Pot–Ieng Sary believed, quite correctly, that by getting them used to the "cruelty game" quite early, these *yotheas* ["soldiers"] ended up by delighting in massacres and thus in waging war.
>
> During the three years of my "house arrest" in Phnom Penh, I watched the *yotheas* entrusted with guarding my "camp" permanently delight in prac- ticing their "game of cruelty" at the expense of animals . . . and, at the same time I often heard them complain at not being sent to the front "to bash the Viets." . . .*

Today it is fashionable for scientists to speculate about "genetic engineer- ing" as a means of producing desirable types of "special-purpose" humans. Pol Pot was out for the same results—to produce killer-robots by more primi-

---

* Norodom Sihanouk, *Chroniques de guerre et d'espoir* (Paris: Hatcette/Stock, September 1979), p. 69. My translation from the original French—W. B.

tive means. Sihanouk returns to this theme several times, and because of its implications, it provides some of the most blood-chilling passages of his book:

> The young recruits started to "harden their hearts and minds" by killing cats, dogs, and other "edible" animals, by clubbing or bayoneting them. Even after the victory of April 17, 1975, when they had no human beings to kill or torture, the Khmer Rouge kept up their "form" by plunging animals into the "fires of hell." I witnessed an example at the Royal Palace, where I was placed under "house arrest." The *kammaphibal*—political commissar charged with looking after "royal prisoners"—and his "team" took great pleasure in catching mice, locking them up in a cage, and setting fire to it. They greatly enjoyed the spectacle of the mice rushing in all directions, desperately and vainly trying to find a way of escape, then the final agony of these beasts being burned alive. This was a daily spectacle. . . .
>
> Another "game" consisted of torturing monkeys whose "sufferings resembled those of humans." They cut off their tails with axes. They put a chain around their necks, slowly strangling them as they were forced to run behind their torturers, who pulled gradually harder on the chain. The poor monkeys uttered heartbreaking cries. The spectacle and the cries were insupportable, but the young *yotheas* thought it highly amusing.
>
> The atrocities committed between 1975–77 by the Khmer Rouge against innocent Thai villagers can be explained by this thirst for cruelty by the Khmer Rouge, conditioned for years at amusing themselves by the sufferings of man and beast.*

Sadism, paranoia, xenophobia, and megalomania—all were forms which the Great Madness of the Khmer Rouge assumed. In his choice of the name *Angkar* as the supreme authority for all acts and edicts there seems little doubt that Pol Pot wanted to identify his regime with the prestige of the Angkor Empire. The reason for the attacks on Vietnam and Thailand was to restore part of the territory of ancient empire. In checking the incidents along the frontiers in late 1978 and 1979, I found it difficult to accept the statements of captured Khmer Rouge troops that their aims were the seizure of the Mekong Delta from Vietnam and even the capture of Saigon. It seemed too farfetched, and always reluctant to inform my readers of anything of which I am not myself convinced, I never even reported it. I put it down to the delusions of an illiterate soldiery or the fantasies of their often equally illiterate commanders or briefing officers.

When one has read Sihanouk's book and, above all, the *Black Paper* issued by the Khmer Rouge's Ministry of Foreign Affairs, no other conclusion is possible than that at least Pol Pot, Ieng Sary, and their military commander, Son Sen, had deluded themselves that it was possible to take on the Vietnamese Army—and beat it. They even boasted that it was their mili-

---

* *Ibid.*, pp. 136–37.

tary exploits which had defeated the United States in Kampuchea *and* *Vietnam.* In fact, as Sihanouk points out, it was Giap's forces that played the decisive role on four crucial occasions in defeating the U.S.-backed regime of Lon Nol. But as Sihanouk reveals, Pol Pot took the credit as if it were due to his own "military genius."

> In all seriousness, Pol Pot, Ieng Sary, Khieu Samphan, and others went on the air . . . to claim that with rudimentary and primitive arms, their troops had succeeded in wiping out almost all the enemy infantry divisions, his armored units and air squadrons.
> Certainly it is good to be patriotic, but to deliberately adopt a chauvinistic attitude and one of bad faith in order to deny to the North Vietnamese allies and comrades-in-arms the preponderant role—to say the least—that they played first in stopping the American and Saigon invaders, then in rolling them back in 1970, 1971, and 1972, is not only to insult them but to insult history itself. It is something which adds little to the stature of the authors of such claims.*

Time and again Sihanouk refers to the insane illusions of Pol Pot and the handful around him that they, not the Vietnamese, were the real architects of the American defeat in Indochina. It was a myth encouraged in Peking and echoed by many Maoists in the West:

> Unfortunately Pol Pot allowed his head to be turned somewhat too soon about "his" victories, to the point of comparing himself with the great conquerors of the past, Alexander of Macedonia, Caesar of Rome, the Corsican— Napoleon—and the Nazi, Hitler. . . .
> In September 1975, returning for the first time to "liberated" Cambodia, at the invitation of the Khmer Rouge leaders, I was astonished to hear Khieu Samphan, Son Sen, and others tell me—with broad smiles and very satisfied airs—that their troops were "dissatisfied" with the "party" because the latter was not giving them the green light to recover the *Kampuchea Krom* (Lower Cambodia) and the frontier districts with Thailand. . . .†

That the Khmer Rouge leaders had carried self-delusion to such a degree as to believe this, or at least to persuade their followers that this was so, is clear in their *Black Paper,* in which the main thesis is that the Vietnamese revolutionary forces were at the point of total collapse in March 1970 and were saved only by the anti-Sihanouk coup which permitted the invincible Khmer Rouge to take charge. The state of affairs in South Vietnam on the

---

* *Ibid.,* pp. 64–65.
† *Ibid.,* p. 79. *Kampuchea Krom,* which means "Lower Kampuchea," is, in fact, the Mekong Delta of South Vietnam, where among about 8 million Vietnamese, there are about 500,000 of Khmer origin.

eve of that coup, described in the eighty-nine-page *Black Paper*, is compa-
rable only to the illusions of General Westmoreland on the eve of the Tet
offensive.

> Before the coup d'état, the Vietcongs could not take refuge in their own
> country simply because they had not liberated the slightest plot of territory.
> The 3rd defence belt of Saigon set up by the U.S. and the Thieu clique,
> stretched as far as up to Kampuchea's border. It was from Kampuchea's ter-
> ritory that the Vietcongs went out fighting the U.S. and Thieu's clique. That
> was a fact known to everybody. . . .*

Immediately after the coup, according to the *Black Paper*, Pham Van Dong
arrived in Peking with as "his main objective to have the Communist party
of Kampuchea help and defend the Vietnamese forces in difficulties." If
there was any group in ignorance of what was going on in their own country
and in South Vietnam, it was the Khmer Rouge. At the time of the March
18, 1970, coup Pol Pot and Ieng Sary were in Peking; Khieu Samphan, Hu
Nim, and Hou Yuon were in Hanoi. As a fighting force they were non-
existent, and as a political organization they had virtually no popular support
whatsoever. Having imprudently launched an armed struggle against Sihanouk, in 1967 and 1969, the Khmer Rouge forces were thoroughly defeated.
Some survivors sought refuges in old bases along the borders with Thailand
and Vietnam which had been used during the anti-French resistance struggle.

In early 1967 I was approached by a leading Khmer Rouge cadre in
Phnom Penh to extend my support for national liberation movements to the
armed struggle about to be launched against Sihanouk. I refused on the
grounds that (a) there could be nothing "national" about it since Cambodia
was not under any foreign domination, (b) there was no internal oppression
of a nature to justify armed action or rally the peasantry to support it, and
(c) the overthrow of Sihanouk would be stabbing the Vietnamese in the
back and the most useful gift possible to the United States. The angry reply
was: "You cannot ask one country to hold back its revolution in the interests
of that of a neighboring country." In fact, it was absurd to speak of a "revolutionary situation" in Cambodia at that time.

In its version of the situation in Vietnam, at the time of Pham Van Dong's
visit to Peking, the *Black Paper* states:

> The Vietnamese were then in the following situation: Ahead, the U.S.
> imperialists and the army of Thieu's clique had wiped out the Vietcong

---

* *Black Paper: Facts & Evidences of the Acts of Aggression and Annexation of Vietnam Against Kampuchea.* Department of Press and Information of the Ministry of
Foreign Affairs of Democratic Kampuchea, September 1978, p. 34. Quoted from the
official English version.

forces from South Vietnam. Now the U.S. and the troops of Lon Nol's clique hit them from the rear. The U.S. carried out deadly bombing on Kampuchea's territory, all along the border zones, bringing down the Vietcong bases. At the same time they dropped troops with prefabricated blockhaus [sic] behind the Vietcongs. In a word the Vietnamese recorded a fundamental setback.*

What really happened in Peking is another of those tantalizing bits of history, revealing, among other things, Chou En-lai's methods of attempting to force Mao's hands when he believed he was off course. This version was related to me by Sihanouk shortly after the event and is incorporated in the book *My War with the CIA* we wrote together. Sihanouk had been in Moscow, about to leave for Peking, when the Soviet prime minister, Alexei Kosygin, told him in the car on the way to the airport that he had been deposed. At Peking Airport there was Chou En-lai and the entire diplomatic corps, whom Premier Chou said he had convoked to emphasize that "You remain the head of state. The only one. We will never recognize another." (In fact, and this is not in the book because neither of us knew it at the time of writing, Chairman Mao favored accepting the *fait accompli* and recognizing Lon Nol.) In the car leading from the airport, Sihanouk informed Chou En-lai that he was planning to fight Lon Nol and was advised to think things over for twenty-four hours, but just as Kosygin had promised Soviet support in case he fought back, Chou En-lai promised Chinese support. Sihanouk reaffirmed his decision within twenty-four hours, and in our book he stated:

> Reports in the Western press were to the effect that China hesitated for some days—according to Lon Nol's absurd version, weeks even—before deciding to assist me. But within 24 hours of my final decision, I had issued my first statements over Radio Peking. How could I have done that had the Chinese not decided to support me? †

What Sihanouk had, in fact, was Chou En-lai's private assurance that he would have Chinese support. On the day following Sihanouk's arrival in Peking, Pham Van Dong also arrived. As Sihanouk described it:

> The opening conversation with Pham Van Dong went something like this:
>
> "How can we help?"
> "Military instructors," I replied. "We have no lack of manpower and the Chinese have already promised arms. We lack trained cadres. You have the best in the world for the type of war we have to fight."

---

* *Ibid.*, p. 38.
† *My War with the CIA, op. cit.*, p. 29.

"I'll tell Giap to send you a couple of thousand of the best we have," replied Pham Van Dong.

We discussed at length the best ways of coordinating the struggle of the three peoples of Indochina. . . .

Later, I spoke with Chairman Mao for a couple of hours. . . . He questioned me at length about Lon Nol, whom he had met during the previous 1 October festivities. . . .*

When Pham Van Dong met Chou En-lai, he was dismayed to learn of Mao's conviction that Sihanouk had no hope of leading successful armed resistance and that Lon Nol should be recognized. Pham Van Dong did his best to convince Chou that with Vietnamese help on the battlefield and Chinese help with arms, Sihanouk would win out. He also met with Saloth Sar—the name Pol Pot used in those days—urging the Khmer Rouge to respond positively to the appeal which Sihanouk would launch for a united front to wage armed struggle against Lon Nol. The first public statement of Chinese support for Sihanouk oddly enough came not from Peking, but from Pyongyang. On returning from Pyongyang, Sihanouk relates:

I again met with the Soviet Chargé d'Affaires and pointed out to him that China's support was now open and official and that I would appreciate a similar statement by his government. "But the statement of support was not made on Chinese soil," he replied. "I have no objection if Premier Kosygin would make a similar statement on Polish or Czech soil," I riposted.†

It is a reasonable speculation that the Soviet chargé suspected that Chou En-lai was pushing his own policy—as I believe he did five years earlier with the offer of combat troops to Vietnam, also made outside the country—which would be authentic only when it had the stamp of Peking, thus Mao's endorsement. Official support came only with the immediate recognition of the resistance government set up in Peking on May 5, 1970. By that time Mao had got a message in the language he understood. The Vietnamese, at the specific request of Sihanouk and the Khmer Rouge, had provided the new-fledged armed forces with the most marvelous takeoff conditions any resistance movement could dream of by completely liberating Cambodia's eastern provinces and handing them over to the resistance administration.

It was the Khmer Rouge who dominated the armed forces from the beginning, Khieu Samphan having been named minister of defense and commander in chief of the armed forces. As a second bonus to ensure that the armed struggle got off to a good start, Hanoi facilitated the return of veterans of the anti-French struggle, who had been evacuated to North Vietnam

---

* *Ibid.*, pp. 30–31.
† *Ibid.*, p. 33.

after the 1954 Geneva Agreement. These included nearly 1,000 members of the Khmer Communist party. Sihanouk describes what happened to them:

> According to Khieu Samphan, after acrimonious discussions, the Viets handed over to the Khmer Rouge leadership the 5,000 Khmer Vietminh cadres "educated" in Hanoi between 1954–70, as well as pro-Sihanouk units . . . trained by Vo Nguyen Giap's officers. These Khmer-Vietminh cadres and the Sihanouk units were "Polpotized" but, still according to Khieu Samphan, the greater part of them were "irredeemable" and thus had to be eliminated.*

According to one of the veteran Communists I met during my May 1979 visit, there were altogether about 1,200 of them when the armed struggle started against Lon Nol, including 300 who had remained inside the country under Sihanouk. As far as he knew, he was one of 30 who had survived.

His view of the monstrous purges during the anti-Lon Nol struggle and at an ever intensified tempo afterward was that this was a replay on a gigantic scale of something which Pol Pot, Ieng Sary, Son Sen, and their closest cronies had tried to do from 1954 onward. They had been students in Paris during the anti-French war, only Pol Pot returning just before it ended. They arrived with a hodgepodge of ill-digested notions of Marxism, Trotskyism, Anarchism, Maoism, Existentialism, despising the then leaders of the Khmer Communists as ignorant country bumpkins without theoretical knowledge. Gradually the "Paris Set," by various methods and helped by the assassination of the then general secretary in dubious circumstances, took over the leadership. Among the results was the launching of armed struggle against the wrong enemy in 1967–68.

Pol Pot and Ieng Sary spent much of the period of the anti-Lon Nol war in Peking, returning after it was over as passionate advocates of the Great Proletarian Cultural Revolution, of which they seemed to have imbibed only the use of unrestrained violence to smash everything—culture, religion, traditions, customs, morality—of the old society and the most barbarous methods of crushing all opposition and potential opposition.

The end result of the Great Madness is approximately 3 million people killed or starved to death, economic and social structures almost totally destroyed, and a traumatized people gradually trying to put their own lives and that of the country together again. The Khmer Rouge regime will go down as one of the most evil in history, and a lot of my left-wing friends are going to be embarrassed at having defended it so ardently and for so long.

After Sihanouk arrived in France at the end of November 1979, I asked him if his Chinese friends had given any explanation for having left him in deadly peril of his life until the very last possible moment before the

---

* *Chroniques de guerre et d'espoir, op. cit.,* p. 52.

Pol Pot forces were forced to flee Phnom Penh. He laughed, shortly, bitterly, and said, "Madame Chou En-lai explained that as Kampuchea was an independent and sovereign state, China could not intervene in its internal affairs. It's preposterous. China ran everything in the Kampuchea of the Khmer Rouge. . . ."

He also revealed, by implication, that Chairman Mao knew quite well what was going on under the Pol Pot regime. In October 1975, just before Sihanouk and part of his family returned to Phnom Penh, Mao told Khieu Samphan in Sihanouk's presence that he, his wife, Monique, and the two children of their marriage were not to be killed. It says something for Sihanouk's courage that he still insisted on returning.

During our hourlong conversation he was surprised and somewhat moved to learn that a Vietnamese-Cambodian commando group had attempted to rescue him and his family on the eve of the capture of Phnom Penh, out of concern that Pol Pot would kill them before abandoning the city. He commented:

"I knew the Khmer Rouge feared something like that because they kept changing my residence. In the last days, the latest house to which they moved us was encircled by an entire regiment of troops, and the room in which Monique and I slept was floodlit with strong searchlights, day and night—it was impossible to sleep."

The commando group attacked the wrong building, in fact, and most of them were wiped out.

32

Summing Up

To the month, September 1979 from September 1939, my fortieth journalistic birthday was spent in Havana, covering the sixth summit of the nonaligneds. According to the demonologists, it was to be the arena of a political gladiatorial contest between two Titans, both of whom I greatly admired. Oddly enough, since they were to fight it out for the leadership of the nonaligned movement, they both were prestigious—but maverick—Communists. As a maverick journalist I could not be attracted by both. Titleholder, Josip Broz Tito, eighty-seven years. Challenger, Fidel Castro Ruz, fifty-two years. Old versus new, youth versus age. Belgrade, where the movement was born eghiteen years earlier, versus Havana, where the demonologists predicted it would be buried. In preliminary skirmishes the contest had been expressed as between Tito's "equidistance" in relations with the socialist and capitalist worlds and Castro's "natural allies" thesis of tilting toward the former.

Less than two weeks before the curtain was raised, Castro-backed Sandinista guerrillas won out in Nicaragua, and it seemed clear that the days of the U.S.-backed oligarchy in neighboring El Salvador—both countries on the doorsteps of Cuba and the United States—were also numbered. The conference opened with Hurricane David and ended with Hurricane Frederick, both of which, after considerable damage to Cuba, whirled around in Castro skies and then roared off to vent their wrath on the United States.

Between nature's assaults was Hurricane Carter—the CIA's discovery of a "brigade of Soviet combat troops" in Cuba, poised for an invasion of the U.S.A. As a headline counterattraction to the summit, it was unbeatable— at least in the United States. Short of having it moved away from Havana, which Washington, supported by Peking, Belgrade, and sundry other cap-

319

itals, had expended much energy and taxpayers' money to achieve, it was the next best thing. In fact, it proved to be a damp squib, and Carter spent some uncomfortable weeks in wriggling out of the corner into which Zbigniew Brzezinski had painted him. The impending Castro-Tito contest conjured up a contest of another type which I have never been able to forget, neither its elemental nature nor its symbolism.

I was traveling in an ancient taxi, wheezing its way up a road carved out of the arid, boulder-strewn country between Baramula and Srinagar, the sensually beautiful capital of what was then India's Kashmir Province. Warned that I should be alert to a possible sniper's shot from Muslim rebels or a boulder pried loose by them from the upper slope, at one moment my attention was fixed on the downslope which ran parallel to, but high above, the racing Jhelum River. On the grassy bank of a gorge which fell sheer into the rocky riverbed were two bulls, their horns locked in combat, one young, the other old, their forefeet rooted firmly in the earth, shoulder muscles bulging. As I watched spellbound, Goliath gave a sudden lunge and twist of his horns, hurling young David to certain death on the rocks below. With twitching skin and muscles and a twirl of his tail, he strolled toward the females on the riverbank, spittle dribbling down his chin and his scarlet penis half out of its sheath.

Every detail remained etched in my mind, and the symbolic connotations raced through my brain like newspaper headlines. Future Destroyed by Past! Youth's Premature Challenge Ends in Tragedy! The incident surfaced again in the lobbies of the splendid conference complex built for the Havana summit. Delegates, diplomats, journalists—their minds seemed to be concentrated on a single thought: the forthcoming Tito-Castro confrontation. One was bound to slaughter the other—such was the general anticipation. Several of my veteran colleagues made no secret of the fact that they were on hand just to cover that one spectacular joust. It had to be conceded that Tito had contributed to the dramatic buildup to the event by arriving days earlier than any other head of state with a suite that included 160 diplomats and 143 journalists.

One aspect which obviously recalled the scene of the bulls' duel was that the youngest of the founding fathers of the nonaligned movement was now challenging the oldest for supremacy. They had some important things in common. They had won their countries' independence by leading bitter armed struggles against almost impossible odds. Both were outsiders among the nonaligneds in that they did not belong to the Afro-Asian groups of countries which had met in Bandung six years before the founding summit in September 1961, to act as midwives for the nonaligned movement.

For many years, especially after the disappearance from the scene of founding fathers of the caliber of Nehru, Nasser, Nkrumah, and Sukarno, Tito was the unchallenged leader of the nonaligned movement. Yugoslavia assumed that this was a permanent, indisputable fact of international life, and essential elements of the country's foreign policy and economic planning were based on this. Among the nonaligneds, Yugoslavia was a relatively developed country, and it gradually carved out an economic fief for itself, based on catering to the needs of the underdeveloped or developing world, above all, in Africa. The possibilities of expanding markets as more and more countries won their independence seemed unlimited. Then a cloud, no bigger than a puff of cigar smoke, appeared on the horizon. Cuba, through its military missions, was helping national liberation movements win their countries' independence, paying with its own blood in some cases and apparently without seeking economic payoffs.

Whatever criticisms the West had regarding Cuba's role in Angola, for the nonaligned Africans Cuba had knocked the stuffing out of the South Africans and that was GREAT. I had accompanied Prince Sihanouk on a trip to some African countries in May 1973, and in brief conversations with Presidents Kenneth Kaunda of Zambia, Marien Ngouabi of Congo-Brazzaville, and Sékou Touré of Guinea-Conakry, I had been impressed by the depth of their mistrust and fears of South Africa. Later, at international conferences dealing with African affairs and in my visits to Angola and Mozambique, it became clear that no leaders of newly independent African states, especially in the southern half of the continent, felt they could relax and consider their countries' independence inviolate as long as South Africa, with its odious apartheid policies, remained the strongest military force in the area. The bogeyman image was too well implanted and flouted by South Africa itself to be lightly dismissed.

I had been at the fourth nonaligned summit in Algiers, in September 1973, when Castro's suggestion that the member countries lean more toward their "natural allies" of the socialist world was received rather coldly, while Sihanouk's interjection as to why Fidel did not use his influence with the Soviet Union to secure Soviet recognition for his resistance government, rather than that of Lon Nol, was warmly applauded. But by the time of the fifth summit at the Sri Lanka capital, Colombo, in August 1976, Castro's stock had risen enormously. Why? He had taken on the bogeymen and beaten them. I did not attend the Colombo summit, but I knew that the Political Declaration included a paragraph commending the "Republic of Cuba and other States which assisted the people of Angola in frustrating the expansionist and colonialist strategy of South Africa's racist regime and of its allies." It was undoubtedly because of this meritorious activity in non-aligned eyes that Havana was chosen as the site for the sixth summit and Castro automatically became the chairman of the nonaligned movement for the three years following September 1979. As Cuba's star waxed within the movement, that of Yugoslavia waned, partly because of a too obvious jealousy at Castro's increasing prestige. Havana would be a test.

The lighthearted way in which the annihilation of one by the other was discussed over daiquiris and coffee in the press bar was repulsive but inevitable. There were three key issues on which the champions took opposite positions. Should Pol Pot continue to represent Kampuchea? Should Egypt be expelled for having signed the Camp David Agreement with Israel? Should the movement align itself behind Tito's "equidistance" or Castro's "natural allies"?

Castro had an advantage of being on home ground and of speaking first as the president-elect of the movement. Tito had enormous prestige as the movement's father figure and for having survived, against seemingly impossible odds, in defending his own country's independence and nonaligned positions. And he had scored a number of points in advance for his courage and energy, at eighty-seven, to have made the trip to Havana to fight the good fight.

When it came to the test, Castro and Tito were too big to divert policy differences into personal contest, thus disappointing the "Young Turks" on both sides—not to mention the journalists. By his opening speech, it was clear that Castro was seeking consensus, not confrontation, within the movement, although he had some harsh words for what he considered its enemies outside:

"The Yankee imperialists and their old and new allies—in this case I refer to the Chinese government—did not want this conference to be held in Cuba.

"They also engaged in dirty scheming, saying that Cuba would turn the movement of the nonaligned countries into a tool of Soviet policy. We know only too well that the U.S. government even got hold of a copy of the final draft declaration, drawn up by Cuba, and made feverish diplomatic contacts in an effort to modify it. We have irrefutable proof of this. . . .

"Throughout our revolutionary life, no one has ever tried to tell us what to do. No one has ever tried to tell us what role we should play in the movement of nonaligned countries. No one told us when or how to make revolution in our country, nor could anyone have done so. By the same token no one except the movement itself can determine what it should do and when and how to do it. . . ."

The speech was followed with exceptional interest, not only because it was the keynote report which laid down the guidelines that would govern the period of Castro's chairmanship but also because it revealed his political credo as developed during his first twenty years in office. There was justified concern on the mainland of the Americas as to whether Fidel was going to bang the drums of war or offer a cigar of peace. In general, it was the latter, but he was also uncompromising as far as support for revolutionary and national liberation struggles was concerned.

But there was no encouragement for adventurist policies which could endanger peace in the region—or anywhere else. On the contrary: "The struggle for peace and for a just economic order and a workable solution to the pressing problems that weigh on our peoples is, in our opinion, increasingly becoming the main question posed to the movement of nonaligned countries. . . .

"We must demand peace, détente, peaceful coexistence, and disarmament. We must demand and win them because they will not come about by spontaneous generation, and there is no alternative in today's world, if we are to preserve the very existence of mankind."

It was a well-received speech, interrupted some twenty times by bursts of applause. After several long conversations with Castro and having listened to his speech and the reactions from the floor, Tito had reportedly rejected the draft prepared by his experts and had written his own much milder version. It reflected the sentiments of an elder statesman who had carefully taken the temperature of the movement and—in making what was predictably his last speech at a nonaligned summit—wished to make a dignified and worthy exit without doing anything to split a movement which was partly his own creation. Even his advocacy of equidistance was mild:

"We have never equated the blocs, either in terms of the time when they were founded or on the basis of other characteristics. We have from the very outset been consistently opposed to bloc policies and foreign domination, to all forms of political and economic hegemony, and in favor of the right of each and every country to freedom, independence, and autonomous development. We have never consented to be anyone's rubber stamp or preserve, as this is incompatible with the essence of the policy of nonalignment."

His analysis of the world situation was not very different from that of Castro's, except that he avoided any criticism of the Camp David Agreement and, without naming Vietnam or Kampuchea, implicitly attacked Vietnam's role in the area:

"We are also very worried by the worsening of the crisis in Southeast Asia, by the outbreak of armed conflicts and the use of force in dealing with existing disputes. . . . Above all, we must not reconcile ourselves to the imposition of foreign will on peoples by military interventions. Such behavior is totally incompatible with the principles of the Charter of the United Nations and the policy of nonalignment. Thus, here again, we see a way out of the crisis in the withdrawal of all foreign troops from the territories of other countries and in respect for the independence, security, and peaceful development of all countries in that region. . . ."

There was no applause during the speech, but a standing ovation when he finished, which must have warmed his old heart. (Later he presumably drew comfort from the fact that his Havana speech was also valid for Soviet intervention in Afghanistan when it took place a few months later!)

Had there been umpires to judge the results of the five-day summit, they would have to have given a "thumbs-up" decision to Castro. They included a "vacant seat" for Kampuchea, which in effect meant the expulsion of the Khmer Rouge; deferred judgment on Egypt's expulsion, pending a final decision by the movement's Coordinating Committee—under Cuba's chairmanship—within eighteen to twenty-four months; qualified approval for the "natural allies" thesis. "Anybody ever hear of an imperialist country giving guns to a national liberation movement?" asked Mozambique's Samora Machel.

Youth predominated at the conference, not only in terms of length of membership, starting with Nicaragua, but in the age of many of the most eloquent participants. The old founder members were in disarray: Egypt with an expulsion order hanging over it; India without a real government; Kampuchea not represented; Indonesia, Ghana, and others without the dynamic leadership of a Sukarno, a Nkrumah; and Yugoslavia defending minority viewpoints. It was not like the old days, when hot war, cold war, détente, peaceful coexistence were the issues on which it was easy to align the nonaligneds!

It was the voices of comparative newcomers like Didier Ratsiraka of Madagascar, Michael Manley of Jamaica, Maurice Bishop of Grenada, and obviously Daniel Ortega Saavedra of Nicaragua, the newest of them all, which brought fresh ideas and drew the most applause. My feeling was that either the Havana summit would pump fresh life into the nonaligned movement, or it would plunge into a sharp decline, the beginnings of which were already perceptible. From the group of twenty-five leaders who met in Belgrade in September 1961, united by the fact that they mainly represented countries that had recently won their independence which they were determined not to imperil because of conflicts between the major powers, the movement now included ninety countries with widely disparate interests, policies, and ideologies. Was it to degenerate into a chummy club, whose members met every three years to pass vague resolutions on matters of mutual concern, or a decisive force corresponding to its numerical membership and possession of the greater part of the world's strategic raw materials?

Conditions of membership were essentially that an applicant was not militarily allied to any of the big powers, nor were there foreign military bases on its territory by *its own volition*. Ideological options were not part of the criteria; that is why Communists Tito and Castro could take their turns as chairpersons with Egypt's Nasser, Zambia's Kaunda, Algeria's Boumedienne, and (briefly until her government was defeated) Sri Lanka's Madame Sirimavo Bandanaraike. The four in between the Tito-Castro sandwich (plus a fifth, Junius Jayewardene, Sri Lanka's president, who continued Madame Bandanaraike's term as movement chairperson) were far from being Communists.

As the movement grew numerically, it became a pressure group of importance at the UN and within other international organizations. On disarmament, decolonialization, racism, and the basic issues of peace and détente —member states spoke with almost one voice. But it lacked an adhesive element to unite the components into an effective tool to impose fundamental changes in the international order of things. Perhaps Castro, supported by a nucleus of radical states with the former Portuguese colonies, Vietnam, and other newcomers in the vanguard, could do it.

The master concept was to transform political independence into true economic independence by setting up the movement's own economic and financial institutions, banks, transport and shipping lines, industries—starting with fertilizers and insecticides and the processing of locally produced raw materials and moving into medium and heavy industries based on those raw materials. It was based on replacing the nonproductive north-south (have-have nots) dialogue by south-south (have nots-have nots) pooling of resources and economic development programs. The idea had been a gleam in the eyes of the founding fathers, who, at the inaugural meeting, had inscribed the need for a "new international economic order" among the aims to be achieved. But nothing had been done about it. If Castro, with his dynamic leadership and clear mandate from the sixth (Havana) summit, failed to get the new economic order on the rails during his chairmanship, it would be a major defeat for the movement and for him.

These were some of my reflections as I was installed in a one-bed ward of Havana's Fajado Hospital, the day following the end of the conference, which I had almost missed. At the end of a harrowing few weeks in Vietnam and Kampuchea in an August of record heat, even for that part of the world, I had suffered a total loss of appetite for six days. There was just no way in which I could get any food down. The combination of excessive heat and the horrors of what I was hearing each day at the genocide trial *in absentia* of Pol Pot and Ieng Sary—with a few visits to confirm the evidence —was more than my digestive functions could cope with. By the time I reached Ho Chi Minhville on my way out I was almost in a state of physical collapse. After a near blackout at the hotel reception desk, I was whisked off for a hospital check. Symptoms—sudden loss of appetite and fits of dizziness. Grave faces converged around me, probing with their fingers in my nether regions, nodding their heads after each probe. Off to the X-ray room. Unanimous decision: "You must stay ten days for a complete checkup."

My instant reaction: "Nonsense! I'm leaving tomorrow for Paris, and two days after that for Havana!" That is what I did, in exchange for a pledge to present the preliminary diagnosis and X-ray pictures to medical authorities immediately upon arriving in Cuba. I fully intended to respect this pledge, but in fact, the single suitcase in which I had placed these and other documents during my brief transit in Paris was mislaid at Madrid Airport and never arrived in Havana. However, I had glanced at the "preliminary diagnosis" on the plane between Ho Chi Minhville and

Bangkok and discovered that I was probably suffering from a liver tumor, of which sudden loss of appetite is apparently a symptom. Having been honest enough to report this on arrival, I was given a swift check and an assurance that I would survive the summit, but "better have a complete checkup as soon as it's over." Thus, I entered Fajado Hospital for ten days, subjected to innumerable tests and awaiting the verdict "benign" or "malignant" at the end of it. After the supreme test of having some sort of periscope plunged deep into my innards and being turned upside down and in all sorts of other humiliating positions while a specialist examined my internal functionings, I was declared not only tumorless but in very good shape, not only in respect to my age (I had spent my sixty-eighth birthday in the hospital) but in general.

However, the ten days awaiting the verdict were a rare period of reflection, starting, naturally enough with wondering about where the nonaligneds were at and ending by wondering where I was at. Why had I made such desperate efforts to get to Havana anyway when Paris is marvelous in August-September? The conclusion I came to was that I was an ideological nonaligned, attracted to their summits as Muslims are to Mecca. That there were a few outstanding Communists among the leaders was an added attraction because I was obviously a radical nonaligned. I found their get-togethers far more interesting than the few Communist party congresses I had attended, less stereotyped, less predictable as to results, no lip service to a single higher authority, a much greater variety of creative views expressed.

With the last downpours of Hurricane Frederick pounding at hospital windows and even reading frowned upon by my medical surveillants, there was the most time ever to think over the influences on my life and their results. The old friends met at the summit—Pham Van Dong, for instance, in a memorable dinner at which Vessa and I were the only guests—were precious reminders of those influences.

Those who had counted most, from Kisch to Chou En-lai and Ho Chi Minh, were Communists, as were others later, like Castro, who attracted me at first sight, and Tito, whom I had admired from afar. There were many, many others at different levels and in different countries, including Australia, who had impressed me by their courage, lucidity of thought, and readiness to accept the social and material sacrifices implicit in the sort of struggles in which they were engaged. That I did not become a Communist was accidental. When I left Australia for China in early 1951, my intention had been to return after three months and apply for membership in the Communist party. My first weeks in China only reaffirmed my early impressions of the moral and intellectual qualities of Chinese Communists. But two things happened.

As part of my preparation to become a Communist, I read not once or twice, but thrice *How to Be a Good Communist*, by Liu Shao-chi, later to become president of the People's Republic and still later to be disgraced as Mao Tse-tung's principal enemy during the Cultural Revolution. It was infinitely easier to read than the *Communist Manifesto* or *Anti-Dühring* which had deterred my first approach to membership fifteen years earlier. It spelled out in simple language not only the qualities, disciplines, and obligations expected of a member toward the party, but the responsibilities of the party toward its members. But on the third reading, I realized there was one thing which would prevent me from ever becoming a "good Communist," and that was a passage referring to absolute obedience to all party decisions, even if one was convinced they were wrong. Fifteen years earlier I would probably have accepted even that. Obviously Liu Shao-chi was referring to Chinese party discipline. Perhaps things were otherwise in Australia. I never did find out because the second important reason for my not joining the Communist party was that I did not return to Australia after three months, or after three years, but only after nineteen years, by which time I was confirmed in my position as an independent, nonaligned radical and the world Communist movement had become so fragmented (three parties in Australia, for instance) that a choice would have been difficult.

What confused many of my friends and my enemies—and sometimes caused me problems—was that almost every foreign policy issue which I supported with my typewriter was also supported by some Communist party or another. But this had absolutely nothing to do with disciplinary obligations to any Communist party, nor did it imply that we would be on the same side on some other issue. The assumption that I automatically would be also caused some problems. Some very simple illustrations are that I wore out several typewriters defending the armed struggle of the South Vietnamese people at a time when the Communist party of the Soviet Union under Khrushchev's leadership and many other world Communist parties considered this "adventurous" and incurring the risk of a new world war. I supported North Vietnam's initiative for negotiations to end that war which the Chinese Communist leadership denounced as "capitulationist." I support the North Korean Communist leadership in its struggle to reunify the country and secure the withdrawal of U.S. troops from the South, but I strongly criticize—publicly and privately—continuing North Korean support for the Khmer Rouge, including that at the Havana summit. Had I been a member of any Communist party, I would have been obliged to follow one consistent line on such questions. For me the issues were decisive, not which Communist party—or any other organization— was supporting or opposing those issues.

In stating this easily verifiable fact, I am not advocating a commonly enough held opinion that journalists should remain aloof from politics, not join parties or accept the disciplines that membership implies. Journalists are members of human society with the same rights and duties and social responsibilities as everyone else, including those of political options. Political parties, especially those devoted to changing society instead of exploiting its vagaries, need journalists dedicated to their aims. Any party to be effective must be able to count on the loyalty and discipline of its members.

It so happened that step by step and almost accidentally, I had achieved a sort of journalistic Nirvana, free of any built-in loyalties to governments, parties, or any organizations whatsoever. My loyalty was to my own convictions and my readers. This demanded freedom from any discipline except that of getting the facts on important issues back to the sort of people likely to act—often at great self-sacrifice—on the information they received. This was particularly so during my reporting from Vietnam, the most important of my career, far too important to be swayed by dictates from outside or above. Over the years, and in many countries, I had a circle of readers who did not buy papers for the stock market reports or strip cartoons, but for facts on vital issues affecting their lives and their consciences. In keeping both eyes and both ears open during my forty years' reporting from the world's hot spots, I had become more and more conscious of my responsibilities to my readers. The point of departure is a great faith in ordinary human beings and the sane and decent way they behave when they have the true facts of the case.

Index